Mr. Badwrench

MR. BADWRENCH

How You Can Survive the $20 Billion-a-Year Auto Repair Rip-off

ARTHUR P. GLICKMAN

Seaview Books

NEW YORK

Library of Congress Cataloging in Publication Data
Glickman, Arthur P.
    Mr. Badwrench: how you can survive the $20
billion-a-year auto repair rip-off.

    Includes index.
    1. Automobiles—Maintenance and repair. 2. Con-
sumer education—United States.   I. Title.
TL152.G566 629.28′722 81–80605
ISBN 0–87223–734–6   AACR2

Seaview Books/A division of PEI Books, Inc.

To Sally and Joe

for their faith

Acknowledgments

The scope of this book would not have been possible without the assistance of government consumer protection people throughout the country. I am most indebted to Paul Sailer and Elsie Flaherty of the Federal Trade Commission, John Reistrup and Gail Boyle of the U.S. Department of Transportation and Daniel Jaffee and John Wellinghoff of the U.S. Senate Subcommittee for Consumers. I am also indebted to the staff of the Center for Auto Safety, particularly Joyce Kinnard, but also Clarence Ditlow, Tom Jones, Margaret Daigle and John Hubbard. I would lastly like to thank Michael Taper and Jane Van Antwerp for providing me with free lodging during the writing of much of this book.

The author invites comments on the subject matter in this book in care of:

Seaview/Wideview Books
1633 Broadway
New York, NY 10019

Contents

PART ONE

Mr. Badwrench Has You by the Ball Joints

PART TWO

Getting the Better of Mr. Badwrench

PART THREE
Getting Back at Mr. Badwrench

APPENDIXES

PART ONE

Mr. Badwrench Has You by the Ball Joints

1

"The Granddaddy of

Consumer Problems"

The *Wilmington* (Delaware) *Evening Journal* compares it unfavorably to a game of Russian roulette.[1]

It's "like walking blindfolded through a mine field," says Jim Clarke, a Washington, D.C., television reporter.[2]

Joan Claybrook, former head of the National Highway Traffic Safety Administration, claims it has "surpassed going to the dentist in the level of fear it strikes in the hearts of most citizens."[3]

What is it that has practically the whole country cringing? A close encounter of the third kind? A nuclear power plant meltdown? The possible return of Richard Nixon?

No, it's far worse! It's having to visit an auto repair shop and deal with—ugh—*Mr. Badwrench*.

Who is this feared Mr. Badwrench? Foremost, he symbolizes incompetence. About half of all auto mechanics in the U.S. who work on consumer-owned cars can't competently diagnose and repair even *one* area of your car, such as the brakes or electrical system, admits an industry mechanic certification group.[4] What's more, less than 6% of the nation's mechanics have passed industry-sponsored competency tests in all eight areas of the car.[5]

Mr. Badwrench also stands for a new kind of criminal—a sort of technological-age bandit. If he sizes you up as someone who wouldn't know a ball joint from a beer joint, he may well try to sell you unneeded repairs or even charge you for repairs not done. ". . . the use of fraud and deception may be a standard trade practice and as such is actually destroying the faith many of our citizens have in our country," says

MR. BADWRENCH

William L. Newcomb, Jr., head of the Consumer Protection Division of the Missouri attorney general's office.[6]

The high level of boobery and banditry is reflected by the fact that auto repairs are the nation's number one consumer problem. The U.S. Office of Consumer Affairs reports that automotive complaints—most of them involving repairs—accounted for a whopping 35% of all written complaints the agency received in 1978[7]—the last year for which statistics are available. Auto repairs have also topped the complaint list in many states as well, including Texas,[8] Ohio,[9] North Carolina,[10] Virginia[11] and New Mexico.[12] "They are more numerous than any others, more difficult to resolve satisfactorily, and they appear to be increasing," said Robert N. Hilgendorf, former director of the Consumer and Economic Crimes Division of the New Mexico attorney general's office.[13]

Just mention "auto repairs" to a car owner and get ready for an emotional outpouring. When the Illinois Legislative Investigating Commission announced a probe into the auto repair industry, it got what it called "an avalanche of letters" from car owners whom it described as "angry, confused, hopeful, worried and depressed." Said the commission: "People who had worked hard and saved their money to buy an automobile found themselves stunned with sudden and unexpected bills of hundreds of dollars, usually for auto repair work which was not done, was not done properly, or simply was not needed in the first place."[14]

While fraud and deception do appear rampant in the industry, the Illinois commission didn't find it to be the major problem. "Far and away," the commission said, "the major reason that motorists complain is because of shoddy workmanship. Nothing seems to raise a car owner's blood pressure more than his having to return to the repair shop again and again, to take time off from work, to do without transportation, and still discover that his car has the same problem."[15]

Together, incompetent, fraudulent and unnecessary post-warranty auto repairs are costing American consumers over $13 billion a year, according to Michael Pertschuk, former chairman of the Federal Trade Commission (FTC).[16] That's over $35.3 million a day, making Britain's famed Great Train Robbery, which netted only about $6 million,[17] seem like a third-rate burglary. *That amount also averages out to about $130 a year for every car you own.*[18]

As startling as the $13 billion seems, the auto repair rip-off could easily be $20 billion a year when you consider the following:

1. Most shops hide from you their true labor rate—for a very specific reason. It's a standard industry practice to charge not by the clock hour as you might think, but according to grossly overstated times certain price-fixing "flat rate manuals" say each repair should take. Figure you're being charged for at least 30% more labor than it actually takes to repair your car.

4

2. Not content with flat rate overcharging, some shops, particularly new car dealerships, add on an unjustifiable "miscellaneous shop supplies" charge to your bill. Typically, this is computed on the basis of 5% to 10% of the labor charge or the parts charge or both.

3. The auto manufacturers are cheating new car buyers out of tens of millions of dollars annually in warranty repairs. Nearly one million new car buyers a year spend more than a month trying to get their cars fixed under warranty, often unsuccessfully, according to a study done for the Federal Trade Commission. Also, one-fourth of those with new car warranty problems are dissatisfied with the final results, the survey found.[19] In addition, many auto companies put into effect "secret warranties" for defects which crop up after the regular warranty has expired. The scandal is that only those who complain loudly about the defects are given free repairs; those who don't complain get nothing.

4. Most used car dealers are aware of the mechanical condition of the cars they sell, but try to hide this information from customers or lie about what they know.[20] Hidden defects in used cars are probably costing American consumers over $1 billion annually in unnecessary repairs.

5. The auto manufacturers use too many nonstandardized parts, often force consumers to buy costly whole assemblies when all they need are inexpensive component parts, and tend to design cars so that they are unnecessarily difficult to repair. All this adds about another $2 billion a year to the nation's auto repair bill, according to the National Highway Traffic Safety Administration (NHTSA).[21]

6. The auto companies are extorting tens of millions of dollars a year from car owners by withholding effective and inexpensive bumper systems from the marketplace and then charging exorbitant monopoly prices to replace parts damaged as a result of their no-goodnik bumpers.

7. Auto insurance companies, as a rule, do not pay body shops enough money to adequately repair cars involved in crashes. The insurance companies are also reluctant to pay the full price of a replacement for a car that's been declared a total wreck and not worth fixing.

8. Tire companies frequently refuse to honor their warranties, and some companies, when they do honor their warranty, use an unfair method of prorating the worth of your old tire. Tire companies are also costing consumers millions of dollars a year by refusing to install low-pressure warning systems on their tires and failing to properly inform the public of the true dangers of riding on underinflated radial tires.

9. NHTSA estimates that accidents resulting from defects caused by undermaintenance or improper repairs are costing the public $2 billion annually, while another $2 billion loss results from excessive emissions and wasted fuel due to improper maintenance or undermaintenance. Still another $2 billion is lost, according to NHTSA, through cars being prematurely retired due to inadequate maintenance.[22]

Still to be included is the incalculable dollar loss incurred because bad repairs and delays make it necessary for car owners to take time off from their work and shell out money for additional travel expenses, rental cars and the like.

All in all, it can be safely said that no industries in America equal auto-repair-related industries in terms of incompetence, corruption and public-be-damned attitudes.

Nowhere is this more aptly reflected than in a Louis Harris poll released in 1977. A cross section of American adults were asked to pick the industries they thought were doing a poor job in serving consumers. "Garages and auto mechanics"—one category—came out in a tie for first place with auto manufacturers, each capturing 36% of the population. They were followed in third place by the oil industry, whose service stations account for about one-seventh of the nation's auto repair service and parts market,[23] and in fourth place by used car dealers.[24] Another poll—this one for *U.S. News and World Report*, released in 1978—asked a cross section of American household heads to rank 31 industries (not including auto repairmen) according to their job performance. Ranked lowest was another industry related to auto repairs: auto insurance companies (auto dealers came in 29th, auto manufacturers 26th, and oil and gas companies 25th).[25]

Still two other opinion polls reaffirm the low esteem in which auto repairmen are held. *Money* magazine, in its December 1978 issue, reported that 42.6% of its subscribers rated auto repair service "poor" or "terrible," ranking it next to lowest among 35 services (only the railroads give poorer service, the subscribers said).[26] And an October 1978 Roper Poll showed that 35% and 36% of the population respectively feel they are "almost always" or "quite often" purposely given wrong information or overcharged by auto repairmen and auto dealers, ranking them worst of 13 professions surveyed.[27]

Former FTC chairman Pertschuk calls auto repairs "the granddaddy of consumer problems,"[28] and with good reason. There's probably a greater chance you'll be robbed by driving into an auto repair shop than by walking through New York City's Central Park at 3:00 in the morning whistling "Dixie." This is no idle remark, but is based on a 1979 undercover car operation conducted for the U.S. Department of Transportation (DOT). Undercover cars, needing no repairs at all or minor work like replacing one spark plug, were taken to 62 repair shops at random in Atlanta, Philadelphia, Miami, Nashville, Houston, Brooklyn and White Plains, New York. The results: 53 cents of every dollar spent on repairs was unnecessary; 27% of all repairs were not needed and 51% of the shops either fixed something that didn't need to be fixed or failed to fix something that really did need to be fixed.[29] The latter statistic means that you've probably got only a 50–50 chance of getting your car fixed right.

In response, several industry groups wrote to President Carter accusing DOT secretary Brock Adams, who announced the results of the survey at a press conference, of committing "a national slander." They claimed that the survey was "not statistically reliable" because it involved only 62 repair shops out of 400,000 and 120 repair actions out of almost a billion performed annually.[30]

Their complaint, of course, is nonsense. The results of the DOT undercover survey are quite typical of others that have been done during the past decade and come close to jibing with the findings of diagnostic center studies. Let's take a look at just some of these surveys:

· In 1978, KTVF-TV, Channel 5 in Nashville, took a 1976 Vega to 15 repair shops. The only things wrong were a loose bolt on the left front tie rod clamp and loose front wheel bearings. Only one shop found both defects, but it tried to sell the woman driver an unneeded idler arm.[31]

· In 1977, the Colorado Public Interest Research Group took a 1971 Volkswagen with an intentionally induced loose drive belt to eight Boulder shops which claimed to specialize in Volkswagens. The defect made the car hard to start and lack power on hills and in passing. Only one of the eight shops solved the problem and charged a reasonable fee—$6.50. Four other shops fixed the problem, but also did costly unnecessary tune-ups, charging in all from $34.64 to $63.38. The other three shops charged $5 to $20 but didn't solve the problem.[32]

· In 1976, a *Chicago Tribune* task force, after a three-month investigation of car repair practices, concluded much like the U.S. Department of Transportation that "anyone driving a car stands less than a 50–50 chance of getting the correct repair job at a fair price." Of 52 repair shops tested with various cars and intentional defects, 21 "performed unnecessary adjustments," the newspaper said.[33]

· In a study of 3,567 repair actions during 1975 and 1976, a federally sponsored diagnostic center operating in Huntsville, Alabama, found that 32 cents of every dollar spent on auto repair was unnecessary. For women the rate was higher: 38 cents on the dollar vs. 30 cents for men.[34] (Women generally are perceived by the repair industry as far less knowledgeable about their cars than men and thus are more frequently preyed upon by unscrupulous mechanics.)

As bad as all this seems, there's every indication that the problem is going to get much, much worse. Cars are getting more complex; a large number of competent old-time mechanics are reaching retirement age; qualified young people aren't entering the industry; and the number of repair shops, mainly because of the closing of full-service gasoline stations, is rapidly declining.

MR. BADWRENCH

You would think that since cars are owned by 84.1% of all American households,[35] government leaders and legislators would be fighting non-stop to clean up the problem. If you thought that way, you'd be wrong.

The White House and the federal agencies aren't doing jelly beans about the problem; Congress seems to be safely in the hands of special-interest groups opposed to reform, and the most prevalent law in the states relating to auto repair is the mechanic's lien—a law which enables auto mechanics to keep your car if you refuse to pay for their inevitable incompetent, unneeded, unrequested or fraudulent repairs. Unbelievably, only two states—Michigan and Hawaii—along with the District of Columbia have initiated mechanic competency requirements, and only five states, three cities and two counties license auto repair shops and ride herd on them to conduct their business in an ethical manner.

The federal government, instead of helping the poor taxpayer, is actually ripping him off when it comes to auto repairs. The feds have been spending millions of dollars to study the auto repair mess, even though it was studied to death about a decade ago and every problem brought out. Little of this study money seems ever to result in any concrete changes.

While part of my reason for writing this book is to show you ways to avoid getting gypped and to tell you what to do if you do get cheated, the main message I want to get across is that this whole mess can be cleaned up only with strong government leadership, imaginative legislation and tough law enforcement. As we shall see, the main perpetrators of the auto repair problem are not the little independent shops, but giant corporations, including automobile, auto insurance, oil and tire companies and the big mass merchandising and franchising organizations. In fact, many mechanics and shop owners are as much victimized by these corporations as the consumer is.

In order for change to occur, you and your friends and neighbors must overcome your apathy and organize auto repair reform political lobbies. Right now, there is no national consumer organization dealing with the whole range of auto repair problems. The only group that comes close is the Center for Auto Safety, which was started by Ralph Nader but is now independent of him. The center, however, deals only with auto safety and new car warranty problems and isn't interested in expanding into the whole auto repair field. Indeed, the organization would have a conflict of interest if it did, as some of its funding comes from the corrupt auto insurance industry.

While consumers are poor and powerless, the automotive industry has a lot going for it in terms of money and political influence. The National Automobile Dealers Association, for example, gave over $1.2 million to U.S. congressional candidates in 1979 and 1980,[36] and General Motors' political action committee gave over $200,000 in 1980 to federal, state and local candidates and political parties.[37] Even several former U.S. Government critics of the automotive industry are now on its payroll.

As a result of the industry's political muscle, not only does Congress refuse to pass any auto repair legislation, but it has been attempting to destroy practically the only two things the Federal Trade Commission and NHTSA have accomplished in the auto repair field in the past decade. They are a proposed FTC rule requiring all used car dealers to disclose the defects in their cars and an NHTSA rule requiring bumpers to protect cars in 5-mph crashes. Congress has also been trying to prevent the Federal Trade Commission from regulating the insurance industry.

If fighting all these wealthy interests seems too formidable a task, there is an alternative: Do as I have done and refuse to own a car. The quality of my life has improved tremendously since I sold my car in 1971. I now no longer have to put up with auto mechanics, oil companies and their ilk.

Alas, though I'm sure many of you would like to live a carless existence, you can't for the very reason explained a few years back by Lee Iaccoca, then president of Ford Motor Co. and more recently chairman of Chrysler Corp.:

"With all the congestion and problems, there is nobody, on average, driving less. Nobody has given up driving, including the kids who are talking about ecology. They still are driving.

"You see, most people really have no option. It's difficult to switch to the bus or the railroad because often there isn't any."[38]

2

The Flat Rate Fiddle

Here's a little mathematical quiz for you.

Roberta Grey of San Francisco takes her car into Van Ness Datsun for a number of repairs. The shop has a sign posted saying it charges $35 an hour for labor. The total bill for labor comes to $350. How long did the shop work on her car?

If you divided $35 into $350 and came up with 10 hours, you would be wrong. The correct answer is 6.4 hours.[1]

The new math? Hardly. It's more an example of the auto repair industry's old con game: the flat rate fiddle.

Unknown to most motorists, the vast majority of auto repair shops do not charge by the clock hour, even though they would like you to believe that they do. Instead, they typically charge you for the amount of time listed in one of several flat rate manuals. These manuals list various repair operations for each car and then state how long each repair should take. Unfortunately for the consumer, it's quite common for repair times to be overstated by 50%, 100% or even more, making these manuals perhaps the greatest works of American fiction since *Uncle Tom's Cabin*. This con game is so widespread that a survey of 210 auto repair shops in the Washington, D.C., area turned up 208 shops which charged by this system and only two which charged according to the actual amount of time they worked on a car.[2]

In our little quiz, Van Ness Datsun was not charging customers $35 a clock hour as they might have assumed by the sign in the shop, but $35 a "flat rate hour." The dealership, according to the San Francisco district attorney's office, was either multiplying the amount of time a flat rate manual said each job should take by $35 an hour or else was making up its own flat rate times for each repair—which had no relationship to how long the repairs actually took—and multiplying that by $35 an hour.[3]

Thus Ms. Grey, instead of having to pay $224 ($35 multiplied by the 6.4 hours it actually took the shop to do the work) ended up paying $350 ($35 multiplied by 10 flat rate hours). That's an extra $126!

In reality, Ms. Grey had paid not $35 an hour, but $54.35 an hour ($350 divided by 6.4 hours of actual labor).

The San Francisco woman wouldn't even have been aware of how long her car had actually been worked on had not the San Francisco district attorney's office conducted an investigation of the dealership. The DA's office found her invoice, which had been time-punched by the mechanic who worked on the car. "I had no way of knowing how long it took them to do the work," she said.[4]

In all, the DA's office took a random sampling of 540 Van Ness Datsun repair orders and said that 335 customers, or 62%, had been charged more than the posted rate.[5] The alleged overcharges averaged $11.83 an hour, with one customer being charged as high as $103.58 an hour, according to a civil suit filed against the dealership in March 1978 by the DA's office and the California Department of Consumer Affairs.[6]

While Martin Swig, owner of Van Ness Datsun, argued in defense that flat rate manual charging was an "efficient and ethical nationwide system serving the public,"[7] the lawsuit called it "a device to deceive and to extract more money from unsuspecting customers in need of auto repairs."[8] The dealership settled the case out of court by paying $25,000 in civil penalties and court costs without admitting any guilt.[9]

The Van Ness Datsun affair is unusual in that the dealership posted its labor rate per hour without noting that the rate was based on concocted flat rate manual time and not the actual amount of time spent fixing cars. Usually shops reveal neither their hourly labor rate nor the fact that they charge according to a flat rate manual book or their own fictional flat rate times. That way they can hoodwink the public into assuming their labor time is based on how long the mechanic actually takes to do the job.

If a motorist happens to see through this smokescreen and demands that he be charged by the actual clock hour, he is frequently treated with abuse and contempt.

One irate consumer, in a letter to the Federal Trade Commission, told how he left his car in the morning at a New Orleans dealership because of a loud tapping noise in the engine. At 2:00 p.m. he talked to someone in the service department who told him his car hadn't been worked on yet. At 3:00 he got a call that the car was fixed.

Arriving later at the dealership, he was confronted with a bill which included a $49 labor charge for replacing two pushrods. When he questioned the excessive labor charge for what couldn't have been more than an hour's work, the service manager came out. Here then is what ensued, according to the letter writer: "He stated this is what 'the book' said should be charged for labor. When I asked what the actual length of time spent by the mechanic on the work was and the amount of the hourly charge, he told me he would never accept my car in his shop again as long as he is the manager."[10]

A respected book on auto dealership management, *The Automobile Dealer* by Martin H. Bury, recognizes that flat rate manual charging, on occasion, "will pose a problem" for the dealer—"especially for a 'waiting' customer." One of Mr. Bury's suggestions is that of "deliberately delaying the return of the car to the customer"—something he calls "a practice defensively common in many repair shops."[11]

The Types of Manuals

There are actually three types of auto repair flat rate manuals: those published by the auto manufacturers for their dealers to adhere to when making warranty repairs and, in some cases, retail repairs; those designed exclusively for retail customer mechanical repairs; and those for determining crash repair time allowances.

The auto manufacturers supposedly compute their flat rate manuals by making time-and-motion studies of how long it takes mechanics to perform each repair job on new-model cars. They then shove these manuals down the throats of their dealers, telling them that the labor times in the manuals determine how much labor time they will pay for each warranty repair—no more, no less. For example, the 1981 Ford flat rate manual said the time allowed to replace the alternator on a 1981 Ford under warranty was 24 minutes.[12] In this case, whether a dealership did the repair in one hour or in 15 minutes, Ford paid that dealer for only 24 minutes of labor multiplied by the dealer's hourly labor rate.

In past years, dealership mechanics had little trouble doing jobs faster than the factory flat rate books called for. At a seminar I sat in on at the 1978 convention of the National Automobile Dealers Association (NADA), an association staffer said the last time a study had been done—some seven years earlier—the average dealer mechanic could beat the factory flat rate in 80% of all cases and could do 95 minutes of factory flat rate time in a clock hour.[13] (The manufacturers could afford to give away this extra time because in many cases they were also dictating the hourly labor rate, which they set artificially low).

Several dealers at the seminar felt that the manufacturers had since cut back the time allowances in the manuals to near the time it actually takes to do repairs. Others contended that the auto makers' manuals are still on the lenient side on most repairs, but not on some.

At any rate, it can be argued that the manuals published by the auto factories are probably, on average, still above the actual time it takes to do most repairs.

That brings us to the second type of flat rate manual—those put out by independent publishers for dealers and other repair shops to follow when doing retail mechanical work. These include *Chilton's Labor Guide and Parts Manual*, published by Chilton Co. of Radnor, Pennsylvania, and *Motor Flat Rate and Parts Manual* and *Motor Imported Car Time Guide*, both published by Hearst Corp. of New York City.

It's not known exactly how these publishers arrive at the ridiculous time allocations for each repair. But one thing is certain. They start with the manufacturer's times—which we have already seen are often overstated themselves—and add to them generously. While some additional labor time is justified because it often takes longer to repair older cars because of hard-to-remove rusted bolts, accumulated road dirt and the like, these two companies go way overboard. For example, while General Motors allowed 1.2 hours to rebuild the wheel cylinders on 1975 through 1981 Chevrolets and Corvettes, Chilton allows 2.2 hours.[14]

When dealers, gas station operators and other repair shop owners see the liberal repair times allowed in these independent manuals, they naturally salivate. For here is a made-to-order justification for overcharging you. They also buy the manuals in droves, not only enriching themselves but the flat rate publishers as well (Chilton was recently getting $35 a throw for its manuals).

The manuals are especially benevolent to shops that do tune-ups and brake repairs. These have become two of the most overcharged-for and thus profitable repairs in the industry, largely because Chilton Co. and Hearst Corp. allow vastly more time allowances for them than they could possibly need.

This whole practice of charging according to the phony inflated times in some hokey manuals instead of according to good old clock time is incredible, to say the least, but most repair shop operators consider it perfectly honest. In true Nixonian fashion they say, "There's nothing wrong with that. Everybody does it." Indeed, despite this industry-wide corrupt practice, Dick Cossette, president of Automotive Service Councils, Inc., had the *chutzpah* to tell a U.S. Congress subcommittee in 1978 that the auto repair industry has only "a few bad apples who tend to spoil the image for all the rest of us" and that only a "small minority . . . engage in questionable and possibly fraudulent practices."[15]

Indeed, overcharging through flat rate manuals is such a widespread and lucrative racket that it might be even more profitable than knocking off banks. The New York State attorney general's office, after a survey of invoices at 21 new car dealerships, estimated in 1980 that motorists in the state were being overcharged about $73 million annually through the use of flat rate manuals. Some 56% of the invoices charged for more hours than actually consumed—for an average overcharge of $18.19 per job.[16]

The Mechanic Connection

While we have seen that flat rate manuals are a first-class swindle in that they result in overcharges, a closer look will show that the flat rate system is also the major reason why Johnny can't fix your car properly and why he performs so many unnecessary repairs.

The vast majority of auto mechanics are not paid by the clock hour or the week as you might assume. Instead, they are paid by the flat rate hour. This means that for each flat rate hour the shop charges you, the mechanic earns a flat rate hour of pay. To illustrate, let's say you own a 1975 to 1981 Chevrolet Nova and take it to a repair shop to have the right exhaust manifold replaced. Johnny the Mechanic replaces the exhaust manifold in one hour, but the Chilton manual is consulted, which allows 1.9 hours for the job.[17] The shop charges $30 a flat rate hour, so you are billed for $57.

Meanwhile, just as you are charged for 1.9 hours of labor even though the job took only one hour, Johnny the Mechanic is paid for 1.9 hours of labor even though he worked only one hour. Let's say he earns $7 for every flat rate hour he bills. In your case he would earn $7 multiplied by 1.9 hours or $13.30 for his one hour of work.

This is standard operating procedure throughout most of the auto repair industry, varying only by the split between shops and mechanics. Some shops, as in our illustration, pay their mechanics so much a flat rate hour. Others might split the labor charge 50–50 or 60–40, with the shop getting the higher percentage.

Under this setup, a mechanic working on flat rate, or "piecework" as it's sometimes called, can accumulate 11, 12, 16 or more flat rate hours in an 8-hour day. At $7 a flat rate hour, for example, a mechanic who collects 16 flat rate hours in a day would earn $112, while one who bills 9 flat rate hours would take home only $63. A Wisconsin dealer flat rate investigation turned up one mechanic who billed customers for 594 hours of labor when he worked only 262 clock hours.[18]

Under this type of system the mechanic is actually working on a commission basis with two major inducements: (1) to try to sell you repairs that "the book"—the industry lingo for a flat rate manual—allows extravagant time allowances for (doesn't matter if you need the repairs or not) and (2) to rush through work in an effort to "beat the book" by a healthy enough margin to make a decent living.

The system especially encourages mechanics to make as many repairs as possible on the car in front of them, particularly in the same area of the car where they are working. This is because the flat rate allowance for each repair usually includes time for the mechanic to drive the car into his stall, get out his tools, remove certain parts to get at the repair area, retrieve parts, make the repair, replace the parts that were removed, put his tools away and drive the car out of the stall.

Thus, once a mechanic has some parts removed from your car to get at a repair, there's a tremendous temptation for him to want to replace more parts in the vicinity, because he can charge you the full flat rate allowance for each additional repair. It's common for a mechanic in this situation to replace a part unnecessarily so he can pick up an extra hour or more of flat rate time for perhaps an extra ten minutes of work.

It also becomes more profitable for a mechanic to do five repairs to one car than one repair to each of five cars, because he doesn't have to spend time moving the car and getting and putting away tools after each repair.

Flat rate mechanics also have an incentive to say they repaired something which they didn't, since they can pick up additional flat rate pay for doing nothing. Mechanics have been known to bill a customer for replacing their alternator, and, instead of doing the repair, making their old alternator look new by quickly steam-cleaning it with what's known in the industry as a "flat rate gun."

Dealer Flat Rate Mechanics

Flat rate mechanics at new car dealerships have yet another incentive to cheat you: The auto companies hold down their wages.

While a dealer mechanic might be able to earn high *Chilton* or *Motor* time allowances for doing retail repairs, he is forced to work with the factory flat rate manual and its comparatively low time allowances when doing warranty work.

Using our previous example of the 1981 Ford, we find that a dealer mechanic who replaced the alternator under warranty would have been paid for only 24 flat rate minutes of labor while if he did the exact same repair for a retail customer using the *Chilton* manual he would have been paid for 48 flat rate minutes.[19]

Beginning in mid-1978, a change in warranty reimbursement occurred which has even further held down the wages of many mechanics. Up to that time, dealers were complaining that the auto companies not only were making them use stingier flat rate manuals when doing warranty work but were also paying them less per hour than they were getting from retail customers. General Motors, Ford, Chrysler and some other companies then struck a deal. They agreed to pay dealers the same hourly rate they were getting for retail work if they charged retail customers by the factory flat rate manuals and posted a sign in the service department informing retail customers of the labor rate. Reportedly, about half of GM's dealers went along.[20]

The change has made many dealer mechanics unhappy, since they are now paid for retail work according to the lower time allowances of the factory manuals. Mechanics in Chicago were so upset that they went on strike for several weeks, demanding and getting a higher hourly wage to compensate.

Because the auto companies have imposed a time limit for each repair on its dealers, most dealers, in turn, have imposed the same time limit on their mechanics. Often when an auto company wants to cut warranty costs it lowers its flat rate time allowances, which results in a reduction of pay for dealer mechanics. Andrew Kenopensky, automotive coordinator of the International Association of Machinists and Aerospace Workers, the nation's largest auto mechanic union, says auto company flat rate time allowances are often so lousy—especially on big operations like engines and transmissions—that dealer mechanics sometimes refuse to do such repairs and might even quit their jobs if pressed to do them.[21] Unhappy with low factory flat rate time, many dealer mechanics strike back by trying to cheat the auto companies, or—if that doesn't work—to cheat retail customers.

To cheat the auto companies, dealer mechanics will add repairs to warranty orders that they didn't actually do and pick up extra flat rate pay. One dealer mechanic told me that when a particular defective part crops up frequently in a new car, it presents a perfect opportunity to get back at the auto companies for holding down their wages. When a mechanic comes across a car without the defect, according to my informant, he'll mark on the repair order that it did have the defect, and, without touching the part, will collect his flat rate time for the repair. The problem for the dealer mechanic is that there's a limit to how much he can get away with. The auto company might get suspicious if too many warranty claims are filed and start an investigation. Also, some auto companies require replaced warranty parts to be returned to them or conduct regular audits in an effort to uncover such goings-on.

Therefore, it is a safer bet from the dealer mechanic's standpoint to cheat retail customers, who usually have no way of knowing whether a repair was needed or not or whether it was actually performed.

Carrot and Stick

The flat rate system actually amounts to a carrot-and-stick approach to paying mechanics. The mechanic is paid at a comparatively low hourly rate, but is given the chance to earn what he really deserves in the first place if he rushes through his work and perhaps cheats a little here and there in his quest to accumulate flat rate hours.

Despite the leniency of the *Chilton* and *Motor* manuals, collecting flat rate hours isn't always as easy as it seems. For if there's little or no business in the shop, the mechanic may earn little or nothing with the possible exception of a low guaranteed wage. Mechanics are also penalized for shop inefficiencies, since time spent not repairing cars is money out of their pocket. Mr. Bury, in his book *The Automobile Dealer,* figures the average dealer mechanic spends less than six hours of an eight-hour work day in productive activity.[22]

Mechanics also complain that under the flat rate system the service manager or the dispatcher—the person who assigns each car to a mechanic in a large dealership—may rob them of earnings by not passing out the lucrative jobs fairly. Often they give the plum jobs to friends or to those mechanics who will give them a kickback.

With the flat rate pay system, the shop owner wins no matter what happens. If the mechanic continually beats the flat rate allowance by a wide margin, it means tidy profits for the shop owner. If the mechanic can't beat the flat rate time on a particular repair, the shop owner pays him nothing for any additional time it takes him over the flat rate allowance. If there's lots of business, the shop owner has someone available who can handle it and help him make money; if there's no business, he has a body present whom he doesn't have to pay. If there are "comebacks"—returns because of bad repairs—the mechanic is obligated to correct the problem without any pay for his time.

The Paradox of the System

One of the great paradoxes of the flat rate system is the fact that many shops, despite using flat rate manuals to overcharge you, are not making much money on their labor rate, and the average mechanic, despite earning extraordinarily high wages for particular flat rate repairs, is not making the kind of money his skills deserve.

The reason for this is twofold: (1) Repair shops are generally poorly managed and waste so much productive time that they often need to overcharge people and penalize their mechanics in order to make up; and (2) shops are largely making their money from the flat rate system through the sale of unnecessary parts—the profits from which are not usually passed on to mechanics.

Mechanics Speak Up

It's becoming more and more obvious that the flat rate pay system, if not outlawed, could spell doom for consumers and the auto repair industry as well. Aside from the implications for fraud, it promotes speed and not competence as the primary objective of each repair, discourages diagnosis and road testing, forces experienced mechanics into premature retirement, makes it difficult to carry on apprenticeship programs and generally discourages young people from entering the industry.

While most in the industry defend the system, there are a few brave souls willing to speak out against it. "The piecework system is responsible for more stealing and shoddy repairs than any other factor involving your car," says Tom Peterson, a mechanic and service writer for over 25 years. Under the system, he adds, "a conscientious mechanic would starve, and his family with him." He explains further:

"First-class mechanics get that way by about eight years of hard work and schooling. They must be trained in automatic transmissions, alternators, electrical motors, wiring systems, engines, doors, windows, exhaust systems, power steering, front and rear suspension systems, air conditioners and their controls, brake systems including power cylinders, and many other complicated and intricate units. They must spend $1,000–$2,000 on tools and several hundred dollars a year to maintain them.

"Having done all that, the mechanic is about 28 years old and has to start cheating in order to stay alive. He must cut his work short, and in effect steal by claiming he did things he didn't do and elaborating on what he did."[23]

Glenn C. Garrett, a Los Angeles area mechanic, is especially concerned about the effect of the flat rate pay system on diagnosis. He declares: "The sole reason for a mechanic to raise the hood on a car nowadays is not to find and repair the problem, but to finish the 'job' as fast as possible. Thus, the mechanic's pride, craftsmanship and diagnostic skills go out the window."[24]

While a thoughtful and thorough diagnosis is frequently necessary to locate what's wrong with your car, the flat rate manuals allow no time for this procedure. That's a major reason why the repair shop often returns your car with the same problem you took it in to have fixed. The manuals basically allow time to perform specified repair functions and say nothing about how long it might take to check out various possibilities before deciding what repair to make. "By not recognizing diagnosis as a legitimate service to the customer, the flat rate system in effect discourages diagnosis," says a National Highway Traffic Safety Administration report by Booz Allen Applied Research, Inc.[25]

To illustrate, suppose your engine is acting up. "There could be a thousand reasons," says a mechanic. Yet a flat rate mechanic would be reluctant to check out all the possibilities because he couldn't charge you for his diagnostic time. What he can charge to you, however, are the time allowances for making one or more repairs. As a result, what often happens is that the mechanic, without doing any diagnosis, will replace a part and collect the flat rate time for doing so. If that doesn't solve the problem, he replaces another part and gets the flat rate allowance for that, and so on until the problem goes away. Regardless of what minor thing might be troubling your engine, the mechanic might just do a tune-up, which gives him a liberal time allowance, and hope that will solve the problem.

Then too, flat rate mechanics have no incentive to fix parts, since the flat rate manuals either allow no time for it or better reward them if they replace a part instead of fixing it. Many new or rebuilt carburetors are put on cars when the old one could have been fixed at much less cost to the customer.

Replacing parts unnecessarily due to the flat rate system is such a common practice in America that it has spawned a whole cadre of pseudo-mechanics known in the industry as "parts hangers," who have the competence neither to diagnose problems nor to fix parts. They just know how to hang parts on a car. Repair shop operators like this because they typically can make a $40 profit on every $100 worth of parts sales.

Some Discouraging Words

Not only does the flat rate structure discourage mechanics from using diagnostic skills, but it also discourages them from developing such skills in the first place. "The incentive for the mechanic to develop diagnostic skills is lacking, since the skills required are relatively difficult to develop and the financial reward is questionable," says a paper prepared by staff members of Booz Allen Applied Research and the National Highway Traffic Safety Administration.[26] This lack of diagnostic knowledge is a major reason why so few auto mechanics in this country can pass competency tests.

It even happens under the flat rate system that the more complicated the job a mechanic is capable of doing, the less he's paid. Sam Laddon, a retired Wheaton, Maryland, body shop operator, says the flat rate system penalizes the journeyman auto body mechanic who can repair heavy collision damage by allowing proportionally fewer flat rate hours in relation to actual time spent than for repairing less complicated damage.[27] Likewise, the mechanic who can completely overhaul an engine or trace difficult electrical-system problems usually collects proportionally less flat rate time for his efforts than mechanics who get the easier flat rate gravy jobs like tune-ups and brake repairs.

The flat rate system also discourages road testing by mechanics. A flat rate mechanic is not about to take your car for a spin, since he's not getting paid for his time. Therefore, he often repairs a car blind without actually experiencing for himself what is wrong. Then, once he's finished with the repairs, he doesn't make a road check to make sure the problem has gone away. That's another reason why you so often get your car back with the same problem it had when you brought it in. Warranty work in particular is almost never road-tested by a flat rate mechanic, since he would lose his shirt doing it.

Another minus for the piecework pay system is that it discourages capable young people from entering the industry. Tom Peterson, the auto service veteran, tells how the flat rate system breaks the will of the mechanic. The mechanic's job, he says, "is so demanding mentally and physically (they have to race the clock every hour), that by age 45 either the mechanic or his income is going to drop. Most mechanics must quit at that age—and there goes any hope of a pension. With such prospects, no wonder fewer and fewer young people want to learn the trade."[28]

Many prospective entrants into the trade are also turned away by another aspect of the flat rate pay system: its negative effect on apprenticeship programs. "Apprenticeship won't work in a flat rate shop," says union coordinator Kenopensky. He explains that journeymen mechanics, concerned with beating the book in order to make a living, don't want to take the time to instruct apprentices.[29]

DeForrest E. Cline of the U.S. Labor Department's Bureau of Apprenticeship and Training doesn't go as far as Mr. Kenopensky but admits the flat rate system "is certainly a deterrent" to apprenticeship programs. "We'd like to see an hourly wage for journeyman mechanics," he says, adding that apprentices should get a percentage of the journeyman's wage. Mr. Cline says the idea of paying mechanics an hourly wage is going along "slowly but surely," but that "it will take another 10 or 12 years before it's a fact."[30]

Piecework and Mechanics Don't Mix

While a case might be made for paying agricultural workers by piece-work—how many bushels of apples or oranges they can collect in a day—or paying garment workers by how many shirts or dresses they turn out in a day, automobile mechanics are in a totally different ball park.

Auto mechanics work with a very complicated piece of machinery said to have 15,000 parts. With the exception of a few who work in a very narrow specialty field, most mechanics are not part of a repetitive assembly-line operation. A mechanic might be called on to repair an engine malfunction in the early morning, work on a transmission problem before lunch, fix an air conditioning unit in the early afternoon and mend an electrical short before quitting for the day.

Auto mechanic work is also different in that the task to be performed is not always readily apparent. An apple picker knows he must pick apples. But an auto mechanic doesn't always know immediately what repair he has to make to cure an ailing car. Before a mechanic even begins working on your car he must be able to diagnose what's wrong with it—something that takes time and thought, which you should be very willing to pay for. A mechanic who can replace a part quickly is useless to you if he replaces a perfectly good part.

Safety also must be considered. A major disadvantage of the piecework system has always been the tendency of workers to sacrifice quality for quantity through excessive speeding. Your life and the lives of those around you depend on your car being repaired carefully and correctly, not in a hasty, slipshod manner. A Philadelphia man, an auto mechanic since 1942, wrote to Ralph Nader in 1975 saying he would like to see the "flat rate or the piecework system eliminated by an act of Congress" because "there is no safety in fast work."

"Since 1962," he said, "I have worked at my present position as a front end specialist paid by the hour and have come to realize the enormous safety factor in the hourly wage. Fast rushed work in the repairing of automobiles under the flat-rate system creates a hazard on the highways. I would like to see every automobile repair center in the United States on an hourly wage as soon as possible."[31]

In most other occupations where the piecework system has been used, a major advantage claimed has always been the weeding out of inefficient and mediocre workers. In the auto repair field, the piecework system has had almost the opposite effect. It has weeded out some of the most skilled workers who can earn better money with less pressure elsewhere and has left us with largely inefficient and mediocre mechanics—the parts hangers.

A panel convened by a Los Angeles area service managers' association in 1977 urged that auto mechanics be paid according to skill level and industry certification test achievements instead of flat rate manuals. "If mechanics were paid according to their worth," John Olsen of Merlin Olsen Porsche-Audi in Encino was quoted as saying, "then unqualified mechanics wouldn't exist."[32]

Defense of the System

Despite all the horrible consequences of the flat rate system, it is still defended by most people in the industry, particularly Chilton Co. and Hearst Corp. Here are some of the arguments for the defense and my responses.

1. *Flat rate manuals are needed to give consumers accurate estimates.*

The reasoning here is that the shop, by looking in a flat rate manual, already knows the precise labor time it will charge when you ask for an estimate. If the shop charged by the clock hour, the actual labor charge might be different from the estimate.

This is pure baloney. What good is having an accurate estimate if it's based on Chilton and Hearst time allowances which are astronomically overstated?

Actually, once a shop has done a particular repair on a particular car, it knows exactly how long it should take and doesn't need the help of Chilton or Hearst. Dealerships, which work on the same line of cars all the time, and specialty shops, which do only one or two kinds of repairs, should especially have enough experience to give accurate estimates without the help of flat rate manuals.

I contend that if the manuals stated the actual time it takes to do repairs, few shops would buy them. Perhaps, to help shops estimate repairs done for the first time, Chilton and Hearst could publish books citing anything out of the ordinary about each particular repair.

2. *The customer is protected under the flat rate system because he doesn't have to pay for any labor time exceeding the flat rate time allotment.*

Supposedly, if the flat rate manual allows one hour to replace a widget and the mechanic takes an hour and a half to make the repair, you pay for only one hour.

The major hole in this argument is that it's highly unlikely that a mechanic can't beat the flat rate time, so you almost always overpay.

Also, because shops know few of their customers are aware of how their labor charge is computed, it's not unusual for them to charge over the flat rate allowance. When the Illinois governor's office took five cars with deliberately loosened alternator belts to 20 shops in 1974, it found "the average cost of repair in our 20 shops for this minor malfunction was 300% of the maximum rate allowed by Chilton's Flat Rate Manual." In black communities, the cost averaged 800% above the maximum Chilton rate allowed for the repair.[33]

It seems that many shops try to win both ways with flat rate manuals. If they do repairs in less time than the manuals call for, they charge you the full flat rate allowance and may even show you the manual to prove you are being charged for the "correct" time. If they can't beat the manual on a particular repair, they might charge you whatever they feel like charging.

3. *The flat rate mechanic has an incentive to do the job right the first time because he's obligated to do any comeback work at no pay.*

While comeback work is a constant worry of the flat rate mechanic, his main incentive is to do the job as quickly as possible and replace as many parts as possible. Because he doesn't take the proper time for diagnosis, a flat rate mechanic might protect himself against the car's being returned by replacing everything in sight, figuring the odds are in his favor that one of the repairs will correct the problem.

There's also the possibility that when you bring your car back because it wasn't repaired right, the mechanic might redo the repairs without pay but then try to charge you for additional repairs to make up for his loss. There's a chance too that neither the shop management nor the mechanic will be anxious to accommodate you on a comeback and may refuse to touch your car.

4. *If consumers were charged by the clock hour, a person who got a fast mechanic would pay less for the same repair than a person in the same shop who got a slower mechanic. That isn't fair.*

Those in the business who use this argument are true hypocrites. Here they charge everyone the full flat rate manual time for each repair—which represents not how fast the average mechanic can do a job, but how fast the slowest mechanic can do a job—then they say they can't see how they can charge clock time for their slowest mechanic.

Actually, I have no objection to a shop's charging a flat fee for a particular repair as long as it's based on the average speed of its mechanics. What I object to is the labor time being determined by Chilton Co. or Hearst Corp. or any outsider.

5. *If mechanics are paid an hourly wage, they'll goof off and take their good old time doing repairs.*

This could well happen in some cases, but a shop with goof-off mechanics would have to give such high estimates for repairs and charge such exorbitant prices that it wouldn't stay in business very long.

Shop management—like any type of management—always has the

prerogative of simply firing anyone who goofs off. Mr. Kenopensky says International Harvester Co. heavy-duty truck mechanics are paid by the clock hour and that the company "will not tolerate a man not proficient." He hardly ever hears complaints about the competence of International Harvester mechanics. Also, he adds, unlike mechanics in dealerships, who, because of flat rate pay system conflicts, are constantly changing jobs and tend to be young, Harvester mechanics tend to be old experienced hands with many years of service in the same place. "If it works in truck service facilities, I have no reason to believe it wouldn't work in auto repair shops," says Mr. Kenopensky.[34]

6. *Repair prices will soar if the flat rate system is abolished.*

This might happen for some repairs, but I don't think it will be bad for the consumer.

First, if consumers were billed for the actual time taken, prices for tune-ups, brake jobs, transmissions and other repairs for which the flat rate manuals allow gravy time allowances would fall as consumers saw the present exorbitant hourly charges for these repairs.

Second, there would be more competitive pricing all around, which would tend to bring prices down.

Third, even if prices for particular repairs went up because of higher wages paid to mechanics, many of the incompetent, unnecessary and fraudulent repairs would be eliminated, bringing a net savings to consumers. The Illinois Legislative Investigating Commission said a common theme running through its consumer complaints about auto repairs was: "I would not have minded paying the bill, even though it seemed high, if the repair had been done right."[35]

Is It Legal?

Is the fact that repair shops charge for labor by using a common flat rate manual "legal pickpocketing," as one irate Lincoln owner called it after being forced to overpay $50 for labor?[36] Or is it illegal—perchance a price-fixing violation of the U.S. antitrust laws, which are supposed to be enforced by the Federal Trade Commission and the U.S. Justice Department?

The U.S. Senate Antitrust and Monopoly Subcommittee began an investigation into the auto repair industry in the late 1960s principally because of the antitrust implications of the flat rate manuals. It found that not only were the manuals responsible for a lack of pricing competition among shops, since all were using the same manuals, but also that the flat rate system was artificially holding down the wages of mechanics.

At that time the *Chilton* and *Motor* manuals not only listed their fictitious time allowances for each repair, as they do now, but also told shops exactly what to charge for each repair based on a uniform labor rate used throughout the books. Chilton dropped the price instruction in 1974, and Hearst followed.

Even without telling the exact price to charge, the manuals today still effectively fix part of the price by giving the repair time to be charged. As it now stands, practically any repair shop you go into might insist that you pay the same exorbitant *Chilton* or *Motor* time allowance, and there's not much you can do about it.

However, the Federal Trade Commission can do something. The FTC has been pretending for more than 50 years that this abhorrent trade practice and price-fixing scheme doesn't exist. The seeds of the flat rate system were planted in 1919—five years after the FTC began operations. In 1919, shops in Philadelphia and Memphis independently posted *their own* flat rate for various repairs. Then Chevrolet came along in 1922 and published its own flat rate manual (presumably for dealers to follow when doing warranty work), and other manufacturers soon copied the idea. In 1926, Chilton came along and consolidated the auto company flat rates into one book while making its own changes.[37]

About the closest the inept FTC has come to taking a stand on flat rate manuals occurred in 1968. Late in the previous year, the National Automotive Radiator Service Association asked the commission for an advisory opinion on whether it could publish, without violating the antitrust laws, a flat rate manual to be used by its members for radiator, heater and air conditioning repairs.[38] The commission wrote back on February 16, 1968, saying it had turned down the request for the following reason:

"There is implicit too grave a danger that the association's manual would facilitate price fixing between competing radiator repair shop operators. The Commission points out the well-established antitrust principle that price fixing by competitors is illegal per se. The public expects to derive benefits from different prices offered by competing service operators."[39]

That advisory opinion immediately raises a basic question: If it's illegal to start a new flat rate manual that *might* facilitate price fixing, why isn't it also illegal to use flat rate manuals already in existence which do in fact cause price fixing and have for over 50 years?

Unbelievably, the FTC didn't get around to investigating the antitrust price-fixing implications of flat rate manuals until April 1976. The investigation wasn't very vigorous and was dropped in December 1977 with no action taken. A written summary of that investigation by an FTC staff attorney is a study in wishy-washiness. On one hand it says that "there may be antitrust questions present," but then suggests it would be better if the commission issued a trade regulation which would require shops that use flat rate manuals to disclose that labor charges are not based on actual time worked. However, the report also implies that if the commission did issue such a disclosure regulation, it could be construed as an endorsement by the FTC of a price-fixing scheme.[40]

There *is* the possibility that flat rate manual price fixing is so unique that it may elude the antitrust laws. Competing repair shops aren't necessarily getting together and conspiring to fix prices; rather, it's a third party—the flat rate manual publisher—that is manipulating prices.

Even this third-party price-fixing is denied by Chilton and Hearst. They both argue that shops are free to charge for any repair time they wish and the fact that shops follow their manuals to the letter has nothing to do with them.

The truth is that not only does Chilton expect shops to charge exactly what it tells them to, but it has long encouraged them to do so. A look at the 1935 *Chilton Flat Rate Manual*, the earliest one I was able to find at the Library of Congress, shows Chilton already engaged in what I, a nonlawyer, would define as a conspiracy to fix prices of auto repairs and to overcharge the American consumer. Here's what Chilton said in the front of the manual:

"Labor prices as listed are based in general on an hour rate of $1.80. It is the belief of the compilers that these figures represent the minimum rate which will provide a fair profit under average conditions or overhead. *We therefore strongly recommend that the operations be sold at the labor prices quoted,* but if overhead conditions in a particular establishment warrant a higher or lower rate the conversion table on inside of back cover may be used" (italics mine).

Reform

It's time our legislators and law enforcement officials did something about this rotten system. These are the major reform alternatives I propose:

1. The paying of auto mechanics by the flat rate system or any commission system should be outlawed. At the same time, to keep prices under control, repair shops should be given government help to make their operations more efficient and tax incentives to hire apprentices and buy labor-saving devices.

2. Congress should amend the antitrust laws to make third parties who assist competitors in fixing prices prosecutable for engaging in a

price-fixing conspiracy. Also, competing businesses which make use of a third party's help in fixing prices should be prosecutable.

3. Congress or the Federal Trade Commission should prohibit the auto companies from putting a time limit on their dealers for doing warranty repairs. Also, dealers should not be allowed to put a time limit on mechanics when doing warranty work or to force mechanics to redo warranty work at no pay. The manuals and the mechanic pay system are an "unfair trade practice," which the FTC has power to prohibit, because they result in poor-quality warranty work and the refusal of dealers and mechanics to do warranty repairs. Unable to impose time limits, the auto manufacturers will have an incentive to improve the quality and efficiency of their dealers' service departments, since they would then have to pay for any incompetence or inefficiencies.

4. The Federal Trade Commission or the Justice Department should file price-fixing suits against General Motors, Ford, Chrysler and possibly other auto companies on two fronts.

First, their practice of requiring dealers to use their flat rate manuals when computing retail labor charges price-fixes part of the retail repair bill and limits repair price competition between dealers for the same line of car. Linda H. Lee, a public relations woman for the Ford Parts and Service Division, openly admitted to me in a letter that this is happening. She wrote:

"Basically, by establishing standard allowances for each repair operation, dealers are provided with a uniform basis for pricing their work whether it be customer paid or warranty reimbursable.

"It allows dealers to provide customers with an accurate estimate of how much a job will cost. This estimate will be consistent wherever the customer goes—the only variable being the individual dealer's labor rate."[41]

Second, the auto company manuals set a minimum base of flat rate time for the entire auto repair industry. Both Chilton and Hearst admit that their manuals are based on the auto company manuals. Hearst, in its 1978 *Motor Parts and Time Guide*, says that "the operation times reported in this publication . . . are primarily based on data supplied by the vehicle manufacturer." Chilton, in its *Chilton's 1981 Labor Guide and Parts Manual*, says: "Among the factors they [Chilton editors] consider in determining CHILTON TIME" is "the time allowed by the respective car manufacturer for its authorized dealers to perform specific operations on cars under warranty conditions."

5. The publishers of flat rate manuals could be required to thoroughly substantiate the times listed in their manuals. The staff of the FTC's Bureau of Competition has considered this approach.[42]

6. All repair shops in the country could be made to come out of the closet with their pricing policies. The lead of New York State should be

followed here. New York requires shops which charge by a flat rate manual to post a sign saying something like this:

LABOR RATE
$20 per hour
Computed by
Motor
Flat Rate Manual[43]

New York State also requires that "if flat rate time is used the consumer shall be shown relevant time rates as listed in the manual, on request." In addition, the state mandates that "written estimates must indicate the hourly labor charge and how it's computed, i.e., by clock hour or flat rate. If flat rate, the manual used must be specified."[44]

In addition to what New York requires, shops that use a published flat rate manual could be required to disclose on their invoices the actual or approximate time spent on each repair.

What to Do Meanwhile

Unfortunately, there's not much you can do until the government steps in, but you can try the following:

You could attempt to find a shop that charges by the clock hour and pays its mechanics the same way, but that's like trying to find a Hostess Twinkie in a health food store. (In Savannah, Georgia, and Charleston, Beaufort and Hilton Head Island, South Carolina, you might try Trouble-Shooters, Inc.) The next best thing is to make sure, before you contract for a repair, that you understand exactly how the labor charge is to be computed. That way, if the shop is charging you flat rate, you can at least prevent them from charging you more than the flat rate time. Also watch out for any shop that has both the *Chilton* and *Motor* flat rate manuals. They'll probably try to charge you according to which one gives the most liberal time allowance. Let's say you own a 1976 Buick Apollo and the shop replaces both front wheel cylinders. The shop might look in the *Motor* manual and see that it allows 1.8 hours[45] and then look in the *Chilton* manual and see that it allows 2.1 hours,[46] and charge you for 2.1 hours. (The factory flat rate on that repair is 1.5 hours.)

If you've been cheated under the flat rate system, you should consider suing. For example, if the shop puts on the repair bill that it has charged you for so many "hours" of labor and bills you for more hours than the repairs actually took, sue in small claims court (see Chapter 20) for the difference. The shop will have a hard time explaining the phony and corrupt flat rate system to the judge. A judge might also be sympathetic if you sue a shop because it has charged you the full flat rate time for two or more overlapping repairs.

You might also consider filing a class action price-fixing suit on behalf of all consumers. For help in such a suit, contact Public Citizen Litigation, a Ralph Nader group (see Appendix C).

Another avenue open to you is to complain bloody murder to the two federal agencies supposed to be enforcing the antitrust laws: the Federal Trade Commission (see Appendix B) and the U.S. Justice Department (see Appendix L).

Realistically, only the politicians can change this corrupt system, and they'll try only if they feel the heat from you. If you would like to see a congressional investigation of auto repair flat rate manuals or perhaps an amendment to the antitrust laws specifically outlawing this type of price fixing, then write to the U.S. Senate and House judiciary committees (see Appendix L). If you'd like to see the auto repair flat rate pay system abolished, write to the chairmen of the U.S. Senate and House labor committees (see Appendix L). Send copies of your letters to your congressman and two senators (see Appendix L).

You should also complain about the flat rate system to state and local officials and legislators, particularly your attorney general (see Appendix B).

3

The Chain Store Hustle

It's hard to resist their advertisements.

FRONT END ALIGNMENT $12   BRAKE SPECIAL $37   TUNE-UP $25

These and similar ads are the trademark of nationwide department and discount stores as well as tire company stores and various other chain-owned or franchised auto repair outlets.

Many of these firms are known all over the country for offering the best bargains on auto repairs. And indeed they are bargains if the shops do the work advertised and only that work. However, such specials are often merely come-ons to get you into the shop to sell you additional highly profitable repairs—many of which are quite unnecessary. Also it's been learned that in many "package" deals such as brake overhauls and tune-ups, either an incredible number of usable parts are thrown away or some of the repairs or services offered as part of the package are not performed.

Reports coming out of a federally sponsored diagnostic center project and talks with government auto repair investigators, experienced mechanics and other industry observers lead me to believe that, as a group, chain and franchise stores are perhaps the biggest auto repair rip-off artists of them all. This is not to say, however, that there are not some honest and competent chain and franchise operations or moral individual shops within such organizations.

Despite the "specials" and reputation for low prices, a rudimentary analysis of data from five federally funded diagnostic centers indicates, according to a U.S. Department of Transportation official, that "above-average repair costs" are most likely at specialized chain stores and at mass merchandising stores such as but not limited to Sears, Roebuck & Co., Montgomery Ward & Co., J.C. Penney Co. and K-mart Corp.[1]

Joseph Ralph Pisani, as part of his doctoral thesis at the University of Maryland, conducted extensive interviews of mechanics in Prince George's County, Maryland, and Travis County, Texas. "Repair shops," he concluded, "believe automotive service centers of retail chains to be the least trustworthy and the least careful in performing repairs." Independent shops, according to Mr. Pisani, were rated best by both mechanics and consumers.[2]

An East Coast consumer protection agency investigator told me he suspected that mass merchandiser auto repair facilities "are more in the business of selling you [unnecessary] parts than in fixing your car." And an investigator for a California district attorney's office claims that "mass merchandisers pay low wages to nonunion employees" and that many give those employees a commission on either the total repair bill or on every part sold. "The pay structure is directly related to overselling practices," he says.

The Alabama Findings

The most penetrating account of mass merchandiser auto repair practices was amassed by the University of Alabama in Huntsville, which operated one of the five federally funded diagnostic centers. The university did a thorough analysis of 836 engine, brake, alignment, suspension and steering system repairs performed by five national merchandising chains in the Huntsville area. It found that 213 of the repairs, or 25%, were unnecessary. The university, in its official report on the study, itemized the unnecessary repairs for each of the stores. However, the names of the companies were expunged and letters substituted in their place, such as chain store A, B, C and so on. Nevertheless, I was able to obtain the names of the chains and the percentage of unnecessary repairs for each:

Chain Store	Total Repairs	Unnecessary Repairs	Rate of Unnecessary Repairs (%)
Woolco	58	27	47
Ward	90	28	31
Penney	86	24	28
K-mart	165	38	23
Sears	437	96	22[3]

The Huntsville project also did a special analysis of repairs involving front and rear disc brakes or drums, front and rear brake linings, rear wheel seals, control pivot arms, idler arms, lower ball joints and shock absorbers. It found that 46% of these repairs done at the above five chain stores plus a regional chain outlet were unnecessary and that 44 cents of every dollar spent for these repairs at the six shops was wasted.[4] The only type of repair shops that had a worse record for these repairs were 12 area tire dealers,[5] including some operated by national tire companies and regional chain outfits. Some 48% of the repairs at the tire dealers were unnecessary, resulting in an economic loss to consumers of 45 cents on the dollar.[6]

In still another analysis, this time of 2,463 repairs done at repair shops, the Alabama project found that tire dealers and mass merchandising chains were the repair facilities most likely to take advantage of women. At tire dealers, 36% of the repairs obtained by women were unnecessary, compared to 26% for men. At the chains, women paid for unneeded work on 32% of their repairs, vs. 24% for men. In comparison, service stations actually treated women better than men; independents treated both evenly, and car dealers performed only slightly more unnecessary repairs for women than men.[7]

Quota Selling and Commissions

Evidence exists that at least some of the big chain stores are or have been engaged in "quota selling"—forcing mechanics to sell so many of a particular part every month—and in giving mechanics and service writers commission inducements. These practices, of course, lead to the sale of many unneeded parts and services.

Apparently, this has been going on for many years, with very few chain store mechanics—past or present—willing to blow the whistle on the scam. However, the Oregon attorney general's office did manage to interview a man in 1973 who had been employed as a mechanic 10 years earlier at a Firestone Tire & Rubber Co. store. He said he was fired because he refused to sell unneeded repairs.

"They . . . would say we have a quota to meet, so many brake shoes, so many tires," the mechanic said in a signed statement. "I had so many [ball joints] to sell per month. There was an implied directive to either sell them or lose your job."

His boss had talked a woman into getting a new set of brake shoes. "I took the wheels off," he stated, "and it wasn't needed at all. Her brake shoes were just as good as the ones he wanted put on and I refused to put them on. On Friday, I was terminated."[8]

In 1973, a California investigator looking into the auto repair operations of Goodyear Tire & Rubber Co. interviewed a mechanic who had worked for the company for about four years and left because—as he put it—he was tired of "screwing the public."

He said Goodyear had a high-pressure commission policy which employees had to adhere to or lose their jobs. A mechanic working for Goodyear received an hourly wage, and if he doubled his monthly hourly wage in parts and labor billings, he would receive a 16% commission on everything above that figure.

The former Goodyear mechanic also told of competition being set up between various stores with monthly quotas set. Another former Goodyear employee explained that his store was assigned a quota by the area manager and that the store manager in turn assigned him a quota.[9]

Through extensive investigation, I have found a shocking pattern of unscrupulous behavior by major auto repair chains and franchise organizations—enough to warrant a major congressional investigation into these companies. Here are my findings for each company.

K-mart Corp.

A common trick among chain stores is to advertise a low-cost front end alignment special. Then, when customers bring in their cars, they're told falsely that the alignment can't be done unless other more costly repairs are performed first. Or else they're simply conned into authorizing unnecessary repairs to other areas of the car to make up for the low-cost special. It's this sort of trickery that Michigan authorities say they uncovered with K-mart Corp.

In 1977, a motorist took his 1972 Plymouth Duster into a K-mart repair facility in Lansing in response to an ad offering front end alignments for $7.47. Once there, however, he was told that his car had defective ball joints and the mechanic refused to perform the alignment unless the ball joints were replaced.

Somewhat suspicious, the motorist said he would think about it and drove directly to the state's Bureau of Automotive Regulation, which licenses and regulates auto repair shops. There his car's ball joints were found well within manufacturer's specifications.

Under arrangements with the bureau, he took his car back to K-mart, had the work done and got back his old ball joints. The bureau again tested the ball joints and found them to be satisfactory.[10]

The case was settled under a voluntary agreement whereby K-mart admitted no violation of the law, but nevertheless agreed to pay a $7,000 fine and to refund the customer about $80 for repairs.[11]

Cases against five other K-mart auto centers in Michigan—mostly involving the alleged sale of unnecessary repairs in 1977 and 1978—were settled when K-mart, without admitting guilt, agreed to pay the state $15,000 and reimburse one customer $114.63.[12]

That's not all! K-mart has also gotten into big trouble in California, Nevada and Kansas.

The Alameda County (Oakland), California, district attorney's office said it sent an undercover car with new ball joints into three different K-mart auto centers in 1974, and, in each one, personnel tried to sell new ball joints. Investigators also got statements from employees that they replaced shock absorbers, tie rod ends and mufflers unnecessarily.[13]

The DA's office found that the K-mart centers were using a Lomac Ball Joint Tester, which is supposed to be used with a dial indicator gauge in order to give an effective reading on the wear of a ball joint. However, investigators said, K-mart employees weren't using the dial indicator and were still telling customers that their ball joints were defective. The DA charged that the "use of the Lomac tool without the gauge was simply a ruse to make customers believe that their vehicles were in need of new ball joints."[14]

In a stipulated settlement in 1978, K-mart admitted no guilt but agreed to pay $15,000 in penalties and to spend an additional $78,492 in 1978 educating and training its mechanics throughout California.[15]

Over in Sacramento County, California, the district attorney's office filed suit against K-mart in 1976 alleging that the company misrepresented the need for repairs, engaged in false and misleading advertising, charged customers for adjustments and repairs which weren't done and failed to comply with the state's auto repair law.[16] That case was settled with K-mart agreeing to pay $4,728 in investigative costs.[17]

In Orange County, California, authorities investigated 13 K-mart auto repair facilities in 1980 and said they found violations of state law in all 13. The company was accused of such things as doing unnecessary and incompetent brake drum turnings and advertising brake repair specials for all four wheels and then telling customers that only two wheels needed repairs, charging them close to the advertised price for four wheels. As part settlement, K-mart, without admitting guilt, agreed to pay civil penalties and investigative costs of $50,000.[18]

In Nevada, the Washoe County (Reno) district attorney's office said it sent an undercover car into a K-mart center in 1980 and was sold a new master cylinder when the old one just needed to be tightened. K-mart, without admitting guilt, paid $1,583 in penalties and investigative costs.[19]

In Kansas, the Sedgwick County (Wichita) district attorney's office alleged in 1980 that K-mart had unnecessarily replaced a master cylinder on an undercover car. Unfortunately, according to the DA's office, the evidence was misplaced and the case had to be dismissed.[20]

Sears, Roebuck & Co.

Sears auto repair centers have been in trouble with the law in such states as California, Texas, Vermont, Maryland, Nevada and Wisconsin.

The company got itself into hot water in two California counties—Orange and Sacramento—for sales practices regarding "coil spring spacers." These are plastic doodads which are supposed to lift up sagging springs. Sears was charging about $23 for a set of four installed, although Charles D. McFarland, assistant Orange County district attorney, doesn't think they could have cost Sears more than a couple of dollars and can be installed in hardly any time at all.[21]

The Sacramento DA's office accused Sears of selling these spring spacers without any measurement being taken to demonstrate their need. Customers were told, according to Roger Robinson of the DA's fraud division, that a front end alignment couldn't be performed unless the spring spacers were installed. This could be true, he said, if the curb height of the vehicle isn't correct. But in order to determine that, he said, it's necessary to measure the distance from the ground to one or two points on the bottom of the car's frame or chassis—something Sears wasn't doing. The correct distance varies according to the car. "Sears was selling a helluva lot of them [spring spacers]," according to Mr. Robinson, with some of its stores selling more in a week than many other repair shops would sell in two years.[22]

Under a 1978 stipulated settlement with Sacramento County, Sears, without admitting wrongdoing, agreed to pay costs and civil penalties of $10,935, to follow the proper guidelines in selling spring spacers and to fully explain what's involved to customers.[23]

In the Orange County case, the DA's office accused Sears of not only selling spring spacers unnecessarily but also of misleading customers by calling them "stabilizers."

An undercover car was taken into several Sears repair centers in Orange County about 20 times, and, according to Mr. McFarland, drivers were sold "stabilizers" in the "great majority of cases."[24]

For those alleged misdeeds and others, Sears, without admitting guilt, agreed in 1978 to pay costs and civil penalties of $80,000.[25]

Sears got off much easier than that in the other states.

In Texas, Sears in 1976 was criminally convicted of deceptive business practices in Harris County Court and fined $500 as the result of a Houston TV station's sending an undercover car into one of its auto repair centers. The company replaced a new set of front shock absorbers which were made to look used and charged for a front end alignment which wasn't done.[26]

In Vermont, a woman went into a Sears auto center in Burlington in 1977 to obtain a front end alignment and was told, according to a suit filed by the state attorney general's office, that it couldn't be done without first fixing or replacing the ball joints and tie rod ends. The woman became suspicious, because one ball joint and one tie rod had been replaced just the week before. She had a state motor vehicle inspector look over her car. He found Sears' representations untrue. Sears settled the case by, among other things, paying $1,750 in costs and penalties.[27]

In Maryland, in separate 1980 incidents, two motorists became suspicious that they were sold unnecessary brake repairs at a Sears center. They took their old parts to the Montgomery County Office of Consumer Affairs, which said it found in both cases that Sears had replaced perfectly good brake pads. Under pressure from the agency, Sears refunded the customers $83.46 and $84.92 respectively, and, without admitting guilt, signed an agreement with the county not to sell unnecessary repairs in the future.[28]

In Nevada, the Washoe County district attorney's office filed criminal charges against Sears in 1980. A woman investigator drove a car into a Sears center, complaining that the brake warning light was on and that the brake pedal felt low. She was told her master cylinder, four shock absorbers and an idler arm were defective and was charged $251 for repairs. In fact, said the DA's office, the master cylinder and front shock absorbers were new and the rear shocks and idler arm were in good working order.[29] This case hadn't come to trial when this book went into production.

In Wisconsin, Sears in 1980 paid $2,000 in penalties after an investigation by the state's Division of Consumer Protection found that the company had failed to supply customers with copies of auto repair estimates and orders as mandated by law.[30]

Goodyear Tire & Rubber Co.

Goodyear, between 1973 and 1978, was accused of auto repair rip-offs by government agencies in at least four states, costing the company over $100,000 in penalties.

In 1973, Goodyear was accused by the Santa Barbara County, California, district attorney's office of using wheel alignment specials for $9.95 as "part of a sophisticated scheme . . . to entice the automobile owners to come in to the Goodyear locations so that Goodyear employees, through fradulent misrepresentations, [could] sell them unneeded and unnecessary replacement parts and services." As in previously mentioned cases of this type, Goodyear was charged with making "numerous and frequent misrepresentations concerning the replacement of 'ball joints.' "[31] Many unnecessary repairs were performed on a state undercover car, according to the DA's office.[32]

In a stipulated settlement, Goodyear agreed to pay a penalty of $80,000, close its Santa Barbara store for 10 days and fire the employees involved.[33]

In Missouri, the attorney general's office charged in 1975 that Goodyear mechanics were inducing customers to buy unneeded repairs and were even going so far as to "alter, damage and/or to destroy certain auto parts" so that new parts could be sold. The company was also accused of falsely advertising that it employed "service specialists" and "trained professionals" and of misrepresenting that tires were on sale for limited specified dates when in fact they were frequently on sale and often sold regularly at the sale price.[34] Far from being trained professionals, the Goodyear mechanics "appeared to be high school dropouts with very little training," according to William L. Newcomb, Jr., chief counsel of the attorney general's Consumer Protection Division.[35]

As part of a consent agreement, Goodyear, while admitting no wrongdoing, agreed to pay $18,000 to the state for investigatory costs and to vastly improve the competency of its mechanics in Missouri.[36]

Wisconsin officials in 1978 accused Goodyear of advertising a brake relining special for $40.88 which it had no intention of doing at that price. State inspectors said when they tried to have their brakes repaired at Goodyear for the advertised price, they were told that they wouldn't get an adequate brake job for that price and that additional repairs should be purchased.

In a consent order, Goodyear agreed to disclose conspicuously in its brake repair ads any parts and services that were not covered by the price but likely to be necessary and to itemize the parts and services included in the advertised brake repair price.[37]

In Kansas, the Sedgwick County district attorney's office did two 1978 undercover operations against a Goodyear store in Wichita. In both cases, employees tried to sell unneeded repairs before they would do wheel alignments. In addition, one investigator was sold $83.76 worth of unnecessary brake repairs.[38] Goodyear in this case admitted guilt and agreed to pay $2,794.70 in costs and penalties.[39]

Firestone Tire & Rubber Co.

WMAL-TV in Washington, D.C., sent an undercover car to two Firestone stores in 1973 and found all sorts of devious practices. The car was put into fine condition and outfitted with new, but deliberately rusted, front shock absorbers. After passing the Virginia state inspection, the car was driven by a woman to a Firestone store in Fairfax, Virginia. She said she was leaving on vacation and asked for a brake and front end check. The store did $65.10 worth of unnecessary repairs, including a front end alignment and the replacement of a ball joint and two shock absorbers. The service manager also tried to sell her a brake job, saying the linings were 85% worn—a statement that wasn't true.[40]

A few days later, the car was once again put into tip-top shape and outfitted with four new but very dirty shock absorbers and other new but dirty parts. The only defect was a damaged left rear drum. The car was taken to Firestone's Riverdale, Maryland, store. This time, a male driver said he was buying the car for $1,000 less what it would cost to put it in good operating shape. He got a bill for $201.75, which included charges for four new shock absorbers, new tie rod ends and tie rod sleeves, the fourth alignment the car had undergone that week, new front brake drums and grinding of the new drums. They also tried to sell him two new rear tires.

Not only were the repairs unnecessary, but the grinding of the drums hadn't been done, leaving the car in a dangerous condition. The left wheel bearing dust covers were just barely hanging on and the mechanic had improperly installed both front bearing retaining nuts—a condition which could have destroyed the front wheel bearings in 100 miles or so.[41]

As a postscript to this adventure, Firestone tried to keep the undercover operation from being shown on TV. The company was sent a transcript of the Firestone segments prior to airing and sent back what newscaster Jim Clarke called a "battery of lawyers." The lawyers, Mr. Clarke said, "put great pressure on the [broadcasting] company to cancel it." The lawyers apparently backed off after they learned everything that was said during the undercover operation was recorded on tape. Mr. Clarke told me in 1978 that the Firestone lawyers were extremely intimidating and that he had been a reporter for 20 years and hadn't experienced "more pressure before or since on a story."[42]

In 1978, the Sedgwick County, Kansas, district attorney's office said it was sold over $165 worth of unnecessary repairs when it sent two undercover cars into a Firestone service center in Wichita. Alternators were replaced unnecessarily on both cars.[43] A district court judge fined Firestone $1,000. He ruled that while no intentional fraud was involved, Firestone had failed to properly train its mechanic in the use of a diagnostic machine on which he had relied.[44]

In 1979, the Alameda County (Oakland), California, district attorney's office caught a Firestone store subcontracting out tune-up work without telling customers—a violation of state law. Firestone paid $4,000 in costs to settle the case.[45]

J.C. Penney Co., Inc.

Sometimes chain stores find it convenient to have incompetent mechanics. Then when they're accused of replacing parts unnecessarily they can plead that there was no intention to defraud but that the mechanics involved didn't know what they were doing. J.C. Penney took this approach in Alaska.

The state attorney general's office charged that the company's Anchorage store in 1975 replaced the rear brake drums on a 1971 Ford station wagon after informing the owner that the drums couldn't be turned and still conform to Ford standards. However, the drums, according to the charges, were in good working condition and in any event could have been turned and still have conformed with Ford's standards.

Penney, as a defense, said that it had hired a brake specialist about two months before and an assistant shortly afterward and that neither was aware that Fords, Mercurys and Lincolns have non-standard-diameter brake drums.

In an assurance of voluntary compliance, the company agreed to refund the price of all work done on the brake drums of Ford Motor Co. cars beginning with the date the "brake specialist" was hired and to pay the State $1,700 in attorney fees.[46]

In Sacramento County, California, the district attorney's office, after conducting undercover operations against Penney in 1976, alleged the company violated 11 state laws and regulations. Among the charges: engaging in false and misleading advertising and representing untruthfully to people who brought their cars in for minor repairs and adjustments that additional parts were worn and in need of repair or replacement.[47] In settlement, Penney, without admitting guilt, agreed to abide by the laws and regulations of California and to pay costs and civil penalties of $6,711.[48]

In 1980, the Washoe County, Nevada, DA's office accused Penney, just as it did K-mart and Sears, of selling an undercover agent an unnecessary master cylinder repair. Penney, without admitting any wrongdoing, settled the case by paying $1,601.50 in costs and civil penalties.[49]

Montgomery Ward & Co., Inc.

The Los Angeles city attorney's office charged in a civil suit that Ward failed to rebuild calipers or wheel cylinders, bleed brakes or turn drums despite advertising that such services would be provided as part of a brake repair package. In a 1976 stipulated judgment, Ward agreed, among other things, to pay $15,000 in penalties and to perform all advertised services.[50]

Earl Scheib, Inc.

"I will paint any car for $29.95," proclaimed Earl Scheib in a famous advertisement. However, the San Diego and Orange County, California, district attorney's offices charged in 1974 that such an offer was false or misleading, as were these other claims made by Mr. Scheib's company: that their auto painting was guaranteed for five years against fading; that $10 worth of body repair would be performed free with each paint job; that a long-lasting glasslike finish was baked onto every car in an infrared drying tunnel; that cars repainted were completely hand-sanded; that all body repairs were performed by specialists with years of experience; and that their auto painting and body repair were quality work.[51]

In a consent judgment, Earl Scheib, Inc., without admitting guilt, agreed to pay $60,000 in civil penalties, and, among other things, not to represent that it will paint any vehicle for $29.95 or any other price unless it actually will without requiring customers to purchase more goods or services.[52]

Midas-International Corp.

Midas, with more than 950 franchised muffler shops in the U.S.,[53] has been under a Federal Trade Commission consent order since 1960.

At that time, the commission charged the company with falsely advertising and promoting that its mufflers were unconditionally guaranteed for the life of the car on which they were installed. In reality, the commission said, the mufflers were only guaranteed for as long as the purchaser owned the particular car, and the guarantee was not unconditional, but had several limitations not revealed in the advertising. Midas, which was under different ownership then, admitted to the charges and agreed, among other things, not to misrepresent the nature or extent of its guarantee.[54]

While I've not found any actions taken by law enforcement agencies against Midas since the FTC consent order, I have come across several consumer complaints which indicate that at least some of the company's franchisees are engaging in unscrupulous practices.

A man from a retiree community, in a 1978 letter to the FTC, tells a wonderful story of consumer persistence against a bunch of rip-off artists. He said he called up a Midas Muffler Shop and got a quote on a new tail pipe for $12.95 installed. I'll let him now tell the rest of the story:

"I brought the car in and the mechanic put it on the lift and got a clipboard and paper and pencil and started his ritual. He finally came up with an estimate of $92 *and change!* I said, 'Just the tail pipe, please.'

"Well, of course he put the pressure on and became very adamant that all this work was necessary. I said, 'Just the tail pipe, please,' again, and he got his 'turnover' man, who went through the same spiel. I said, 'Just the tail pipe please and for Christ's sake let's get at it!'

"They both started the same spiel again, but after I threatened to call the police they finally condescended to install the tail pipe but with all kinds of dire predictions about what was going to happen to the exhaust system and to me and my passengers from the leaks and rattles, etc."

The windup was that he got his tail pipe installed for $12.95 and had no further problems with the exhaust system. But he paid a price more than money for his refusal to be conned. "My blood pressure soared 20 points that day and I was in bed for two days recovering," he said.[55]

Let's now look at some particular repairs that are often done unnecessarily and incompetently by chain and franchise outlets.

Brake Repairs

If you value your life and your money, think twice about having brake repairs done at national department and discount store chains or at tire company stores.

Your life is at stake because of the poor quality of the mechanics these companies tend to hire. "If someone's a good mechanic he's not going to [work at] Penney or Sears," says Richard Alexander, auto investigator for the District of Columbia Office of Consumer Protection. He explains that the supervisors at mass merchandiser repair facilities are often qualified mechanics, but that the people who do the actual work are mostly "trainees." A trainee, he says, may learn how to fix the brakes on the most popular models but "there might be something he doesn't know about a Volvo that might cost you your life."[56]

Horror stories abound concerning the poor quality of brake work done at chain outlets.

A Houston area man, in a letter to the Federal Trade Commission, complained that a complete brake job at a Firestone company store in 1976 "would've cost my life had I not acted in time." He said he had trouble driving after the brake job and went to another repair shop where it was discovered that the left front caliper had been punctured, which could have frozen the wheel.[57] Another motorist, in a 1976 letter to the U.S. Office of Consumer Affairs, tells of a mechanic at a Goodyear company store in Tennessee who, during a brake job, apparently put a bearing on backward and messed up the axle trying to get it off.[58]

If the above doesn't frighten you away from tire company stores and chains for brake repairs, maybe the following will. A study of 1,233 brake repairs[59] by the University of Alabama diagnostic center found that tire dealers, including tire company stores and regional tire retail chains, "have a consistently greater unnecessary brake repair rate than any other type of repair facility,"[60] followed by the department and discount store chains.[61]

Some 38% of all brake repairs done by tire dealers and 32% done by the merchandising chains were unnecessary compared to an average of 25% for all repair shops.[62] In addition, the university found, it appears that tire dealers and chains especially take advantage of women on brake repairs. Some 54% of the brake repairs purchased by women at tire dealers weren't needed vs. 34% for men. At chains, it was women 46% and men 26%.[63]

Many of the unnecessary brake repairs at tire dealers and chains appear due to "package" brake specials offered by these companies. A National Highway Traffic Safety Administration report says that "when an owner buys a package deal, his repair bill is, on the average, double what it would have been if he had bought only the repairs he needed."[64]

Here then are a few guidelines for minimizing brake repair costs:

DRUM AND DISC TURNING

Between $235 million and $395 million is wasted annually on brake drum or disc turning, according to estimates by the University of Alabama's diagnostic center.[65] The center examined 376 drum and disc turnings and found that almost 60% weren't needed.[66] In another sampling, the center found about 26% of the front drums and 11% of the rear drums had been turned beyond the manufacturer's recommendations.[67] When this is done, it shortens the life of the drums or discs and means they have to be replaced sooner than necessary—and they don't come cheap.

The center recommends you have the drums turned only if they are scored due to metal-to-metal wear by more than 0.020 inch.[68] With the typical drum turning costing $5 to $10 a wheel, this could save you a small bundle.

BRAKE PEDAL

If your pedal is too low when you apply the brakes for a hard stop, all that's usually necessary is a simple adjustment of the brake shoes.[69]

MASTER CYLINDER

If the fluid in the master cylinder reservoir is low, the cause could be evaporation. If no other failures are noted, you may just have to add fluid. That's all.[70]

WHEEL CYLINDERS

If your brake system is relatively new or has been recently overhauled and one cylinder is leaking because of a defective or damaged part or a cracked forging, you don't need to have the other three cylinders fixed. However, if one cylinder needs to be repaired because of wear or aging, the others probably need to be repaired as well.[71]

Besides being wary of brake specials because you may not need all the repairs in the "package," you should also be cautious because you might need *more* repairs than are offered. Be especially wary if the advertised price includes the repair or servicing of disc brakes, but doesn't include the rebuilding of brake calipers or the installation of new or rebuilt wheel cylinders. That $45 "special" could end up costing you $500.

Tune-Ups and Emission Control

In an effort to conserve gasoline and reduce pollutants, your car should be properly tuned at all times. But what kind of repair shop should you patronize for tune-up work?

The answer is probably *not* tire dealers and chain stores—if University of Alabama findings are any criteria. At tire dealers, consumers spent 47 cents of every emission repair dollar for unnecessary work—the highest dollar loss of any type of repair shop[72]—and the chains had a 42% unnecessary repair rate—the highest percentage of any type of repair shop.[73]

Once again, the problem may have to do with "package" deals. U.S. Department of Transportation (DOT) officials figure lots of money is being wasted on unnecessary repairs as part of tune-up specials. They contend that many tune-ups are sold when the problem may be a faulty spark plug or some other minor malfunction.

For example, if your car is losing power and getting bad mileage, the cause could be as simple as one improperly gapped spark plug. All the shop need do is either regap the spark plug or replace it with a new one. However, when DOT in 1979 took cars with only one defective spark plug to 18 repair shops and explained the resulting symptoms, only two shops did the correct repair and only the correct repair. Of the remaining

16, three did unnecessary repairs of $121 to $180 and the 13 others averaged $39.24 in unneeded repairs.[74]

A DOT diagnostic inspection project in Phoenix did an experiment in which it took 57 cars which failed its exhaust emissions inspection and performed the *least-cost* repairs necessary for the cars to pass the inspection. The average cost per car was $16, compared to an average of $25.79 for those who simply took their cars to repair shops of their choice or did it themselves.

The experimenters found that 65% of the repairs required no parts, but just adjustments of carburetor idle mixture, timing and dwell. Only 20% needed points and only 13% needed spark plugs. It was also found that major improvements in miles per gallon could be achieved with relatively inexpensive repairs.[75] In fact, if your repairman is honest and competent, there's a good chance he can bring your car up to emission standards for $10 or less.[76]

A good repair shop should tell you precisely what is out of whack. This is the procedure followed by the highly respected Automobile Club of Missouri diagnostic centers. "We never say, 'Your car needs a tune-up,'" according to John N. Noettl, a club official. "We'll say, 'Your No. 3 plug wire is bad' or 'You need your timing set!'"[77]

This is something to think about before going to one of the increasing number of chain repair shops that deal exclusively in tune-ups. They might be set up to do tune-ups and no lesser repairs, or it might be that their mechanics are so low-skilled that they only know how to do a tune-up and aren't capable of diagnosing what specifically might be ailing your car. Indeed, Andy Granatelli, chairman of Tuneup Masters, a fast-growing West Coast chain, confided to an Associated Press reporter, "We take guys that, frankly, nobody else would hire."[78]

Realistically, things don't look good for those of you whose cars are required to pass periodic emission control inspections. The five DOT diagnostic centers and the Automobile Club of Missouri have found emissions to be the most frequently misrepaired subsystem.[79] Carburetors especially pose a problem for mechanics. "The vast majority of the repair industry is unable to identify and, therefore, repair carburetor outages effectively with the equipment they have," says a University of Alabama report.[80]

Another problem is defining exactly what a tune-up is. "No one really knows," says Allen Richey, executive vice-president of the Automotive Services Association in Austin, Texas. "There is no real understanding by either the garage industry or the consumer of what constitutes a 'tune-up' whether it be labeled as a major tune-up or a minor tune-up."

Mr. Richey, who represents repair shops in seven South Central states, says a tune-up for one facility could be "simply the replacement of points, condenser, and the setting of the vehicle's dwell and timing" while at another facility it may be those things plus cleaning or adjusting the carburetor.[81]

What's needed is a trade regulation defining just what a "major" and "minor" tune-up must include. Such a definition, according to Mr. Richey, "would benefit both the industry and the consumer" with the consumer being able to "objectively compare the prices offered for the job."[82]

Meanwhile, heed the definitions given by *Motor Trend* magazine when comparing tune-up prices. The magazine says you should expect to get at least the following during a "minor" tune-up: "New spark plugs, new points, new condenser. A check of the ignition wiring, vacuum advance, leads and coil. A replacement distributor cap if needed. Timing adjustment. Cleaning of the gas filter. Cleaning or replacement of the carburetor air filter. Adjustment of the carburetor. A check of the smog equipment."

A "major" tune-up, says the magazine, should involve the above plus cleaning, overhauling or replacing the carburetor. It could also include tightening and adjusting the fan belt and cleaning the battery terminals. Some shops, in addition, might pull the distributor, "strobe" it on a machine and adjust and/or rebuild it.[83]

Also check to see if the price you're being quoted for a tune-up is for both parts and labor. "That bargain $24.95 [tune-up] may be nothing but parts," warns *Motor Trend*. "Or it may be just labor, with all parts extra."[84]

Ball Joints

"Ball joints is one of the major huckster-type repairs," says Harry Johnson of the Consumer Fraud Division of the Alameda County, California, district attorney's office.[85]

The classic way repair shops—especially chain outlets—try to bamboozle motorists into unnecessary ball joint repairs is described by Mr. W of Hartland, Wisconsin, in a letter to the Milwaukee Better Business Bureau. He said he responded in 1972 to a Firestone ad in the *Milwaukee Journal* for an $8.88 front end alignment.

"After my car was placed on a hydraulic lift," he said, "the store's assistant manager told me he had some bad news. He asked me to accompany him to my car.

"There, another man (who was to have done the alignment) wiggled my left front wheel slightly and told me I needed new upper ball joints.

Cost: $49.95, not including the $8.88 for the alignment. The mechanic told me that unless the ball joints were replaced he could not guarantee the alignment. Seconds after he said that a third man joined us and warned me that unless the ball joints were repaired it was likely that my wheels would fall off."

Mr. W didn't bite because he had had the front end of his car closely inspected at a diagnostic center two days before and it was determined all he needed was a front end alignment and a wheel balance.[86]

Many people, unfortunately, do fall victim to this classic swindle. The truth is that when a car is on a lift or jacked up and the front wheels are off the ground, it's natural for the front wheels to wobble when wiggled. Also, if a shop tells you, as it did Mr. W, that it can't align your front wheels because your ball joints are worn, the California Bureau of Automotive Repair suggests, "Try another alignment shop."[87]

Actually, there is only one method of determining whether your ball joints are worn unless they have built-in wear indicators. That method is to make a measurement with a special instrument, such as a dial indicator or caliper rule. The California Bureau of Automotive Repair requires all repair shops, before replacing a ball joint, to measure it and write down the measurement on the customer's invoice along with the manufacturer's allowable wear or looseness of the old ball joint.[88] After the rule went into effect, according to Douglas Laue, deputy director of the bureau, ball joint sales reportedly dropped overnight by 85%.[89]

Regardless of where you live, don't let any mechanic replace your ball joints without giving you first in writing the measurements of your ball joints and the factory tolerance. Mr. Johnson, the consumer fraud investigator, says you shouldn't have to replace your ball joints "before 70,000–80,000 miles in most cars."[90]

The Federal Trade Commission is considering a trade regulation concerning ball joints similar to the rule in effect in California. However, consumers must apply pressure for it to become a reality.

Steering Repairs

There are three main steering components frequently replaced unnecessarily, especially by mass merchandising chains and tire dealers: control pivot arms, idler arms and tie rod ends. The University of Alabama examined 23 control pivot arm repairs done by the chains and said 19, or 83%, were absolutely unnecessary.[91] Don't have these parts replaced without a second opinion.

Tire Chain Repairs

Tire dealers have been increasingly getting into repairs because of low gross profit margins on tires—usually about 25% to 30%[92]—and unconscionably high profit margins on such repairs as mufflers, brakes, shock absorbers and tune-ups. "Our profit margin is up around 70% on muffler business," boasts Bob Kisling of Kisling Tire Co. in Linday, California, in a trade paper ad. He goes on to say that "we also found the muffler work creates new customers for the tires, shocks and repair services we sell here."[93]

While there's nothing wrong with adding complementary product lines to one's business, the temptation presented by high-profit repairs is often too much for some tire sellers to resist. When you bring your car in for new tires, they may try to sell you all sorts of repairs you don't need.

An outrageous example of this was reported by free-lance writer Moira Johnston in a *New West* magazine article dealing with the extremely high failure and return rate of Firestone 500 steel-belted radial tires. One of her sources, a Firestone salesman named Mark, told her the company had held a big sales meeting in 1977 to stir up the salesmen on the virtue of the firm's new 721 radials. The 721 series was replacing the 500s, which were being returned at a fast clip after people noted defects or had accidents with them. Mark said someone at the meeting pointed out there was money to be made when people brought in their defective 500s for adjustment. The salesmen were advised, according to Mark, that when the car was on the rack to change the tires, they do a "safety inspection" and then recommend such things as shock absorbers, brake jobs and tune-ups. They were told, Mark said, there was $40 to $200 a day to be made on such "add-ons."[94]

Bargains and Advertising

"Beware of bargains," Albert Porcelli of the New York–based Auto Body Craftsmen's Guild told a *New York Times* interviewer. "If an outfit puts up a big sign, 'free wheel alignment check,' ask yourself why should they want to do that for nothing."

Mr. Porcelli advised to "go more on recommendation than on what you see advertised. A good man doesn't really have to advertise. He's busy without advertising and looking like he's giving things away."[95]

This gets to the crux of why tire centers and mass merchandising chains do so many unnecessary repairs. Explains a University of Alabama report:

"Service stations, car dealers and independent shops do not normally advertise their repair services. They would generally depend upon good will and performance to draw their customers back. Chains and, particularly, tire dealers depend heavily on advertising with specials and loss-leaders. They probably view their customers as very occasional ones who have no loyalty to their shop. . . . Such an attitude is not likely to generate a positive approach to the consumer and the risk of additional repairs is enhanced."[96] In other words, if customers who get ripped off after responding to these ads don't come back, the companies don't care because their advertising continually draws in new people.

The Alabama report also pointed out that the "tire dealers even have evidence of a customer's loyalty (or lack of loyalty) by the brand of tire he has on his vehicle."[97]

The lesson here: If an advertised special is hard for you to resist, at least get a second opinion if the shop tries to sell you additional repairs.

Not only should you be wary of responding to advertised repair specials of the chains and tire companies, but you should also be wary of even going into one of their service centers while an advertised special is on. A 1974 University of Pittsburgh report on chain auto repair practices in the Pittsburgh area found that "there is a strong suggestion that chain outlets will suggest or push for fixing or replacing parts that are on sale at that particular time."

This conclusion was reached after the university had two mechanics thoroughly go over a 1973 Chevrolet Malibu and then took the car, which had no defects, to 13 chain stores. The driver in each case asked for a safety inspection prior to going on an extended trip. Seven of the 13 shops tried to push "sale" items on the investigators. The following five shops, they said, made strong selling attempts: Two Kaufmann's Department Store outlets run by Firestone suggested that they buy two new tires which were on sale; two Sears stores tried to sell unneeded alignments which were on sale, with one of the stores going so far as to perform an unauthorized alignment; and a Goodyear store told them they needed two front shock absorbers, which were on sale for $12.95 each.[98]

You should also be wary of anyone who calls you on the phone to come into a shop for a free checkup. Frost & Sullivan, Inc., a consulting firm, says this is a ploy used by franchised installation specialists. They get your name by employing "spotters" who look for older cars likely to need parts replaced and then track you down through your license plate number.[99]

Fighting Back

I believe that what I have shown you in this chapter is only the tip of the iceberg of the widespread corruption and incompetence that exist in the auto repair operations of some of America's biggest retailers.

If you wonder why the news media haven't done more in reporting and uncovering this corruption, it might be that they fear retribution from some of their most prominent advertisers. In 1979, according to *Advertising Age*, Sears was the nation's third-largest advertiser, spending $393 million; K mart was sixth with $287.1 million; Mobil Corp., owner of Montgomery Ward, 20th ($165.8 million); and J.C. Penney Co., 38th ($122 million).[100]

It's also curious that the federal government hasn't done anything about these companies. Law enforcement officials in California and a few other states have been nailing these companies, but that does little good for auto owners who live where officials are not so diligent.

Since the Federal Trade Commission, which should be looking after these companies, has not been doing its job, I think the U.S. Justice Department should be brought in. I propose that Congress pass legislation outlawing various fraudulent activities by firms with auto repair operations in more than one state. To enforce the legislation, an auto repair fraud unit should be set up within the Justice Department to run periodic undercover car operations against these firms and to infiltrate companies suspected of quota selling.

Not only are many chain and franchise auto repair operations directly defrauding the public, but they set the tone for the whole industry. As the Sacramento County, California, district attorney's office put it in a civil suit accusing K mart of corrupt auto repair practices: "Numerous competitors have been injured since they must either adopt defendants' unlawful practices to successfully compete or lose substantial business to defendants."[101]

If you've been ripped off by a national or regional chain or franchise organization or if you once did the ripping off as one of their employees, contact the Federal Trade Commission (see Appendix B) and one or more of the consumer protection organizations in Appendixes A and B.

A list of the addresses of chain and franchise companies is in Appendix I.

4

Big Oil Shafts You Again:

Crime Along the Interstates—

and Whatever Happened

to "Service" Stations?

"We stopped for gas," explained the retiree from Greensburg, Pennsylvania, as he began to describe what happened to him and his wife while driving to Florida along Interstate 75 in Georgia. "The attendant found one of our front shocks leaking, so we agreed to replace the two front shocks.

"While the car was on the rack, he pointed out to us weak spots on three of our tires. Since our spare tire was not satisfactory, he quoted $56.73 per tire of good quality plus tax and less a trade-in of $9 per tire, for four tires."

The total bill for this routine pit stop at an Exxon station, excluding gasoline, came to $266.34.

The couple had been fleeced. But, like many such travelers, they didn't realize it until they were out of the state. And even then they didn't realize the extent to which they had been taken. They thought they had simply been overcharged for the tires. This occurred to them when they got to Ocola, Florida, that evening and saw an Exxon newspaper ad for the same tire at $31.49 plus $3 for whitewalls.

The retiree wrote to Exxon Corp. asking for the difference between the advertised price and what he had paid. In typical oil company fashion,

Exxon wrote back saying that the station owner was an independent businessman and that they had no control over the price he charged for tires.

The Pennsylvania man let it go at that until several months later when he saw an article about gas station rip-offs along I-75 in Georgia in the *News Bulletin* of the American Association of Retired Persons. He wrote to the association describing his experience and asked if it could get him back the amount of money he had overpaid for the tires.[1] He was then told that most likely none of the $266.34 expenditure was necessary and that he had been completely bilked. Under pressure from the association, Exxon agreed to refund the man $150.[2]

50-Percenters

It's not uncommon for gas stations adjacent to Interstate highway interchanges with heavy vacation traffic to cheat motorists out of $60 to $500 a throw.[3] Many station attendants even go so far as to slash tires and damage parts in order to sell repairs.

The offending stations are not a bunch of off-brand pirates either. In most cases, they're franchisees of the major oil companies—the same people who are driving honest operators of full-service gasoline stations out of business and replacing them with their own retail self-service stations which do no repairs.

The actual persons who do much of the freeway fleecing, according to law enforcement officials, are known in the trade as "50-percenters." They are people who hire themselves out to service station operators for no salary but get to keep half of whatever they take in. The amount of money many make for themselves and the station operator is enormous. The CBS program *60 Minutes* interviewed a man named John, who at one time operated corrupt gas stations along an Interstate highway in the Southwest. He said a 50-percenter "could possibly make the owner three or four hundred dollars a day and himself too" and that "they work about, I'd say, six or seven months out of the year and make their fifty or sixty thousand dollars, tax-free."[4]

In all, the American Petroleum Institute estimates that service stations' malicious damaging of car parts and shortchanging on gasoline is a $100 million-a-year racket[5]—a figure which might be conservative.

There is even alleged to be a school to train these roadside swindlers. Georgia investigators say their informants have revealed that a man with a master's degree in psychology operates somewhere out of New Mexico offering a cram course on the subject. For a fee of several hundred dollars, each pupil is taught which people to victimize and how to psych them out. The prime targets are "senior citizens" as well as "big spenders" who drive big late-model cars and flash a string of credit cards. Those who drive compact or older cars and display frugal tendencies are considered bad risks. Students are also taught, according to Georgia officials, to exude trust by being neat and courteous and to keep the station clean and tidy. They're also taught to get the occupants away from the car—sometimes by offering them coffee or soft drinks—while they do their evil deeds.[6]

Besides older people and big spenders, women traveling alone or with children are prime targets of many crooked station attendants, since they are highly susceptible to scare tactics. Victims are almost always people with out-of-state license plates, while local people are left strictly alone.

The 50-percenters, says Tim Ryles, administrator of the Georgia governor's office of consumer affairs, are "a very distinct subculture." He says they call each other by such nicknames as Dirty Jack or the Tire Surgeon or the Hawk. The lifetime ambition of the last, says Mr. Ryles, is to cut all the tires on a Greyhound bus.[7]

In 1977, Mr. Ryles' office received 322 worthy-of-investigating complaints about I-75 rip-offs in his state[8]—probably only a fraction of the number actually fleeced. Things got so bad that year that the American Automobile Association issued a nationwide travelers' alert[9] and in January 1978 the *Atlanta Journal* dubbed the Georgia highway "Rip-Off Road."[10] *60 Minutes* in 1978 took a car into four gas stations along I-75 in Georgia and was sold $476.25 worth of unnecessary repairs in three of them.[11]

Georgia has drastically reduced the problem, but vacationing motorists are still exploited there as well as in Arizona, New Mexico, Texas, Nevada, Florida, California, Nebraska and many other states. While Georgia officials are very open about what's happening, officials in some of the other states are trying to hide the problem. For example, I called Anthony B. Ching, chief counsel of the Arizona attorney general's Economic Protection Division, to discuss the situation there for this book. He refused to talk, saying, "We'd rather not be associated with a book like that."[12]

Tricks of the Trade

Here are the types of tricks to watch out for while traveling along the Interstate highways:

THE TIRE TRAGEDY TALE
Typically, the attendant will offer to check your tire pressure—sometimes on the premise that your tires look low. He will then puncture one or more tires with an icepick or with a pointed screwdriver called a

"honker." The instrument is often concealed under a rag. A variation is to slash your tires with a cut-down putty knife while you go to the restroom or aren't looking.

The real pros will puncture or cut all four tires. Others might do no damage but try to convince you that all your tires are bad. Jerold V. Fennell, Nebraska assistant attorney general, said he had a case where an attendant took four perfectly good top-quality Michelin radial tires off a car and sold the driver four cheap 4-ply tires.[13] One woman, traveling on I-15 between Barstow, California, and Las Vegas, was sold five tires, including the spare, according to California officials.[14]

A former New England gas station attendant, in a *Mechanix Illustrated* article entitled "Confessions of a Turnpike Pocket Picker," said even when someone came into his station with a legitimate flat tire, every ruse in the book was used to get him to buy a new tire. Customers were told the flat couldn't be fixed either because of the condition of the tire or because the station had run out of patching cement. Few people want to chance driving without a good spare, and so, our confessor said, "most people thus confronted bought a tire . . . at the top price."[15]

THE BLEEDING SHOCK ABSORBER

60 Minutes, using a concealed camera, actually filmed this trick at a Shell station along I-75 in Georgia. While the driver went to wash up, the attendant was shown taking a bottle which contained oil from his pocket and hiding it in his rag. He was then shown going to the side of the car away from the stationhouse, bending down and squirting oil onto the shock absorbers. A puddle of oil then formed under the car.

When the driver returned, the attendant told him, "You have brake fluid, or something, leaking on the front of this. Something like it." After a short exchange, the attendant said, "Stay here and we'll raise it up on the hoist." After doing that, the attendant told the driver that one of the shock absorbers was busted and that the puddle was "fluid from the shocks" because "the seal ruptured in there." The driver was sold two new shocks, since it's not wise to have one new and one old shock absorber on the same axle.

Later, an attendant at a Gulf station, after apparently slashing a tire, told the driver that one of his shock absorbers was bad. But instead of trying to sell him two shock absorbers, he recommended four.

"If one of those is bad, all four are bad," he said. Another attendant said, "It's like buying one shoe and not buying the other one."[16]

A variation of this ruse is for the attendant to push up and down on your car's fender a few times and then tell you the shocks are bad. You can verify the truth of this by doing your own shock absorber test, checking each wheel at a time. What you do is stand over a wheel and, pushing down with your hands, bounce the body of the car up and down a few times and then let go while the body is either down or up. If the car returns to the center and stops, your shock absorbers are OK.

THE PLOP PLOP FIZZ FIZZ BATTERY

While you're not looking, the attendant will drop Alka-Seltzer tablets into the battery cells and then replace the caps. Within minutes, an explosion will occur, blowing off the caps, creating smoke and scaring the hell out of you. The attendant will then try to sell you a new battery.

COOKING THE ALTERNATOR

How would you like your alternator—barbecued or salted? The first delicacy is prepared by the attendant squirting a homemade barbecue sauce onto your alternator, causing lots of smoke and unpleasant odor. He then tells you this means you need a new alternator. If you fall for this trick, he'll remove your old alternator, paint it, put it back in your car and charge you for a new alternator. Salting an alternator is when the attendant distributes metal filings around the alternator and then tells you that the filings mean your alternator has excessive wear and needs to be replaced.

THE WATER PUMP CHUMP

The attendant will loosen the main nut on your water pump, making it leak badly. He'll then try to sell you a new water pump. Once you agree to the repair, he'll just tighten the nut and charge you for a new water pump.

Some attendants will simply wait until a driver pulls into the station with smoke billowing from under the hood to sell a new water pump. In many cases, the problem might be caused by something as simple as overheating from hard driving, low coolant level, a loose fan belt or a radiator hose leak.

THE REAR END RUPTURE

The attendant will squirt some oil on the underbody of your car's rear end, direct your attention to the drip and convince you that you need expensive rear end repairs costing several hundred dollars. Usually, all the attendant does is steam-clean away the oil.

SHORTSTICKING

The attendant will check your oil and push the dipstick down only far enough so that it registers a quart low, or else stick it in all the way but wipe off part of the oil with his thumb or a rag. You are then shown the dipstick to convince you that you need oil. Sometimes instead of adding the oil you don't need, the attendant will take an empty oil can, cover the hole with a rag and then pretend to pour the contents into the crankcase.

THE SPARK PLUG BUG

The attendant loosens a spark plug wire while checking under the hood, causing the engine to miss. He then sells you a new set of spark plugs. Some stations don't even give you new spark plugs in this situation —they merely clean the old ones, put them back in the car and charge you for new ones.

THE FAN BELT SLICER

Again, while under the hood, the attendant slices the fan belt with a knife hidden under a rag and then sells you a new fan belt.

FUEL PUMP FOLLY

An oil-and-gas mixture is sprayed on the fuel pump. The attendant then points to the mixture dripping on the ground and recommends a new fuel pump.

THE GAS IN THE CAN TRICK

"When a dude pulled in for a fill-up and left the car to go to the john or the phone, he was asking to get hit" with this trick, according to our New England gas pump jockey. He said attendants, instead of filling the tank completely, would pour some of the gas into a can. Sometimes they put in $4 worth of gas and charged for $5 worth if the person didn't check the total on the gas pump.[17]

Motels and Towing

Some highway repair robberies are pulled off in conjunction with getting you to stay in motels or having your car towed long distances.

One station in southern Georgia regularly worked the rear end ruse in the evening so that they not only could get $450 for repairs but could also get their victims to stay at a nearby motel owned by the station operator.[18]

The towing trick was pulled by a California service station operator until officials busted him. When a car came in overheating, he would tell the motorist that he had a cracked block. He would then convince the motorist that no one in the area could fix it and that the best place to have it repaired was a garage in Las Vegas. He would then talk the motorist into letting him tow the car into Las Vegas—a two-hour trip that he charged over $100 to make. Unknown to his victim, not only was nothing wrong with the block and not only did the car not need towing, but the station operator owned the garage in Las Vegas, which socked the motorist with a big repair bill.[19]

The Texaco Star

The crooked practices outlined here have been going on for years with not enough being done to curb them. The major oil companies, for the most part, attempt to deny responsibility for such acts; local law enforcement officials often look the other way; state law enforcement officials often have neither the legal clout nor the money to deal with the problem; and the federal government is doing absolutely nothing about it.

The oil companies, after spending billions of dollars over the years in advertising their brand-name service stations, typically claim that their dishonest franchisees are "independent businessmen" whom they have no control over. Texaco Inc., for example, advertised for years that "you can trust your car to the man who wears the star." But let's see what happens when a consumer complains about being ripped off by the man with a Texaco star.

Professor W. John Weilgart of Luther College in Decorah, Iowa, tells of going into a Texaco station in Colorado because the generator on his VW bus wasn't charging. He said he asked the station operator to simply recharge the battery so he could get to a Volkswagen dealer. However, the operator unscrewed his generator without having a replacement "to hold me a virtual captive for four days, so I would stay in his motel," the professor charged. He said he was forced to pay an outrageous $175.66 for repairs and soon afterward the car began to smoke, causing him to spend another $100.22 in repairs at a VW dealership. Professor Weilgart traveled a little farther and the generator installed by the Texaco station burned out, causing him to spend still another $118 in repairs. The professor said the Texaco man assured him the generator was a genuine VW part, but the VW dealer, which made the replacement, said it wasn't and therefore there was no warranty on it.[20]

Professor Weilgart complained to Texaco, which referred him to Joe Clark Oil, Inc., a Texaco distributor. R.H. Bradley, secretary/treasurer of that company, denied any responsibility, saying the station owner "is an independent businessman and does not report to or have any connection with Joe Clark Oil Co. The only item we sell to [him] is gasoline and diesel fuel and this is on a cash basis, thus we have not a voice in the operation of his business."[21]

A similar response was received from O.P. Treadwell, assistant manager of Texaco's Denver Resale Marketing Division. "Retailers are neither agents nor employes of the Company," he said, "but rather are independent businessmen whose conduct we cannot legally control." Nevertheless, Mr. Treadwell said, as a result of his contacting Joe Clark Oil, which contacted the station owner, Professor Weilgart would get $175.66 refunded if he returned the defective generator.[22]

This was no help, since the defective generator had been thrown away. Commenting on his experience and the subsequent runaround, Professor Weilgart said that "to me it [represents] the whole decadence of this society."[23] He also had this to say about gas station franchisees being independent businessmen: "If he [the retailer] is truly independent, as Texaco now maintains, he should have no Texaco sign and should be free to buy any oil."[24]

Agreeing that oil companies should be made responsible for the actions of their franchised gas stations is Mr. Ryles, Georgia's consumer protection chief. "The logo of the oil company is up there," he says; the stations accept credit cards issued by the oil company and the oil company advertises to entice people to do business with its stations. "There's Bob Hope on television telling you about Texaco and then you pull into a Texaco station and you get Jack the Tire Ripper."[25]

Not only that, but in many cases the dealer doesn't even sell the gas of the company whose logo towers over the station. "If you go to an Exxon station you have no guarantee you're going to get gas refined by Exxon," says Hank Banta, former assistant counsel of the U.S. Senate Antitrust and Monopoly Subcommittee. "In fact, the odds are against it."[26]

Mr. Fennel, the Nebraska consumer protection chief, says oil companies won't do anything about complaints against their service stations unless a person raises enough hell. But he figures 90% won't complain at all and maybe only one in 100 will be persistent enough to get something done. "Some people just write it off," he says, while others say nothing because they're too embarrassed that such a thing could have happened to them. "Old people are really afraid" to complain, Mr. Fennel contends, because they feel others will think they're not competent to take care of their own affairs.[27]

Of course, the oil companies could clean up the problem overnight by policing their franchisees and canceling the franchises of crooked operators. However, says Mr. Ryles, "as a general rule the pressure has to come from us" before the oil companies will do anything.[28]

The job is made even harder for consumer protection people since few states have licensing authority over repair shops and criminal convictions are hard to get. One reason that it's tough to get convictions is that the victims are almost all out-of-staters. "By the time they figure out they've been ripped off they're back home," says Mr. Fennel. He says he doesn't have the funds to bring people back from all over the country to testify.[29] Likewise, most consumers would rather write off their loss than spend more money and time to come back and testify.

Even if a victim does appear in court, often there's not enough evidence for conviction. That's because as a rule people don't keep their old parts, nor do they get receipts with the station's name on it.[30] An examination of old parts could prove that there was either nothing wrong with them or that they had been intentionally damaged.

The traditional way of nailing corrupt repair shops by sending in undercover cars doesn't always work either. The "50-percenters" are extremely sharp and can often smell a setup. Richard Matysiak, an automotive investigator for the Georgia governor's Office of Consumer Affairs, says they take note of such things as new bolts in the license plates, recently changed tires and thumbprints on the hubcaps. "Anything that doesn't look right they'll stay away from," he says.[31]

Sometimes stations even get tipped off to an undercover operation. An official in a Southwestern state attorney general's office told the Federal Trade Commission in 1974 that "confiding [in] local enforcement agencies can be disastrous" when doing undercover work. "In most police departments and state police and highway patrol agencies officers are on close terms with the local service stations as they do business with them on a daily basis," he said. "Intentionally, or unintentionally, we have been burned by attempting to cooperate with the local police agencies."[32]

Even if a state does manage to get rid of the "50-percenters" they simply set up operations in another state. Many of them live in trailers for easy mobility.

The Federal Solution

Since these crooks move from state to state and rip off people traveling out of their home state, and since the national oil companies are involved, this is really a problem the federal government should be tackling. However, I have found no one in Washington doing anything about it.

Once again we see the Federal Trade Commission not doing its job. The FTC should be fining the oil companies $10,000 each time they fail to fully investigate a consumer auto repair complaint or fail to take action against a corrupt operator.

The FTC should also be looking into an allegation made by Mr. Ryles that the oil companies have twice as many stations along I-75 in Georgia than the traffic can bear, thus forcing many station operators to engage in fraudulent activities in order to survive.[33] High station rents and low profits on gasoline also force operators of service stations near Interstate highways to cheat customers on repairs.[34]

As a further means of cracking down on these highway hustlers, Congress should enact a law making it a federal crime to cross state lines to engage in auto repair fraud or for any person who works at a gas station on or within 5 miles of an Interstate highway to maliciously damage any parts of a car in interstate travel or use deception in order to sell auto parts, repairs and maintenance items. After such a law is enacted, the U.S. Justice Department should set up a task force to root out these auto repair criminals. The Justice Department might even be able to infiltrate the ranks of the 50-percenters and make wholesale arrests. Meanwhile, the Internal Revenue Service should be investigating this racket for income tax evasion.

Protecting Yourself

The first step in protecting yourself on out-of-state trips is to have your car completely inspected before you go and have all needed repairs taken care of. That way, any repair the gas station attendant recommends can be viewed with suspicion.

The next step is never to leave your car unattended in the service area of a gas station and to watch the station employees like a hawk. If the attendant opens your hood or checks your tires, be looking over his shoulder. It's best to use restrooms in restaurants whenever possible so that you don't have to leave your car unattended at a gas station. If you must use a service station restroom, park your car far away from the gas pumps and service bays. To avoid being sold unnecessary oil, keep a rag in your car and check the oil yourself.

If you have the least bit of suspicion about a recommended repair, get a second opinion. If you suspect foul play, call the police or the sheriff or a consumer protection agency (see Appendixes A and B). A Michigan motorist's quick action in notifying authorities led to the closing of a station along I-75 in Georgia. He became furious when told all four tires on his car—after only a few hundred miles of use—were dangerously damaged. He took out a warrant for the arrest of three men, charging them with criminal destruction of property.[35]

In Georgia, look for a golden triangle symbol on the gas pumps of stations along I-75. This means the station has been approved for good business practices by the Georgia Association of Petroleum Retailers.

If you're a member of the American Automobile Association, I would suggest that while traveling you have repairs done at garages which perform AAA road service. This will give you some clout if the repairs aren't done right or the garage gyps you. A complaint to the AAA might get you restitution.

If you do get repairs done at an unfamiliar gas station, make sure you get an itemized written estimate, your old parts back and an itemized receipt which clearly identifies the name of the station and its location.

You should also pay your bill with a credit card issued by the company whose petroleum products the station sells. That way, as W.H. Ligon, managing director of the Texas Service Station Association, explains, "When you get your statement, all you have got to do is pull that credit card out [and] write a simple note to the oil company, 'I was dissatisfied with this work. I am not going to pay the bill.' Send it back to the oil company; the oil company will charge it back to the dealer and never say a word to you about it."[36] It may not be as simple as that, but oil companies are less likely to want to alienate a steady credit card customer than someone not loyal to their brand.

There is even a federal law—the Fair Credit Billing Act—which legally allows you to withhold payment on an oil company credit card bill if there's a dispute over repairs performed at a franchised service station of the oil company issuing the credit card.[37] This means you must use a Mobil credit card at a Mobil station, a Gulf credit card at a Gulf station and so on. Under more restricted circumstances, the law also allows you to withhold payment if you use other types of credit cards to pay for repairs. More on the law in Chapters 15 and 20.

A tipoff that you're being fleeced by a gas station is if the attendant refuses to accept an oil company credit card and insists on either cash or charge cards like American Express, Visa or MasterCard.

Complaining

If you've been cheated by a gas station on or near an Interstate highway, complain to the oil company and the organizations listed in Appendixes A and B. Also contact the national office of the American Automobile Association (see Appendix I) so that it can warn other travelers about rip-off stations to avoid. You can find the names of most oil company chief executive officers and their business addresses by looking in Moody's or Standard and Poor's directories of corporations. Many libraries carry them.

When complaining to an oil company about how one of its franchised operators ripped you off, defuse their inevitable argument right in your letter. Tell them something like: "Please don't tell me the station opera-tor is an independent businessman. You advertise your station's services and products and you should be responsible. If you don't accept that re-sponsibility I will petition the Federal Trade Commission to file suit against you for unfair and deceptive trade practices."

Whatever Happened to "Service" Stations?

While the big oil companies are reluctant to do much about the service stations that rip off consumers, they've been closing down thousands of honest stations with the fervor of a vice squad closing down bordellos. In their place, the oil companies have opened up their own self-service gas stations that provide no preventive maintenance checks and no repairs.

Some dealers who have been in business 20 years or more have been simply told to pack it up and get lost. While there were about 204,500 gas stations performing repairs in 1972, the number had dropped to about 106,500 by 1979.[38] Frost & Sullivan estimates the number of gas stations performing repairs will dwindle to 50,000 in the late 1980s.[39]

The oil companies contend that the move to self-service is saving con-sumers a bundle of money, but skeptics feel the savings might be false and short-lived.

Self-service stations sell gas for several cents a gallon cheaper than the full-service line at regular stations. On the surface this looks like a tre-mendous savings. Mr. Banta of the Senate Antitrust Subcommittee says a 1-cent-a-gallon reduction in gasoline prices nationwide translates into a $1 billion savings for consumers.[40]

However, the American Automobile Association warns that the savings could be illusory for many motorists. The California State Automobile As-sociation (CSAA), an AAA affiliate, says that the failure of motorists to perform simple maintenance on their cars—partly due to the increased use of self-service gas pumps—may be leading to a rash of mechanical and tire problems.

The CSAA reviewed 747 diagnostic clinic reports in November 1978 and said it found "a surprising number of deficiencies that should have been corrected with rather simple maintenance. . . . Simple things like oil and radiator levels, fan belts, hoses and tire pressures aren't being checked enough."

The most common deficiency—found in 31% of the cars surveyed—was dirty or corroded battery cables, which the organization said "can lead to electrical system shorts and starting failures." Second was failure to change oil frequently enough (27%), a possible cause of engine damage. Third was worn tires (16%), which could cause skids and blowouts. Other deficiencies were worn belts (15%), low engine oil (12%), overdue transmission fluid change (12%), low tire pressure (12%), low battery water (11%), worn heater hoses (10%) and low transmission fluid (6%).[41]

"The few cents per gallon a motorist saves constitutes no savings at all when neglect of his vehicle results in a major breakdown," says Glenn T. Lashley, editor of *American Motorist*,[42] an AAA publication. If you aren't in the habit of properly maintaining your car yourself, the AAA suggests you use the "full service" island every third or fourth fill-up.[43]

The AAA is also concerned about the effect self-service-only gas stations are having on emergency services. With fewer and fewer gas stations offering towing or a mechanic on duty, you could find yourself in big trouble should your car break down away from home.

Jim Campbell, executive director of the California Service Station Association, also sees another bad aspect of no-service gas stations as far as the consumer's pocketbook goes. He believes consumers could lose what they save on gas by being forced to have their cars repaired at new car dealerships instead of at neighborhood gas stations. In the San Francisco area, dealers in 1981 were charging $35 to $45 an hour compared to $20 to $32 an hour for service stations, he said.[44]

The Oil Company Conspiracy

As it now stands, the oil companies are mostly interested in retaining stations which sell 80,000 to 100,000 gallons of gasoline per month. Mr. Campbell says the average service station in California sells only 37,000 gallons per month and that the cry of the oil companies is "80,000 or bulldoze." He is especially concerned that the oil companies want to run these new high-volume self-service stations themselves instead of giving present franchise operators a chance to run them.[45]

Indeed, there are some who see the oil companies' desire to muscle in on the retail market as one of the main reasons for the abandonment of the neighborhood full-service gas station. They look at it as a long-range plot by the oil companies to raise gasoline prices instead of lowering them. "History clearly indicates," says Maryland State Senator C. Lawrence Wiser, "that those savings are short-lived and that as soon as the oil companies can consolidate their monopoly position at the retail level, not only will the independent dealer have been driven on out of business, but the consumer will pay the much higher prices which monopolistic companies are able to extort from the public."[46]

To help prevent this from happening, Maryland in 1974 enacted a law which prevented oil companies from taking over any more stations and required them to divest themselves in time of all stations they then operated.[47] The oil companies challenged the constitutionality of the law, but it was upheld by the U.S. Supreme Court in 1978.[48] Florida, Delaware and the District of Columbia have similar laws.[49]

Shell Auto Care

All is not lost. Several oil companies are actually emphasizing "service" at many of their service stations with special franchise repair programs. These include Shell Oil Co. ("Auto Care"), Texaco ("Texacare"), Atlantic Richfield Co. (Arco "Auto Service Plus") and Standard Oil Co. of California (Chevron "Hallmark"). Also, Exxon Corp. has company-owned "Car Care Centers."

Shell, first with the concept and foremost in the field, has won praise from consumer advocates for offering one of the best consumer protection packages in the entire auto repair industry.

In order to qualify for the program, Shell dealers must agree to have at least one mechanic trained, tested and certified for doing tune-ups, brake overhauls, wheel alignments and air conditioning repairs. Initially, the mechanic has to pass tests given by Shell, but after the dealer has been in the program for a year, the mechanic must pass tests given by the National Institute for Automotive Service Excellence, an independent testing organization. Auto Care stations are also required to have an engine analyzer, wheel balancer, wheel alignment machine and air conditioning charging unit.[50]

To protect consumers, Auto Care dealers must give a written estimate in advance of any repair work, get permission from customers to exceed the estimate, return all parts replaced, give a written warranty that the repairs will be free from defects in materials and workmanship under normal use for 90 days or 4,000 miles (whichever comes first) and agree to have any disputes resolved by a neutral third party.[51] Only those Shell dealers with "Auto Care" signs belong to the program.

Despite the benefits, I do have a word of caution about the program. It is, in effect, a franchising arrangement where participating dealers pay Shell, according to *National Petroleum News*, a one-time fee of $675 and then $100 a month for joint advertising.[52] With someone taking $100 out of the till every month, some Shell Auto Care dealers might just resort to selling unnecessary repairs to make up for it. Indeed, WTVF-TV in Nashville, in 1978, took a 1976 Vega into a Shell Auto Care dealer and got badly ripped off. The car needed only the two front wheel bearings tightened and a bolt tightened on the left front tie rod clamp and perhaps an alignment—work that should have cost no more than $36. However, the Shell station's bill came to $150 and included the installation of four tie rod ends and an idler arm which weren't needed.[53]

5

How AAMCO and Others

Beep Beep You

on Transmission Repairs

"This transmission is going to have to come out of here," said the service writer of a franchised AAMCO shop in Chicago. "It's an internal problem."

Dipping his fingertips into the oil in the transmission pan, he told the customer, "Look at this! Those are metal filings. This transmission is being eaten away inside."

The cost of this diagnosis was $45, which the service writer said would be refunded if repairs were made there. He then gave the customer a choice of having the transmission rebuilt for $340 or $486—the latter being "guaranteed for life." The $340 repair was chosen and performed.

Unknown to the service writer, the customer was part of a *Chicago Tribune* task force investigating the auto repair industry. The car—a 1974 Chevy Nova—had been examined prior to being brought into the AAMCO shop by William Cecil Armstrong, an auto repair instructor at Waubonsee Community College. He found it in fine shape except for a minor induced defect—a punctured vacuum hose which caused the car to shift roughly.

What then of the metal filings? "That's one of the oldest tricks in the business," Mr. Armstrong told the *Tribune*. "There are always going to be metal filings in the fluid, but when they show them to people, they get hysterical. There was nothing wrong with the transmission."

Was this a fluke? Did they just happen to pick a bad-apple AAMCO franchisee? To find out, the task force took the same car with the AAMCO reconditioned transmission and with the same induced defect to another AAMCO shop. "It keeps losing power . . . and it goes whusssh," explained the reporter.

"Your transmission is going to have to be rebuilt," the manager told him. "It'll cost you $394 plus tax, with a six-month guarantee. Or if you want it custom-rebuilt, it's $489, guaranteed for as long as you own the car."

The reporter declined to have the car fixed and was charged $31.50 for the diagnosis.

The *Tribune* then took a 1973 Ford Maverick to a third AAMCO shop. This time a vacuum hose was purposely pulled loose, making the car hard to shift. Mr. Armstrong estimated that the defect—located outside the transmission—should cost $10 to fix. After an AAMCO mechanic had road-tested the car, the manager told a reporter, "It's an internal problem. You can't drive it anymore or it'll get worse. We'll have to tear it down to find the problem."

The manager charged $46 for an examination, after which he said, "The clutch plates are no good, the pump is bad—it doesn't circulate the fluid." He offered to rebuild the old transmission for $391 with a six-month guarantee or to custom-rebuild it for $489 with a lifetime guarantee.

A fourth AAMCO shop found the real problem and charged $9.25 for repairs.[1]

Three out of four AAMCO shops trying to sell unneeded and ultra-expensive transmission jobs in this 1976 investigation may appear alarming, but it was an improvement over what the New Orleans Better Business Bureau found two years earlier.

The BBB took five different General Motors cars to five different AAMCO shops. Each car was rigged by stripping the governor gear, which is located outside the transmission. This caused the cars to stick in low gear. All five AAMCO shops said the problem was inside the transmission and recommended repairs ranging from $292 to $454.84. The transmission expert who induced the defect said the repair should have cost about $40. At least four of the five shops charged $23 to inspect the internal workings of the transmission, although it was unnecessary to do so.[2]

These undercover studies are not the only hint that AAMCO is trying to deceive people about transmission repairs. For more than a decade, the parent company, AAMCO Transmissions Inc., and its franchisees have been in trouble with the Federal Trade Comission and law enforcement agencies all over the country.

This is not to say that there aren't honest AAMCO franchisees or that you can't get a fair deal at AAMCO. Undercover operations by the *New York Times* in 1976[3] and the Pinellas-Pasco (Florida) state attorney's office in 1980[4] found the AAMCO shops visited to be aboveboard. Nor is this to say that you can't get burned by other automatic transmission shops, because you most certainly can. The *New York Times* found that 11 of 21 non-AAMCO shops visited with simple transmission problems made or recommended expensive repairs.[5] WTVJ-TV in Miami, in visiting 11 shops—none of which were AAMCO outlets—got five estimates for overhauling the transmission of a car with a simple induced defect.[6]

It seems that transmission repairs, by their very nature, attract con men. "It's an area where people have little knowledge," says Joseph P. O'Sullivan of the Reno County, Kansas, attorney's office. "Because of the ignorance of the consumer it can lead to tremendous fraud."[7] Indeed, the unknowing motorist whose car won't shift or shifts badly can easily believe that his car is in need of $250 to $600 worth of repairs, though the problem may actually be minor.

What makes AAMCO so worthy of special attention is the fact that it's the nation's largest transmission repair operation with over 800 centers[8] and has become practically a household name through extensive advertising.

The Early AAMCO Scam

To understand where AAMCO's coming from, let's look at its beginning.

The company was incorporated in 1963, and its early training manuals for franchisees contained no material on repairing or rebuilding transmissions. Three early franchisees told the Federal Trade Commission that their training was devoted almost exclusively to sales techniques and that they received no technical training. It wasn't until late 1966 or early 1967 that the company got around to issuing a service guide to its franchisees.[9]

In the 1960s, AAMCO advertised that most transmissions could be repaired with a simple adjustment of bands or linkage for $4.50 or with a little more work at $13.75. Actress Zsa Zsa Gabor and former baseball manager Leo Durocher were used to pitch these prices in TV commercials.

The Federal Trade Commission, however, charged that these were "bait and switch" ads intended to draw motorists into AAMCO shops where they would be high-pressured into very expensive and unnecessary repairs. Company literature obtained by the FTC supported this. The AAMCO training manual said the selling of simple repairs was "not recommended." It further advised:

MR. BADWRENCH

"It is AAMCO's policy that the purchase of an AAMCO custom rebuilt transmission be suggested to every customer who enters your shop. If you follow this simple rule not only will you have more satisfied customers but the profit picture of your operation will exceed any of your fondest expectations."

The manual, which included dialogues to help meet possible consumer resistance to the lifetime-guaranteed transmission, also told franchisees that "all transmissions with high mileage should be (and can be) replaced with the AAMCO custom rebuilt transmission with a lifetime guarantee."[10]

Examination of company correspondence by the FTC indicated that AAMCO was strongly interested in seeing that each franchisee maintained an average repair order of $180[11]—a figure which is high at even today's prices.

A former franchisee told the FTC that he and other franchise holders were instructed by AAMCO not to quote a price to the customer until the transmission was completely disassembled. "You have the customer in a fix," he told an investigator. "You try to sell the highest job first."[12] This practice is still in existence today.

The Federal Trade Commission said it found another widespread AAMCO scheme in the 1960s. Franchisees would talk a customer into letting them disassemble the transmission to find out what was wrong. That might cost $23. They would then tell the customer that the transmission needed an expensive rebuilding job. If the customer balked, he would be told that it would cost another $23 or so to have the transmission reassembled and replaced in the car. If the customer objected, the FTC said, his transmission would be put in a carton in the trunk and he would be forced to call someone to tow the car away.[13]

What did the FTC do about all these AAMCO activities of the 1960s? It gave the company what amounted to a feather-slap on the pinkie. The commission allowed AAMCO, without admitting any guilt or paying any fine, to sign a consent order on July 29, 1970 agreeing, among other things, that it would not engage in deceptive advertising or sales practices; that it would sell only those parts and services which were actually needed; and that it would police its franchisees to make sure they followed FTC-imposed guidelines.[14] By September 15, 1971, AAMCO itself had admitted that its franchisees had violated the consent order 233 times.[15] Nevertheless, the commission took no further action against the company then and has done nothing since despite widespread evidence that the company and many of its franchisees are robbing the public blind.

While the FTC hasn't lifted a finger against AAMCO, here's what several attorneys general and district attorneys' offices around the country have been doing:

TOPEKA AND WICHITA, KANSAS

The general manager of a Topeka AAMCO shop, who used a written sales pitch provided by AAMCO national to sell an undercover agent unneeded repairs, was convicted in 1973 of deceptive business practices, and Transmission Specialists, Inc., the AAMCO franchisee, pleaded nolo contendere (no contest) to a felony theft charge.[16]

The Kansas attorney general's office got an expert to restore the transmission on an old car and then short out the $7 passing gear switch under the dash, causing the car to be always in passing gear. The agent was sold $350 worth of repairs.[17]

When news of the bust came out, employees of the AAMCO shop in Wichita, which was owned by the same company, came forth and said the same kind of things were going on there. This time the owner, the general manager and Transmission Specialists, Inc., were all convicted of theft and given fines.[18]

More recently, the Sedgwick County district attorney's office filed charges in 1978 against an AAMCO franchisee in Wichita, Stanley Clayton, for ripping off two customers.[19] The shop admitted guilt, agreed to refund the customers a total of $92.70 and to pay $647 in penalties.[20]

SACRAMENTO, CALIFORNIA

An AAMCO shop, without admitting guilt, paid penalties in 1973 of $14,500 after being charged by the district attorney's office with, among other things, showing customers worn parts said to be from their transmissions when in fact they were from some other transmissions.[21]

HOUSTON, TEXAS

In 1973, the owner of three AAMCO shops, without admitting guilt, agreed in part to pay civil penalties of $1,000, reimburse certain customers and discontinue several practices alleged by the offices of the state attorney general and Harris County district attorney. Among the allegations: The shops, on occasion, took transmissions out of customers' cars for diagnostic purposes, and then if the customers refused to authorize repairs, replaced them with different transmissions.[22]

DALLAS, TEXAS

Lawrence R. Santella, an AAMCO shop manager and former New York City policeman, was convicted of felony theft in 1978 for billing a customer $334 for a transmission overhaul when in fact the transmission had not been taken out of the car, but instead had been painted. Mr. Santella received probation for his crime.[23]

HOLLYWOOD, CALIFORNIA

A local AAMCO shop, in a 1977 agreement with the California Bureau of Automotive Repair, admitted to violating state law and closed its doors for two weeks as a penalty. The shop charged the owner of a 1970 Toyota for parts that weren't installed, including a vacuum modulator which her type of car didn't even use. The shop also charged an undercover operator for a new governor gear when in fact the entire governor had been replaced with a used one.[24]

SAN MATEO COUNTY, CALIFORNIA
The owners of AAMCO shops in Redwood City and Daly City, two San Francisco suburbs, without admitting guilt, agreed in 1978 to pay penalties of $10,000 each. The district attorney's office alleged, among other things, that they sold undercover agents unnecessary rebuilt transmissions for $380 and $580 respectively. In addition, AAMCO national agreed to pay a penalty of $20,000 and to monitor its franchisees in the future.[25]

MODESTO, CALIFORNIA
An AAMCO franchisee, Valley Industries, Inc., agreed in 1978, without admitting guilt, to pay a $9,000 fine and make restitution to two customers. In addition, AAMCO national agreed to pay $17,000 in penalties. The Stanislaus County DA's office alleged the franchisee had made several misrepresentations during two undercover operations, including that parts had been replaced or reconditioned when they had not.[26]

FRESNO COUNTY, CALIFORNIA
Two employees of an AAMCO franchisee were convicted and sent to jail in 1978 for making false or misleading statements in connection with the sale of transmissions. The franchisee itself was fined $5,000 and AAMCO national paid $25,000 in penalties. The DA's office said it sent three undercover cars into the shop and each time unnecessary transmissions were sold, costing from $300 to over $500.[27]

BURLINGTON, VERMONT
The Vermont attorney general's office, after receiving numerous complaints about an AAMCO franchisee, Burlington Automatic Transmission Co., in 1976 notified AAMCO national, which sent in two undercover cars, each with induced $4.50 defects. The shop tried to sell major transmission work for $248 and $420 respectively.[28] The franchisee agreed, as part settlement, to pay $4,500 in penalties.[29]

FLINT, MICHIGAN
The Michigan attorney general's office, in a 1978 action, accused an AAMCO franchisee, Consolidated Transmissions of Flint, of ripping off 13 people. The shop, alleged the AG's office, went so far as to do unauthorized repairs on some cars ranging from $283 to $490 and then

send the owners notices of garageman's liens on their cars and a warning of daily storage charges if they didn't pay up.[30] The case was still in litigation when this book went to press.

Since this fraudulent activity is apparently widespread, I asked George T. O'Brien, Jr., a Federal Trade Commission compliance officer, why the commission hasn't cracked down on AAMCO. He explained that the company could be fined up to $10,000 for each violation of the consent order, but hasn't paid a cent because of a loophole. He said as long as AAMCO national itself doesn't violate the order, adequately polices its franchises and takes action against any franchisees which do violate the order, there's nothing the commission can do. He added that he was satisfied that AAMCO was keeping its end of the bargain. "We're trying to get them to police their own act," he said.[31]

So here we have the federal government's leading consumer protection agency letting the fox guard the chicken house. Unlike the FTC, many state and county investigators don't buy the proposition that AAMCO national is trying to run an honest ship and that those franchisees who've been snared during undercover operations are merely fish who eluded the company's own nets.

"AAMCO's selling approach to automatic transmission repair, in my opinion, is sophisticated and high pressure to the point that it becomes a wicked device in the hands of unscrupulous franchise holders especially when legitimate business slows down," observed one state investigator. The AAMCO franchisee, he added, "has a built-in system where he can bilk people blind and they would never know it."[32]

Let's now look at how that built-in system works.

The AAMCO Scam Today

The first thing that should raise suspicion about the company is the fact that its emphasis isn't on attracting topflight mechanics to purchase its franchises, but in attracting high rollers who have big bucks to plunk down. In fact, AAMCO will sell you a franchise even if you've never seen a transmission. "Absolutely no mechanic experience required," says a company business opportunity advertisement in the *Wall Street Journal*. The ad goes on to say, "we provide the marketing techniques, constant management advice, and a six week home office training course."[33] Thus, while it might take a mechanic six years or more of repairing transmissions until he feels he has the skills to open up his own transmission shop, an AAMCO franchisee acquires the skills in six weeks.

This willingness of AAMCO to sell its franchises to people who are not mechanics with a lifetime commitment to repairing cars means that a lot of fast-buck artists get franchises. According to consumer protection people, your chances of finding a good and comparatively honest transmission franchise outlet vastly decreases if the franchise holder is not a mechanic. An auto club official who has observed the work of seven AAMCO franchisees in his market area told me only two were good and trustworthy and both of those were run by conscientious mechanics.

What new franchisees are taught in their six-week course, according to industry insiders, is how to psych people out and relieve them of their money.

Most people who come into an AAMCO shop are an easy mark because they've been attracted by the heavy amount of advertising the company does and most certainly are not familiar with its sordid reputation and run-ins with the law.

If you listen closely to AAMCO's commercials, you'll realize they tell you almost nothing. The company no longer advertises that most transmissions can be fixed with simple adjustments or repairs (although they can be), thus avoiding charges of bait-and-switch advertising and violation of the FTC consent order every time one of its franchisees tries to sell unnecessary repairs. Instead, AAMCO tries to be as noncommittal and uninformative as it can possibly be in its advertising. The other transmission franchisors do the same. "The type of advertising done by transmission franchise organizations is frequently very clever in terms of establishing brand loyalty," says Frost & Sullivan, Inc., a market research firm. "However, we see very little 'reason why' advertising discussing meaningful advantages of one specialist over another in terms of quality control, price, guarantees, etc."[34]

The reason that price is omitted from AAMCO advertising is that the company's prices, as we shall see shortly, are exorbitant. The ads do offer a free multi-check 19-point test and free towing. What many people don't realize is that the free check is no more than a simple diagnosis of the problem and doesn't cover disassembling the transmission, and that anyone who offers free towing is probably going to make it up somewhere else—either by charging more for repairs or by selling unnecessary repairs.

While the AAMCO ads proclaim that "when we give you a price, it's a firm price," AAMCO franchisees are trained to withhold pricing information from you until they have you in a bind.

Typically, the shop, if it doesn't do a minor repair, will tell you it can't give you a firm price until it disassembles your transmission and sees what the problem is. This is rubbish. The shop almost always knows at this point exactly what it's going to do. Regardless, it might even minimize the problem to get you to agree to spend about $50 to have your transmission disassembled.

Once you agree to the disassembly and your transmission is taken apart, they've really got you. Only now do they give you the "firm" price: usually a choice of two services—the "custom rebuilt" for maybe around $580 with a lifetime guarantee or the "banner" reconditioning service for about $460 with a six-month guarantee. As an inducement, you may be told that the dismantling fee will be forgotten if you have the work done there.

The psychological pressures on you at this point are enormous. You don't want to have to lose $50 and still not be any closer to having your car repaired than before. Also, you probably don't know where else to take the car. If you knew of a reputable transmission shop, you wouldn't have brought your car to AAMCO in the first place. Then too, you probably have no idea how much transmission work should cost and thus have no way of knowing that the prices being quoted to you are outrageous.

At this time, the shop is likely to try to high-pressure you into the more expensive of the two repairs. Susan Cooney of Evanston, Illinois, testifying before the Illinois Legislative Investigating Commission in 1975, said that an AAMCO shop employee pressured her into the "custom" repair for her 1970 Maverick by saying better parts would be used, that she would "never have to spend another dime on the transmission" and that she would get a lifetime guarantee. It was only after shelling out $463 for the "custom" service that she was told she would have to bring the car back once a year and spend $13.75 to have the transmission inspected or the guarantee wouldn't be honored. Even after she shelled out all that money, her car had the same problem it had when she brought it in.[35]

I have found not only that it is often unworthwhile to pay the extra $80 or $100 or more for the AAMCO custom rebuilt service, but that the prices for both services are practically a crime.

The major difference between AAMCO's two services, other than differing guarantees, is that the "custom rebuilt" includes the replacing of all steel clutch plates—even if it's possible to refinish them at far less cost—while the "banner" service, according to AAMCO, doesn't require replacement unless the plates are "warped, burnt or scored."[36]

As for AAMCO's $500 and $600 jobs, Jack Shapiro, an assistant attorney general in Maryland who has thoroughly investigated the transmission business, told me in 1978 that 90% of transmission rebuilding should be done for no more than $250—possibly as high as $300—"based on a fair value of labor and a fair markup on parts."

He says, "Don't get taken by the word 'rebuilt.' It implies a standard of repair that is high when really it isn't.... They're selling a word without substance.... They're getting away with markups of up to 300%, 400%."[37] In 1981, it cost transmission shops in California only $63.90 for parts to rebuild a General Motors Turbo Hydra-Matic 350 automatic transmission to minimum requirements of the state's transmission re-building regulation (see Appendix M). The actual clock time for doing the job is about 6½ hours, including 3 hours to remove and replace the transmission.

Shocking AAMCO Statistics

The assertion by the FTC that AAMCO national is trying to do something about franchisees who do major repairs when minor repairs would do is refuted by the company's own sales statistics which were supplied to the FTC in 1977.

A computer printout of the company's mid-Atlantic region covering the period January 1, 1977, to September 16, 1977, shows that 42,378 cars were serviced, bringing in gross sales of $9,150,999. A little work on the calculator shows that this averages an astronomical $215.94 a car. The printout also shows that 54.5% of the cars underwent "major service."[38]

In comparison, the average job at an independent transmission shop in 1978 was about $150 nationally except for the San Francisco area, where it was around $175, says Robert Cherrnay of the Automatic Transmission Rebuilders Association.[39] Even $150, contend critics, is high for an average. I couldn't get a straight answer from any transmission shop owners as to what percentage of the cars they see are *really* in need of major repairs. I'm sure it's less than 30%.

As bad as AAMCO's averages seem, some franchisees far exceed the average, according to the computer printout. For example, the average repair at AAMCO shop 21410 in Rochester, New York, for the nearly nine-month period was $308.80, with 85.3% of all repairs being "major."[40]

What's most fascinating about AAMCO's printout is that wide variances in averages can be seen in the same areas. For example, shop 02603 in Bethesda, Maryland, a Washington, D.C., suburb, had an average repair of *only* $147.77 and *only* 28.4% of its work was major. On the other hand, shop 23900 in nearby Silver Spring, Maryland, had an average of $222.56 and slightly over half its repairs were major.[41]

Protecting Yourself

The first step in avoiding the transmission rip-off is to take proper care of your transmission. Every two years or 24,000 miles (or more often if you live where there's year-round hot weather), have the transmission oil and filter changed and see to it that any necessary minor adjustments are performed. Also, between maintenance periods, get into the habit of checking your transmission fluid level about once a month and adding fluid if it's low. Your transmission has a dipstick just as your engine does. Consult your owner's manual for the proper way to test the fluid level.

If you follow the above procedures, chances are any problems with your transmission will be minor.

The next rule is to never assume you have a transmission problem. What you may perceive as transmission trouble may be something altogether different. Take as a lesson what happened in 1978 to Mr. A of Concord, California.

He said he was driving home from work in his 1973 Pontiac Grand Prix when, as he accelerated, "the engine appeared to strain and make a louder and louder noise similar to a car straining to climb a steep hill in low gear."

He left the car the next morning at an AAMCO shop because, he said, "my initial impression was that I may have a transmission problem." He said he got a call back later that morning telling him that the problem was definitely in his transmission and that a price couldn't be quoted until the transmission had been completely dismantled. He got a call back later in the day saying that the transmission would have to be rebuilt and was quoted a price of $580 and two lesser figures of $465 and $400. After mulling it over for more than a day, Mr. A decided to go ahead with the $580 repair. However, after the repairs were completed, he found that his car had the same problem as before plus additional troubles. He said he took the car back to AAMCO and explained the original problem to a mechanic, who diagnosed the trouble as a faulty engine fan clutch assembly. The franchise owner fixed the fan clutch assembly and the problem went away. "I was now thoroughly convinced," said Mr. A, "that the only problem I had ever had was this comparatively minor defective part and that the replacement of my transmission was totally unnecessary." He stopped payment on his check.[42]

This should teach you, if you think you have a transmission problem, to take your car to a general mechanic and let him diagnose it. If he confirms it's a transmission problem that he can't handle, then and only then go to a transmission expert.

What kind of an expert should you choose? Investigator O'Sullivan, who went to auto mechanics school at the same time he was going to law school, says, "The more you get away from the franchise operation, the less the hard sell." He suggests: "Go to a smaller guy who has his name on the door."[43]

Wouldn't you rather deal with a skilled mechanic who owns his own shop and has enough business without advertising than patronize someone who may have gotten into the transmission profession by answering a Cottman Transmission ad which said, "No mechanical skills needed now or ever"? You can also figure that franchised shops are generally going to charge more because they've not only got to make back the money they paid to get the franchise, but they've also got to pay the franchisor a percentage off the top. AAMCO shops reportedly must pay around 7½% to 8% of their gross sales to the national company.

If you're in a quandary over which independent transmission shop to try, then pick one that belongs to a national or state trade organization. Members of such organizations often have more pride in their work than others and may be under peer pressure to make amends if anything goes wrong. The most prominent trade group in the transmission field is the Automatic Transmission Rebuilders Association (ATRA). The 900-plus members of the association have an agreement among themselves to guarantee each other's work for 12 months or 12,000 miles. This means that if an association member in one city repairs your car and something goes wrong in another city, a member in that other city will fix your transmission for free. All you need do is call the original shop collect from the other shop and tell it what's wrong with the transmission, and the shop will take it from there. To locate members of the association, look for the "ATRA" symbol in ads under "transmission" in the yellow pages, or contact the national office (see Appendix I).

Before doing business with any transmission shop, check out its reputation with the Better Business Bureau, local consumer protection agency and local consumer groups (see the Appendixes). If they give their OK, call up the shop and ask what it will charge you for rebuilding or replacing your transmission and the terms of the guarantee. If the shop won't tell you or quotes sky-high figures or has a lousy guarantee, try another shop.

Once you've found a shop that seems OK, take your car there, but be very cautious. The Maryland attorney general's office says that selling unnecessary repairs and misleading customers are "practices which are alleged to be common throughout the automatic transmission repair and rebuilding industry."[44]

Remember, no matter how serious you may think your transmission problem is, the odds are in your favor that relatively minor work will have it back in operation. For example, don't get hysterical if your car won't shift and the problem came on gradually. You may have noticed that it took your car a few moments to go backward when you put the gear lever in reverse. Then you noticed that it gradually took more and more time until the car wouldn't shift at all. This could be caused by the simple fact that you didn't change the fluid and filter when you should have and the fluid got so dirty it just wouldn't go through the filter anymore. A simple change of fluid and filter could send you on your way again. If your transmission won't shift out of low gear and the engine is idling roughly, the problem could be so simple you could fix it yourself: a disconnected vacuum hose. Turn off the engine and look under the car. If you see a rubber hose dangling loose, simply reconnect it, being careful not to get burned.

If the shop says it has to disassemble your transmission before it can tell you what's wrong with it, consider taking your car elsewhere for a second opinion even if it means paying an extra towing charge. One reason: The odds are against an internal malfunction, especially if your car has low mileage and you've reasonably maintained the transmission.

Before giving the go-ahead for having your transmission disassembled, get in writing how much you will be charged if your transmission needs to be rebuilt or replaced, the terms of any guarantee and the cost to reassemble your transmission if you decline to have recommended repairs performed. If the shop refuses to do this, go elsewhere.

Also go elsewhere if the shop offers to install a rebuilt transmission in your car or to rebuild your old transmission without meeting the standards required by the California Bureau of Automotive Repair (see Appendix M).

If everything the shop puts in writing looks reasonable and the California standards are to be met, let the shop proceed with dismantling your transmission. Afterward, if the shop wants to do a full rebuilding job, question them about its necessity. Ask if perhaps the transmission just needs to be resealed. Also ask if the price could be lowered by perhaps servicing instead of replacing the clutch plates.

In addition, stand your ground if the shop wants to replace your torque convertor, which is located outside the transmission but works in conjunction with it. It seems to be a standard industry practice to replace torque convertors unnecessarily, and they don't come cheap—a rebuilt one can cost over $100. Make sure before the shop replaces your torque convertor that it has been gauged and checked for possible reuse. If found usable, it should simply be flushed, serviced and reinstalled in your car.

After repairs, be sure to get back all replaced parts, just in case you need to prove that parts were replaced unnecessarily. Also get an itemization of what parts were replaced.

I would suggest, to protect yourself further, that if given a choice between having your present transmission rebuilt or having a rebuilt transmission installed, you consider the former. While installing another transmission is quicker, the shop has your old transmission and thus you're left with no evidence in case you want to prove later that there was nothing seriously wrong with it.

Sometimes the mere fact that a shop wants to install another transmission can indicate a swindle at hand. A common auto repair fraud is "silver-streaking" a transmission, which the National District Attorneys Association defines as telling a customer that "a new or rebuilt transmission has been installed when, in fact, the bottom of the old transmission has merely been sprayed with silver paint and no work has been done."[45]

Also be leery of any shop that says it's going to install a "new" transmission in your car. Chances are they don't mean a "brand-new" transmission but a rebuilt transmission that will be "new" only to your car.

Fighting Back

The only way to start cleaning up the automatic transmission repair industry—a business with over $2 billion in annual sales[46]—is to make some heads roll in the Federal Trade Commission. Not only has the commission done nothing about AAMCO, but it also shows no interest in promulgating trade regulations which would reform the industry.

As for AAMCO, the FTC should stop relying on the company to police itself and should be out carrying on its own investigations against AAMCO shops. The FTC should also be fining AAMCO national each time one of its franchisees is caught violating the consent order. I believe that when a national company advertises the services of its franchisees, it should be responsible for the actions of those franchisees. If the state of California can get monetary penalties out of AAMCO national each time one of its franchisees is caught red-handed, there's no reason why the FTC can't do the same.

On the trade regulation front, the FTC could adopt the California transmission rebuilding standards and also require all repair shops, before dismantling a transmission, to inform the customer in writing of the cost of its various rebuilding services and the guarantees that come with each. This will end those surprise $400, $500 and $600 snow jobs for which AAMCO is famous. Mr. Chernnay of ATRA says a transmission expert usually knows when he test-drives a car whether or not the transmission needs to be rebuilt. "Very rarely is there a surprise," he says.[47]

If you have a complaint against AAMCO or any other transmission franchise organization or would like to see a national trade regulation concerning transmissions, write to the FTC (see Appendix B).

Since the FTC doesn't help resolve individual complaints, also contact one of the consumer protection agencies listed in Appendix A or B.

Lacking any transmission standards out of the FTC, work to get your state or local government to enact the aforementioned regulations. Also try to get your state to enact a law mandating a minimum one-year prison sentence for those convicted of fraud in connection with rebuilding or replacing automatic transmissions.

The addresses of transmission franchise organizations are in Appendix I.

6

Dealer Service:

The Mr. Goodwrench Fraud

What has General Motors Corp. done in answer to complaint after complaint about its dealers' service departments, including repair problems not solved without repeat visits, cars not returned when promised, dishonest practices and excessively high prices?

Actually it has done little about these problems, but instead has tried to convince you that it has by spending millions of dollars on a slick and sleazy advertising campaign called "Mr. Goodwrench."

These advertisements for GM service, like the service itself, are full of deceptions.

For example, there's that balding, grandfatherly-looking Mr. Goodwrench who appears mostly in the print ads. Chances are you wouldn't want him working on your car. For he's really the art director at D'Arcy-MacManus & Masius—the advertising agency that created the Mr. Goodwrench ads.[1] Then there's that young virile Mr. Goodwrench in the TV commercials. He's no more an auto mechanic than Betty Crocker. He became Mr. Goodwrench not by passing a mechanic certification test, but by passing a screen test. He's actually a professional actor.[2]

The deception in the Mr. Goodwrench promotion, however, goes much further than using phony mechanics. The ads are carefully worded to give you the illusion of substance where none exists. "Mr. Goodwrench knows you want your car fixed right the first time . . . and delivered on time," say the ads, which, if you read or hear them carefully, promise neither. The reason that there are no such promises is that GM dealer performance in these two areas is rather dismal. An extensive survey of how often repair shops fix a car right on the first try was undertaken in

1977 by the Washington (D.C.) Center for the Study of Services. Customers of 34 GM dealerships in the Washington area said the average dealership repaired their car right on the first try only 58% of the time. At one dealership—Ourisman Chevrolet Co., Inc.—only 23% of the customers surveyed said the dealer got the repairs right on the first attempt.[3] Also in 1977, Manusco Chevrolet in Skokie, Illinois, did a survey of its own service customers and said 34% rated the dealership poor in having the work completed right the first time.[4] The Washington Center for the Study of Services also did a survey in 1975 on how often particular repair shops deliver the car when promised. The average GM dealer surveyed did so only 75% of the time.[5]

The GM ads go on to say that Mr. Goodwrench, in order to fix your car right the first time and deliver it on time, "has GM Service School training available to help him do both jobs." While it's true that the training is "available," far too few mechanics take advantage of it.

The impression that the ads signify an improvement in GM mechanic competence and training isn't true at all. Mr. Goodwrench "is not a training program," a GM public relations man told me candidly, but "a promotion for selling parts."[6] Indeed, the whole campaign was devised not for the GM service section but for the GM Parts Division.

"You want genuine GM parts," proclaims Mr. Goodwrench as he gets to the crux of the TV commercials. If you're consumer-smart, you'll want nothing of the kind. "Actually," an industry insider told marketing consultants Frost & Sullivan, Inc., "the car manufacturers don't make many of the parts they sell—they buy them from the same [suppliers companies like Sears use]. Car manufacturers have been extracting high prices based on a mystique of 'genuine parts' . . . the whole thing is a rip-off of the public! . . . Smart car owners are not fooled."[7] One dealer told Frost & Sullivan of having the choice of buying shock absorbers from the auto factory for $9.50 each or lifetime-guaranteed shock absorbers from Gerlik for $3.27.[8] While GM claims that participating Mr. Goodwrench dealers are getting competitive prices on fast-moving items like shock absorbers and spark plugs, GM dealers, as well as other car dealers, are generally under tremendous pressure to buy a large percentage of their parts from the factory at inflated prices or face retaliation. The retaliation might take the form of not getting prompt delivery of the fastest-selling cars or harassment with warranty claims.

A 1975 survey by the National Automobile Dealers Association shows just what kind of rip-off "genuine" GM factory parts are. When 134 General Motors dealers were asked how GM compares to other parts suppliers, some three-fourths felt that GM prices were worse while product quality was the same. A vast majority of the dealers also thought that other suppliers were much better or the same in regards to service, availability and return privileges.[9]

Another deception in the Mr. Goodwrench ads is the very claim that "GM made it possible for Mr. Goodwrench to have competitive prices on the parts you're most likely to use—such as plugs and shocks." Despite this claim, your chances of going into a GM dealership and getting competitive prices on such parts are probably only slightly more than 50–50, if that. While the ads point out that "you'll find Mr. Goodwrench at more than 6,000 GM dealers across America," they omit mentioning the fact that GM has some 11,555 car dealers.[10] This means almost half of GM's dealers aren't involved in the Mr. Goodwrench promotion, which requires dealers, among other things, to buy fast-moving parts in large quantities in order to get discount prices.

The Mr. Goodwrench commercials also try to convey the impression that GM dealer service personnel are honest and trustworthy. One commercial shows a woman taking her ailing car to Mr. Goodwrench, fearing that she's in for an expensive repair bill. But Mr. Goodwrench, much to her relief, finds that a very minor thing is causing the problem. What are the chances of this actually happening at a General Motors dealership? Probably pretty remote, judging by a 1973 Michigan attorney general's office investigation. The AG's office had the graphite removed from a spark plug wire and then went around to various dealers to see what they would do. At each dealership, an undercover investigator explained that the car was "running rough and missing" and that it had recently been tuned. Four out of six Oldsmobile dealers badly ripped the investigator off, and a fifth overcharged slightly. For what shouldn't have been more than a $10 repair, the dealers charged $10.08, $11.44, $24.81, $27.85, $36.71 and $38.54.[11]

In a more recent survey—this one done under a federal contract by the University of Alabama at Huntsville—515 repairs done by GM dealerships in Huntsville were examined. It was found that 136 repairs, or 26%, were unnecessary. An Oldsmobile-Toyota dealership had a 36% unnecessary repair rate.[12]

GM itself doesn't believe its dealers' mechanics are competent, honest or professional. Otherwise why would the company restrict them to flat rate time limits and constantly be on the lookout for fraudulent warranty repairs?

We have seen thus far that the Mr. Goodwrench advertising campaign is almost totally without substance, or, in the words of Esther Peterson, former consumer adviser to President Carter, "largely Madison Avenue puffery."[13]

Now comes time for the real clincher. After conducting this phony advertising campaign to lure unsuspecting people into its dealership service departments, guess what General Motors has to say to those who took the bait, ended up with bad repairs or got cheated, and then complained to the company? Typically, GM tells such persons that it's not the company's responsibility because dealers are "independent business-men" whose retail service practices they have no control over. In other words, "Tough luck." GM even spells out this position in a booklet called *A Guide to Assist Owners of General Motors Vehicles:* "It must be kept in mind that dealers are independent businessmen and therefore in some areas such as sales transactions and nonwarranty service, General Motors cannot take any direct remedial action."[14]

This is pure corporate hogwash. The truth is that General Motors has the power to force its dealers to do practically anything it wants—even do handstands up the Washington Monument steps if it so desires.

GM dealers, when doing retail repair work, are far from independent businessmen. After all, General Motors forces them to pay exorbitant prices for parts which they're forced to stock; to take a loss on warranty work, or at least to make less profit on warranty work than retail work, thus forcing retail customers to subsidize warranty work; and, for many dealers, to adhere to the GM flat rate manual when doing retail repairs if they wish to be paid for warranty work at their retail hourly labor rate. Also to be considered is the fact that General Motors is part owner of many dealerships. In 1977, GM had financial interests in 345 dealerships, representing about 3% of all its U.S. dealers.[15]

The Feds Goof Off

The deceptive Mr. Goodwrench advertising campaign and General Motors' refusal to accept responsibility for the actions of its dealers when doing retail work is just another example of the Federal Trade Commission's failure to do its job. As I've said before, if a corporation advertises the services of its franchisees, it should be made responsible for the actions of those franchisees.

I propose that the FTC, as part punishment for the Mr. Goodwrench campaign, should force General Motors to clean up its entire dealer service system and to fully investigate all complaints against dealers and take appropriate remedial action. Also, since General Motors won't hesitate to terminate the franchises of dealers who don't meet sales quotas, I suggest the FTC force GM to also terminate the franchises of dealers whose service departments perform bad repairs or engage in fraud.

Dealer Repairs—Bad News

It's not hard to conceive that mechanics at dealerships—be they outlets for GM, Ford or whatever company—would be the best persons to take your car to. After all, they're specialists in one line of car, they have access to valuable technical bulletins from the factory not always available to nondealer mechanics, they're equipped with some of the finest tools and machinery, they have factory schools they can attend to keep current, they're better paid and have better working conditions than most other mechanics, and many of them have passed mechanic certification tests.

Nevertheless, you're more apt to get an inadequate repair at a new car dealership than at any other kind of repair facility. At least that's what the five federally sponsored diagnostic centers discovered during 1975 and 1976.[16] Those findings have been confirmed by the Automobile Club of Missouri diagnostic center in St. Louis.[17]

One explanation of this apparent contradiction is that dealers tend to get the tougher repair jobs. Indeed, chain stores, which have some of the least qualified mechanics in the industry, did the most adequate job, according to the five diagnostic centers,[18] and probably for the opposite reason: They do only the simplest jobs.

Even so, other surveys point to something inherently rotten about dealer service:

· The Washington Center for the Study of Services found dealer service departments twice as likely to be rated inferior by consumers as independent repair shops.[19]

· The California Bureau of Automotive Repair did a survey in 1977 in which it found that dealers franchised by General Motors, Ford, Chrysler, Volkswagen, Datsun and Toyota generated 18% of the agency's complaints although they represent only about 5% of the registered shops in the state. The survey didn't include warranty complaints. Officials said part of the reason for this imbalance could be explained by the fact that each dealer does a high volume of work compared to most other types of shops and that people who patronize dealers tend to be from higher income groups and are more prone than poor people to complain when they're dissatisfied.[20]

· The University of Alabama in Huntsville, as part of the federal diagnostic center project, examined 1,476 repairs done by Huntsville dealers and found that one-fourth of them were unnecessary.[21]

Project officials made two very interesting observations from their statistics. First, they found that dealers with the fewest unnecessary repairs did 70% more business than would have been expected based on the population of their brand of car.[22] Second, they found that dealers in the small towns outside of Huntsville had a significantly lower unnecessary repair rate than dealers in the city—17% compared to 25%. This, officials said, "suggests that the car dealers in the small towns may be more sensitive to the effects of unnecessary repairs on their reputations."[23] (This seems to be a phenomenon applicable to the entire auto repair industry. Says a Kansas consumer protection worker: "In the rural communities a crook is not going to survive.")

The Big Why

Why is dealer service so often corrupt and incompetent?

A lot of the problem is due to auto executives who screw dealers, who in turn screw consumers. Also to be considered is that many auto makers and most dealers are primarily interested in sales and consider service an unwanted orphan.

Former U.S. Representative Bob Eckhardt of Texas attributes a lot of the problem to a conflict of interest. He figures auto dealers are in business mainly to sell cars and that "to a certain extent, the less satisfactory it is to maintain a car, the more desirable it is to buy a new one."[24]

To ensure that their retail repair service will be as unsatisfactory as possible, dealers have devised an ingenious system of service department management.

At a typical metropolitan area dealership everything is large and impersonal. There may be 25 or 30 mechanics, but, in most cases, you're not allowed to talk to them. Instead, you're forced to talk to what's known as a write-up man or service writer. He is then expected to communicate your problem to the mechanic, and, quite often, to diagnose what's wrong with your car as well. The problem is that most service writers have only limited mechanical expertise and couldn't diagnose their way out of a litter bag. Those hired for these jobs, admits Paul Scranton of Northwood Institute, a major training ground for auto industry management, are "more people-oriented than mechanically oriented."[25]

Dealers claim they don't like to use mechanics as service writers because they're not good "communicators." This is balderdash. The truth is that dealers like to hire smooth-talking salesmen who can talk you into all sorts of repairs you don't really need. As an incentive, most service writers are paid a commission—typically about 5% on all retail work they write up or sometimes 3% of the repair bill plus $1 per flat rate hour sold. In Fairfax County, Virginia, just outside Washington, D.C., Dean Tistadt of the Department of Consumer Affairs took a survey of 38 dealerships in the county and found that 36 paid their service writers a commission. He called the practice "an open invitation to unnecessary repairs," especially "when there's no work in the dead of winter."[26]

I see no way that dealers can justify paying these people in white smocks a percentage of the take. After all, you either need a repair or you don't. Nevertheless, a Ford dealer once tried to defend the practice by telling me he paid his service writers a 10% commission so they would have an incentive to give prompt service and not goof off. "If I paid them hourly, they'd stand around and pick their nose or something," he said. I, for one, would prefer to deal with a service writer who picks his nose rather than one who picks my pocket.

Most dealership mechanics complain bitterly about service writers, principally because they know so little about what's wrong with a car and make so much money. "It's quite possible to make more money with a pencil than $4,000 or $5,000 worth of tools," complains Andrew Kenopensky of the Machinists Union.[27]

Once the service writer has talked you into repairs you don't need and put down on the repair order either his inexpert diagnosis of the problem or your inexpert diagnosis, your repair order is sent to a dispatcher, who assigns your car to an available mechanic. The mechanic who gets the repair order then has to try to fix your car without ever being able to question you about specific symptoms or being able to afford—because of the flat rate pay system—to take the car for a road test. As if all this weren't enough to ensure bad and unnecessary repairs, the mechanic then has to race through the job to collect his flat rate time.

When the car is finally repaired, it is rarely road-tested to see if the repairs were done right. It's usually you who ends up doing the road testing—after you've paid the bill.

And what about that bill? Expect it to be ever so high. After all, you're not only subsidizing the auto companies' warranty repairs and paying for grossly overpriced "genuine" parts, but you're also supporting a whole host of nonproductive service department personnel, including the service manager, the service writers, the dispatcher, the foreman, the car jockeys (low-paid help who drive cars to and from the parking lot), the cashiers and more. In fact, the average dealer service operation employs one nonmechanic for every mechanic.[28]

It's this kind of corrupt and inefficient system that caused Representative Eckhardt to comment at a congressional hearing, "I have always felt the faster you get away from the dealer the better off you are."[29]

Dealer Dirty Tricks

Beside paying service writers a percentage of the bill and mechanics a flat rate commission, there are lots of other questionable practices that go on in dealership service departments. Here are three of them:

THE PARTS COMMISSION
Some dealers pay their mechanics a commission on additional parts they sell beyond what the service writer puts on the work order. This

is another open invitation to sell unneeded repairs. A dealer at the 1978 National Automobile Dealers Association convention boasted that he initiated a pool whereby his mechanics could earn an additional 50 cents to $2 for selling additional work. He said the whole thing cost him $89.50 and brought in $2,800 in parts and service work.

THE OIL ADDITIVE

Motorists who get their car's oil changed at dealerships invariably find themselves charged for an oil additive that they not only didn't ask for but don't need. The only reason it's added is that mechanics can redeem a ring at the bottom of each can and get 25 cents. Dealer mechanics, says Samuel Mesnick of the Contra Costa County, California, district attorney's office, "find a need for it in everything but their own cars."[30] Some dealers have been known to cover up the fact that they're charging for an oil additive by listing only the additive's part number on the invoice.

SHOP SUPPLIES

Many dealers, not content with merely charging you for parts and labor, tack on a phony charge to your bill, usually called "miscellaneous shop supplies" or "shop materials." The charge—usually 5% to 10% of the total parts bill or total labor bill or both—is supposed to cover, contend dealers, such things as rags, screws, bolts and other small items used up in repairs. Some dealers have a maximum shop supplies charge of $5 to $10 per repair bill, while for others the sky is the limit.

This practice is so widespread that 36 of 38 dealers surveyed in Fairfax County, Virginia, were adding the charge to bills,[31] as were over 60% of the dealers in the entire Washington, D.C., area surveyed in 1975–76[32] and 50% or more of the dealers in the Atlanta area surveyed a few years earlier by attorney Donald A. Weissman.[33]

As far as I can determine, only the city of Washington, D.C., forbids this practice,[34] although the law hasn't stopped some dealers from doing it anyway. (Dealers tend to be flagrant law violators. The Massachusetts attorney general's office reported in 1978 that its investigators had visited 470 new car dealers at least once and had found violations of consumer protection laws at 458 of them.[35])

Is such a practice legal, however, where no law specifically prohibits it? Probably not. It seems to exist only because most law enforcement agencies have been lax in doing anything about it. One notable exception has been the New York State attorney general's office. It got two New York City dealers to discontinue the practice and make restitution to consumers.

One of the dealerships was operated by Daimler-Benz of North America, Inc. The AG's office found that the company had imposed a "miscellaneous shop supplies" charge of 5% of the total cost of parts whether or not any supplies were used, or, if they were used, regardless of their actual value. The company agreed to make restitution of $22,000 to about 4,000 customers who were assessed the charge in 1974. The other dealership, Jaguar-MG of New York Inc., had charged about 700 customers a 4% "miscellaneous shop supplies" charge for about two years beginning in June 1971, the AG's office said.

"These assurances [of discontinuance] were obtained by this office," says Assistant Attorney General Earl S. Roberts, "upon the general proposition that a firm may not make a charge for parts not supplied, and certainly not in the absence of any prior agreement by the customer with full knowledge of the charges to be added."[36]

Dealing with the Dealer

If you're foolhardy or desperate enough to take your car to a large dealer service department, there are ways to protect yourself.

A dealer mechanic told me the best thing to do is to stick with one mechanic and let him do all the work on your car. That way he'll get to know both you and your car and probably won't cheat you. In fact, said the mechanic, he'll probably do extra work for you for free, especially if you compliment him when he's done a good job. The mechanic also told me that many people make the mistake of giving the service writer money or gifts in hopes of getting good service and not being ripped off. Instead, you should reward the mechanic who always works on your car. Slipping a dealer flat rate mechanic a fiver will give him an incentive to do a more conscientious repair job.

It's important that you deal as little as possible with the service writer unless you know that he was a top-notch mechanic at one time and doesn't work on a commission. Whatever you do, don't let the service writer put his diagnosis on the repair order. Make sure he puts down what you tell him the symptoms are and when they occur and nothing else. For example, make him put down "car idles rough after warmed up" and not something like "tune engine." That way the mechanic will know what your problem is and perhaps can fix it with a simple adjustment. The notation "tune engine" has already committed you to an expensive repair.

In the same vein, don't let the service writer put down "check battery" or "check alternator" or for the mechanic to check anything. This is telling the mechanic how to go about his diagnosis—all of which might be unnecessary and costly. Again, if he knows the symptoms, the mechanic might be able to go directly to the problem. Also, don't let the service writer put on the repair order notations to fix broad categories, such as "repair transmission" or "repair exhaust system." This could result in replacement of your whole transmission or exhaust system when only minor repairs are necessary.

There's also a right and wrong time to take your car in for repair to a dealership. The worst time is the early morning when most people are dropping their cars off en route to work. It's best to try in the afternoon when the pace has slowed down and the service writer has time to spend with you and can perhaps even road-test your car.

Complaining

If you have a complaint against a new car dealer service department, you might try to get it resolved through AUTOCAP—a dealer complaint handling program (see Chapter 19 and Appendix H). Arguments against Ford dealers in some areas can be arbitrated by special panels (see Chapter 19).

If you write to an auto company about dealer service (see Appendix H) and get a letter back saying the dealer is an "independent businessman," send a copy of both letters to the Federal Trade Commission and your state attorney general's office (see Appendix B). Ask them to take action against the auto company for refusing to take responsibility for its franchisees' activities.

You should also ask state and local government officials to outlaw service writers' commissions or at least force shops to disclose such commissions on a prominent sign. In order to get restitution for consumers, request that "shop supplies" charges be outlawed and that lawsuits be filed against shops which make such charges.

7

The Four-Headed Screw:

Body Shops,

Auto Insurance Companies,

Bogus Bumpers

and Crash Parts Prices

Poor Mrs. Adriana Caruso! There were only 178 miles on the odometer of her new $3,349 Ford Pinto when a truck ran a stop sign and struck the car, causing extensive damage.

She had the car looked at by a body shop of her choice, which appraised the damage at $2,715. However, her insurer, Allstate Insurance Co., the "good hands" people, said it would allow only $1,720 for repairs. In fact, Allstate gave Mrs. Caruso—a Queens, New York, resident—an ultimatum: Either take a check for $1,720 or have the company's chosen shop repair it for that price. Up a creek, she chose the latter.

Two months later she got her car back. It was plagued with all sorts of defects, including doors that didn't fit properly, a rear quarter panel that didn't curve smoothly, a vinyl top that hadn't been fixed, water leaks, wind noises and more. She took the car back to the shop that had given the $1,000-higher estimate and the shop owner said he found 36 defects. He also found that $285 in parts which Allstate had authorized to be replaced had not been replaced and that a used door had been installed instead of a new one which had been authorized.

Mrs. Caruso refused to allow the Allstate-imposed body shop to try to make good on the repairs and declined an offer from the dealer who sold her the car to buy it back for $500. Instead, she appeared at a hearing conducted by the New York State legislature and told her story. After articles about her troubles appeared in the newspapers, Allstate agreed to refund her the purchase price of the car less her $100 deductible and to take the car off her hands.[1]

Other motorists, without a legislative hearing at which to air their grievances against body shops and auto insurance companies, aren't as fortunate as Mrs. Caruso. For example, a Germantown, Maryland, man whose car was involved in an accident in May of 1977 still didn't have a completely repaired car 10 months later, with neither the insurance company nor the body shop willing to take responsibility for extensive engine damage. "This horror story has got to end," he wrote the insurance company involved. "At this point I am ready to explode."[2]

Exploding or jumping off a bridge is often the only alternative for consumers caught in the crossfire between auto insurance companies and body shops. In most states, laws regulating insurance-related auto repairs are generally weak or nonexistent, and complaining to the state insurance commissioner is often of no help because many of them come from the insurance industry and plan to go back to it once their term of office is over.

As a result, consumer dissatisfaction with auto insurance companies and body shops is high. *Consumer Reports,* in a poll of its subscribers released in mid-1977, found 19% dissatisfied with body shops chosen or recommended by an insurance company and 11% dissatisfied with body shops they chose themselves.[3] A 1973 Louis Harris survey showed that 19% of the adult population had an unsatisfactory experience the last time they filed an auto insurance claim, and 45% said the insurance companies paid their damage claims "with some delay" and another 9% said "with an unreasonable delay."[4]

With an estimated 24 million cars undergoing collision repairs annually,[5] this means several million Americans a year are having serious problems with crash repairs. In addition, many millions more are getting short-changed on body repairs and don't even know it. This is because they don't have the expertise to know what repairs a car needs nor the expertise to examine a repaired car to make sure all work was done that was supposed to have been done and done well. Says a Maryland body shop operator: "There is more incorrect and unsafe body work done than any other kind of repair."[6] Gerald Schramski, a Coast Guard warrant officer in Miami, tells the story of his daughter's being involved in an accident in 1974 in which the insurance company appraiser authorized a new fender and hood. The car was involved in another accident in 1976 and pieces of putty started falling out of the fender. It was discovered that the repair shop back in 1974 had not replaced the fender and hood but merely bumped out the dents and filled them with putty.[7]

This kind of thing is so common that the amount of unsatisfactory crash repairs could prove to be astronomical if anyone were to extensively check them out. In England, the Automobile Association—the British equivalent of the American Automobile Association—has a program of inspecting members' cars after collision repairs, and a spokesman told me that only "about 20% of accident repairs are wholly satisfactory on the first check."[8]

Back in America, Allstate Insurance said a survey it took in New York State in 1975 showed that customers didn't get what Allstate paid for one-fourth of the time. The following year, State Farm Mutual Automobile Insurance Company made a check of 43 cars in the North Miami area for which it had paid out $10,477 to body shops to buy new parts. It found that $3,968 worth of parts hadn't been installed.[9]

The Estimate

If you want proof that collision repairs is a shady business, take your damaged car around to 10 or 15 body shops and see what kind of estimates you get. You would assume that the estimates would be pretty close to each other, considering that most shops, because of insurance company pressure, charge about the same for labor and have the same parts prices. But it never seems to work out that way.

The *Miami Herald* in 1977 took a 1973 Plymouth Fury III with a banged-in left front end and fender to 15 different body shops. It received estimates ranging from $457 to $746. No two estimates were the same. Twelve of the shops had the same $10 hourly rate but estimated the work would take anywhere from 15.5 hours to 29.6 hours. Parts prices for the 15 shops ranged from $195 to $412. A few shops estimated the fender could be straightened with nine hours of work ($90 labor), while some of the other shops wanted to install a new fender for $128.59 plus $25 labor. An independent appraiser hired by the *Herald* was able to find a used fender with attached parts for $85 and allowed two hours of labor or $20 to have it installed.[10]

While the repair-or-replace variation accounted for some of the difference in estimates received by the *Herald*, there were other reasons as well. One body shop operator had an arrangement with another body shop operator to give a higher estimate than his so his estimate would look good to the insurance company. Two shops looked at other estimates and gave lower ones. Several shops quoted wrong prices for parts because they used outdated parts catalogues or misread the catalogues. One shop wanted to install a new bumper for $110, while others wanted to charge $68 to $74 for a rechromed bumper. Eleven of the 15 shops included unnecessary front wheel alignment in their estimates, while four shops omitted necessary frame repairs. One shop included a $6.56 estimate to replace door chrome that had been lost in a previous accident.[11] About the only traditional unscrupulous practice missing was that of one body shop operator's giving an estimate and then filling out pads himself from two other body shops, giving higher estimates.

As a postscript to the *Herald* survey, the newspaper's independent appraiser got each of the shops to agree to fix the car for $445, or $12 lower than the lowest estimate.[12]

Estimating collision damage is subject to so much fiddling that even adjusters for the same insurance company might vary all over the board. Elizabeth Wolf, a reporter for *Hammer and Dolly,* a publication of the Washington Metropolitan Auto Body Association, found this out after her 1971 Volkswagen squareback was hit by a car driven by a woman who was insured by Government Employees Insurance Co. (GEICO). She took her car to four different GEICO claims centers and got a different estimate at each. They ranged from $121.70 to $207.63. The car was also taken to eight different repair shops, and, again, there were no identical estimates, with prices ranging from $136 to $249.48. Not wanting to get her car repaired at a shop of GEICO's choosing, Ms. Wolf insisted to the company that a shop which gave her an estimate of $200.59 do the work. However, GEICO refused to accept that estimate and after some haggling offered her a check for $178.80, which she reluctantly accepted. "Insurance companies have a way of wearing you down," she said.[13]

Body Shops and Insurance Companies

For a deeper understanding of why you, the consumer, often have so many problems with body shops and auto insurance companies over crash repairs, we need to take a close look at the relationship between the two businesses. Perhaps the best description of that relationship was put forth by *Miami Herald* reporter Arnold Markowitz. "The two industries," he said, "live together nervously, like suspicious strangers forced to share the only bed in the last hotel room in town."[14]

S. John Byington, while deputy director of the U.S. Office of Consumer Affairs, put the relationship this way: "Insurance companies are understandably interested in paying the least possible amount for repairs to protect underwriting profits and to keep premium rates low," while, on the other hand, "the repair shop owners are understandably interested in making a decent living."[15]

Who then is the bad guy when you tell a body shop operator that an insurance company is going to pay the bill and the estimate suddenly shoots up? Says Mr. Byington: "To insurance companies, the auto repairers are the culprits because they allegedly try to pad the bill. To repairmen, the insurance companies are at fault because they allegedly try to undercut the price on the estimate. Within this vicious circle, however, it is the consumer who really loses."[16]

The consumer loses because the two sides aren't on equal bargaining terms; the insurance companies have tremendous economic clout over the body shops. A Georgia schoolteacher whose car was smashed in 1978 said she questioned the body shop operator as to how he could sign his name to a statement that he could adequately repair her car for $1,600. She said he became very nervous and told her: "My livelihood depends on the insurance companies. I don't dare dispute them. If I did, I wouldn't have any business. They would just go and find another body shop man in this area that would sign it. They would put me out of business."[17]

The Maryland body shop operator quoted earlier put it this way: "We have a choice not to take the job and starve to death or take the job at their price and the hell with what kind of job the consumer gets."[18]

Anthony J. DeRosa of the Independent Garage Owners Association of Illinois complains that "for an auto repairman to repair a car and stay within the insurance company estimate, he must install used or marginal safety parts. Needed repairs discovered in the course of the repair job often go unmentioned since no compensation will be forthcoming from the insurance company."[19]

The "Preferred" Shop

One way auto insurance companies keep body shops in line is by having what's known as "preferred" or "captive" shops in their hip pockets. These are shops so desperate for business that they sell their souls to the insurance companies by agreeing to do repairs according to their estimates, often without ever seeing the car.

While practically all the major auto insurance companies have such arrangements, they are most frequently utilized by drive-in claim centers. Here a company adjuster checks over your car, gives an estimate and then perhaps directs you to a particular repair shop or gives you a choice of several shops which will do the repairs for his estimate. (The adjuster might also give you a check for the estimated price.)

Whether a shop is or isn't "preferred" can make a big difference in the quality of work performed. "To break even or make money," says Mr. Byington, the former consumer official, "these 'captive shops' must make up the money by doing inadequate repairs. This has resulted in the consumer receiving a car that is not fully fixed or, worse yet, unsafe to drive."[20]

It is not uncommon for consumers to get cars back from "preferred" shops with the front end out of alignment, the body seams not recaulked, rechromed bumpers installed instead of new ones, poor paint jobs, headlights not aimed, rattles, leaks and so on.

Many insurance company adjusters, if you don't like the choice of their shop or their estimate, will tell you that you can have the car repaired at the shop of your choice but that you will have to pay the difference in price out of your own pocket.

One of the heaviest users of the "preferred" shop system is Allstate Insurance Co. Winfield C. Rhoads, home office property claims director of the company, says one-third of Allstate claimants go to a shop recommended by the company or choose from a list of recommended shops. Mr. Rhoads doesn't like the name "preferred shops." In true 1984 Newspeak fashion he calls them "competitive shops" even though they don't offer competitive prices, and, according to him, they accept 75% to 80% of Allstate's estimates without adjustments.[21]

Some states have outlawed the practice of directing consumers to specific shops, but the insurance companies either do it anyway or get around the laws by giving such low estimates that only their preferred shops will do the repairs for their price.

"The Game"

An anthropologist looking into American society would find one of the strangest social relationships between auto insurance companies and body shops, for they play a very weird and phony game with each other.

"The claims settlement system," says Henry Benck, operator of a body shop in suburban Chicago, "is based upon a fairy tale flat rate system which bears only passing resemblance to truth" plus a low, insurance-industry-imposed labor rate which "forces the shops to engage in a massive scheme of offsetting, padding and other shortcuts in order to obtain a fair price for repairs."[22]

Body shops, like mechanical repair garages, generally use flat rate

manuals when computing labor charges. However, there's a big difference in how they're used. While shops doing mechanical repairs eagerly
use flat rate manuals so they can overcharge people, many body shop
operators aren't excited about using the manuals but are forced to adhere
to them by the insurance companies, much as auto dealers are forced to
adhere to flat rate manuals by the auto companies. Also, while the
collision manuals, like the mechanical flat rate manuals, are quite liberal
in their time allotments, there's one difference in computing labor rates.
The shop that does mechanical repairs can set whatever hourly rate it
wants provided the free market will pay it. The body shop operator
isn't so fortunate. He doesn't operate in a free market but in one con-
trolled by the insurance companies, which account for the great bulk
of his business. While a mechanical repair shop might be able to
charge $25 or $30 or even more per flat rate hour for repairs, most body
shops in the country are restricted by insurance companies to charging
anywhere from $12 to $16 per flat rate hour.

Insurance companies generally insist that their adjusters follow religiously either Glenn Mitchell Manuals Inc.'s *Collision Estimating Guide*
or Hearst Corp.'s *Motor's Crash Book Guide* or the two organizations'
special foreign car estimating guides. If, for example, the *Mitchell Imported Collision Estimating Guide* says the time to refinish the front door
of a Toyota Corolla is two hours,[23] that's how much time the insurance
companies instruct their adjusters to allow—nothing more and nothing
less.

The manuals are used so the insurance companies can have a uniform
system of judging repair costs and can hire people to adjust claims who
have never repaired a damaged car in their lives and don't really understand what's involved. This way insurance executives who don't
know anything about repairing cars can keep tabs on their adjusters who
don't know anything about repairing cars. Says Gilbert N. Tanner of
the Washington (D.C.) Metropolitan Auto Body Association: "I am an
expert, so I know how much it is going to cost me to do a job. I don't
need a guide. But insurance companies don't hire experts. They hire
people they can train to read guides."[24]

While many body shop operators are content to live with the collision flat rate manuals, some aren't. Mike Orrico, president of Quality
Auto Body Shop, Inc., in Westmont, Illinois, says that the Mitchell
manual "is supposed to be a simple guideline to replace all parts, but an
adjuster will not allow for frozen nuts and bolts, mud- and tar-covered
nuts and bolts, bent parts that have to be pulled or pushed aside to get
to the nuts and bolts or the extra time needed to first pry open a hood
or a door." Mr. Orrico also complains that not enough time is given
shops to prepare a car before repairs start, such as cleaning road tar, wax

and scum off a panel in order to get a decent paint job. Nor, he says, is enough time allowed for color-matching paint.[25]

While body shop operators say they can beat the flat rate allowances by 50% to 60% most of the time, it still doesn't give them much of a labor charge if the insurance companies restrict them to $12 to $16 a flat rate hour.

Even if body shops beat the manuals by an average of 50%, it still gives them only $18 to $24 a real hour—not very much considering the enormous skill required. It's noteworthy that in the summer of 1978 it cost about $24 an hour in the Washington, D.C., area to fix a freezer made by General Motors' Frigidaire subsidiary at an authorized dealer.[26] Yet, in the same metropolitan area, Motors Insurance Co., another GM subsidiary, was paying body shops only $12 an hour based on flat rate manuals, or an effective rate of about $18 a real hour for something that takes much more skill than fixing a freezer.

This is where "the game" gets really interesting. The insurance company adjusters know that the body shops can't survive doing work at a pitiful $12 a flat rate hour or even $18 a real hour. But they also know that their bosses won't permit them to write an estimate without using the flat rate manuals. So what the adjusters usually do is "find more time" for the shop. This means the adjuster will add repairs to the estimate which aren't necessary and which he knows won't be done. Mr. Benck, the body shop operator, says another method is for the adjuster to inflate the hourly times on judgment items which aren't in the flat rate manuals, such as straightening a panel. He explains further: "It possibly could be a three-hour job; we inflate it to four or five to compensate for the $12 an hour rate that we use . . . this is done knowingly with your adjusters from the insurance companies."[27]

When such fraud is taken into consideration, plus beating the book, plus shortcuts and other forms of cheating, the $12 labor rate in the Washington, D.C., area becomes an actual rate of $20 to $30 an hour for most independent body shops and $25 to $37 an hour for dealer body shops, according to industry sources.

Another part of "the game" is the parts discount. Not content with screwing body shops out of a fair labor charge, auto insurance executives often demand and get discounts on parts as well. Many independent body shops buy their parts on average at the retail price less 25%. This means they buy a $100 part for $75. But then the insurance companies come along and demand discounts of usually 5% or 10%—leaving the body shop owner with hardly any profit. Shops are under tremendous economic pressure to give these profit-robbing discounts. John Daniels, a St. Louis body shop operator, explained in 1978 that with the prevailing discount rate at 10% in his area and with 95% of his business coming from insurance companies, "if I lowered my discount rate I think I'd have to fold my tent and leave."[28]

Mr. Rhoads, the Allstate executive, says if a shop didn't grant a discount "it would be more difficult" to do business with it and that the discount is taken into consideration when writing estimates "almost all the time."[29]

Naturally, many body shops are going to try to cheat to make up for the discounts, and the adjusters, understanding their situation, will go along. One body shop repairman told me bluntly that if the criminal laws were enforced, "you could lock up every body repair shop operator in the country for obvious fraud."

While much of the fraud is of the gentleman's agreement type whereby adjusters try to make amends for the idiotic labor rate and parts discount, it sometimes goes beyond that. Some shops don't do repairs that the insurance adjusters expect them to do. On the other hand, body shop operators in New York State complain that they are often forced to give insurance appraisers kickbacks and payola.[30] Then there are times when crooked appraisers and crooked body shop operators get together to defraud the insurance companies. A body shop operator told the *Miami Herald* of an independent appraiser suggesting he "discover" a non-existent windshield crack, bill the insurance company $200 for a new windshield and split the money 50–50.[31]

It is even possible that "the game" induces many body shops to buy parts stripped from stolen cars. The shops, to compensate for insurance company penny-pinching, install the stolen parts and then charge the insurance companies for higher-priced new parts. The National Automobile Theft Bureau estimated in 1978 that 38% of all crash parts used to repair cars were stolen.[32]

Sometimes consumers join the fraudulent game between body shops and insurance companies. Not wanting to pay their $100 or $200 deductible, many consumers work up a scheme with the body shop to pad the repair bill with $100 or $200 of nonexistent repairs. Consumers also try to defraud insurance companies by trying to get them to pay for damage caused in previous accidents.

The Bad Hands People

Consumer Reports, after polling its subscribers on their experiences with their own auto insurance companies, came up with special criticism of Allstate Insurance Co., a subsidiary of Sears, Roebuck & Co.—the firm which has been cited again and again for engaging in unethical auto repair practices.

The poll, released in mid-1977, found that 25% of Allstate policy-holders were dissatisfied with the repair shop chosen or recommended by the company—6% higher than average. Also, 11% were dissatisfied with their own repair shop when Allstate paid the bill. The magazine rated Allstate worse than average in handling customer claims as well as in handling non-claim service and suggested, "You're not in good hands with *Allstate*."[33]

Other insurance companies judged to have given worse than average service were GEICO, Liberty Mutual Fire Insurance Co. and Liberty Mutual Insurance Co., Sentry Insurance A Mutual Co. and Travelers Indemnity Co.

Only four insurance companies were judged to give "much better than average" service—Amica Mutual Insurance Co., Erie Insurance Exchange, New Jersey Manufacturers Insurance Co. and United Services Automobile Association. All four greatly restrict those to whom they will sell a policy.

Rated better than average were insurance operations connected with three AAA clubs—the California State Automobile Association, the Automobile Club of Southern California and the Automobile Club of Michigan—plus three regular insurance companies: State Automobile Mutual Insurance Co., State Farm Mutual Automobile Insurance Co. and United States Fidelity and Guaranty Co.[34]

(The complete ratings can be found in the latest *Consumer Reports* annual buying guide or the July 1977 issue of the magazine. Both are available at many libraries.)

While getting poor marks from consumers, Allstate and GEICO were racking up unconscionable profits in 1977. Allstate made a net profit of $352 million,[35] possibly accounting for over 40% of all Sears, Roebuck earnings that year,[36] and GEICO had a net profit of $58.6 million.[37]

Why is the auto insurance business so profitable? Ask Anthony Feola of the Auto Body Craftsmen's Guild in New York and he'll tell you it's because "insurance companies collect high dollar for premiums and pay out low dollar for repairs."[38]

Totaling Your Wreck

When an insurance company decides to "total" your wreck, there's a good chance it'll turn you into a total wreck. That's because it never wants to pay you the full cost of replacing your car.

To illustrate, let's see how "totaling" works first with an old car and then with a relatively new car.

A Livonia, New York, man had been driving his 1970 Plymouth Duster some 340 miles a week on business and claimed the car was "in excellent mechanical condition" and "was economical and very reliable." Then, in December 1977, he skidded off an ice-covered road and hit a utility pole.

Since he had been paying $60 a year in collision insurance—in event of just such an accident—he said he was "flabbergasted" when the Travelers Indemnity Co. adjuster told him the value of his car was $272 and that, less his $200 deductible, his settlement was going to be $72. He said he found a dealer who could have sold the same model car locally for $650.

Irate at such shabby treatment, especially after paying for his policy with Travelers for six years without a claim, he began firing off letters of protest all over New York State and to Washington, D.C., although, he said, "I have never written complaint letters or petitioned for anything before."[39]

Alice T. O'Rourke of Alexandria, Virginia, got the same kind of treatment from Travelers Indemnity Co., only this time it involved an almost brand-new car.

Mrs. O'Rourke took possession of her 1978 Fiat X1/9 in October 1977 after plunking down $5,836 for it, including $4,200 from a bank loan. Forty-six days later a hit-and-run driver ran the car off the road and through a guard rail. A Travelers adjuster decided to "total" the car and said he would give her $4,165, which wouldn't even pay off her loan, let alone give her enough money to buy the same model of car again. The adjuster told her that her car had "depreciated," although she found that even a 1977 Fiat was selling for $4,600. Since it had taken her 1½ years to save the down payment, she didn't have enough money to hire a lawyer, nor did she have, she said, "the stamina and fortitude to fight an insurance company."

This story had a happy ending only through the intervention of the *Washington Star's* Action Line column. The newspaper contacted the insurance company, which called Mrs. O'Rourke and offered her $5,200. While she was mulling over the offer, the *Star* printed her complaint and quoted the company as saying the car was worth $5,200 to $5,500. She got the $5,500.[40]

As these examples show, the way insurance companies total a car is one of the more thieving tricks up their sleeves. Instead of paying you what it would cost to buy a comparable car, they try to get away with paying you the wholesale value of your car, which is about 30% under retail, or else what's called the "actual cash value" of your car. The latter is a Newspeak term which has nothing to do with the value of your car but is halfway between the wholesale and retail prices. For example, the 1973 Plymouth Fury III used in the *Miami Herald* shop survey was listed in the *Red Book*, a used car price guide, at $2,075 retail and $1,500 wholesale. That would put the "actual cash value" of such a car in average condition at $1,787.50.[41]

Even if insurance companies would pay you the full retail book value of your car, it doesn't necessarily mean you could replace your car for that price. First, you would have to find someone with a comparable car actually willing to sell it for that price. Second, in most states you would also have to pay a sales tax on the car as well. That could increase the price by 6% to 8%.

How does an insurance company decide whether or not to total your car? It's very simple. The company figures out how much it will cost to fix your car and how much it is worth as salvage. If the cost of fixing is the same as or exceeds the "actual cash value" of your car less its worth as salvage, the company totals it. As an example, let's say the "actual cash value" of your car is $4,000 and the scrap value is $400. This means the insurance company would lose $3,600 if it scrapped the car. Therefore, if the car can't be fixed for less than $3,600, it's hello scrapyard.

Mr. Rhoads, the Allstate exec, estimates that between 7% and 8% of claims settled by Allstate are totals, accounting for 23% to 25% of dollars paid out for claims.[42]

The Horror of *1984*

We've had the throwaway Coke bottle and the throwaway razor, but sometime between 1982 and 1984 we are going to have the ultimate in American opulence: the throwaway car.

This is because, if present trends continue, there will be few skilled auto body mechanics around and more car bodies will be made with materials not easily repaired.

Auto body repairmen, because of the heavy lifting and physical exertion involved in performing their trade, start thinking about retirement or at least reducing their workload around age 50. The National Association of Independent Insurers (NAII) reported in 1977 that the average body repairman was between 40 and 50 years old and "that within five to seven years there will be a tremendous personnel shortage in the auto body repair industry."

NAII attributes the shortage to the piecework pay system and its negative effect on apprenticeship programs, the reluctance of shop owners who pay an hourly wage to train new men, inadequate trade school training and "a paucity" of government and industry training programs.[43]

Auto body repairmen agree with NAII's dire prediction. "We are too rapidly moving toward extinction," says the Chicago area's Mr. Benck. "Our trade and skills are drying up."[44] Body repairmen also agree with NAII's list of causes for this predicament, except they add one conveniently overlooked by the organization: the auto insurance companies themselves. "The insurance industry," says Mr. Benck, "is digging its own grave."[45] Many body shop operators contend that young people don't want to enter the trade because they don't like the idea of the insurance companies' holding down their wages and forcing them to commit fraud in order to make a decent living.

Even if the demise of the professional auto body mechanic could somehow be averted, there's still a good possibility that you might have to throw away your car after a minor accident because more and more body parts will be unrepairable.

Already, for example, General Motors' Endura bumper can't be re-chromed because it's made of plastic. Also aluminum hoods, deck lids and bumpers now being put on cars are very difficult to repair. Then too, forget about trying to fix fiberglass body parts. Not only are they rather unstraightenable, but body shops are reluctant to grind fiberglass because the dust particles are harmful. Thus, a small dent in the Corvette fiberglass body may mean that the whole part has to be thrown away. Also pushing us down the road to the throwaway car is the fact that moldings, grilles and wood-paneled doors usually can't be repaired and that the sheet metal used nowadays is so thin that it tears upon straightening.

Crash Parts Prices

Another industry also has its hands deep in your pockets when your car is damaged: the auto manufacturers.

American automakers, in particular, have developed one of the great money-making schemes of all time. First they design their cars so unnecessary damage is inflicted during crashes, and then they clean up on the sale of replacement parts, which they hold a monopoly on and which they sell exclusively through their dealers at outrageously high prices.

A study by the Alliance of American Insurers found that it would cost $26,418, including labor, but excluding sales tax, to replace all the parts on a 1979 Chevrolet Impala bought new for $5,741.[46]

Even more shocking, *Money* magazine found in 1976 that while a current model Oldsmobile Cutlass coupe sold new for $4,553, it would cost

$3,475, excluding labor, to replace all the so-called crash parts—i.e. bumpers, hood, doors, headlights, roof, etc.[47]

The price of individually bought parts is so high that it's even possible for a car dismantler to buy a new car left over at the end of a model year, take it apart and sell the parts piece by piece for twice the amount he paid for the car.[48] Some monopoly parts like doors and hoods—basically hunks of metal—often retail for more than clothes dryers and refrigerators—far more complicated pieces of machinery that are subject to much competition.

The cornerstone of being able to get such outrageous prices for pieces of metal has been the proliferation of models and annual style changes. The American auto companies start by making lots of models which are much the same inside but cosmetically different on the outside. They then make sure that few of the cosmetic parts can be interchangeable among models. Next, every year they change just about every sheet metal part—sometimes ever so slightly—so that a part from one year won't fit cars made in any other year. This all produces a hyped-up need for thousands of different crash parts and makes it uneconomical for independent parts manufacturers to come in and start stamping out these parts, because there's not enough volume for any particular part. Thus each of the U.S. auto companies has been able to enjoy a monopoly on crash parts and raise prices at will, which they often do.

At one time, back in 1967, the four U.S. auto companies got up to 370 different models.[49] In the 1981 model year, the total was down to a still economically wasteful 239 models, with GM alone accounting for 115 models.[50]

A classic example of a trumped-up model difference is the Plymouth Duster and the Dodge Dart. C.W. Joiner, a Chrysler official, called them "basically the same car" designed to appeal to two different markets.[51]

Philip E. Benton, Jr., while general manager of Ford Motor Co.'s parts and service division in 1976, said that while "skin interchangeability" among Ford's car lines was "not satisfactory," it "is obvious that we have to maintain a . . . differentiation among products."[52] He disclosed that 251 skin sheet metal parts were required for 16 selected 1976 models out of a possible 334 parts, meaning that 75% of the parts were not interchangeable.[53]

While the American automakers have a monopoly on their crash parts, the same is not true for some of the foreign car companies such as Volkswagen, Datsun and Toyota. Robert M. McElwaine, president of the American Imported Automobile Dealers Association, explained why:

"Independent parts manufacturers have entered into this business because the imported cars have not gone in for the proliferation of models that domestic manufacturers have spawned, nor are the imports subject to annual or even biannual model changes. Therefore, they need only a few dies, and they are not outmoded in a year or two."[54]

Actually, according to the Federal Trade Commission, about 30% to 40% of the crash parts sold by the U.S. auto companies are made by independent manufacturers. However, says the commission, they use tooling owned by the automakers and to obtain that tooling must agree to sell all parts produced to the contracting automaker.[55]

Crash Parts Price Increases

The considerable amount of competition among car makers for the sale of cars tends to keep new car prices down, but there is no such competition in the sale of crash parts—which allows crash parts prices to soar through the roof.

The President's Council on Wage and Price Stability said that while the price of new cars increased 22.2% between January 1971 and February 1976, crash parts prices for new model cars increased 60.4%. While part of the difference could be explained in quality changes of the parts, including improved bumpers, the council noted that "the differences are too great to be explained solely by product improvement."[56]

The council also found that the two U.S. manufacturers with the fewest new car sales—Chrysler and American Motors—increased their prices for 1971 model year crash parts far more than General Motors or Ford. Between January 1971 and January 1977, dealer net price for American Motors 1971 model crash parts went up 85.6%, and for Chrysler 75.2%. In comparison, GM's prices went up 51.5% and Ford's 45.3%, and the Consumer Price Index rose 47.1%.[57]

All four U.S. auto companies seem to raise crash parts prices during recessionary periods—when it's hard to raise prices of new cars—and to especially soak the owners of small cars.

Between January 1, 1974, and January 1, 1976, when new car sales took a nosedive, crash parts prices increased well over 39%, according to the President's Council.[58]

The council also found that between January 1971 and January 1977, prices of crash parts for new model subcompacts rose almost twice as fast as prices of crash parts for full-size cars.[59]

This "soak the small car owner" trend was also discovered in a study by the Auto Body Craftsmen's Guild in the New York City area. It found that the cost of replacing 25 crash parts on a 1974 Chevrolet Vega increased 36% from February 1974 to February 1975, compared to a 12% increase in crash parts prices during the same period for the 1974 Cadillac

Eldorado. Most dramatic was the price increase for a Vega front hood. It skyrocketed 63% while an Eldorado front hood went up only 4%.[60]

Crash Parts and "Totaling"

Every time an auto company raises the price of its crash parts, you're exploited in two ways. First, it means that it will cost you more to fix your damaged car, or, if an insurance company is footing the bill, it will drive up your insurance costs. (About 75% of auto premium dollars are going for repairs and only 25% for injuries to people.[61]) Second, the more crash parts prices rise, the greater the likelihood an insurance company will declare your car a "total" and will force you to buy another car—often at a financial loss.

Body shop operators report that many Vegas were totaled simply as a result of the tremendous increase in crash parts prices for the car in 1974.[62] Thus we can see that a company like General Motors, by raising the prices of its crash parts, can create potential customers for its new cars.

In the example of the $5,741 Impala that would cost $26,418 to repair, it must be remembered that repair costs are in proportion to the $26,418, not the $5,741. If there's damage to only 10% of your car, the repair bill could be $2,642. Thus, says the Alliance of American Insurers, "even moderate damage can make a car not worth repairing, especially if it is three or four years old."[63]

If you have a make of car which goes through style changes every year, the car is depreciating fast at the same time the crash parts prices are rising fast, and so it will only take a few years and a minor accident to result in your car's being totaled.

Defense of High Prices

The auto companies defend the high prices of crash parts by contending that the parts must be warehoused for long periods of time, and, if produced after a model run, are subject to high per-unit production costs.

Nevertheless, the prices of crash parts are still unjustifiably high, and storing these parts or manufacturing them in limited quantities would be unnecessary if the auto companies stopped engaging in wasteful annual style changes and phony "skin" differences in models.

The pure economic waste generated by this system can be seen in the following statistics supplied by General Motors in 1976. The company said it had about 13,000 crash part numbers—over half of which had annual sales of fewer than 300 units during a then recent 12-month period and over 75% of which had sales of fewer than 700 pieces each.[64] GM alone, according to the Federal Trade Commission, designed more than 5,000 different crash parts to fit its 1968–72 model year cars and light trucks.[65] Ford in 1976 stocked 7,800 different crash parts.[66]

Alternatives to New Parts

Two alternatives to using new crash parts would be more repairing and less replacing, or the installation of used parts. However, there are problems with both.

Repairing often isn't a viable alternative because of a shortage of body repairmen with the necessary skills and the fact that the auto companies provide little or no repair information to many of the 30,000 independent body shops[67] which repair about half[68] of the nation's damaged cars.

Substituting used parts for new parts also has many shortcomings. For the first two years after a model is introduced, used crash parts are in short supply and are often just as expensive as new crash parts.

As used crash parts become more available, the price drops and may gradually reach half that of new parts after four or five model years. After six or seven years, the price might drop to one-fourth that of new parts.[69] But salvage dealers don't like to sell individual parts until a car is maybe nine years old. Instead, they sell mainly assemblies or "clips." For example, if your car is front-ended and needs just a few of the front end parts, chances are the body shop—if it is going to install used parts—will have to buy what's known as a "front clip"—all the sheet metal from the cowl to the grille. That often makes it more economical to buy a new part or two if that's all that's needed.

Beyond that factor, used parts can also present a headache for the repairman. They may be dented or rusted or not fit properly. If bought in a clip, the excess material has to be removed by a blowtorch. Used parts may also have to be sanded and painted before they're ready to be installed, whereas a new part just has to be zipped on.

For these reasons, plus the fact that new parts are generally more profitable to the body shop and result in greater consumer satisfaction, many body shop operators try to avoid used parts as much as possible. Most body shops are especially critical of rechromed bumpers, which they contend don't always come out with the same contour as new bumpers and are hard to align.

Monopoly Distribution

Not only do the automakers have a manufacturing monopoly over more than 90% of the crash parts sold in the United States,[70] but their dealers have a wholesale distribution monopoly. This adds even more to the price of crash parts and gives dealers an unfair competitive advantage over independent body shops because:

1. They can buy parts cheaper. A part that retails for $100 could cost the dealer from $39 to $57, while the independent body shop would have to pay $70 to $75.[71]

2. They can control the supply of parts. Body repairman DeRose claims that "some dealers, to keep the competition down, will tell you they do not have the parts [when they really do]. A lot of them do that, especially on foreign cars."[72]

This dealer monopoly system exists because of incredible bungling over the years by the Federal Trade Commission. In 1979, an FTC administrative law judge ruled that General Motors' wholesale compensation plan was illegal and discriminatory and ordered the company to come up with a new plan.[73] The case was still in litigation in 1981.

Crash Parts Shortages

Almost as scandalous as the wholesale compensation system is a wholesale shortage of crash parts.

The U.S. Office of Consumer Affairs says most of its complaints about crash parts shortages deal with two-to-four-month waiting periods, with waits of six months or longer not uncommon.[74]

Allstate's Winfield C. Rhoads says cars being tied up due to lack of parts "is a way of life. . . . Very seldom is a complete order filled."[75]

The problem is most acute for foreign cars. The U.S. Office of Consumer Affairs reported in 1976 that 46% of its complaints about delay in obtaining replacement parts involved foreign cars[76] (at the same time, imports accounted for about 18% to 22% of U.S. car sales).[77] Robert Durban, manager of material damage at Reliance Insurance Co., said getting a quarter panel for low-volume sellers like BMW, Mercedes, Volvo, Porsche or Saab might take "a month of Sundays."[78]

(Not only are foreign parts hard to get, but Rick Marchitelli of the Automotive Legislative Council of America says, "It seems that for no apparent reason, foreign vehicle parts are extremely expensive for both mechanical and body repairs."[79])

For American cars, crash parts are particularly hard to get in the first few months of a model year. That's because the auto companies use all or practically all such parts on the assembly line and don't set any aside for the replacement market. Pity the poor soul whose new car gets hit as he drives it home from the showroom. It could take six months or more to get the necessary replacement parts.

The auto companies and their dealers even have an incentive to make sure there's a constant shortage of crash parts: It helps them sell new cars. There are three ways this comes about:

1. *More rental cars are sold.* When motorists' cars are tied up at the body shop, they often have to rent cars. Thus, the greater the number of cars that are tied up and the longer they're tied up, the more new cars there are sold to auto rental firms.

2. *Impatient motorists buy new cars.* Says former U.S. Senator Frank E. Moss: "The frequently unreasonable amount of time needed to obtain replacement crash parts may place such a heavy inconvenience on a consumer that out of desperation he is driven to replace that car with a new model."[80]

3. *More cars are stolen and dismantled.* Rufus "Tinker" Whittier, who spent 15 years stealing cars, told *Money* magazine that it's common for cars to be stolen for their parts because of distribution delays. He explained: "Somebody smashes into the front of your new car and the body shop don't have fenders. They say, 'You're going to have to wait a couple months.' But I have a friend who'll get the parts next week, and at a discount."[81] The auto companies, of course, can then sell a new car to the guy whose car was stolen.

P.T. Barnum Bumpers

Auto executives over the past two decades have gone to great lengths to ensure that the bumpers on their cars don't protect anything except their enormous crash parts profits.

The success of their efforts is reflected in the results of crash tests conducted on 1980 model cars by the Insurance Institute for Highway Safety.

The institute crashed each of 12 compacts and subcompacts front-into-rear with another model of the same car at 10 mph, which is jogging speed. Five cars incurred no damage (Plymouth Horizon, Ford Mustang, VW Rabbit, Chevy Chevette and Honda Civic DX), while the other seven sustained front and rear damage of from $102 to $222. The most costly to fix was the Buick Skylark, which incurred $65 in front damage and $157 in rear damage.

Even more shocking results were obtained when the same cars were crashed into an angle barrier at 5 mph—the speed of walking. The average car sustained $175 worth of damage. The most costly to fix were the Honda Civic DX ($455), Datsun 210 ($394), Chevy Chevette ($285) and Buick Skylark ($274).[82]

"Technology has been available for years to preclude *any* damage in these sort of crashes," says Albert Benjamin Kelley, senior vice-president of the institute. "It simply is not being applied to the fullest benefit of the consumer."[83]

What then of all those ballyhooed bumpers that have been appearing on cars since around the 1973 model year? Aren't they supposed to be protecting cars in such crashes?

Actually, the only requirements for bumpers on 1973 through 1978 model cars is that they protect various "safety systems," such as head-lights and taillights, in various barrier-hitting or pendulum-swinging tests of 5 mph or less, regardless of how much damage is done to the bumper itself or sheet metal or non-safety parts.[84] For example, while the 1976 Chevrolet Impala meets the bumper safety standard, the Insurance Institute for Highway Safety found in late 1975 that the car, when crashed 5 mph front into a barrier, incurred $132 in damages—$105 of it for parts and materials.[85]

The bumper standard for 1979 models was tougher because it went beyond "safety systems" protection and included "property loss" protection. The 1979 cars were required to provide 100% protection to all *non-bumper* parts of the car in 5-mph *direct* barrier crashes and pendulum impact tests and 3-mph corner pendulum tests.[86]

The standard for 1980 and later models, as imposed by the National Highway Traffic Safety Administration (NHTSA), is somewhat better, but still quite weak. It prohibits *all* damage to the car and its bumper systems in the above 5-mph tests with the exception of small bumper dents. It doesn't take into consideration corner impacts such as bumping into a pole at a shopping center at 5 mph.

Despite the leniency of the 1980 standard, the U.S. Senate voted in the summer of 1979 to roll back its scope to 2.5 mph—half the speed of walking—and to keep it that way until September 1984. Fortunately, the House of Representatives didn't go along.

I don't know which senators voted for this outrage against the American consumer, because there was an unrecorded voice vote. The main instigator, however, was Senate Majority Leader Robert Byrd of West Virginia, acting not on behalf of the American consumer, but on behalf of Houdaille Industries, Inc., a bumper manufacturer in his state.

Houdaille claimed that a 2.5-mph bumper standard was more cost-effective than a 5-mph standard. This was disputed by three studies, including one by the Insurance Institute for Highway Safety that contended a 7.5-mph bumper would be more cost-effective than a 5-mph bumper.[87]

Nevertheless, in 1981, President Reagan proposed lowering the bumper standard to 2.5 mph, contending it would save the automakers $650 million a year.

At the center of the controversy are the bumpers that many of the auto companies have elected to use to meet federal bumper standards. Many are needlessly heavy, frilly and expensive, and some actually cause more damage in high-speed crashes than the ineffective bumpers of the 1960s.

A State Farm study, released in early 1976, found that while the front bumper of a 1970 Ford LTD cost $68.20 back in 1970, the front bumper for the 1976 model cost $334.50—an increase of 390%. "The reason for this tremendous increase in bumper prices is the complexity designed into the new bumpers," said Thomas C. Morrill, State Farm vice-president. "This is being done—ostensibly—to meet federal requirements, but it isn't necessary. Lightweight models that comply with the requirements

Insurance Institute for Highway Safety
1980 Model Low Speed Crash Test Results

	5 mph front into barrier	5 mph front into angle barrier	5 mph rear into pole	10 mph front into rear			total damage all tests
				front damage	rear damage	damage to both	
SUBCOMPACTS							
Plymouth Horizon	$ 0	$ 85	$ 0	$ 0	$ 0	$ 0	$ 85
Ford Mustang	0	70	42	0	0	0	112
Volkswagen Rabbit	0	186	126	0	0	0	312
Chevrolet Chevette	0	285	141	0	0	0	426
Toyota Corolla	0	143	363	0	107	107	613
Honda Civic DX	0	455	175	0	0	0	630
Datsun 210	0	394	191	171	0	171	756
Averages	$ 0	$231	$148	$ 24	$ 15	$ 40	$419
COMPACTS							
AMC Concord	$ 0	$ 3	$ 0	$102	$ 0	$102	$105
Chevrolet Citation	0	0	136	75	136	211	347
Ford Fairmont	0	0	293	0	202	202	495
Chevrolet Malibu	0	201	191	49	167	216	608
Buick Skylark	0	274	152	65	157	222	648
Averages	$ 0	$ 96	$154	$ 58	$132	$191	$441
Overall Averages	$ 0	$175	$151	$ 39	$ 64	$103	$428

Results are rounded to the nearest dollar.
A labor rate of $14 per hour, slightly lower than the prevailing average labor rate in the U.S., was used.
Criteria for bumper face bar damage were based on the DOT Part 581 Bumper Standard.

are being used on some new models such as the Volkswagen Rabbit and the Chevrolet Chevette."[88]

Dr. William Haddon, Jr., president of the Insurance Institute for Highway Safety, argues that many cars have bumper assemblies designed with needless cosmetic filler panels and stone-protecting shields "which raise both the initial cost of a motor vehicle and cost of damage repair."[89] Here were the replacement costs, as of October 1977, of some of these needless filler panels, which cover up the shock absorber units: 1977 Datsun 610, $112.85; 1977 Ford LTD, $68.40; 1978 AMC Matador, $62.35, and 1977 Oldsmobile Cutlass, $54.50.[90] The stone shields, according to bumper inventor Paul Taylor, president of Tayco Developments, Inc., are not only needless but collect snow and slush in the wintertime which could either damage the bumpers or cause them to lose their shock-absorbing capabilities.[91]

More significantly, many of the "new" bumpers are so poorly designed that they cause more damage at high speeds than the pre-1973 model bumpers. "At high speed 'hits,'" says the National Association of Independent Insurers, "these energy absorbing bumpers due to the manner in which they are mounted, contribute to increased repair costs. Because the energy absorbers are fused to the frame, at high speed 'hits' this design causes more cars to be considered 'totals,' in view of the high repair cost, than were 'totalled' before the development of these bumpers!"[92]

All in all, a 1977 report by State Farm points out that despite the bumper safety standards and a significant decline in the replacement of bumpers and the parts they're supposed to protect, "the real world experience has been that the cost of front and rear repair has continued to escalate." While the report didn't give the exact reason for the increase, it did hint at the tremendous increases in bumper system prices. A survey of 1975 models, it said, found more than 25% of the total parts dollar was being spent on bumper system components.[93]

The Available Technology

We've now gone through more than a decade in which technology has been available to provide consumers with bumpers that are low in cost, give far better protection than the 1980 standards and reduce damage in high-speed crashes. To wit:

· Gerald J. Lynch, chairman of Menasco Manufacturing Co., told the U.S. Senate Antitrust and Monopoly Subcommittee in 1969 that his company had developed an energy-absorbing bumper system which could withstand as much as 23-mph bumper-to-bumper shocks with no damage, reduce shock and damage by 82% at 30 mph and have a beneficial effect at even higher speeds. His system called for four telescoping shock isolators mounted in an "M" pattern at the front and back. He estimated the eight shock isolators needed per car could be manufactured for "less than $25." Menasco at the time had designed shock mitigation devices for Polaris and Minuteman missiles and for aircraft landing gear.[94] The auto companies weren't interested.

· Paul Taylor, the president of Tayco Developments, told the U.S. Senate Commerce Committee in May 1971 that he and his son, Douglas, had developed 5-mph energy-absorbing bumpers. He said he tried to sell the bumpers to Ford and other auto companies for about $25 each, but was turned down cold. Mr. Taylor demonstrated to committee members that a 1971 American Motors Hornet station wagon equipped with his bumper could crash into a concrete wall at 5 mph without any damage to car or bumper.[95]

· In 1977, the Insurance Institute for Highway Safety crash-tested a 1977 Gremlin—front into an angle barrier—at 5 mph and found the car was damaged to the tune of $236. Another Gremlin was then fitted with a bumper system designed, built and tested within about 45 days by Mr. Taylor's firm. The car was then crashed into an an angle barrier at 5 mph and at 7 mph front into a barrier with no damage to car or bumper.[96]

· A Norwegian bumper manufacturer, A/S Raufoss, claimed in 1977 that it could produce a no-damage 10-mph lightweight aluminum bumper system for less than $60, compared to the $163 cost quoted by Houdaille Industries for only a 5-mph no-damage bumper. The company also claimed that its 10-mph bumper would reduce damage at higher speeds.[97]

· Minicars, Inc., and Calspan Corp. have been developing research safety vehicles under contract to NHTSA. The Minicars vehicle suffers no damage in 10-mph crashes and no damage past the replaceable nose module at 20 mph.[98] Calspan's vehicle, with front and rear bumpers made of resilient foam, can guard against damage in 8-mph frontal and 5-mph rear barrier impacts and reduce damage to other cars as well in low-speed collisions.[99] In fact, Calspan's research vehicle was rammed into the side of a 1975 Plymouth Fury at 8 mph with no damage to the research vehicle and little damage to the Plymouth. With ordinary bumpers, there would have been several hundred dollars' worth of damage to both cars.[100]

Let's face it! The auto companies have installed expensive, cost-absorbing bumpers instead of inexpensive shock-absorbing ones as part of a massive propaganda campaign to con the American public. They want us to believe that the old no-protection bumpers were better, that high no-damage standards are either impossible to meet or not worth the cost, that government bumper regulations are driving up the cost of cars and repairs and that cars with good bumper systems would have to look like tanks. Of course, none of this is true. The auto companies are simply interested in maintaining their enormous crash parts profits and seeing to it that your car is totaled prematurely.

It must be remembered that every year the auto companies can delay the enactment of tough bumper standards, they profit from crash part sales for years to come. For example, General Motors, by withholding 5-mph bumpers from its 1971 Impala, has cleaned up on monopoly crash part sales for that model. The Insurance Institute for Highway Safety found that not only had the car incurred $197 in damaged parts and materials in a 5-mph front-into-barrier test conducted in the last quarter of 1971, but the price of the parts and materials had escalated 41% to $277 only four years later.[101]

Bumper Mismatch

A problem with pre-1980 models is that of bumper mismatch. The auto companies varied the height off the ground of their bumpers from model to model. For example, a Los Angeles woman complains that the bumper of her 1977 Vega "is only good when one bumps into a wall or another Vega. Otherwise it is too low to do any good at all."[102]

GM Crash Parts Sales

General Motors won't reveal its crash parts profits, but you can be sure they're sizable. The company has, however, estimated that crash parts by dollar volume constitute 25% of all parts sales to dealers.[103] GM also says that crash parts sales in 1975 were 1.2% of total domestic automotive sales.[104] That would put 1975 crash parts sales at $313.6 million.[105]

Car Information Act

The Motor Vehicle Information and Cost Savings Act of 1972 not only required the Department of Transportation to come up with property-loss bumper standards, but also to devise methods of comparing damage susceptibility, crashworthiness, ease of diagnosis and repair, and insurance costs among different makes and models of cars and to then establish procedures for dissemination of this information to consumers.[106]

Practically nothing was done to implement these requirements during the Nixon and Ford presidencies, and the Carter administration, despite lots of activity on this front, failed to come up with any standards. The information to be disseminated is designed to help consumers make more enlightened buying decisions and to encourage auto makers to produce cars which are more damage-resistant, safer, and less costly to service, repair and insure.

We have already seen that the federal requirement that automakers disclose the miles per gallon for each model has not only influenced buying decisions, but has also encouraged the automakers to increase the miles per gallon that their cars can get.

Insurance industry claims and loss statistics offer an especially promising way to evaluate cars. The Highway Loss Data Institute—associated with the Insurance Institute for Highway Safety—has found substantial differences in models when rated according to claims frequency, average loss payment per claim, relative injury claim frequency, etc. Allstate since 1976 has been giving rate increases and decreases to some policyholders based on whether their particular model is more or less profitable to insure than the average in its market class.

Reform

The problems involving the four-headed screw are only going to be solved by extremely tough legislation, regulations and antitrust law enforcement.

Most essential is that the following changes be made to NHTSA's bumper standard as suggested by the Insurance Institute for Highway Safety:

1. A bumper system should "be able to prevent damage to itself and its car in 10-mph front-to-rear direct and angled car-to-car impacts, both with and without the pitch-dive effect of one or both cars being braked just prior to impact."

2. The barrier test requirement should be raised from 5 mph to 7.5 mph.

3. A bumper system should be limited "to considerably less than 4 percent" of a car's total weight.[107]

As far as insurance companies go, Congress should repeal or change the McCarron-Ferguson Act of 1945. This law exempts insurance companies from federal prosecution for antitrust violations, and, according to some interpretations, also exempts them from federal regulation. Congress should at least amend the law to allow the federal government to go after the auto insurance companies for price-fixing of crash repairs, especially by forcing shops to use flat rate manuals. Congress should also allow the Federal Trade Commission to regulate some of the seedier practices of auto insurance companies, particularly the way consumers are gypped when their car is totaled.

The federal government should also be seeking ways to bring down the costs of crash parts and increase their availability. The most effective way to do this would be to put an end to wasteful annual styling changes and proliferation of models. Perhaps a certain percentage of each company's crash parts could be required to be interchangeable among models.

A less radical approach would be to force the auto companies to disclose on new car stickers the cost of each crash part and the total crash part price. Such disclosures would not only tend to bring down crash part prices after the public sees how absurdly high they are, but it would set up a sort of competition in what is basically a monopoly market. If two cars were selling for about the same price, but one car's crash part prices were way higher than the other car's, consumers might choose the car with the lowest crash part price tag. For example, the Auto Body Craftsmen's Guild in 1975 found that while the Ford Pinto's sticker price was about $23 less than the Chevy Vega's, the cost for Pinto crash parts was almost $200 more than the cost for Vega crash parts.[108]

To discourage the auto companies from raising crash parts prices indiscriminately, Congress should require them to submit all such price increases to a government agency. The agency, in turn, should be required to computerize the information and put out press releases periodically citing abnormally high price increases and comparing crash part prices of cars—both new and used.

Congress should also require the auto companies to provide free loaner cars to persons whose cars are tied up for more than two weeks because of the unavailability of crash parts. In addition, Congress should make the car makers sell crash parts to independent body shops, dealers and others at the same prices and terms.

On the state level, legislation is especially needed to put consumers, body shops and auto insurance companies on an equal footing. Here are my suggestions:

1. Prohibit insurance companies from directing a consumer to a particular repair shop or a group of shops.

2. Mandate binding arbitration in cases where an insurance company offers a lower payment than the amount for which the consumer's body shop is willing to do the work.

3. There should be state inspections after crash repairs have been completed to ensure that cars have been repaired correctly and honestly

and are safe to drive. In Iowa, for example, a policeman can direct that a car involved in an accident be given a state safety inspection after repairs.[109]

4. Insurance companies should be prohibited from forcing body shops to follow flat rate manuals, to charge less for crash repairs than the going rate for mechanical repairs or to give parts discounts.

5. Insurance companies, when they total a car, should be required to pay the full purchase price, including sales tax and any other fees, of a comparable car.

6. Insurance adjusters and appraisers should be required to pass a minimum competency test.

7. Insurance companies should be required to give you an itemized copy of their appraisal, specifying where new, used or rebuilt parts are to be used. The body shop's invoice should also have the information itemized.

8. Motorists should not have to get more than one estimate for damage, and insurance companies should pay the reasonable cost of that estimate.

9. No insurance company should be able to insist that a claimant use a drive-in claim center, and insurance companies should be subjected to heavy fines for directing a claimant to drive a car to such a center if the car has safety defects as a result of an accident.

10. Insurance companies, if they are to appraise damage to a car, should be required to give consumers a written appraisal within seven days of being notified. Once an agreement has been reached on the amount of payment, the insurance company should have a check in the mail within five business days if the consumer desires to be paid in cash. If the insurance company is to pay the body shop directly for repairs, a check should be in the mail within five business days of the satisfactory completion of repairs. Mr. Orrico, the Westmont, Illinois, body shop operator, says insurance companies often take 30 to 90 days to send body shops a check.[110]

11. Insurance companies and body shops should be prohibited from requiring customers, when they come to pick up their cars after repairs have supposedly been done, to sign a release absolving them of any further responsibility.

12. Shops should be required to tell customers in writing their storage charges prior to accepting their car. No shop should be allowed to levy storage charges if the bill or quality of work is in dispute.

13. Tow trucks should be required to state all charges on the door of the truck.

Protecting Yourself

Protecting yourself from thieving insurance companies, body shops and auto companies begins with the choice of car you buy.

If you buy a car with P.T. Barnum bumpers, figure that car may cost you in the long run several hundred dollars more than one with good bumpers. Remember, with some cars, backing into a pole at the supermarket at 6 mph could cost you $100 or more.

If you're buying a 1980 used car, look over the crash test results included in this chapter and avoid those cars with ineffective bumpers. You can obtain earlier or more current crash test results by writing or calling the Insurance Institute for Highway Safety (see Appendix I).

You should also avoid buying any model that changes style annually. Once you commit yourself to a frequently restyled car, you're not only at the mercy of the auto makers' extortionary crash parts prices, but your car depreciates faster and could be totaled sooner than cars that keep the same sheet metal shapes from year to year.

If you don't like the possibility of your new car's being tied up after an accident for months because of a lack of parts, here's a little trick to try before buying the car: Call up the dealer's body shop and ask how long it will take to get a bumper assembly, grille, grille header panel, right fender and right headlight assembly for the car. If they say a couple of months, don't buy the car.

Your next step in the protection process is to choose an insurance company that will treat you fairly and promptly when you have a claim. Check the *Consumer Reports* annual buyer's guide or the July 1977 issue.

What's contained in your insurance policy is also important. Many people think that their collision policies automatically entitle them to a rental car and towing should their car be disabled. Not so. You need special "endorsements" with your policy specifying such coverage. If you own more than one car, you need such endorsements for each car, and you must pay an extra premium for them.

If your car is fairly old, consider dropping your collision and comprehensive coverage. The insurance companies will pay out so little money if your car is totaled that this kind of policy on older cars is often just not worth the money.

As for body shops, I would strongly recommend going to one that belongs to a trade organization. Members of such organizations are usually not too fond of the insurance companies and may help you in fighting them. One of the most consumer-oriented organizations around is the Auto Body Craftsmen's Guild in Glendale, New York. The most prominent national associations of auto body repair shop operators are Automotive Service Councils, Inc., and the Automotive Service Industry

Association (see Appendix I for addresses). Look in yellow-pages ads under "Automobile Body Repairing & Painting" for members of various associations.

I'd also suggest you choose only those shops that will guarantee their work in writing and that you stay away from any shop that offers to save your deductible. If they're willing to cheat the insurance company, then they're willing to cheat you.

You've also got to be wary of tow truck operators who "happen" to arrive on the scene of your accident and want to tow your car to a particular shop. These guys are often rip-off artists who listen to accident reports on the police radio and then speed to the scene of the crash. In some cases, police officers call them when there's an accident in return for a kickback. Such tow truck operators often tow cars to shops that do less than quality work and engage in all sorts of chicanery.

Now some advice on how to deal with problems in the settlement process.

Never go to a drive-in claim center without first getting a written estimate from at least one body shop. This will give you an idea of the extent of damage and how much it will cost to fix. If the adjuster offers you a check for the damages, don't accept it unless you're certain your car can be repaired for that amount. Never go to a drive-in claim center if your car has safety defects or if it's inconvenient.

Insist that your car be repaired at the shop of your choice and not at one of the insurance company's "preferred" shops. If your shop's estimate is higher than the insurance company wants to pay, there may be an arbitration clause in your insurance policy which you can invoke. This allows you and the insurance company to each appoint an appraiser, and the two of them, if they can't agree on a fair price, can together appoint a neutral third party to arbitrate the dispute. You may want to appoint your body shop operator as your appraiser. Another alternative in such cases is to sue the insurance company in small claims court for the difference in estimates.

If an adjuster directs you to a particular shop or gives you a choice of shops, make him put in writing that he is doing so and that he will guarantee the repairs. Says Robert E. Mackin, assistant insurance commissioner of California: "We have always taken the position that where the insurance company has directed a policyholder to a particular shop for repairs the insurer acts as the guarantor, meaning that it has to make good if the repair shop does a poor or fraudulent job." Mr. Mackin adds, however, that "the problem we encounter in most such cases is that the policyholder has no evidence of the fact that the company directed him to a certain shop."[111]

Before giving the go-ahead for any repairs, make sure you get a written itemized list from the insurance company of what repairs it has authorized and a similar itemized list from the body shop of what repairs it is going to do. Make sure the lists agree. Once the repairs are completed, make sure the body shop gives you another itemized list of what repairs it did and which parts were installed, including a notation of which were new and which were used. Next, check the list against what the shop was supposed to have done.

When you go to pick up your car after repairs have been completed, don't accept the car if there are any obvious flaws or without taking a road test to catch any operating defects. Insist everything be repaired before accepting the car and never sign any document releasing either the body shop or the insurance company from any further responsibility.

If your car is totaled and the insurance company isn't willing to pay you enough to buy a similar car, either invoke the arbitration clause of your insurance policy or sue in small claims court for the difference. It's a good idea to keep a record of all maintenance and repairs done to your car so that should your car be totaled you could show a judge that you had properly maintained the car and had invested money in it.

If you're having trouble getting money out of the other person's insurance company, realize that you don't have to bother with the person's company. You could sue the person himself in small claims court and then let *him* deal with his insurance company to get the money back. Another alternative, if you have collision coverage, is to file a claim with your own insurance company and let it deal with the other guy's insurance company.

If your car is damaged in a crash, but still drivable, make sure the body shop has the needed parts before you drop off your car for repairs. Otherwise, your car might just sit for a month or more waiting for parts while you could be driving it.

Another bit of advice is to take all valuables out of the car, including the trunk, before leaving your car at a body shop. Otherwise, you may never see them again.

Once you've committed your car to a body shop, keep calling regularly to inquire when it will be ready. If you don't, the shop might take its own sweet time.

If your car is fairly new and the insurance company wants to install used parts, strongly object.

It's also important that you refuse to entrust your car to any shop that plans to sublet the work. Some new car dealers reportedly will farm your car out to the lowest bidder among back-alley shops. New car dealership body shops must also be watched carefully because they might try to pressure you into forgoing repairs and instead buying a new car. *Automotive Age* quotes Dick Hassan of Granite Dodge in Quincy, Massachusetts, as saying: "We make it a practice to talk to anyone here with a bill over $200 and tell them to trade it."[112]

Complaining

In most states, if you have a problem with either the insurance company or the body shop, there's little effective way to get your complaint resolved. Many state consumer protection agencies don't get involved in this area because they figure it's the province of the state insurance commission. But state insurance commissions are often so useless in resolving consumer complaints that one industry observer asks, "Where do you go to complain about your insurance commission?"

A list of state insurance commissions is in Appendix F. For the names and addresses of auto insurance company executives, consult the annual *Best's Insurance Reports: Property-Casualty,* available at many libraries.

Several states, cities and counties license or regulate auto repair shops, and so problems with body shops can be referred to the licensing and regulatory authorities listed in Appendix A. One of those regulatory authorities—the New York State Department of Motor Vehicles—even licenses insurance company drive-in claim centers. Such centers are subject to suspension, revocation or denial of their licenses for knowingly issuing false or misleading estimates or unreasonably impeding or delaying your right to a fair recovery for damages.[113]

Another alternative is to complain to Professional Insurance Agents, a trade association of independent insurance agents (see Appendix I). It has set up a "consumer line" to help people with insurance problems and is especially interested in mediating insurance company–body shop disputes.

If you're interested in political reform, your beefs about auto insurance companies can be sent to the Ralph Nader-affiliated National Insurance Consumer Organization (see Appendix C).

8

Even *You* Could Be a

"Mechanic on Duty"

It was a hot and muggy Saturday night in Boston when Andra Hotch-kiss, after having a service truck man jump the defective battery on her car, pulled the vehicle into a Gulf station with a "mechanic on duty" sign out front. She asked the lone "mechanic" who was on duty if he had a replacement battery. He said he did and so she shut off the engine, not worrying that the car probably wouldn't start again. As a test, she tried to start the motor again, but got no juice. The "mechanic" then told her that although he had a battery, he wasn't going to install it. He then changed his mind and came back with a battery, which he tried to install without success. It had side terminals instead of top terminals, which her car required.

While the "mechanic" went to wait on gasoline customers, Ms. Hotch-kiss started to take the battery out of the car herself, but the "mechanic" came over and began doing it, dropping nuts and bolts into the engine compartment in the process.

The "mechanic" then found the proper replacement battery, but put the clamp on wrong so that it wouldn't hold the battery down tight. Ms. Hotchkiss' brother, Ralf Hotchkiss, who was with her, fixed it properly. After all that, the car wouldn't start nor would the lights go on. It was discovered the battery was bone dry. Ralf told the "mechanic" to put in battery acid, but he came back with battery water and began pouring it in. Ralf stopped him. (All batteries should be filled originally with an acid that is part water. The reason you add water to a battery in use is that the water in the acid evaporates.) The "mechanic," undeterred, again tried to put water in the battery and again Ralf stopped him.

Just then, a car came into the station overheating. The "mechanic" went over to the car, unscrewed the radiator cap and was sprayed with boiling water. An ambulance came and took him away to a hospital, leaving the station unattended. Ralf looked around the station for battery acid, but couldn't find any, and so the car had to be left over the weekend.[1]

This 1978 incident illustrates how easy it is for anyone to pass himself off as an auto mechanic in Massachusetts or practically anywhere else in the United States. "Anyone with a borrowed screwdriver is a mechanic who says he is in California," Peter Carberry, executive vice president of the Automotive Service Council of California, told a State Senate committee in 1974.[2]

Unbelievably, only Michigan,[3] Hawaii[4] and the District of Columbia[5] have any kind of mechanic licensing law. And, of the three, only Michigan requires that all auto mechanics have at least minimal knowledge of whatever repair they're performing.

Meanwhile, the National Institute for Automotive Service Excellence (NIASE), an industry mechanic certification group, admits that about half of the more than 500,000 mechanics who work on consumer vehicles are not competent to perform the full range of diagnostic and repair functions in one or more vehicle systems.[6]

This percentage of Mr. Badwrenches can be expected to increase as cars become more complex and competent mechanics retire or go into other fields.

Let's explore why things are so bad, the pitiful measures being undertaken to reverse the trend and the dramatic action that needs to be taken to increase the number of competent mechanics.

The Mechanic Shortage

There is such an acute mechanic shortage that William D. McLean, manager of educational programs for the Motor Vehicle Manufacturers Association, said in mid-1977 that the U.S. needed to recruit and train about 745,000 new mechanics in addition to the 446,000 then employed in the consumer section. More than 270,000 mechanics, he said, would have to be trained or retrained in tune-ups alone "before the entire U.S. vehicle population can be maintained according to manufacturers' specifications."[7]

While a ratio of one mechanic for every 87 "household-owned" vehicles is considered desirable,[8] the ratio in 1977 was only about one mechanic for every 238 vehicles.[9] This is a steep drop from a ratio of 73 cars per mechanic in 1950 and 129 cars per mechanic in 1965.[10] Even more startling is that in early 1978 there was only one "test-ready" mechanic—a person capable of diagnosing and repairing correctly at least one area of the car—for every 500 consumer-owned vehicles, according to Dr. McLean.[11]

The ratio, instead of shrinking, can be expected to expand even more as older experienced mechanics retire without competent young people taking their place and as the vehicle population continues to increase. It's estimated that 90,000 new mechanics are needed each year just to replace those who retire or leave the profession.[12] Meanwhile, the number of cars in operation, which stood at less than 69 million in mid-1965,[13] grew to 104.7 million in mid-1979[14] and is expected to grow by one estimate to 120.7 million in 1985.[15]

Despite the demand, few capable young people are interested in entering the industry, and those who are interested often don't have the necessary talents to fix today's complex cars.

"Every year there are tens of thousands of people entering the automotive field," says Allen Richey, executive vice-president of the Automotive Service Association in Austin, Texas. "Unfortunately," he adds, "very few of them are qualified."[16] He says only about one in 25 entering mechanics has gone to a training school before starting work.[17]

The Future Is Bleak

"Where is the next generation of mechanics coming from?" despairingly asks Robert Wiens, head of the California Bureau of Automotive Repair.[18] Mechanics certainly don't seem to be coming out of auto company training programs, vocational schools, community colleges or even U.S. Labor Department apprenticeship programs.

The auto companies are doing practically nothing to train new mechanics. For example, Ford Motor Co., which made 18% of all cars registered in the U.S. as of July 1, 1979,[19] and whose dealers employ about 66,000 mechanics,[20] says it provides annual job-entry training "to approximately 200 newly hired dealership technicians."[21] Chrysler Corp.'s MoTech—a one-year training school—graduates only 400 a year.[22]

Although large numbers of people are going through vocational school and community college training courses, they offer little hope for the future. Rick Marchitelli of the New York Auto Body Federation says that 90% or more of those taking auto repair vocational school training are not interested in becoming mechanics, but are merely "hobbyists" who want to learn how to work on their own cars.[23]

Of those vocational school and college students who are serious about a career in auto mechanics, many can't make the grade. The College of Alameda near Oakland, California, somewhat typifies what is happening nationwide. Hector Corrales, counselor on transportation education at the college, told me in 1978 that there were 200 students in the college's two-year auto mechanic program and a waiting list of 175 more. Yet he expected only about 20% to graduate. Mr. Corrales says the students have usually tinkered with cars and have the idea they'd like to be mechanics, but "they don't have the stamina and they don't have the discipline" and they're "not equipped for test-taking—they can barely read or write."

To be a mechanic today, he says, one needs to know math and how to read technical literature and to have a good memory as well. "In addition to being able to work with your hands," he points out, "you have to remember minute detail, you have to concentrate."[24]

The same type of situation exists at lots of vocational technical schools, where many if not most of the students are high school dropouts. *Motor/ Age* magazine did a random sampling of technical schools in 1978 and said almost all instructors confirmed "that there is a problem in the reading and mathematical skills of their students." Most instructors said they had to lower their standards to accommodate these deficiencies. "This means," says the magazine, "that students, in some cases, are graduating and attaining jobs with little or no idea of how to read an aspirin bottle label, let alone a service manual."[25]

It's unlikely, too, that the number of badly needed mechanics will come out of government apprenticeship programs. The U.S. Labor Department shelled out over $4 million during a 22-month period in 1977–78 to the National Automobile Dealers Association (NADA), Automotive Service Councils, Inc., and International Association of Machinists and Aerospace Workers[26] just to set up and administer auto mechanic apprenticeship programs and to recruit and screen applicants. The programs involved college and on-the-job training, with none of the money going to the apprentices themselves or to pay for their training.[27] The $4 million produced only about 8,500 apprentices, which was far short of original expectations.[28]

The program involving the auto dealers was a complete boondoggle. NADA spent nearly $2 million to recruit only 2,404 apprentices.[29] Equally as scandalous, the dealers admitted they didn't recruit people with a lifetime commitment to repairing cars, but those who wanted to become service department managers.[30]

Why the Good Guys Stay Away

It appears that only those qualified young persons with "grease in their blood"—as one collegiate automotive instructor put it[31]—enter the trade. Here's why:

LOW WAGES AND FRINGE BENEFITS

To be an auto mechanic today requires "more skill and training than any other blue-collar worker in America," claims Andrew Kenopensky of the Machinists Union.[32] Yet the pay and fringe benefits are generally below many other blue-collar jobs. Even the guys who work on the automobile assembly line make much more money than auto mechanics and get lots more fringe benefits. In mid-1979, job offers for auto assemblers ranged from $5.35 to $7.72 an hour vs. $3.13 to $6.88 for auto repairers.[33]

The low wages can be generally attributed to the lack of unionization (only about 10% of the nation's new car dealers have collective bargaining agreements with mechanics,[34] and there's practically no unionization at nondealer shops); the auto manufacturers holding down wages for doing warranty work; the auto insurance companies holding down wages by not dealing fairly with body shops; and the flat rate pay system.

THE FLAT RATE SYSTEM

Someone who considers himself a professional is likely to be put off by a payment system which encourages slipshod repairs and cheating and causes physical and mental strain.

BAD IMAGE

The industry has perhaps the worst image of any profession in America. Even being a member of the Mafia is more respectable than being an auto mechanic.

POOR STARTING OPPORTUNITIES

Young people complain that shops don't want to hire them because they're inexperienced, or else, if they are hired, they're given coolie-type work to do.

The main problem seems to be the reluctance of shop owners to take on those in college/on-the-job apprenticeship programs—the major reason why the Labor Department program has been such a bust. Many shop owners have the idea that it will cost them money to take on an untrained person and then they'll have no guarantee that the person will stay after his training is over. There's also the problem that flat rate mechanics don't want to jeopardize their own earnings to help apprentices.

MR. BADWRENCH

DeForrest E. Cline of the Labor Department disagrees with repair shop owners. He figures that an apprentice with no prior experience will cost the shop owner money for the first six months and then make money for him during the next 3–3½ years of his training.[35]

HARD, DIRTY AND UNSAFE WORK

Auto repairers must often work in tiring and uncomfortable positions; lift heavy objects; work in dusty, greasy, drafty and noisy buildings where fumes from vehicles are often present; and occasionally perform repairs outside in bad weather.

Dangers are everywhere. Liquids, such as battery acid and hydraulic fluids, may cause burns or skin irritations. Injuries may result from power tools or from slips and falls because of oil, grease and tools on the floor.

There are even serious illnesses that can be contracted from auto repair work. Of increasing concern is the danger of asbestosis and cancer from exposure to asbestos fiber and dust—material found in brake linings brake pads and clutches. It's a common practice in many repair shops to clean brake assemblies with an air hose or by banging the brake drum on the floor. In both cases, harmful asbestos dust is released into the air.

According to the Bureau of Labor Statistics, 10.5% of workers in repair shops and garages suffered substantial job-related illness or injury in 1974.[36]

Why would a young man with mechanical ability want to put up with such awful working conditions when he could perhaps fix business machines? The 1980–81 edition of the U.S. Labor Department's *Occupational Outlook Handbook* describes that job as dressing in business clothes and visiting offices to fix their machines. It mentions that injuries are uncommon.[37] The pay in 1978 for experienced repairmen and specialists was from $200 to over $300 a week.[38]

UNPROMISING FUTURE

The work is so hard that many mechanics must retire prematurely. Also, the older one gets, the harder it gets to beat the flat rate manuals, and thus income tends to drop.

FAST-CHANGING TECHNOLOGY

"Just as a repairman becomes proficient with one year's models, Detroit puts that model out of style," complains Anthony J. DeRosa of the Independent Garage Owners Association of Illinois.[39] A Washington, D.C., area mechanic explains how this discourages entry into the trade: "The mechanic stays a year or so behind because he has to relearn each year because there are so many changes made in all the different manufacturers' cars. They just keep changing them, so therefore I think it keeps new guys from getting into them, because they can learn to lay bricks, for example, and do that inside of a couple of years—and they're good at it and it doesn't change."[40]

The problem is exacerbated by the many drastic changes made in cars to decrease pollution and conserve fuel.

LACK OF SERVICING INFORMATION AND IN-SERVICE TRAINING

The auto companies are constantly telling their dealers how to solve various repair problems that crop up, but most of this information never gets to nondealer shops, which account for about 93% of the nation's repair garages.[41]

Beside being privy to more information than nondealer mechanics, dealer mechanics are often the only ones to take advantage of factory training courses. Sometimes such courses are offered only to dealer personnel, or, if they are open to others, shop owners can't afford to send anyone. Even dealers are not always enthusiastic about sending their mechanics to such classes, because they have to pay their wages, food and lodging while they're away and lose their production. Dealers are also afraid that after investing money to train their mechanics, they risk losing them to other dealers.

More Mr. Badwrenches

Car technology is changing so rapidly that even today's qualified mechanics could find themselves tomorrow's Mr. Badwrenches. Herbert S. Fuhrman, president of the National Institute for Automotive Service Excellence (NIASE), says, "I don't know that anybody is ever fully competent because the state of the art changes so fast."[42]

Indeed, the car repairmen of the future are going to have to be skilled in electronics, which proficiency tests show to be the "area of greatest weakness in the contemporary mechanic work force," according to Dr. McLean of the Motor Vehicle Manufacturers Association.[43] Grant Chave, manager of service programs for Ford Motor Co.'s Parts and Service Division, says electronic components, which are the coming thing, "tend in most cases to be part of complex systems that make diagnosis more difficult."[44] Ford estimates that by 1985 about 12% of the car's value will be in electronics.[45]

Dr. McLean also sees new materials adding to the burden of unqualified mechanics. "Careless insertion of spark plugs in an aluminum cylinder head can lead to disaster much more easily than in a cast-iron head," he says.[46]

Another opportunity for mechanics to mess up your car will be the increasing requirement that cars undergo periodic emission control inspections. There are just not enough qualified people around to do this work. Congress, in its stupidity, legislated much-needed auto emissions requirements without setting up a massive mechanic training program to go with it. In New Jersey, where cars must undergo an annual emissions test at a state-run facility, a 1978 study found that 25% of the vehicles that failed the emissions tests were not repaired well enough to pass a retest.[47]

Licensing Auto Mechanics

It seems incredible that the auto repair profession, which performs life-and-death work, is largely unregulated while members of other less critical occupations must pass competency tests and be licensed. As an illustration, let's take the state of Virginia, where auto repairs accounted for 24% of all consumer complaints in the year ended June 30, 1978.[48] While Virginia doesn't license auto mechanics or auto repair shops, it does license hairdressers, professional engineers, boxers, insurance agents, real estate agents, hearing aid dealers, nursing home administrators, driver training instructors, speech pathologists, social workers, librarians, harbor pilots, contractors, employment agencies, security guards, certified public accountants, and more.[49]

The Virginia Commission for Professional and Occupational Regulation, which was set up to advise the leglislature on which jobs should be regulated by the state, concluded after public hearings and much study that the state should at the very least set up a program of voluntary certification of mechanics.

In its 1974 report, the commission said if auto repair abuses "existed in an area which did not so directly involve the safety and lives of the citizens, this Commission might have suggested court action and better consumer information programs to deal with questions of competency and honesty. The truth is, however, that shoddy workmanship is a hazard to more persons than the unwary customer. The shoddy job and the untrained worker can ruin the lives of many families."[50]

Despite this report, the Virginia legislature still allows anybody who can fit into a pair of overalls and spell "mechanic on duty" to work on the brakes and other safety-related parts of any car in the state.

In California, the state legislature has also done nothing about licensing auto mechanics even though: (1) The Automobile Club of Southern California told a state senate committee in 1974 that it had conducted a study of vehicle defects and found "that as many as 23% of the defects . . . originated from faulty service or repair operations,"[51] and (2) the state's Bureau of Automotive Repair, which licenses repair shops, says it gets more complaints about incompetence than anything else[52] and is powerless to do anything about it. Douglas Laue, deputy chief of the bureau, says the major problem is caused by those who don't come close to competency.[53]

Let's now take a look at the mechanic certification programs in existence and see what's wrong with them.

Anti-Consumer NIASE

The automotive industry, in an effort to defeat state licensing of auto mechanics, set up the National Institute for Automotive Service Excellence (NIASE), which runs a voluntary certification program. Every spring and fall all over the country, NIASE gives auto mechanics written multiple-choice tests developed by Educational Testing Service, the same company that makes up the College Entrance Examination Board's famous Scholastic Aptitude Test. Questions are changed for every test. There are tests in eight areas of the car—engine, automatic transmission, manual transmission and rear axle, front end, brakes, electrical systems, engine tune-up, and heating and air conditioning. Every time a mechanic passes a test, he gets to wear a hash mark on his uniform denoting the specialty for which he's qualified. If a mechanic passes all eight tests, he gets to wear a "certified general mechanic" arm patch. Retests are given every five years. There are also tests for auto body repairers and painters and heavy-duty truck and bus mechanics.

While the program does serve a worthwhile purpose in giving needed recognition to some undoubtedly competent mechanics, it is much criticized both within and outside the repair industry.

"A written test doesn't prove competency," says Mr. Kenopensky of the Machinists Union. He believes the only true way to judge competency is to give a hands-on test where the mechanic has to actually diagnose and repair a car. He says he knows of persons who have passed NIASE's automatic transmission test "and received their hash mark who have never taken a transmission out of a vehicle or overhauled one."[54] Los Angeles area mechanic Glenn C. Garrett contends the tests challenge "the mechanic's ability to read and write English rather than his knowledge of automotive systems."[55] Passing score on the tests is 60%.[56]

NIASE also suffers from guilt by association. While its stated goal is "to organize and promote the highest standards of automotive service in the public interest,"[57] some of the companies and industries it has been associated with since being founded in 1972 have done nothing but abuse consumers and mechanics alike. The seed money came from the major

U.S. auto and truck makers and the National Automobile Dealers Association. Later on, according to NIASE president Fuhrman, the imported car makers, oil companies, various parts manufacturers and distributors and others "also contributed generously."[58] While NIASE is now self-supporting, among its 36-person board of directors in 1980 were representatives of General Motors, Chrysler, American Motors, Volvo, Shell, J.C. Penney and two parts manufacturers. There were also four new car dealers and one consumer representative, who was also the only woman on the board.[59]

It's my opinion that the auto and oil companies, car dealers and parts makers are supporting NIASE in order to lull consumers into a false sense of security while they protect their profits. All of them have lots to lose if the law should require all mechanics to be competent and honest. State licensing would bring an end to many corrupt practices.

Dealer mechanics, not wishing to jeopardize their licenses, would make sure that retail and warranty work were done properly with no hanky-panky. Despite the fact that large numbers of dealer mechanics have passed NIASE's tests, new car dealerships rank high on the list as far as incompetent and fradulent repairs are concerned. Indeed, there seems to be no relationship between the number of NIASE-certified mechanics a dealer has and the competency of its service department. The Washington Center for the Study of Services in 1977 surveyed 69 customers of JKJ Chevrolet, Inc., a Vienna, Virginia, dealership where 28 out of 35 mechanics were NIASE-certified. Only 65% said the dealership did work properly the first time. Meanwhile, a survey of 21 customers of Paul Brothers Oldsmobile, Inc., in Washington, D.C., which had no NIASE-certified mechanics, found that all had their cars fixed right the first time. Only 25% of JKJ's customers rated the dealership service department "superior," while 71% of Paul Brothers' customers considered that dealer's service department "superior."[60]

Meanwhile, the powerful oil companies don't want state licensing because they fear they would have to close up more of their service stations for lack of competent mechanics.

Those in the parts business aren't anxious for licensing because their sales would drop drastically if all mechanics had to be competent and honest.

Besides the special interests it caters to, NIASE has another fatal flaw as far as consumers are concerned. It isn't interested in decertifying mechanics who cheat the public or perform incompetently. In fact, a consumer brochure put out by the organization asks the question, "Should consumer complaints be directed to the institute?" It then answers: "No. The institute has neither the staff nor other resources that it would need to deal with complaints."[61] Apparently, however, NIASE *is* receptive to hearing from consumers if they have good things to say about its certified mechanics. It even printed a letter from a satisfied customer in one of its newsletters.[62]

Don Price of the Automobile Club of Southern California has criticized the NIASE voluntary program because it tends to recognize "those mechanics who are already trained without necessarily encouraging others who are less qualified to upgrade their skills."[63] By November 1979, less than half of the nation's mechanics who work on consumer cars had taken any tests and only 25% of the country's mechanics had passed one or more tests.[64]

Michigan, Hawaii and D.C.

If critics are right that the NIASE written test is somewhat of a fraud because it doesn't prove competency, then Michigan's written test criteria is a double fraud.

Under Michigan law, all mechanics, except trainees, must be certified for whatever repairs they are to perform.[65]

To become certified, the state's Bureau of Automotive Regulation requires mechanics to pass either NIASE's test or its own test. The catch is that the bureau lowers the passing score on the NIASE test, and its own test, which is much easier, also has a low passing score.

In fact, the bureau's own multiple-choice test is so easy and has such a low passing score that Gene Weingarten, a reporter for the *Detroit Free Press,* said he passed the engine repair exam "even though I know next to nothing about how cars work or what makes them break down." He got 59% of the answers right, and only 50% is a passing score. "I'm so dumb," he said, "I don't know how to change the oil in my own car, or jump a pooped battery."[66] James Hunsucker, deputy director of the bureau, called Mr. Weingarten's certification "a fluke."[67] The Michigan tests are so easy to pass that the state certified 76.5% of the mechanics tested in one or more specialty area.[68]

Actually, what Michigan is trying to do is quite commendable. It's attempting to set minimum standards to get rid of the total incompetents and to encourage low-skilled mechanics to study and perhaps get training in order to be able to pass the tests. The problem is that Michigan officials are asserting that those who pass its tests are "master mechanics." This makes a mockery out of the whole concept of licensing.

The District of Columbia adds more dignity to the licensing approach. It requires that each repair shop have a licensed "supervisory inspector" for whatever types of repairs it performs. To become a supervisor, a mechanic has to pass the NIASE tests in his specialty areas. Unfortunately, this law isn't being enforced, as no one checks to see if each shop has a licensed supervisory inspector. The problem seems to be that too many shops would have to close down for lack of qualified mechanics.

The only other mechanic licensing law in the country—in Hawaii—also has its drawbacks. The law has a grandfather clause which exempts from taking proficiency tests anyone who worked as a mechanic for at least two years prior to January 1, 1976, and was registered with the state by June 30, 1976. All other persons, except trainees, must pass both a written or oral test and a performance test in order to work as an auto mechanic.[69] This is, of course, patently unfair. It allows the incompetents who meet the grandfather clause requirements to stay in business while limiting their competition.

Connecticut, while it doesn't license mechanics, can take action against the license of a repair shop for incomplete or improper repairs.[70]

The Solution

As much as I dislike licensing of professions, the situation is so desperate that *we must license auto mechanics* under the auspices of state consumer protection agencies. But how do we do it without aggravating an already severe mechanic shortage?

My proposed solution would be a threefold approach: (1) registration of all mechanics, with a minimum competency test; (2) tough written and hands-on tests for brake mechanics; and (3) tough written tests for voluntary certification in all other areas.

I favor following Michigan's example as far as requiring all mechanics to pass a minimum competency test in order to be registered. (It would be essential that the public understand that just because a mechanic has passed a registration test doesn't necessarily mean he is an expert mechanic.) Then, if the mechanic continually misrepaired cars or engaged in fraud, he would be deregistered and tossed out of the profession. This type of program should increase the number of quality people who will want to enter the industry. Says Mr. Hunsucker of Michigan: "If the bad actor, the rip-off, the incompetent is eliminated from the marketplace, so much the better for the honest, competent operator."[71] He points out that over 8,000 persons failed Michigan's brake test and contends that "you have to start somewhere."[72]

An alternative registration plan has been considered in California. The idea would be to require all auto mechanics to register with the state and then to deregister those who perform faulty or unsafe repairs or engage in fraud or dishonesty. Under the plan, a mechanic who performed one unsafe or perhaps several faulty repairs would be given a test involving fixing an actual car. If he passed, he could keep his registration. If he failed, he wouldn't be able to work as an auto mechanic until he was properly trained so that he could pass the test.[73] The drawback here is that it doesn't encourage all mechanics to go for training.

Either type of registration would solve a major dilemma for law enforcement officials. Under the present system, says Robert Leonard, former president of the National District Attorneys Association, "most of the problems . . . in this area [auto repairs] go unresolved, since in most cases criminal prosecution is very, very difficult. . . . How can we tell if the job is . . . done by a person who is incompetent or an actual fraud?"[74]

Indeed, the major defense used by most mechanics when accused of corrupt repair activities is to plead incompetence in order to get off the hook. If mechanics were required to be registered, a pleading of incompetence would do little good, since it could get them thrown out of the profession. Thus, the consumer would win no matter which way the mechanic turned. As a report by the Wisconsin governor's Council for Consumer Affairs points out: "In the end it makes little difference to the consumer whether he is the victim of a burglar or a bungler."[75]

Higher Competence

To recognize those mechanics with above-average abilities, I would provide for tougher voluntary certification standards. The simplest thing for a state to do would be to require mechanics to pass the NIASE tests in their specialties in order to become state-certified mechanics. By using the NIASE tests, governments wouldn't have to spend any money for testing and the public would be assured of uniform criteria for certification from state to state. There would be advantages over simple NIASE certification to both consumers and mechanics. Consumers would have the state to handle their complaints against certified mechanics. Mechanics would benefit by being able to proclaim themselves government-approved mechanics, which would bring them lots of business and increase their earnings.

Because they're so critical to safety, I would make brake repairs an exception and require that they be performed or at least supervised only by those who've passed the NIASE brake test and possibly even a hands-on test. So that persons don't get stranded because there's no certified brake specialist around when they need brake repairs, states could do as Michigan has done and allow consumers to sign a waiver to have a non-certified mechanic work on the car in case of emergency.[76]

In addition, I would like to see created an elite class of "master mechanics." To get certified, a mechanic would have to complete an apprenticeship program approved by the U.S. Labor Department and then pass both written and practical tests. This is similar to procedures for becoming a journeyman or master mechanic in many parts of the world, including West Germany, Austria, Denmark and Sweden, where auto mechanics are thought of as craftsmen and not idiots. Many parts of Canada also have such a program.

Other Essentials

While registration and certification will tend to attract more capable people into the industry, it's really only a Band-Aid solution to the problem. Other things must be done in conjunction with it. Here's what I consider essential:

1. The flat rate pay system must be abolished.

2. The economic power of the automakers and insurance companies should be diluted so that they can't hold down the wages of mechanics.

3. The federal government must set up a massive apprenticeship program combining schooling and on-the-job training. Mr. Marchitelli says he would like to see an extensive vocational school training system set up that would cater only to those who are working mechanics and not "hobbyists." He thinks the money could come from redirecting government funds now going to teach the hobbyists.[77]

4. Shop owners must be given tax credits as an incentive to hire apprentices, send experienced mechanics to training courses and improve working conditions.

5. A national pension plan should be set up for auto mechanics who work in shops that don't offer pensions.

6. A national program should be set up to improve the reading and mathematical abilities of students with auto mechanic skills.

7. The auto companies must be required to disseminate repair information at a nominal fee to *all* repair shops. The federal government might even consider setting up a computerized system whereby any needed repair information could be wired immediately to special centers set up in all major metropolitan areas.

8. The auto companies must be forced to cut out superficial model changes and to make their cars easier to repair.

Finding Certified Mechanics

While certification by the National Institute for Automotive Service Excellence (NIASE) doesn't necessarily prove that a mechanic is competent, it's the best criterion we've got, so you may as well take advantage of it. Unfortunately, NIASE refuses to publish a directory of its certified mechanics. The reason presumably is that dealers, auto companies and others fear the unions would try to organize the certified mechanics. NIASE at one time published a list of shops that employed certified mechanics, but presumably abandoned that because mechanics move around so much from shop to shop.

To find NIASE-certified mechanics, look for special display signs at repair shops. Since not all mechanics at a shop displaying the sign may be certified, insist that only a certified mechanic work on your car—not one of the shop's other mechanics. Also make sure the mechanic is certified in the area of the car that you want fixed. A certified brake mechanic might know little about your transmission problem.

It's also a good idea to write down the name of the certified mechanic in case you later want to lodge a complaint against him. While NIASE doesn't want to hear complaints, send them anyway (see Appendix I), with a copy to the Consumer Federation of America (see Appendix C).

Besides NIASE, there is another industry certification program, called Certified Automotive Repairmen's Society (CARS). CARS, associated with Chilton Co., certifies by correspondence and not, like NIASE, at monitored testing centers. Therefore, it doesn't carry the weight of NIASE certification. Nevertheless, there are redeeming aspects of the program. A CARS-certified mechanic is at least someone who was conscientious enough to pay $90 for training and testing material. Also, in order to qualify even to take the tests, he has to have had four years of work experience or two years of work experience plus proof of satisfactory completion of an accredited auto mechanics' vocational/technical program. CARS certifies mechanics in two categories only: general automotive mechanic and auto body repairman. Retests are given every three years. To find a CARS-certified mechanic near you, write to the organization (see Appendix I).

State Licensing Complaints

If you live in Michigan, Hawaii or Washington, D.C., send your complaints about government-certified mechanics to the agencies listed in Appendix A.

Hawaii residents should patronize only state-certified mechanics, which will force those who escaped certification by virtue of the grandfather clause to become licensed voluntarily. Washington, D.C., residents should patronize only those mechanics who are certified as supervisory inspectors.

How Mechanics Lien on You

We have seen that the auto repair profession is full of thieves and incompetents. Yet there exist many archaic state "mechanic lien" laws which allow any auto mechanic to keep your car if you refuse to pay the repair bill—even if the repairs were done incompetently or dishonestly or weren't required or weren't authorized. Laws in some states even allow mechanics to sell the cars they keep to satisfy the lien without even so much as a hearing.

A classic abuse of this law is told by Dennis J. Van Valkenburg, formerly of Silver Spring, Maryland. He had expected to drive to North Carolina to spend Christmas of 1977 with his girlfriend's family. On the morning of December 22 his car failed to start. He called a repair shop, which towed the car in. Mr. Van Valkenburg said he authorized the shop to conduct a preliminary investigation and told them he would call back later in the day to find out what was wrong and decide whether he wanted repairs made.

He called back at 3:30 p.m. and was chagrined to learn that the shop had done a tune-up for $36.63—even though the car had been tuned up seven weeks earlier—in addition to recharging the battery. The total bill, he was told, would come to $67.63, including a $27.50 charge for towing.

Mr. Van Valkenburg said he was then told that the shop was closing for the day and to call back the next morning to find out when he could pick up the car. He said he told the shop not to do any more work on the car unless he authorized it.

However, when he called back at 10:31 a.m. the next day—December 23—he was told his car was being worked on and to call back in an hour. Highly irritated, he went down to the shop to see what was going on and arrived at 11:45 a.m. He was then presented with a bill for $95.50. He was told there had been additional trouble with the car.

Our hapless consumer protested the bill, but was told to pay up if he wanted his car back. Mr. Van Valkenburg said he would pay under protest since he desperately needed his car. He then presented his Master Charge card, which the firm advertised it accepted. The shop, however, refused to accept the card and demanded $95.50 in cash. Our victim said he didn't have the cash and wouldn't be able to get it before the firm closed for the holidays in 35 minutes. He was then told to come back with the cash on December 27 if he wanted his car.

After being forced to spend the Christmas holiday at home, Mr. Van Valkenburg went back to the shop on December 27 and was presented with a reduced bill for $84.04, which he paid under protest. After all that, he found that the car didn't even run well. The motor idled too fast and continued to run after the ignition was turned off. It got worse as he drove it, and he had to pay another shop to give the car a proper tune-up.

Mr. Van Valkenburg eventually sued the Scrooge shop in small claims court, and, in an out-of-court settlement, got most of the money back.[78]

This case raises a profound question: Why in a society where people must have a car should a bunch of botch artists and con artists be able to hold that car for ransom? To take away an American citizen's car is akin to cutting off someone's legs in an unmotorized society. Many Americans would find it hard, if not impossible, to get to work or school, shop for food, visit friends or relatives or take a vacation without their car. A 1977 U.S. Census Bureau study found that 87% of the nation's household heads get to work in a private auto.[79] The auto also accounts for 86.2% of all travel between cities, according to a 1979 Census Bureau report.[80]

Also, why should an auto mechanic be able to take a possession of yours worth perhaps several thousand dollars in lieu of perhaps a $50 or $100 payment—without so much as even a hearing?

"The mechanic's lien," according to Matthew E. Marsh, an expert on the subject, "is peculiarly American," having first come into existence in Maryland in 1791.[81] Of course there were no auto mechanics at the time, but the same principle applied to work by master builders. The rationale behind the law, says Mr. Marsh, is that "those who improve the property of others have a right to look at the property upon which they have bestowed their labor, services or materials as security for payment."[82]

Today, auto mechanics who don't improve a car but make it worse can still take advantage of the law.

It seems that a further rationale for the mechanic's lien law was to protect the poor workman against the rich property owner. The basis for this thinking no longer exists. The situation today might be reversed where the repair shop operator is a wealthy auto dealer or a multimillion-dollar corporation while the auto owner is a relatively poor person. A survey of dealers by *Automotive Age* found that 99.04% of them had a net worth of more than $100,000.[83] Meanwhile, according to the Census Bureau, 37.3% of American households earning under $3,000 a year and 52.8% of the households earning between $3,000 and $6,999 annually owned, in 1977, *at least* one car.[84]

If the mechanic's lien laws were abolished, undoubtedly there would be deadbeats who would refuse to pay legitimate bills. However, auto repairmen could be like other businessmen and refuse to service the car of anyone they suspect won't pay them, or, if they do work and aren't paid, sue for what they think is owed them and let a judge decide whether the bill was fair or not.

T. Pollard Rogers, in a *St. Mary's Law Journal* commentary, suggests a compromise whereby the shop couldn't take possession of your car but could still hold a lien on it until the dispute was settled in court. As he put it: "Automotive mechanics should have the basic protection afforded by a creditor's lien; however, the right to retain possession and foreclose on the automobile prior to a judicial determination creates an unduly harsh remedy, and in effect, encourages fraudulent practices within the industry."[85]

Some states, like Maryland,[86] Virginia,[87] Florida[88] and North Carolina,[89] have tried to solve the problem by allowing motorists to recover possession of their car until a hearing by posting a bond with the court. In Maryland and North Carolina, the bond is for twice the amount of the lien, and in Virginia and Florida for the exact amount. Other costs may also be involved. North Carolina, as an alternative to the bond, allows car owners to pay the court the exact amount of the lien to hold until a hearing.

Florida has gone further than the other states in that once a consumer takes out a bond to get his car, it's up to the shop to sue the consumer to get the money and not vice versa. In fact, the shop has 60 days to file suit, and if it loses the consumer may be entitled to damages, court costs and reasonable attorney's fees.

All this helps, but still presents an undue hardship on consumers. What if you need your car and the courthouse isn't open? Or, more likely, how do you get to the courthouse without your car? A further shortcoming of these laws is that they usually don't require shops to post a conspicuous sign telling customers their rights in such situations. Mr. Van Valkenburg, for instance, didn't know Maryland had such a law until I told him several months after the incident.

Several other states disallow a mechanic's lien under certain circumstances. Alaska disallows a lien on unauthorized repairs.[90] Louisiana limits a mechanic's lien, where an estimate is given, to the amount of the estimate.[91] Washington State prohibits a lien on any unauthorized service or parts; on any parts for which the shop refuses to return the old parts to the customer; and on any used, rebuilt or reconditioned parts installed without disclosure to the customer.[92] California,[93] Michigan[94] and Hawaii[95] require auto repair shops to be licensed by the state before being entitled to impose a lien.

There have been many legal challenges to the mechanic's lien laws, but consumers have won only partial victories—mostly in the area of preventing shops from selling a car prior to a hearing. Perhaps the greatest victory was won in California. In a suit brought by Isabel Adams, whose car was retained and later sold by a repair shop after a dispute over the repair bill, the state supreme court ruled that mechanics could no longer sell a vehicle held on a lien to satisfy a repair bill. However, the court ruled that an auto repairman has the constitutional right to retain possession of a car when the owner, for any reason, refuses to pay.[96]

Reform

If you would like to see a massive auto mechanic apprenticeship program, appeal to your governor, the chairmen of the U.S. Senate and House labor committees and the U.S. Secretary of Labor (see Appendix L). Also appeal to your governor for reform of mechanic's lien laws.

9

Repairability: Should Designers, Engineers and Auto Executives Be Hanged?

"People are at the mercy of repairmen and repairmen are at the mercy of automobile engineers," Robert C. Alexander, onetime chief of California's Bureau of Automotive Repair, told a Washington consumer conference in 1974.[1]

That statement is even truer today. For despite more than a decade of protests that automobiles aren't being designed to facilitate repair and inspection, little has been done about the problem.

The National Highway Traffic Safety Administration, in a report on its diagnostic inspection demonstration project in five cities, said while there were "numerous cases" found of inaccessibility hindering repair and inspection, it could document "only a few specific instances" where "accessibility appeared to be a designed-in feature."[2]

The National Association of Independent Insurers, in a survey of 28 body shop operators, found that "the characteristics of automobile design which contribute to increased repair costs by far outweigh the characteristics which contribute to reduced costs."[3]

It seems that Detroit designs its cars so that they're easy to assemble, although not necessarily easy to repair, and appeal to the often irrational whims of new car buyers. "The industry that must service the car isn't the primary concern," says an engineer.

To be sure, a few models have been designed with service in mind, and the American manufacturers have done a commendable job in cutting down the amount of maintenance necessary on many of their cars. Nevertheless, auto repairmen aren't impressed.

Ex-Congressman Bob Eckhardt of Texas has found numerous examples of design that really irk mechanics. Among them:

· To remove the transmission from some Pintos, the mechanic must first remove the gearshift and handle. This, in turn, involves removing the seats, console and floor covering—a job which takes two to three hours.

· In order to get access to the distributor of many Vegas, it's necessary to remove the air conditioner compressor.

· On some late-model cars, it's necessary to remove the fender to get at the heater blower.

· Door hinges come welded in place on some model cars. As a result, a torch must be used to get the door off. Then, once off, it's difficult to align the door properly and weld it back on.[4]

There's hardly anything worse than a consumer's wrath when he finds out his dreamboat—because of nightmarish design—is going to cost him a bundle just to maintain. Take, for example, W.V. Martin of Montgomery, Alabama. He said he was one of those "unsuspecting members of the public" who bought a 1975 Chevrolet Monza and later found out that for the repair shop to change the spark plugs, "they have to disconnect the engine from the chassis and jack it up on one side and that the labor cost alone for changing spark plugs is $24."[5]

Insurance executives are squawking too. While cars with unicoupe construction may be easier to assemble, they're so difficult to repair that they're being totaled at a 60% greater rate than average. In 1980, unicoupes represented 34% of the cars on the road and 54% of the cars in salvage yards.[6]

Undetachable Parts

To increase your repair costs and the auto industry's profits, many cars are being designed with two or more parts permanently attached to each other. Thus, if something goes wrong with one part, you've got to replace at least two parts.

A government regulator told me he was highly upset when he went to replace the muffler on his 1973 Chevrolet and found that he couldn't replace just the muffler. The exhaust system was designed as one piece from the engine to the tail pipe and so it cost him $130 to replace the whole thing.

Owners of late-model GM cars are equally incensed by the fact that the voltage regulator is built into the alternator. Thus, if something goes wrong with the voltage regulator, instead of being able to replace it for $15 or so, they have to shell out over $100 for both regulator and alternator.

Nonavailability of Parts

A growing gimmick of auto companies is to make sure various parts assemblies can't be fixed by refusing to sell the components.

In a far-reaching investigation, the Suffolk County, New York, Consumer Affairs Office, said it found "almost total unavailability of low-cost individual parts" and that where such low-cost parts are available, "some dealers have stated that it can take two to three weeks to order them." According to James J. Lack, former head of the office, "this forces the consumer to either purchase high-cost component assemblies or make do without the use of an automobile, if the consumer can persuade a dealer to order the individual part needed. In an area such as Suffolk County where 83% of the work force depends on the automobile to get to work, the choice, unfortunately, is obvious—consumers pay and pay."[7]

Insurance executives are especially outraged that many auto makers will sell only a whole door and not the door skin, which is one-third the cost. About 75% of the time, damage to a door in a crash is confined to the skin.[8]

Apparently complaining to the auto companies about not-for-sale parts does little good. I came across two letters written to Ford Motor Co. five years apart complaining about the exact same thing: the unavailability of small component parts for the Lincoln power antenna unit. Jack D. Paulson, a Sacramento, California, lawyer, wrote to Ford in 1972 complaining about not being able to purchase a couple of small gears for the antenna unit which "from appearance . . . are similar to ones found in toys for children ranging from $1 to $2 per toy." He said he was told by the dealer that he would have to buy the entire power antenna unit for over $40.[9] Lawrence Park, president of Mansfield State College in Mansfield, Pennsylvania, and owner of a 1975 Lincoln, complained to Ford in 1977 about parts for the antenna and was told, in effect, to buzz off. He wrote back saying, "I know that the motorized antennas have to be assembled some place and that parts are used in the assembling. It wouldn't take a great deal of imagination to believe that these separate parts could be available with a very minimum of effort. I therefore conclude that your purpose is not service but company convenience or profit only."[10]

If not being able to buy small components irks you, then you ain't seen nothin' yet. C.W. Higgins, chairman of the Automotive Parts and Accessories Association, said in 1978 that "in the past, most service dealt with repair work, however, in five years much of a mechanic's time will be spent diagnosing malfunctions and replacing faulty components with new modules."[11] This means mechanics will be taking whole sections out of the car and replacing them, and that is going to be extremely expensive.

Orphan and Limited-Edition Parts

An ancillary parts problem is presented by so-called orphans—discontinued lines of cars—and "limited editions"—special cars with short production runs. Not only can't owners of such cars get small components, but they're lucky to get any parts at all. That's because once a car is out of production, the parts supply tends to dry up. This works well for the auto companies. If the owner of such a car can't fix it for lack of parts, he's a prime candidate to buy a new car.

The Parts Deluge

Even without the small parts the auto companies refuse to sell, the parts distribution system is being strained to the limit. This is due to a proliferation of different parts plus the need just to keep over 100 million cars and trucks running.

The story can be told in the following statistics. Back in 1951, when life was much simpler and there were only a few basic car models, Ford Motor Co. had 29,000 different parts in its distribution system.[12] In 1978, the number of different parts was 203,000, with only about 15,000 regarded as high volume.[13] Combine the Ford total with that of General Motors (325,000 parts in 1976),[14] Chrysler (150,000 in 1976),[15] American Motors (78,000 in 1978)[16] and the imports; then consider that there must be enough of these parts to service tens of millions of vehicles, and you get an idea of the mess we're in today. "The sheer number of parts is staggering," says Bill Webster, vice-president of Federal-Mogul, an auto parts maker.[17]

What's more, *Motor/Age*, a trade magazine, says the problem will get much, much worse. "Parts proliferation," says the magazine, "looks as though it's going to be a way of life." The major cause will be continuous changes in parts in order to meet stringent air quality and fuel conservation standards. In fact, says *Motor/Age*, the auto companies will be "adopting new materials and new design concepts in every part of the car and in all its subsystems and parts."[18]

Here are some other factors, says the magazine, that will be causing all sorts of headaches in the parts distribution system in the 1980s:

· Cars will be kept longer, requiring a full supply of parts for additional back-model years.

· There is expected to be a steady increase in vehicle population.

· A greater percentage of inventory will have to be given over to parts for light trucks, vans and four-wheel-drive vehicles, and these parts are more difficult to handle than car parts.

· Parts will be increasingly made of metals and materials other than iron and steel, causing handling problems for distributors and mechanics. Nonmetallic parts, for example, may be subject to damage by water absorption, gases, solvents and ultraviolet radiation and are more vulnerable to impact damage than metals.

· More and more parts will be converted to the metric system.[19]

"There will be many new parts required to service the future vehicle population," says Bob Johnson, an executive of Dana Corp., an auto parts supplier. "It appears that the part numbers required to service these vehicles would be at least a third more and could possibly double."[20]

Critics of the auto companies complain that a large portion of today's parts total shouldn't be necessary. Anthony De Rosa of the Independent Garage Owners Association of Illinois estimates that 60% to 70% of all components could be interchangeable, dramatically reducing the number of different parts. Among these, he says, could be exhaust pipes, distributors and distributor caps, alternators, fans and fan belts.[21]

Other Problems

Additional repairability problems are being caused by the fact that some cars can only be fixed with special tools and that many new materials being used in cars, such as aluminum water pump bodies, make it difficult or impossible to rebuild some parts. Remanufactured parts have traditionally saved consumers 20% to 40% against the cost of new parts.[22]

Towing and Design

Many auto designers apparently think that their cars are so invincible that they'll never need to be towed. Thus they aren't designed to be towed with standard American wrecker equipment.

The American Automobile Association warned in 1979 that imports with front-wheel drive and automatic transmissions present serious towing problems. There were reports of tow truck drivers picking up Volkswagen Rabbits with automatic transmissions from the rear and causing up to $1,600 in damage. The Fiat Strada could suffer equal damage.[23]

It seems that foreign cars are especially susceptible to damage while being towed because they're designed for chain or cable towing used in Europe and Japan. Such towing is illegal in the U.S., where towed vehicles must be securely attached to the towing vehicle.[24]

You would think then that the American auto companies, at least, would design their cars so they could be towed from either end by American equipment. Not so. As recently as November 1977, the AAA said only General Motors cars were towable from either end with standard wrecker equipment.[25]

The Cure

To make cars and/or their parts more repairable, available and towable, the very least the federal government should do is require the auto companies to disclose the following information to prospective customers:

1.   The approximate parts cost and labor time associated with various common repairs.

2.   Any nontypical accessibility problems.

3.   All replacement parts of the car not for sale and the cost to purchase these parts as part of an assembly.

4.   A warning if the car can't be towed with conventional towing equipment from either end or if the car can't be towed at 35 mph for 30 miles when resting on the drive wheels.

5.   All normally individual parts which are permanently attached to other parts.

6.   The company's history as far as making parts readily available.

I believe the federal government also has to step in and standardize certain common parts like fan belts, exhaust pipes, etc. The feds should also standardize the location of towing hookup systems and require every car sold in the U.S. to be compatible with conventional towing equipment and to be towable at 35 mph for 30 miles.

Protecting Yourself

Until the above disclosures become law, it's going to be up to you to find out about such things on your own before you buy a car. Talk to mechanics and body shop operators and ask them which are the good and bad cars in terms of inspectability, accessibility and repairability. Compare auto manufacturer flat rate times for various repairs as a clue to accessibility problems. NHTSA, in one study, found that the flat rate time for renewing brake shoes or brake pads on a full-size GM car was 2.6 hours while for a full-size Chrysler it was 3.7 hours.[26] If you're paying $25 a flat rate hour for labor, it would cost you an extra $27.50 to repair the Chrysler.

It's also important, before you let anyone tow your car, that you make sure the tow truck operator knows how to tow your particular model. The AAA puts out two towing manuals annually—one for domestic and one for imported cars. They should be consulted before towing.

Above all, if you want to keep your repair problems to a minimum, avoid power gadgets. Take power windows, for example. Carl Baum, a Brooklyn businessman, bought a 1977 Cadillac Seville with power windows for about $10,000. He started to have problems with the window on the driver's side during the winter of 1977–78. "The problem is simple," he wrote GM's Cadillac Division. "Either it doesn't go down when you want it to, or it doesn't go up when you want it to, and sometimes it does work properly." He said he took the car back to the dealer six times without the window being repaired correctly.

One incident with the window he isn't likely to forget. He said he rolled his window down to pay the toll at the Queens-Midtown Tunnel, couldn't get the window back up and "had to drive all the way to Long Island, New York, with the window wide open in a subfreezing temperature." Another time, while in Washington, D.C., his window wouldn't go up, which made him reluctant to park his car, and so he had to pay a repairman to attempt to raise the window.

His last conversation with the dealer, he said, "consisted of them trying to sell me a new car in place of attempting to fix the window on my present car."[27]

Complaining

If an auto company makes you buy a whole assembly instead of an individual part, consider suing the company in small claims court for what you think is a fair difference in price. Subpoena auto company records showing the cost of the part and its failure rate. Argue that it was reasonable for you to expect when you bought the car that all parts for it would be purchasable. Your case will be strengthened if you can prove that the part has a high failure rate. If millions of people start doing this, it will be cheaper for the auto companies to sell such parts than not to sell them.

You might also complain to the Federal Trade Commission (see Appendix B) about parts availability problems. The commission, although it isn't doing anything about the problem, does say "lack of spare parts" is "one of the most frequent auto related complaints" it receives, with the problem "particularly significant with imports."[28]

10

The New Car Warranty

Merry-Go-Round, or

Ford Has a Bitter Idea

If there is ever awarded a Medal of Honor for heroism above and beyond the call of duty in battling a big, soulless corporation, Eddie Campos and Roger T. Sweitzer are surefire candidates.

Mr. Campos was stuck with a very classy piece of junk—a defective 1970 Lincoln Continental Mark III. It first broke down the day after he bought it and was in the repair shop, according to his account, about 21 times in the next 18 months without ever being fixed right. Exasperated, he took the car to Ford Motor Co.'s Pico Rivera assembly plant near Los Angeles in the summer of 1971 and publicly burned it.

Mr. Sweitzer, on the other hand, purchased a 1972 Ford Pinto on the 30th anniversary of Pearl Harbor Day—December 7, 1971. The car turned out to be almost as disastrous for him as the Japanese bombing of Pearl Harbor was to the U.S. Pacific Fleet. It too began giving him trouble the day after he bought it. The problems, including an oil leak, a bum transmission and bad mileage, continued during months and months of hassles with Ford Motor Co. and several dealers. At first he protested by plastering pictures of lemons all over his car. But that got him nowhere. He claims a Ford representative told him, "What do you want for $3,000?" Finally, in desperation, he took the car to the Pico Rivera assembly plant on New Year's Day 1974, and, together with about

50 other people, sledgehammered it to death. "I would rather put it out of its misery and kill it before it kills me or someone else," Mr. Sweitzer told the auto company prior to the execution.

Not content with their day each of national publicity against Ford, the two men have continued their vendetta against the company. The remains of their two cars are on public display in South Whittier, California. The battered red Pinto with lemon signs all over it rests beneath a sign saying, "Buy your next lemon at your nearest Ford dealer." The charred Lincoln sits appropriately beneath a lemon tree that Mr. Campos planted in 1973.

To this day, neither man regrets his actions. "I got the runaround so much there was no other way," says Mr. Campos. "It was worth it because it cleared my ulcers. . . . I made my point. I've never been sorry for it." While his public burning has yet to win him a much-desired apology from Ford Motor Co., it does appear to have won him the respect of dealers. "Dealers treat me the way I should be treated," he says. "They know who I am."

Mr. Sweitzer says doing in his Pinto "was really a relief. . . . I used to have nightmares about the car. I came close to being killed several times."[1]

Despite their efforts, the battle that these two men gave their cars' lives for still rages on and may in fact be getting worse. ". . . there is an increase in the complaints concerning constant repair," says Herschel T. Elkins, deputy attorney general of California. "Some consumers have had their cars repaired 25 to 30 times without resolution of the problem."[2]

It seems that even the Romans treated the Christians better than the auto companies treat their customers.

"Consumers who buy automobiles receive the worst treatment of any type of consumer," says William L. Newcomb, Jr., the Missouri attorney general's consumer protection chief. "Not only is it true that the automobile is sometimes unsafe, poorly manufactured and deceptively priced, but when the consumer attempts to have his complaint resolved, the problem is ignored or goes uncorrected in many cases."[3]

A survey of consumer warranties prepared for the Federal Trade Commission bears out Mr. Newcomb's assertion. The study revealed that nearly 30% of car purchasers had some problem covered by warranty, compared to 7% for all consumer products; that 30% of car warranty problems took over a month to be resolved, compared to 14% for other products; and that 25% of those who had warranty problems with autos were dissatisfied with the final results, compared to only 8% for all other products.[4]

Lemonscam

You might even compare the methods of the auto companies to a confidence game, which I would call the "lemon drop" scheme. Here's the way it works:

The automakers size up their intended victims carefully with psychological research. They then lure them into dealer showrooms with over $975 million a year worth of advertising messages,[5] offering such things as sex, prestige and even a rocket ship ride if they buy a new car. Millions of people a year swallow the bait. While many swindlers get their victims to withdraw their life savings and hand it over to them, the auto companies go one step further. They not only get their victims' savings, but compel them to agree to hand over future earnings as well (over two-thirds of new cars are sold on credit).[6]

By the time a victim finds out he hasn't gotten a sex object, status, a rocket ship or even a dependable means of transportation, the auto executives have disappeared with his money. Left behind is a smoke screen of unresponsive dealers, abrasive district service representatives and unsympathetic customer relations personnel. Many examples have come to light indicating that the auto companies know their cars are defective but are selling them anyway:

· The Federal Trade Commission said in 1978 that while comedian Bill Cosby was appearing in TV commercials talking about how tough Ford builds its cars, the company was knowingly manufacturing 1.8 million defective cars with a problem known as "piston scuffing"—metal-to-metal contact between the pistons and cylinder walls in engines.[7]

· Ford located the gas tank on its Pintos only 7 inches behind the rear bumper, and it often exploded after a rear-end collision. An internal 1972 Ford memo shows the company figured the cost of making the fix over the long haul would be $11 per vehicle or $117 million, whereas the cost of not making the fix—an estimated 180 burn deaths, 180 serious burn injuries and 2,100 burned vehicles—would come to $49.5 million. This would be a savings to the company of $67.5 million. Ford arrived at its ghoulish figures by multiplying each death by $200,000, each injury by $67,000 and each vehicle by $700. Here is the company's macabre balance sheet of death as contained in the memo:

BENEFITS:
Savings—180 burn deaths, 180 serious burn injuries, 2100 burned vehicles
Unit Cost—$200,000 per death, $67,000 per injury, $700 per vehicle
Total Benefit —180×($200,000)+180×($67,000)+2100×($700)=$49.5 *million*

150

COSTS:
Sales—11 million cars, 1.5 million light trucks
Unit Cost—$11 per car, $11 per truck
Total Cost—11,000,000 × ($11) + 1,500,000 × ($11) = $117 million[8]

After numerous burn deaths and injuries, and after several exposés raised public ire, Ford reluctantly agreed in mid-1978 to recall some 1.5 million 1971–1976 Pintos plus some 30,000 Mercury Bobcats.[9]

A jury in Orange County, California, was so incensed at Ford's casual attitude toward death that it awarded 18-year-old Richard Grimshaw, who was burned over 90 percent of his body after the gas tank ruptured on a 1972 Pinto, more than $127.8 million, including $125 million in punitive damages. The trial judge later reduced the punitive award to $3.5 million.[10]

· Internal Ford documents reveal that company engineers knew for almost five years that engine cooling fans on certain 1972 Ford Torinos, Mercury Montegos and Lincolns would break, posing a serious safety hazard. However, nothing was done about the problem until after a mechanic was fatally injured in 1977 and at least 11 other persons had been injured in separate accidents. The mechanic had been working on a 1972 Torino when a fan blade flew off and slashed his neck and chest. Ford, after the fatality, recalled the 1972 cars plus some 1976 and 1977 cars which might have had the same problem.[11]

· Internal Ford documents, which came to light in 1978, show that the company knew as far back as 1971, without telling the public, that its cars would jump unexpectedly from park to reverse, particularly when the engine was running.[12] Federal officials said in 1980 that they had received over 23,000 complaints about the problem, alleging 98 fatalities. Under pressure to recall the cars involved, Ford in 1980 agreed instead to send some 20 million Ford vehicle owners a sticker warning not to leave the vehicle when the engine is running, to use the parking brake when they park and to make sure the shift lever is placed firmly in the park position.[13]

To understand more of the "lemon drop" scheme, let's take a look at what happens to a new car, particularly an American-built car, from the time it's put together until it's delivered to you.

At the Factory

The motto at the assembly plant is "Praise Henry Ford and Keep That Line Moving." An auto executive wouldn't stop an assembly line for anything—even if his mother was caught in it and was about to be welded to a fender. It's a fact of life that the line moves on even if it means that subquality parts have to be used, a few parts are missing, a weld or two is neglected, a few bolts aren't tightened or some electrical connections are hanging loose.

The extent to which the automakers will go to meet production schedules is revealed in a secret Ford Motor Co. document presented at an internal quality control meeting on November 16, 1973.

The document indicates that Ford at the time was faced with a critical shortage of parts from both its own factories and outside suppliers and was substituting below-standard parts in order to support production. "We are confident that part shortages have had a detrimental effect on our outgoing vehicle quality," the report says.[14]

Another factor that has a detrimental effect on the quality of auto production is the practice of annual model changes. A U.S. Commerce Department report notes that about "a third of all parts used in auto assembly undergo some degree of design modification during an annual model change. Much of the new design is in modification of parts of the outer sheet metal."[15]

Naturally, such constant design change makes it difficult for American manufacturers to control the quality of their cars, especially in the beginning of each model year. In 1978 alone, General Motors, Ford and Chrysler diverted over $2.6 billion which could have been used to improve the quality of their cars into wasteful annual styling changes.[16]

The quality of cars isn't helped much either by the high absentee rate and level of malaise among assembly-line workers. Their work is so soul-deadening that James J. Flink, professor of comparative culture at the University of California at Irvine, says absenteeism has climbed to 13% a day, and even higher on Mondays and Fridays, and that alcohol, drug use and industrial sabotage are commonplace on the assembly line.[17] (The auto companies put the absentee rate at about 6% to 9%.[18])

Once a car comes off the assembly line with defects, there's little incentive for the auto companies to fix it immediately, if at all. First, they don't want to tie up their production facilities fixing cars. Second, the faster they get the car into the hands of the dealer the faster they get their money. Third, they figure whoever buys the car won't notice most of the defects and therefore they'll never have to correct them. Fourth, it's often cheaper to have the dealer do the repair work.

As a result of these factors, it's very common for inspectors or foremen on the assembly line to overlook defects. Irving Bluestone, a retired United Auto Workers vice-president, says he knows of "instance after instance" of inspectors "knocking down" a job because something wasn't done right only to have foremen overrule them in order to get the cars out.[19]

In Transit

Even if a car makes it through the assembly process unscathed, it still could incur transit damage on its way to the dealership. Ford estimated that 5.6% of its 1973 models were damaged in transit, with damage to 7.6% of the cars shipped by rail and 2.9% of the cars sent by "haulaway" trailers.[20]

The problem seems especially acute in the Northeast.[21] In fact, the New York State attorney general's office got after Ford because buyers of its cars weren't being informed of transit damage, and, in some cases, were paying new car prices for substantially repaired cars. Under a 1978 agreement with the attorney general's office, Ford agreed that any new cars which received more than $300 transit damage, excluding such easily replaceable items as wheels, tires, radios, and windshields, would be sold as used cars. The company also said it would urge its New York dealers to inform prospective buyers in writing of any damage under $300 unless it was "insignificant." Ford has now adopted the part of the agreement involving more than $300 transit damage as a national policy.[22]

Pre-delivery

Theoretically, if your new car is delivered to a dealer with defects or transit damage, the dealer is supposed to fix the faults. In practice, many or all of the defects are passed on for you to find; that is, if they don't kill you first.

Consumers Union, publisher of *Consumer Reports*, said it took delivery of 34 new cars in the year prior to April 1977 and found some 856 sample defects—about 25 per car—"not counting the hundreds of purely cosmetic flaws."

These were mainly assembly-line defects and not design defects. Most common were improper inflation, installation and alignment of tires and wheels. Also, loose and dangling wires and hoses were routinely found and rain leaks were much in evidence.[23]

The U.S. Environmental Protection Agency found the pre-delivery inspections of Ford dealers in Washington, D.C., and Atlanta so inadequate that the agency told Ford Motor Co. in early 1978 that henceforth the company would have to inspect and adjust various pollution control items prior to delivery to its dealers.[24]

Two major reasons why dealer pre-delivery inspections are not done adequately are undercompensation from the auto manufacturers and the practice of some auto companies of allowing the dealer to trade away all or part of the pre-delivery allowance when negotiating with customers on the price of the car.

Marvin D. Hartwig, an Iowa City Lincoln-Mercury dealer, said in 1978 that his average return on pre-delivery was $30 to $40 per car. Yet, he added, "we run three to four hours mechanic prep time per car. Our factory warranty rate of $14 per hour doesn't quite cover our costs."[25] A Ford service rep admitted to me that if Ford paid its dealers an adequate allowance for pre-delivery work, it would eliminate most consumer warranty problems.

The New Jersey attorney general's office in 1979 blew the whistle on a practice it called "double dipping," whereby dealers were being reimbursed by the factory for pre-delivery and also charging customers for the same service. The only companies that don't reimburse their dealers, according to the AG's office, are Alfa Romeo, BMW, Fiat, Lancia, Lotus, Mazda, MG, Porsche-Audi, Renault, Triumph and Volkswagen.[26]

Investigators in Contra Costa County, California, found that not only was Concord Dodge, the largest Dodge dealer in Northern California, collecting a pre-delivery inspection fee from both Chrysler Corp. and customers, but it wasn't performing the inspections.[27] Some auto companies are doing some of their own pre-delivery inspections in part to sidestep such practices.

Many auto manufacturers seem to discourage good pre-delivery inspections simply by the type of inspection forms they provide dealers. Many of the forms, such as those for 1978 Ford, Buick and Chrysler cars, don't have little boxes beside each individual item to be checked off. Instead, they have only one checkbox for many inspection operations or describe inspection duties in such broad terms that many items could easily be overlooked. For example, the 1978 Chrysler new vehicle preparation form had only four check-off boxes for the whole car compared to 71 for the 1978 Datsun pre-delivery inspection record.

Datsun also goes a step further than most auto companies to help ensure that the work will actually be done by requiring that a copy of the completed form be given the car purchaser, signed by the pre-delivery mechanic attesting to the fact that he checked and corrected to factory specifications all the items on the checklist. A Datsun form is in Appendix M.

The Warranty Hassle—Dealers' Viewpoint

Aside from pre-delivery inspections, many dealers are also taking a loss on warranty work.

Surveys by the National Automobile Dealers Association (NADA) in

1978 found that General Motors dealers were losing 18 cents for every dollar of warranty work they did[28] and that dealers in general were losing an average of $3.50 on each warranty job.[29]

While much has been done since to try to equalize warranty and retail labor charges, dealers are still making less money on warranty parts than retail parts, and it's estimated that it takes eight minutes more paperwork per job to process warranty work than to process retail work[30] —time the dealers are not being paid for.

These factors serve as a disincentive for dealers to do warranty work, especially when there is plenty of retail work in the shop. But even if dealers were fairly compensated for warranty work, it would still not solve the problem as far as they're concerned.

Dealers surveyed by NADA in 1976 felt that the major warranty problem was not reimbursement—as bad as that was—but the refusal of the auto companies to allow them greater latitude in dealing with their customers.[31] John J. Pohanka, president of NADA at the time, said some auto companies administer their warranties "in an atmosphere of fear and threat to the dealership." He added that the emphasis of these companies is not on consumer satisfaction, but on cost control. This results, he said, in "nit-picking, second-guessing, and factory pressures to reduce warranty claims even though claims are justified."[32]

Increasingly, dealers' hands are being tied by the requirement to get the approval of factory service representatives prior to making warranty repairs. On top of that, auto company practices include subjecting dealers to factory audits which result in their having to pay back warranty money already received, not stocking warranty parts in ample supply at factory warehouses, and procrastinating in providing factory training and technical information for new model cars.

Prior Approval

Dealers surveyed in 1977 reported that 19% of their warranty claims required prior approval by the factory service rep, tying up nearly $1,400 in claims per dealer.[33] Dealers for one line of car report that some 35% of their claims require prior approval.[34]

This wouldn't be so bad if the factory service reps were prompt and competent. Unfortunately, they tend to be slothful and inept. The service reps are often unavailable when dealers need them—the biggest sore point between Ford Motor Co. and its dealers, according to a 1978 survey.[35]

Dealers are often put in the position of telling customers with warranty claims to call the factory service rep and set up an appointment or to come back in one, two or three weeks when the rep is due there for a regular visit. What frequently ensues is described by former Federal Trade Commission chairman Michael Pertschuk: "We have found instances where the manufacturer's zone representative is asked to assist in reviewing a claim or to authorize extensive repairs, but the customer's phone calls are not returned and appointments to meet with the zone representative, set weeks in advance, are broken without notice."[36]

A major reason why factory reps are so frequently unavailable is that they are spread too thin over too many dealerships, according to the 1977 NADA survey. The study also found that job turnover among service reps is high, with the average one staying about 17 months. One manufacturer keeps its reps an average of only eight to nine months.[37]

The best factory reps, an industry observer told me, are guys who have been around as mechanics for 20 or 25 years and still have grease under their nails. However, they're scarce, he says, and have been replaced with young men so unknowledgeable about cars that "most of them would have trouble opening the hood."

Another problem with factory service reps is that they're under tremendous pressure to hold down warranty costs. Some are given monthly budgets they have to work within. That means they'll refuse legitimate warranty claims at the end of the month simply because such claims will put them over their budget.[38] A former General Motors service rep told me he was under no budget, but he was expected to keep his warranty payouts in line with the national average. To do this, he had to turn down justified warranty claims. He said dealers were also under pressure from the area sales rep to keep warranty costs down if they wanted to receive the hot-selling cars. "There was so much dishonesty and out-and-out conniving that I couldn't stand it," he said.

In general, the motto of the factory rep is that the customer is always wrong. While not expert at fixing cars, they are experts when it comes to thinking up excuses for why your car shouldn't be fixed under warranty. "Oh, it's nothing to worry about," they'll tell you. "It's a typical problem in this model and will go away in time." Don't believe it. A variation is to tell you, "You have nothing to complain about. This part is within manufacturer's tolerances. It's the way it was made." This really means that they goofed when they designed the car and either don't know how to correct the defect or do know and don't want to spend the money. Then there's the old standby: The problem with your car, they'll say, is "owner abuse." However, if you've hardly driven the car, they'll tell you the problem was caused because "you don't drive the car enough."

Many times the factory rep will authorize only a temporary repair—designed to last only until the car is out of warranty. For example, transmission expert Robert Cherrnay accuses GM of making "patch type of repairs" for its problem-plagued series 200 transmissions.[39]

Audits

Volkswagen of America and General Motors are notorious for a warranty practice that has been dubbed "search and destroy missions" by some industry insiders. These two companies do an incredible amount of auditing of dealer warranty claims already paid, with the result that many of these claims are denied and the dealer is "charged back" for the cost of repairs.[40] This makes these dealers downright paranoid about doing warranty repairs.

This is not to say that audits and chargebacks aren't always justified. After all, filing false warranty claims is well within the dealer code of ethics. There was even one instance, in a celebrated case known as "Motorgate," where a Chevy dealer defrauded General Motors out of a reported $600,000 through a false warranty claim scheme.[41]

Panting for Parts

Auto companies cost dealers and consumers time, annoyance and money by not making warranty parts readily available. It can take days, weeks or months to get warranty replacement parts. "In some cases, the manufacturer does not allocate enough parts for replacement needs," says Robert P. Mallon, a Tacoma Ford dealer. "In other instances, inefficiencies in the distribution system cause delays in getting the parts to the dealer."[42]

Groping for Guidance

Adding to all the above problems, dealer mechanics are often left uninformed about how to fix new models when they first come out. "Many times the technical literature and the training does not occur until after the cars are introduced," says D. James McDowell, managing director of automotive engineering and road service for the American Automobile Association.[43] A perfect example is GM's Oldsmobile Division. It held no training classes on diesel engines in at least some parts of the country and possibly the whole country prior to introducing its diesel-engine car in September 1977. One Oldsmobile dealer service manager told me in February 1978 that GM had just recently given his mechanics their first course on the engine. Fortunately, not all the auto companies show such contempt for their dealers' mechanics and the people who buy their cars. Saab refused to allow any dealer to sell its 99 turbo model when it first came out unless that dealer sent its service personnel to a special school and bought special turbo repair tools and parts.[44]

Another trouble spot for service department management is that, according to NADA, factory service reps spend only about 47 minutes per month to improve the average dealership's service operation.[45]

Devious Dealer Warranty Practices

While much of the difficulty consumers experience with new car warranties can be traced to the policies of the car manufacturers, dealers aren't exactly Mr. Clean either when it comes to honesty in warranty repairs.

Some dealers will refuse to do warranty work unless you also agree to additional retail work and may even tell you that the warranty will be voided if you don't pay for repairs. Others might tell you that a certain repair isn't covered under warranty, when it actually is. Illinois attorney general William J. Scott said that while investigating a large Dodge dealer, his office found one customer who "was told that the warranty did not cover the needed repairs and he was forced to pay for them in cash. However, a warranty reimbursement invoice was actually sent to Chrysler for payment."[46]

One of the more insidious dealer warranty practices is what's known in the trade as a "wall job" or "sunbath" or "sunshine treatment." This is when the dealer accepts your car for warranty repairs without having any intention of touching it. The car is parked against a wall or out in the sun and returned to you without anyone's having looked at it. Eddie Campos, the guy who burned his car, said he got a letter from a man who took his car to a dealership and then went out to sit in it, reading a magazine, while he waited for the shop to work on it. After some time sitting in the car, his name was paged and he was told his car was ready.[47]

Many times the put-off starts before you even pick up a new car. The dealer will promise you that all defects you notice will be fixed at the first checkup. They rarely are.

Paint Spotting and Rust

Two of the biggest warranty problems in recent years have been paint spotting and premature rusting. The auto companies have tried to blame both problems on environmental factors beyond their control. However, their story is hard to believe.

Typical of a consumer with a paint problem is Mr. D of New Jersey. He bought a 1977 Mercury Monarch in November 1977, and, after taking delivery, noticed black spots covering the entire paint surface of the car. He took it back to the dealer, who refused to repaint the car. The Ford zone manager refused to help either, so he complained some more. On January 12, 1978, he got a letter from J.M. Carter of Ford's owner relations department in Newark saying that zone manager Charles Temple had "diagnosed this condition as being environmental fallout" and there was nothing Ford was going to do about it. What, you may ask, is "environmental fallout"? Mr. Carter defined it as "a general term applied to minute separate particles of matter in the air that eventually settle on exposed surfaces."[48] I would call it a general term to avoid responsibility for an inferior paint job.

In 1978, Massachusetts AUTOCAP, an organization which handles complaints about dealers, got General Motors to back down on its refusal to include paint spotting as part of its one-year or 12,000-mile warranty. The organization said the paint problem is widespread, particularly on metallic finishes such as blue, green and silver.[49]

An even lamer excuse than "environmental fallout" has been given by the auto companies for premature rusting. They say it's caused by increased use of salt on winter roads and not due to any fault of their product.

That would be an acceptable excuse except for two things: (1) This is the space age and the technology has existed for years to rustproof cars against any increased amount of salt; and (2) cars have been rusting out in Florida and other seacoast states where it doesn't snow.

Indeed, car rusting is so bad in Florida that Walter Dartland, the Dade County (Miami) consumer advocate, filed a $700 million class action suit in 1977 against Ford on behalf of 200,000 Florida owners of 1969–74 vehicles. He contended that the cars and trucks of those years rust prematurely and the company should foot the bill for repairs, accelerated depreciation and punitive damages. In an out-of-court settlement in 1981, Ford agreed to compensate owners of rusty vehicles to the tune of an estimated $20 million to $60 million.[50]

An internal Ford document dated October 19, 1973, warned that "there is a serious vehicle rust problem in our 1969 through 1973 vehicles in a maximum corrosion environment." According to Ford, rust was causing metal perforation on exterior appearance panels "one to two years earlier in our cars than competition" and was contributing to "lower resale values of our vehicles."[51]

The automakers now offer extended rust warranties.

Rating Warranty Service

Which are the best auto companies as far as warranty service is concerned? That all depends on which surveys you read. But one thing is clear: General Motors—the nation's third-largest industrial company in terms of sales,[52] with profits between 1969 and 1980 of some $23 billion[53] —is among the worst, if not *the* worst.

A 1976 survey by *Automotive News* of independent firms which process dealer warranty claims found that General Motors is by far the toughest to file a new car warranty claim against. (The survey did say that GM allows its dealers to do a better job preparing cars for delivery than some of the other auto companies.)[54]

Three GM divisions fared very badly in a 1976 NADA survey in which dealers were asked if they thought the consumer's interests were protected by the warranty administration policies of their manufacturer. Scoring worst were Fiat, Oldsmobile, Volvo, Pontiac, Buick, British Leyland and Chrysler-Plymouth. Scoring best were Toyota, American Motors, Mercedes-Benz and Datsun.[55]

GM's Chevrolet division also came out worst in a warranty survey done in 1974 by Boston College. Consumers were asked to rate the warranty protection and service of the various auto dealers and manufacturers. Chevrolet was lowest, with only 52% of buyers showing definite satisfaction. American Motors ranked tops with 89%.[56]

An exception to GM's dismal warranty performance seems to be the Cadillac division. *Consumer Reports*, in its 1976 annual questionnaire, asked its readers to evaluate service during the new car warranty period as to the condition of the car when delivered, overall service quality, whether there were any service problems, the adequacy of repairs, the availability of parts, fairness of charge and courtesy of dealer. Approximately 165,000 readers responded. Scoring best were Cadillac, Mercedes, Subaru, Peugeot, Lincoln and BMW. Scoring worst were Fiat, MGB, Triumph, Capri, Austin, Jeep and Dodge.[57]

Secret Warranties

On August 25, 1972, the Ford Motor Co.'s Customer Service Division sent out a general field bulletin to all regional and district managers of the division, advising them of a warranty extension so secret that they weren't even to tell dealers about it. The bulletin told of a "limited service program" in which Ford would pay 100% of the repair cost for body rust on 1969–72 model cars and light trucks through the first 24 months of ownership and 75% of the cost from the 25th to the 36th month. How were owners of these cars to know of this policy? They weren't to know. The bulletin advised that only those individuals who complained were to be accommodated.[58]

This so-called secret warranty didn't become public knowledge until July 8, 1975—nearly three years later—when the Center for Auto Safety obtained a copy of the bulletin and released it to the press. The next day Ford admitted it had repaired rust damage to 69,000 cars and trucks out of a possible 12 million Ford vehicles eligible for the secret program.[59]

Such secret warranties are not unusual. The Center for Auto Safety estimates that the auto companies, at any one time, are carrying out 300 secret warranty campaigns which are available only to car owners who complain bitterly.[60]

To stop such practices, the FTC in January 1978 filed a landmark complaint against Ford for failing to tell some 55,000 Ford and Mercury owners about a compensation program for the aforementioned "piston scuffing" problem and for advertising that its motor vehicles were durable, reliable and tough when at the same time it was admitting by its secret warranty action that this was not so.[61] As part settlement, Ford agreed in 1980 to publicize any post-warranty free repair programs.[62] Ford, after the FTC complaint was filed, publicly announced it was extending the warranty for piston scuffing to 36 months or 36,000 miles.[63]

The Consumer's Dilemma

You've now gone into hock to buy a new car and you start discovering defects. What will you do?

Complaining to the dealer or auto company could be just a waste of time. The U.S. Office of Consumer Affairs says its correspondence records "are replete with letters from frustrated automobile owners who have been bounced back and forth between dealers, district and regional manufacturer service representatives, and other 'owner relations' personnel, without any semblance of reasonable resolve to their problems."[64]

Then how about complaining to the U.S. Office of Consumer Affairs or some other consumer protection agency? That may be an equal waste of time because they too give consumers the Ping-Pong ball treatment. "All too frequently," says Clarence M. Ditlow III, director of the Center for Auto Safety, "consumers tell us that they are just shuttled from one office to another—from the local consumer protection office which refers them to the state attorney general which refers them to the FTC which refers them to the local consumer protection office, and so on."[65]

The only other major alternative is to sue, but here again the system is set up to discourage you and make you take your lumps. If you're stuck with a "lemon"—an unrepairable car—and want to get your money back or a replacement car, you generally have to give up possession of the car, often continue to make car payments and then maybe have to fight the case in court for several years. "Because people cannot afford to be without a car for that period of time, this offers little relief," says former Federal Trade Commission chairman Pertschuk.[66] Lawyers, in fact, often discourage people from filing new car warranty suits, saying it's just not worthwhile. There's also the problem of getting the money to hire an attorney. Says an Oklahoma college instructor in a letter to his congressman: "I do not have the money to hire an attorney because I am making payments on the new car. So I am turning to you."[67] According to Mr. Pertschuk: "The only suits that really are brought are suits by citizens who are just so damned mad they're willing to go through the process just to see justice triumph."[68]

Federal Warranty Law

Congressional response to the corrupt warranty practices of the auto companies was to pass the Magnuson-Moss Warranty-Federal Trade Commission Improvement Act[69] in 1974. But this legislation has been so weak in protecting "lemon" owners that Tim Ryles, Georgia's consumer affairs chief, says the law has "turned out to be something of a lemon itself."[70]

The act covers all consumer goods over $15 manufactured after July 4, 1975, and doesn't really get down to the nitty-gritty problems unique to automobiles. Those provisions of the act which its sponsors hoped would substantially improve auto warranty service have simply failed to do so.

One of the most promising provisions specified that warranties must be labeled either "full" or "limited," with full warranties offering much more protection. It was anticipated that many auto companies, for competitive reasons, would offer full warranties and that the word "limited" would scare off potential buyers. However, neither of these hopes has materialized. The only company that gives a "full" warranty is American Motors, which accounted for less than 1.5% of the cars sold in the U.S. in 1980.[71]

The main advantages of a "full" warranty over a "limited" warranty in relation to automobiles are: (1) The car company must fix a defective car, without charge, within a "reasonable" number of tries or give you a choice of a new car or your money back; (2) if you sue to get a new car or a refund, you can still use the car while the case is in litigation; and (3) the car company can't limit the "implied warranty" of merchantability or fitness for a particular purpose. An implied warranty is a right created by state law that says, in effect, that your car must be fit for the ordinary purposes for which you bought it. It also gives you protection should a defect show up after the written warranty expires if it was reasonable for you to expect that such a defect wouldn't occur. For example, let's say you bought an American Motors car with a 12-month or 12,000-mile warranty and the engine poops out at 25,000 miles, requiring $800 in repairs. Provided the problem wasn't caused by you, American Motors would probably be obligated to make the repair for free, since it was reasonable for you to assume when you bought the car that the engine would last for more than 25,000 miles.

In certain circumstances, under the Magnuson-Moss Act, the implied warranty can be extended beyond the terms of a written "limited" warranty due to an "unconscionable" act on the part of the seller or because you live in one of a few states that prohibit implied warranties from being limited to a specific period of time. (More on these states shortly.)

A major shortcoming of the Magnuson-Moss Act regarding full warranties is that it doesn't define what constitutes a "reasonable" number of attempts to fix a defective product. It does, however, allow the Federal Trade Commission to promulgate a rule defining "what constitutes a reasonable number of attempts to remedy particular kinds of defects or malfunctions under different circumstances."[72] The FTC has yet to issue such a rule.

The Magnuson-Moss Act has even more shortcomings. If an auto company doesn't adhere to either its full or its limited warranty, the act allows you to sue in state court, but it doesn't guarantee you attorney's fees if you win. The act says you "may" be allowed to collect costs and expenses connected with the suit but allows the court "discretion" in awarding attorney's fees. Without a guarantee of such fees, many people are reluctant to file warranty suits because it may not pay. Also, the Magnuson-Moss Act has a provision for class action warranty suits but the requirements are so hard to meet that the provision has rarely been used. To file a class action, there must be at least 100 plaintiffs, each must be out at least $25 and the total amount in controversy must be at least $50,000. This criterion is hard to meet because of the difficulty of getting together 100 or more people with the same exact problem, the $50,000 requirement and the fact that there's no guarantee of attorney's fees if the suit is successful.

Besides the Magnuson-Moss Act, there is a Federal Trade Commission rule which can be helpful to you if there is a warranty dispute and you financed your car through a dealer. Known commonly as the "holder-in-due-course" rule,[73] it allows you, while the warranty is still in effect, to stop making payments on your car loan while you sue to get a new car or a refund. Unfortunately, the rule doesn't apply if you went out on your own and got a loan.

State Warranty Laws

Ineffective as the Magnuson-Moss Act is, only a handful of states offer new car owners any substantial additional legal coverage when it comes to warranties.

For example, only seven states—Maine,[74] Maryland,[75] Massachusetts,[76] Vermont,[77] West Virginia,[78] Mississippi[78a] and Kansas[79]—prohibit disclaimers or limitations on implied warranties. This gives all auto buyers in these states—even those with "limited" warranties—protection against defects which crop up after the written warranty expires if it's reasonable to assume that such defects shouldn't occur.

Instructions on filing and winning warranty lawsuits are discussed in Chapter 20; methods other than suing for resolving warranty disputes are covered in Chapter 19; and how to buy a car so that you won't have warranty problems is detailed in Chapter 14.

Auto Warranty Reform

It's quite obvious that a cascade of tough federal and state laws is needed to arm consumers against the powerful auto companies and their dealers as well as help dealers get an even break from the manufacturers. "Federal and state laws must make it too costly for the manufacturers not to live up to their standards," says Mr. Ditlow of the Center for Auto Safety.[80]

I don't know exactly how much it would cost the auto companies to honor their warranties fully. But I do know that they spend far more money on needless annual styling changes than they do on warranty payments. Secret Ford documents put the estimated lifetime warranty costs of the company's 1973 model cars at $155.7 million.[81] This is a paltry sum compared to the $463.1 million spent by Ford in 1973 to amortize special tools and dies associated with annual model changes.[82]

Here are my recommendations for federal and state laws which I believe would clean up the auto warranty system overnight:

1. *Mandatory "full" warranties.* All auto companies should be required to give "full" warranties as defined by the Magnuson-Moss Act.

2. *Three tries and out.* The auto companies and their dealers should be given three tries or one month to fix a "lemon" car. After that, they must offer either a replacement car or the return of the purchase price.

3. *Mandatory attorney's fees.* Persons winning auto warranty suits should be entitled to mandatory attorney's fees plus costs pertaining to the suit.

4. *Binding arbitration of disputes.* Consumers with unadjusted warranty claims should be entitled to settle such disputes with binding arbitration if they wish. The Magnuson-Moss Act presently declares that it is the policy of Congress to "encourage" warrantors to set up informal dispute settlement mechanisms.[83] However, the act doesn't require it.

5. *Warranty extension for downtime.* The written warranty period should be extended a day or 34 miles for every full day a warranted car is in the shop, is inoperable or is in need of replacement parts. The Magnuson-Moss Act allows the FTC to make a rule extending the warranty if the consumer is deprived of the use of a product for at least 10 days.[84] However, the FTC has made no such rule. California law requires that a warranty for products selling for $50 or more be automatically extended a day for every full day the product is out for warranty repairs. Also, the warranty is extended until the product is fixed correctly, provided that, in cases where a repair has been tried and failed, the buyer has so notified the manufacturer or seller within 60 days after completion of attempted repairs. If the defect hasn't been fixed after a "reasonable number of attempts," the product can be returned for a replacement or refund less a deduction for usage.[85]

6. *Disclosure of assembly-line defects.* The auto companies should be prohibited from shipping to a dealer any car which is known to contain manufacturing defects or substandard parts, unless a list of the shortcomings accompanies the car. Everything on the list would have to be corrected before the vehicle could be delivered to a customer.

7. *Disclosure of transit damage.* Dealers should be required to disclose all transit damage—both repaired and unrepaired—to all purchasers or prospective purchasers. In addition, any car with transit damage of $300 or more, excluding items such as tires and glass and other easily replaceable items, should be sold as a used car. At present, according to *Automotive Age*, Kentucky, Idaho, Wisconsin and Wyoming require disclosure of unrepaired and repaired transit damage in excess of a certain amount—usually $300 or 6% of the value of the car, whichever is less, excluding glass, tires, etc.[86]

8. *Minimum pre-delivery inspection requirements.* Before a car is delivered to a consumer, specific items should be inspected and adjusted to factory specifications. Also, consumers should receive a copy of the pre-delivery inspection form, signed by the person who made the inspection, asserting, "I certify that I have personally checked and cor-

rected to factory specifications the items indicated in this checklist." A detailed form similar to the one in Appendix M could be required.

9. *Pre-delivery included in sticker price.* Congress should specify that the charge for pre-delivery inspection be included in the base sticker price of each car and that no dealer may charge extra for this service.

10. *Penalties for cover-ups.* Auto executives who conceal information about safety problems in their cars should be subject to a $50,000 fine and a minimum two-year jail term.

11. *Fair compensation to dealers.* Dealers should be fairly compensated for warranty work and pre-delivery inspections. Some 16 states now require auto manufacturers to pay their dealers for warranty work in an amount not less than the charges made by the dealers for non-warranty work.[87] (The auto companies are challenging some of these laws in the courts.)

12. *Quick settlement of warranty claims.* In cases where prior approval of the manufacturer is needed before proceeding with warranty work, the factory rep should be required to rule on the warranty request within three business days. This might encourage the auto companies to set up drive-in warranty claim centers in metropolitan areas.

13. *Disclosure of non-training.* In cases where there has been no factory training or technical information available on a particular model, dealers should be required to disclose these facts to all prospective customers.

14. *Payment limitations outlawed.* It should be made illegal for an auto company to limit any dealer or any factory service rep to a warranty budget that results in the disallowance of legitimate claims.

15. *Warranty repair order and invoice requirements.* To give consumers proof of their exact complaints prior to their warranty expiring, dealers should be required to make out warranty repair orders showing the defects and/or symptoms being complained about and should give a copy of the repair order to the car owner. If a dealership can't take a warranted car for repairs immediately or refuses to perform warranty repairs, it should be required to give the consumer a written acknowledgment of the defects or symptoms. To avoid "wall jobs," dealers should be required to give customers a copy of all warranty repair invoices stating what work was done, what parts were replaced and whether the parts were new, used, rebuilt or reconditioned. If a dealer pulls a "wall job" while at the same time putting in writing that repairs were made, the dealer is open to charges of fraud.

16. *Dealer-manufacturer squabbles.* All squabbles between dealers and car companies involving warranty matters should be settled by binding arbitration.

17. *Free loaner cars.* Puerto Rico law should be followed: It requires a loaner car be made available if a warranty repair takes more than seven

days unless due to "fortuitous causes such as disaster, strikes or any other causes beyond the control of the seller."[88]

18. *Warranting of tires.* The auto companies should be made to warrant tires on new cars. They currently refuse to do this, which subjects new car buyers to the runaround not only from auto companies and their dealers, but also from tire companies and tire dealers (more on this in Chapter 12).

19. *Nixing temporary fixing.* It should be illegal for an auto company or dealer to make only temporary repairs to satisfy a warranty claim.

20. *Notice of warranties.* As is the law in Massachusetts, automakers should be required to give prompt written notice of any defect to both vehicle owners and dealers, whether the warranty is still in effect or not.[89]

21. *Dealer and manufacturer licensing.* State agencies, free of auto industry influence, should be set up to license auto companies and their dealers, to mediate warranty disputes and to have the power to put out of business any auto company or dealer that violates state law.

11

State Inspections:

A Government-Sponsored Rip-off?

In 1975, graduate students at Carnegie-Mellon University took a 1969 Chevrolet Bel-Air with planted safety defects to 20 private garages in the Pittsburgh area which performed mandatory state safety inspections. The results: On one hand, the garages found no more than 54% of the defects, with the average shop finding only 37% of them. On the other hand, the average garage "found" two nonexistent defects per car.[1]

In 1978, the New York State Department of Motor Vehicles, in covert operations to weed out repair shops that were making improper state safety inspections, visited 222 inspection garages and found that only 69 shops, or 31%, were doing a satisfactory job.[2]

Such results bring into question a system operating in over 20 states where privately owned repair shops perform both the state safety inspections and the repairs. Critics of the system contend that such shops often either force unneeded repairs on motorists, go easy on regular customers or just slap on inspection stickers—sometimes charging inflated prices—without actually checking the car.

Part of the rip-off problem stems from the fact that the allowable charge for making the inspections is often so ridiculously low that shops almost have to cheat to make a profit. In New York State, for example, during the time of the above-mentioned investigation, shops could charge only $3 for the inspection, of which they got to keep only $2.75.[3]

As an alternative to inspections by privately owned repair shops, two states, New Jersey and Delaware; two cities, Washington and New Orleans; and several Florida counties have set up government-run inspection stations.[4] These stations inspect cars in assembly-line fashion, but do no repairs. If a defect is discovered, the motorist is free to go wherever he or she wants to have the car repaired. Thus there's no incentive to tell people there's something wrong with a car when it isn't so.

However, even the government-operated system isn't foolproof in avoiding rip-offs. Government stations give only pass/fail grades to various safety systems. Thus, a motorist may be told that his exhaust system or brakes are faulty without being told specifically what needs to be repaired. Thus someone who may only need a tail pipe may be conned by a repair shop into replacing the whole blasted exhaust system. (Government-run emission testing centers work the same way: They tell you only that your car is polluting, not what adjustments or repairs need to be made.)

Nevertheless, the state-run system is far superior to the private garage system. Why then don't the states with private garage safety inspections switch over?

The answer has to do with politics and money. The powerful oil companies and service station operators don't want a change because they're making money out of the present system. In Pennsylvania, it's figured that a license to inspect cars increases gasoline sales alone by an estimated 15%.[5] States are not enthusiastic about government-run inspection centers because of the enormous investment involved, especially land acquisition in urban areas. There's also the problem that inspection centers wouldn't be accessible to people who live in sparsely populated areas.

Actually, state governments needn't invest a penny in building and running assembly-line inspection centers. Private firms could be contracted to finance, build and run the system. The state of Arizona has done this successfully for annual emission inspections. The state contracted with Hamilton Test Systems, a subsidiary of United Technologies Corp., to finance and run a $10 million, 12-station, computerized inspection network in Maricopa (Phoenix) and Pima (Tucson) counties, which have over 75% of the state's population. The inspection cost to motorists is $5.[6] California also contracted with Hamilton Test Systems to set up and run emission inspection centers in the greater Los Angeles area.[7]

The National Highway Traffic Safety Administration (NHTSA) has shown the feasibility of setting up full-scale diagnostic centers which could not only do safety and emissions inspections, but could also check out and report on the condition of your whole car—all for perhaps $15.[8] More on this in Chapter 16.

As for the rural area problem, possible solutions would be to use government-operated mobile inspection units there or keep the private inspection system there, since rural people, as explained in Chapter 6, don't get cheated as much as urban people.

Are Safety Inspections Needed?

There are still over 25 states that do not require at least one safety inspection annually. Most of these states claim that there's no proof that annual inspections would reduce the number or severity of highway accidents enough to justify the cost and inconvenience to motorists. A 1977 report to Congress by the U.S. Comptroller General expresses this view. While stating emphatically that "vehicle defects can and do cause highway accidents," the report criticizes NHTSA for not coming up with any meaningful studies to show that annual inspections would be cost-effective in reducing those accidents.[9]

Nevertheless, two often-cited studies show a shocking number of deaths as a result of vehicle defects. A 1970 study by the California Highway Patrol of 409 fatal one-vehicle traffic accidents found that about 6.4% of the vehicles had mechanical defects which caused the accident and another 11.7% had defects which contributed to the accident.[10] In another study, the Indiana University Institute for Research in Public Safety found that vehicle defects were a definite cause of 4.2% to 4.5% of all accidents and were a probable cause of 9.1% to 12.5% of all accidents.[11] Applying these statistics, NHTSA figures over 2,400 deaths in 1973 were almost certainly caused by vehicle defects.[12]

Undoubtedly, some of those lives could have been saved through safety inspections. But saving lives and reducing auto accidents aren't the sole benefit of annual inspection nor its only justification. A good computerized inspection system, including both safety and emissions checks, could actually save motorists money in the long run. Such a system could reduce breakdowns, increase vehicle longevity, cut gasoline consumption, reduce pollution, provide defect information for various models of cars and catch cars that have not been returned for recall inspections or were stolen.

Arizona officials, for example, figure that motorists will more than make up for their $5 emissions inspection fee. An estimated 30 to 35 million gallons of gasoline are being conserved annually as a result of the state's program, and individual motorists frequently save enough on gas consumption to offset the cost of any needed maintenance. Arizona citizens have also gained health benefits from the program by removal of 250 tons of pollutants from the air daily.[13]

The Swedish Way

Sweden has shown that annual safety inspections can greatly increase the longevity of cars and that the data gained from the inspections can be used to help consumers decide which new or used car to buy.

Inspections in Sweden are done by AB Svensk Bilprovning, a quasi-government company. When Sweden first began mandatory inspections in 1965, the average life expectancy for a car was about 10 years. As a result of the inspections, it increased to about 14 years in 1973–74.[14] While over 35% of the cars 10 years old were scrapped in 1965, the rate was only 10% in 1974.[15]

Data from the inspections are published annually in two booklets, *Weak Points of Cars* and *Life Expectancy of Passenger Cars in Sweden*.

Weak Points of Cars tells what components have high or low failure rates on various cars. It also compares various models of cars as to percentage of faults per cars inspected. For example, from data collected from three months of inspections in early 1975, it was found that 33.3% of the 1972 Datsun 1200s had faulty service brakes and 27.2% of the 1972 Fiat 125s had excessive play in the lower swivel joints. It was also discovered that the Peugeot 204 had the lowest percentage of cars with faults (17.3%) while the Renault 4 had the highest (43.4%).[16]

One of the *Life Expectancy* booklets, calculated in 1975, shows a large difference between life expectancies of various makes. For 1974 models, projected life expectancies ranged from a high of 16.6 years for Volvo and 14.3 years for Volkswagen to a low of 11.6 years for BMC and 11.7 years for Simca and DKW/Audi.[17]

For further information or to obtain copies of the booklets, write: AB Svensk Bilprovning, Fack, S-16210 Vallingby, Sweden.

Protecting Yourself

If you're one of the millions of motorists who have to put up with the private garage system of inspection, there are three precautions you should take besides the usual ones in getting your car repaired:

1. Don't let the shop take off your old inspection sticker until it's ready to put a new one on. That way, if it tells you that you need repairs, you can drive away and get another opinion or a better estimate. Once the old inspection sticker is taken off, you can't legally drive anywhere and you'll be at the mercy of the garage doing the inspection.

2. Don't wait until the end of the inspection period to get your car

checked out. The shop will know that you have no time to shop around for another opinion and may exploit you.

3. If you know that you'll need repairs to pass the inspection, either get them done beforehand at the shop of your choice—not necessarily an inspection garage—or else shop around for the inspection station that will give you the best estimate on the work.

Needed Legislation

If you've had it with the private garage system of inspections, write your governor and state legislators and insist that assembly-line inspection stations be set up that don't perform repairs. In the meantime, insist that private garages be allowed to charge inspection fees high enough so that they can make a profit on the inspections alone.

Also needed is legislation requiring the federal government to put out booklets similar to those published in Sweden. Data on weak points of cars could be obtained from present government-run inspection centers, and national data on vehicle longevity could be obtained from state motor vehicle statistics.

Complaining

If you have the least suspicion that an inspection station–repair garage has ripped you off, complain to the official in charge of inspections in your state (see Appendix G). In Virginia and many other states you can complain to the local unit of the state police, which will come out and investigate.

12

The Robber Rubber Barons

It wasn't exactly nice of U.S. Representative John E. Moss of California, during a 1978 congressional hearing, to accuse the Firestone Tire & Rubber Co. of "merchandising death"[1] for not voluntarily recalling its steel-belted radial 500 tires.

After all, the company had a logical explanation as to why its 500 tires were blowing out like balloons at a New Year's Eve party and had been involved in—at one point—thousands of accidents, hundreds of injuries and 34 known deaths.[2]

According to Firestone, the blowouts were being caused by car owners who had not properly maintained their tires and had let them get dangerously underinflated. Thus, the company was not about to recall the tires. In May 1978, John F. Floberg, vice-president, secretary and general counsel of Firestone, told the U.S. House of Representatives' Oversight and Investigations Subcommittee, which was headed by Congressman Moss, that "any problems associated with this tire are not problems resulting from any deficiency in the design or manufacture of the tire itself, but, rather, from the maintenance habits of a large portion of American motorists."[3]

The Alibi That Didn't Fly

Firestone's defense in this matter—the underinflation alibi—didn't explain why Firestone 500 tires were failing when other manufacturers' radials were not—a point which eventually shamed the company into recalling over 7.5 million tires.[4] But the alibi did raise a whole new set of questions about not only Firestone's ethics but the entire tire industry's morals. It seems the tire companies are not telling the public about the true dangers of underinflated radial tires.

Robert Lee, senior product engineer at Firestone, testified before the House Oversight Subcommittee that driving a radial tire at only 4 pounds per square inch (psi) underinflated is "right on the threshold of danger" —meaning a blowout—and that "it's just a matter of how long." At 6 to 8 psi underinflation, he said, there's going to be "trouble for sure."[5]

In addition, Mr. Floberg told the subcommittee that the effects of underinflation are "irreversible" and that "a tire which has been damaged as a result of having been run underinflated for a period of time may well fail because of . . . cumulative damage even after the tire has been brought up to proper inflation."[6] Underinflation, he said, normally has the effect of concentrating heat and stress at the tire's most vulnerable point —"where the steel cord is bonded to the rubber." If the stress and heat are severe enough, according to Mr. Floberg, "tread, belt or ply separations will eventually occur in the tire."[7]

Also at the hearings, Mr. Floberg was asked if Firestone intended to warn consumers in its advertising that 4 pounds underinflation was the threshold of danger. Unbelievably, he replied that to do so "would be a decision, I suppose, of the advertising department" and not something initiated by those in top management such as himself.[8]

Congressman Moss said if Firestone was right in claiming many failures of its 500 tires could have been avoided by proper inflation then it was "reprehensible in the extreme" that the company didn't inform the public "of the steps they might take to reduce the chance of blowouts."[9]

If anything, Firestone and the rest of the tire industry have gone out of their way to convince the public not to worry if its radials look underinflated—implying that that's the way they're supposed to look. The so-called low-profile look, in which the bottom of the tire lies somewhat flat on the ground, makes it virtually impossible to visually detect underinflation. "The low profile of the radial tire on the road," Mr. Floberg said, has "apparently caused many consumers to believe that there is no need to check air pressure when, in fact, their tires may be dangerously underinflated."[10]

Firestone's silence about the dangers of underinflated radial tires is made even more significant by the fact that Mr. Floberg admitted to the House subcommittee that there are an alarming number of underinflated tires on the road. He cited several surveys, including an NHTSA study showing that "a significant percentage" of tires in use today are "at least 10 psi underinflated," and an Illinois Institute of Technology survey of 2,400 vehicles in the Chicago area which found that 27% of them had tires underinflated by 4 to 16 pounds.[11]

In addition to those surveys, B.F. Goodrich, in a study released in 1977, found 55.3% of cars checked had at least one tire underinflated by 4 pounds or more,[12] and Consumers Union has found that many new cars are delivered to customers with underinflated tires.[13]

With the increasing use of self-service gas stations causing many car owners to ignore checking tire pressure, it behooves the tire industry to warn the public of the extreme dangers of underinflation.

Tire Pressure Warning Systems

The problem of underinflation, which Mr. Floberg said "probably accounts for more radial tire disablements than any other causes combined,"[14] could be entirely eliminated by a low tire pressure warning system.

Two Detroit product liability lawyers, Harry M. Philo and Arnold D. Porter, suggest sinister motives as the reason why the rubber barons won't incorporate such inexpensive warning systems into the valve stem of each tire. "The tire industry," they say, "is presented with a classic problem of big industry: If drivers are properly instructed regarding inflation pressures, or if tires are designed to signal improper inflation, they will last for a considerably longer period of time, thus cutting into the replacement market."[15]

NHTSA has been toying with the idea of requiring all or some new vehicles to have a low tire pressure warning system—either installed on the tire valve or connected to a light on the dashboard.[16] However, the idea has been put on the agency's back burner.[17]

Of course, there's nothing to stop the automakers from installing such a system voluntarily. General Motors introduced a low tire pressure warning system on its 1980 GMC and Chevrolet heavy-duty trucks, but not on its cars. An advertisement for the device tells truckers that it can protect their tire investment and save them fuel as well[18] (proper tire inflation cuts down on fuel consumption).

Messrs. Philo and Porter also contend that many other tire innovations were kept off the market for years, including self-sealing tires, which were patented in 1962; run-flat tires, which maintain reasonable highway speeds for long distances even though totally deflated; and dual chamber tires, in which an inner chamber takes over when the outer chamber fails or is punctured.[19]

The Yo-Yo Tire Warranty

Mrs. A of Wisconsin bought a new 1975 Ford Granada equipped with five Firestone steel-belted radial 500 tires. The tires soon began giving her problems.

"Before there was 12,000 [miles] on these babies," she said, "they had hernias on the sidewalls and big chunks of tread had peeled and flown off while driving. We were changing tires constantly and very much afraid to make any long trips."

She went to her Ford dealer, who denied any responsibility and told her to go to a Firestone dealer. The Firestone dealer was no help either. "As far as the car salesman and Firestone dealer were concerned," she said, "our problem was rather funny and of no concern to them. We wrote the Ford company [and got] the same 'rock head' nothingness."[20]

Many people find themselves caught in a no-man's-land between Detroit and Akron. This is because the auto companies warrant every item on their cars except the tires, which they attempt to palm off as the tire companies' responsibility. This often turns new car tire warranties into a sham, with auto manufacturers and new car dealers claiming that a problem tire is the responsibility of the tire manufacturer or tire dealer, who, in turn, often say it's the automaker's or auto dealer's problem. Tire dealers are often reluctant to replace a tire which came with a new car because they're afraid the tire company won't reimburse them.

Here we have a situation where the auto companies force the tire manufacturers to make tires to their exact specifications and then when something goes wrong with the tires, they tell the consumer, "It ain't our fault." The truth is that the auto companies have so much control over the tire companies that Harry C. McCreary, Jr., chairman of McCreary Tire and Rubber Co., once remarked: "When Detroit snaps its fingers, Akron jumps through the hoop—backward if necessary." He added: "If you are a tire manufacturer, you are not apt to argue very loudly with your biggest customer. You give him what he demands, not what you feel he should have. If you don't like it he can always get his tires from your competitor, right across the street."[21]

Even if you can convince a tire dealer or tire manufacturer that your original equipment or replacement tire is defective, you're still in a bind. The tire companies won't give you cash to go out and buy the tire of your choice; instead, they'll only replace the tire for another of the same kind either for free or on a prorated basis.

This means you might be forced to replace your defective tire with another tire that may have the same inherent defect. Many people who had Firestone 500 tires encountered this problem. Phil Shimmin, director of purchasing for Pacific Theatres in Los Angeles, said he bought a number of Ford LTDs for staff use which came equipped with Firestone 500 tires—many of which failed. He replaced the defective tires on a prorated basis with other Firestone 500 tires, but even some of the replacements failed. Mr. Shimmin said that because "the Firestone dealers were not willing nor prepared to make cash refunds for tires that failed, but only to replace them with new tires," he, "out of concern for the safety of our employes," replaced all the Firestone tires with Michelin tires at a great financial loss to his company.[22]

The rubber barons have other tricks up their warranty sleeves as well. Some tire manufacturers, when they prorate an adjustment for a defective tire, set artificially high prices for the replacement tire, some using the manufacturer's suggested retail price. The deception here is that tires are usually sold below the suggested retail price, sometimes making it cheaper for you to go out and buy a new tire at the going price than to buy one prorated on the rarely followed manufacturer's suggested price. Richard Tallman of the House Subcommittee on Oversight and Investigations told me that out of some 1,500 letters sent to the subcommittee concerning defective Firestone 500 tires, about 25% complained that Firestone hiked its retail price when figuring out the prorated cost of replacement.[23]

A fairer method used by some tire companies is to prorate the replacement cost based on the current selling price of the tire or the price originally paid for the tire.

Another unjust practice among tire dealers is charging consumers for mounting and wheel balancing when they replace a defective tire.

The Phony Spare

One of the few innovations the auto/tire industries *have* produced is the "phony spare," which F. Timothy Eichenberg, former treasurer of Bernalillo County, New Mexico, calls "yet another conspiracy against consumers."[24]

One version, called the "Space Saver" tire, is an undersized spare which weighs less and takes up less space than a normal tire. It became standard equipment on newly downsized 1978 General Motors cars and is designed just to get you to the repair garage. GM warns that when the spare is on, the car shouldn't be driven continually over 50 mph, nor should the car be taken through an automatic car wash, because there's less ground clearance than with normal tires.[25]

What's even more outrageous, according to Mr. Eichenberg, who got stuck with one of these spares when he bought a 1978 Chevrolet Monza, is that once the phony spare is used, it must be deflated in order to be placed back in the trunk, and it must be kept there deflated.[26] What happens, you may ask, if you need to put the spare on your car and there's no air hose available? Don't fear. General Motors has the answer. For about $7.50 it will sell you a can of pressurized carbon dioxide which you can keep in the trunk to inflate the tire. Since the can is unrefillable, GM can charge you about $7.50 every time you have a flat tire.[27]

What happens if you want a real spare tire on one of these cars? Can you simply buy a real tire and mount it on the spare wheel? No, says *Consumer Reports,* "you'll have to buy both a tire and a wheel." The magazine also says that GM won't let you order a real spare with the cars and that a snow tire or snow chains can't be put on the phony spare.[28]

Another type of phony spare, the T-type, which became standard on many 1978 compact and subcompact cars, has many of the same problems except that it can be stored inflated.

High-Speed Tire Failure

Did you know that although your car may be designed to go over 100 mph, your tires may not be? This little bit of information came out in a federal trial in Louisiana where a judge ruled that both Ford and Goodyear were liable for the failure of a tire which blew out at a speed in excess of 100 mph and resulted in the driver's being killed and a passenger's being seriously injured.

Under NHTSA regulations, tire manufacturers are required to test their tires only up to 85 mph, while the car involved in the case—a 1976 Mercury Cougar—could register up to 140 mph. Goodyear, according to the testimony, said that it randomly selected tires for further testing at speeds of 95 and 100 mph, but about 10% of the tires don't survive the 100-mph test.

Despite the fact that the driver was legally drunk and speeding, Judge Eugene Davis found that "Ford should have foreseen that a significant number of ultimate users of its products would drive their vehicles at top speed" and that "Ford, as assembler, was aware of both the design limitations of the tire and the speed capability of the automobile."[29]

Tire Grading System

"We believe grade labeling [of auto tires] will be an impairment to our free enterprise system," Winston W. Marsh, executive vice-president of the National Tire Dealers and Retreaders Association, told the U.S.

Senate Commerce Committee in 1965.[30] Congress wisely recognized that "free enterprise" in the parlance of the tire industry translates into freedom to keep the consumer in the dark. It thus passed the National Traffic and Motor Vehicle Safety Act of 1966, which, among other things, required the Secretary of Transportation to put a uniform tire quality grading system into effect no later than September 9, 1969.[31]

NHTSA, a part of the Department of Transportation, was so slow in implementing the law that Carl Nash, a Ralph Nader associate, brought suit in 1973 to force the Transportation Secretary to promulgate the grading system. The court ordered the system to go into effect by September 1, 1974, but complications and legal challenges by the tire manufacturers forced nearly a five-year delay.[32] Finally, on April 1, 1979 —nearly a decade late—a tire grading system went into effect for bias-ply tires. The system went into effect for bias-belted tires on October 1, 1979, and radial tires on April 1, 1980.

Tires, under the system, are graded according to treadwear, traction and heat resistance. For the first six months after each of the above respective dates, the grades were to be on a paper label attached to the tire tread. After those dates, they were to be molded on the tire sidewall.

Here's an explanation of the ratings:

TREADWEAR

A graded numerical sequence is used which increases in increments of 10, such as 80, 90, 100, 110, 120, etc. The higher the number, the longer the tread can be expected to last. Therefore, a tire with a treadwear grade of 150 can be expected to last 50% longer—at least on a government test course—than a tire with a grade of 100.

TRACTION

The symbols A, B and C are used, with A-graded tires enabling you to stop your car on wet roads faster and in a shorter distance than the other two grades. C-graded tires have poor traction on wet roads.

HEAT RESISTANCE

Here too, A, B and C symbols are used, with A-rated tires the coolest-running and therefore the best. Excessive heat can lead to blowouts and tread separation.

A note of caution: Manufacturers might increase their treadwear rating at the expense of traction and heat resistance, so judge tires on all three criteria.

You can get a free pamphlet, entitled *Uniform Tire Quality Grading*, which further explains the grading system, by writing: General Services Division, Room 4423, NHTSA, 400 7th St. S.W., Washington, DC 20590.

Getting Your Tire Recalled

If you have a tire which you think might have a manufacturing defect, notify NHTSA (see Chapter 19 for toll-free hotline number and address). It could be possible that the tire has already been part of a recall campaign which you weren't notified about, or your call might lead to a recall.

You will need to give NHTSA the DOT number of your tire or tires, so have that information handy when you call. The DOT number is imprinted on the tire just above the rim. Here is one from a Toyota tire:

DOT	EM	H2	BAA	183
Meets or Exceeds Dept. of Transportation Safety Standards	Mfr. and plant	Tire size	Optional symbols	Week and year of manufacture

In this particular case, the tire was manufactured by Bridgestone Tire Co., Ltd., at its plant in Tokyo during the 18th week of 1973.

If the tire you're inquiring about is still on your car, you might have a problem. It seems that tires are often mounted on cars with the DOT number facing the axle. In order to see the number, you'll have to either take the tire off the wheel or crawl under the car with a flashlight.

Besides NHTSA, also notify the Center for Auto Safety about tire defects (see Appendix C).

Legislation Needed

I can think of ten new laws or regulations needed to clean up consumer tire problems. Here goes:

1. Auto manufacturers should be required to warrant the tires on new cars, and they and their dealers should make the decision on all tire adjustments.

2. All tires should be required to have built-in low tire pressure warning systems.

3. Tire companies, when giving a prorated adjustment, should be required to base the adjustment on the price originally paid for the tire or the actual current selling price.

4. Consumers should be given a choice of cash or a replacement when returning a defective tire.

5. Tire companies should be required to reimburse their dealers for

all expenses involved in making warranty adjustments, such as mounting and balancing, and no consumer should be required to pay such expenses.

6. Tires on new cars should be required to pass stress tests at the maximum speed for which a car is designed. As an alternative, a warning sticker should be pasted near the speedometer giving the maximum speed for which the tires were designed.

7. Manufacturers of radial tires should be required to give material to all their customers properly warning them of the dangers inherent in underinflated radial tires.

8. Any dealer who delivers a new car with underinflated tires should be subject to a heavy fine.

9. Tire companies should be required to issue recall notices to those who purchased tires as far back as five years ago instead of the present three years.

10. Tires should be required to be mounted so that the DOT identification number always appears on the outside of the car.

Protecting Yourself

Since the auto companies won't warrant the tires on their cars, you should insist that the brand of tires you want be put on when you buy a new car. *Modern Tire Dealer* says General Motors buys tires from Uniroyal, Goodyear, Firestone and General; Ford from the same companies plus Michelin; Chrysler from Goodyear, Firestone, General and Michelin; American Motors from Goodyear only; and Volkswagen from Michelin, Goodyear and Uniroyal.[33] New car buyers surveyed by NHTSA said Michelin tires gave far less trouble than any others.[34]

Absolutely veto any new car equipped with tires from a manufacturer who has a rip-off replacement policy, and, of course, don't buy any replacement tires from such companies either.

It is also important that you properly maintain your tires so that you avoid problems. A 1979 B.F. Goodrich survey found one out of every 20 tires in danger of imminent failure.[35]

I suggest you read the 13-page 5 *Keys to Better Tire Mileage and Safety*, which can be obtained free by writing: Tire Industry Safety Council, Box 1801, Washington, DC 20013. If you send a check or money order for $2.75 to the same address, you'll get an entire glove compartment kit which consists of the pamphlet, an air pressure gauge, a tread depth gauge and a spare set of four tire valve caps.

It's essential that you own a tire pressure gauge and check your tire pressure every few weeks and before long trips. The pressure should be checked prior to starting out for a drive, according to the Safety

Council, "since pressure can increase up to 6 pounds or more when tires are hot from driving."[36]

Also keep in mind that tire pressure can drop 1 pound for every 10-degrees drop in temperature[37] and that tires are apt to lose about 1 pound of air per month in normal use.[38]

Another tip: Check the tire pressure of your new car before driving it out of the dealership and make sure it's correct.

Watch out for underinflation, but also be on the lookout for overinflation, overloading and balding tires. Overinflation makes tires vulnerable to impact damage and causes excessive wear in the center of the tread. Overloading can cause heat buildup and sudden tire failure. A bald tire, according to Firestone, has a 40% greater chance of going flat or blowing out than a non-bald tire.[39] Firestone, in fact, has found that an alarming number of people are riding around with bald tires. The company inspected a random cross-section of 4,500 tires at places where the tires were removed from the car and found about 25% of them were worn below the treadwear indicators.[40] The treadwear indicators are smooth bands which run horizontally across the tire tread and appear when only 2/32 of an inch of tread is left.

Complaining

Executives of Firestone, Goodrich, Goodyear and Kelly-Springfield are listed in Appendix I. If your complaint is against a tire dealer, contact the National Tire Dealers & Retreaders Association (see Appendix I).

13

Used Car Dealers: Oh How They Hide the Defects

The newspaper ad for a Fort Lauderdale, Florida, used car dealership looked enticing to Ms. S. The ad, which appeared in 1976, showed the picture of a 1967 Dodge window van which was described as a "sharp" 6-cylinder stick shift.

Ms. S and her boyfriend went to see the van and were impressed. "It started up right away," she said. They took it for a 15-to-20-minute road test and were still highly enthusiastic. Commented Ms. S: "It sounded good—[the] motor was clean [and the] oil looked clean."

She bought the van "as is," getting a $400 allowance for a trade-in, plunking down $400 cash and financing another $356.

Two days later, the engine started backfiring and the van had no pickup. Also, the transmission would frequently pop out of second gear. A mechanic checked over the car and found the motor and the transmission shot. It was also discovered, according to Ms. S, that when the rubber mat on the floorboard was picked up, "you could see right through to the road."

Having bought the vehicle "as is"—meaning no warranty—she had no recourse but to pay for needed repairs herself.[1]

Discovering defects within a few days after buying a vehicle from a used car lot is not uncommon. A mail survey by the Federal Trade Commission's Seattle Regional Office of persons who bought used cars from dealers in December 1972 found that 31.6% of the respondents discovered at least one defect within 10 days of purchase. Many of the defects cost them between $51 to $200 to fix.[2]

"Detailing"

The problem seems to be that Americans are softies for looks when it comes to buying used cars. Knowing this, used car dealers go out of their way to improve the appearance of their cars through "detailing"— i.e., appearance reconditioning—and skimp on mechanical repairs.

"Detailing," in fact, is practically an American art form. The Federal Trade Commission staff, in a visit to a specialist in this trade, compared vehicles waiting for renovation with those which had already been reconditioned and found the contrast "startling."[3]

These specialists, according to the FTC staff, even went so far as to spray the interior with "new car smell." In addition, they removed dents and scratches, polished or repainted the outside, replaced torn upholstery or armrests, shampooed the interior, redyed the carpeting, sprayed the trunk with a flocking material, installed a new trunk mat, steam-cleaned the engine compartment and repainted the engine.[4]

The end result, says the FTC staff, is that "the consumer shopping for a used vehicle is confronted with immaculate vehicles and smooth-talking salespeople who strive to assure the customer that the gleaming beauties are in 'mint condition' or 'dependable transportation' while maintaining a wall of silence about defects which may lie beneath the surface."[5] The California Public Interest Research Group, in a survey of 101 San Diego used car dealers, found that 75 of them failed to disclose car defects to potential buyers.[6] National Analysts, in another survey completed in 1977, found that 85% of used car buyers were not advised of uncorrected mechanical problems prior to their purchase. In over half the cases where a defect turned up, the salesperson had said either no problem existed or the problem had been corrected. The rest just kept their mouths shut about the defects.[7]

The truth is that used car dealers generally know about the defects in their cars, they just don't like to tell consumers about them and will often lie about their existence. Dealers generally inspect cars thoroughly before they buy them, so they know what they're getting. Many dealers buy their cars at auctions, where they're given the opportunity to take an hour to inspect a car after they buy it and to take it for a drive. At one major auction, at least, if an undisclosed defect costing over $75 is discovered, the buyer can demand that the sale be rescinded or the price be arbitrated.[8] According to the FTC staff, the used car salesman's knowledge of defects "is sufficient that they can identify vehicles on the lot which they will not sell to their friends."[9]

Some dealers blame the American consumer for this approach to selling used cars. Harvey A. Farberman of the State University of New York at Stony Brook, while doing an on-the-job study of the used car business, found that dealers hold intense antagonism toward used car buyers. A partner in an East Coast used car operation told him:

"They don't know shit about a car. They look at the interior, turn on the radio, check the odometer, kick the tire, push the windshield wiper button, turn on the air conditioner, open up the trunk, look at the paint. What the [deleted] has any of that to do with the *condition* of the car? I mean, the way the [deleted] runs. If I put money into all this crap, I can't put it into improving the mechanical condition. Three weeks later the [deleted] car falls apart and they're on my ass to fix it. Then I got to live with them. They drive me off the wall. Then that broad down at the consumer affairs office wants to know why I don't give the customer a fair shake. Shit, why the hell don't she educate the consumers? It would make things a lot easier."[10]

"As Is"

An estimated 40% to 60% of cars sold by used car dealers are purchased "as is."[11] What many people don't realize is that this disclaimer is quite often a device for unloading lemons.[12]

When you purchase a used car "as is," any defects that might crop up are your responsibility no matter what the salesman told you. It's a very common practice for used car salesmen to tell you something like "If there are any problems, just bring it back and we'll take care of it." Or he might disclose one defect in an effort to make you think it's the only one ("All this car needs is a muffler"). He may even make you think the car has undergone major repairs ("It just had a motor job"). Hardly a court in the country will accept your version of these oral representations when there is a written "as is" disclaimer in your purchase contract. "The purchaser of a defective vehicle sold 'as is' is essentially without remedy, no matter how reassuring were the seller's statements during the sales transaction," says the FTC staff.[13]

The "as is" disclaimer is especially hard on poorer people. They tend to buy older used cars, which are more apt to have defects, and they tend to finance the cars as well. What often happens to such people was described in 1976 by Paul L. Biderman, New Mexico assistant attorney general:

"In our state, the second poorest in the nation, an all-too-familiar pattern has emerged. A buyer goes to a used car lot that offers easy credit; he puts down several hundred dollars in painfully acquired savings to buy a vehicle 'as is'; the vehicle is grossly defective, as emerges only after the temporary repairs made to disguise the problems have worn off; the customer then either surrenders the vehicle after his demands for repair are refused; or the customer runs up costly repair bills, frequently leaving him unable to meet his first payment. Repossession occurs and the process begins all over again with a new buyer, except that the first customer has been divested of his down payment *and* his transportation. In a rural state as dependent on automobiles as New Mexico, this can amount to severe human hardship in any number of ways."[14]

The used car dealers just described are known as "hook artists," according to Victor Snyder, owner of Trader Vic's used cars in Pacioma, California. He says they advertise heavily and are especially looking for those who are new in town with little money and no credit. As soon as a buyer misses a payment, the hook goes out and the car is repossessed. They might sell the same car to 10 people, says Mr. Snyder.[15]

To temporarily mask defects in "as is" used cars, many dealers have some real dirty tricks up their sleeves. One such deception, according to Mr. Snyder, is to pour a can of pepper into the radiator to stop leaks. When the pepper makes contact with the water it swells, plugging up the holes—but only for a short time. Another ruse, he says, is to put extra-thick 90-weight oil in the crankcase to mask engine problems.[16]

Warranty Woes

The Center for Auto Safety, after a survey of used car dealers in Dallas, Cleveland and Washington, D.C., said its "most disturbing finding" was that dealers would divulge details of the warranty only after persistent questioning.

"The most common initial response to the warranty inquiry was to the effect of 'good warranty' or 'full guarantee,'" the center said. "Since the surveyors had been briefed to pursue details such as the length of the warranty and the parts covered, this information was obtained. Many customers, however, do not have the necessary awareness to ensure that the details are fully disclosed before sale."[17]

Even if a used car dealer gives you a warranty or a service contract instead of selling you the car "as is," the terms of the warranty could render it practically worthless, or the dealer may just refuse to honor the warranty.

It's common for many used car dealers to offer you 50–50 split warranties in which you pay for half of any repairs and the dealer pays for half. The catch is that you usually aren't allowed to get the car repaired at the shop of your choice. Instead, the dealer's own mechanics must do the repairs. This is bad news, because the dealer can jack up the cost of repairs to whatever he wants, and make you, in effect, pay 100% of what it would cost you to get the car repaired on your own. Also, the mechanics employed by many used car dealers are not the greatest, and many people report having trouble getting 50–50 repairs performed promptly.

The Safety Factor

A study by Stanford Research Institute of 50 vehicle crashes in which the accidents were caused by probable mechanical defects turned up 11 vehicles that had been recently purchased used cars. The study was done in San Mateo and Santa Clara counties in California.[18]

Unfortunately, California, like many states, doesn't require used cars being sold to undergo a safety inspection. This puts many lives in danger. The Center for Auto Safety, in its survey of used car dealers in Dallas, Cleveland and Washington, found that 15% of used vehicles "are being sold without any inspection of safety-related components."[19]

Mandatory Disclosure of Defects

American consumers unnecessarily pay perhaps over $1 billion annually to repair hidden defects in used cars. Many Americans also pay with their lives for hidden defects. Yet, only one state—Wisconsin—has really tried to do something about the problem.

Used car dealers in Wisconsin must disclose to prospective purchasers whether or not each car has any of 29 possible safety defects and 30 possible other defects, including cracked block or head, leaky radiator, inoperative heater or defroster, or improperly functioning alternator, generator or starter. Cars with defective safety items can't be legally driven in the state, so dealers generally fix them. Dealers also generally fix the other defects or reduce the price of the car.

In addition, each used vehicle at a dealership must carry a window sticker listing, among other things, the asking price, the previous use of the vehicle (privately driven, rental, taxi, etc.), a checkbox if flood-damaged, odometer information required by federal law, and whether the car is being sold with a warranty or "as is" and the terms of any warranty. Big black letters on the window sticker warn prospective purchasers that if there is no warranty they will have to pay the entire cost of all servicing and repair once they purchase the car. (The disclosure statement and window sticker are in Appendix M.)

The impact of these disclosures has been stupendous. A study by the Center for Public Representation found that Wisconsin consumers saved $15.7 million in repair costs in 1976 because of the disclosure law, which went into effect in October 1974.[20] Furthermore, the center estimated it would have cost Wisconsin consumers $40.5 million more in 1976 if they had been forced to pay as much for repairs to used cars as consumers in Minnesota, where there is no disclosure and no safety inspection. Consumers in both states paid about the same price for used cars. In comparison with Iowa, where there is only a safety inspection of used cars, Wisconsin used car buyers saved $5.4 million in repairs, the center said.[21]

Although the disclosure items don't constitute a warranty, dealers often makes repairs free of charge when there is a discrepancy between the disclosure statement and the actual condition of the car.

A more recent study on the effects of the disclosure law, done by two University of Wisconsin professors and released in 1978, found that used car prices since the law went into effect are *lower* in relation to *Blue Book* value than prior to the law.[22] (The *Blue Book* is a used car pricing guide.) This is despite the fact that dealers spend about $15 to inspect each car[23] and fix many defects. Wisconsin used car buyers also save themselves lots of trouble and indirect expenses by seeing to it that defects are repaired before they start to use the car.

The law doesn't cover cars sold by private transaction. As a result, dealers have seen a steep drop in their share of the market, and an increase in the share of private sellers. The Wisconsin Automobile and Truck Dealers Association says dealer share of used car sales in the state dropped from 55.1% before the law went into effect to 33.3% in 1978.[24]

Wisconsin used car buyers have another good thing going for them: a relatively tough state agency that licenses used car dealers, inspects dealerships to make sure they're adhering to the laws and handles consumer complaints (see Chapter 19 for details).

Close behind Wisconsin is the state of Maine. It has a Used Car Information Act which requires used car dealers to give consumers, among other things, a statement "identifying any and all mechanical defects known to the dealer at the time of sale." However, the law doesn't specify that the car be inspected.[25]

Federal Trade Commission Disclosure

The Federal Trade Commission, impressed with the Wisconsin disclosure law, has considered issuing a trade regulation which would require every used car dealer in the nation to disclose what it knows about the mechanical condition of the cars it sells. The proposed regulation would require used car dealers to have a sticker on each car, noting whether each of the 13 systems on the vehicle is "OK," "not OK," or, if no inspection has been performed, "no rating." The systems are engine, fuel, cooling, electrical, brake, steering, suspension, wheels, tires, accessories, frame and body, transmission and driveshaft, and differential. The window sticker would also tell if the car had been flooded or wrecked and give the vehicle's past use (rental car, taxi, etc.), an odometer accuracy statement and the terms of any warranty. The regulation has yet to be promulgated because of political pressure from used car dealers.

Precautions

You should take many precautions before buying a used car. But the most important one is this: Never buy a used car without having a mechanic or diagnostic center go over it before you buy it.

Used car salesmen may try every trick in the book to talk you out of doing this. First, they might try to pacify you with a written warranty or tell you "it's already been thoroughly checked" or assure you that "we'll take care of anything that goes wrong." If you still insist, they might (1) offer the services of their own mechanic; (2) require a nonrefundable deposit; (3) allow an unrealistically short time to have the car looked over; (4) act as if they are insulted because you don't trust them, or (5) reduce the attractiveness of the sale.

If confronted with these tactics, don't buy. The dealer is simply afraid your mechanic will see through the camouflage of "detailing." David Whitgob, former manager of the now-defunct Berkeley (California) Co-op Garage, said over half the used cars given a pre-purchase inspection at the garage had serious enough defects to result in a reduction of the purchase price or a decision not to buy the car.[26]

The mechanical inspection should be done away from the used car lot. If the dealer won't let you take the car off the premises, don't buy.

You should also give the car a thorough inspection yourself and take it for a road test. The chart here, supplied by *Hot Rod* magazine, will give you some pointers.

MR. BADWRENCH

In addition to what's on the chart, be sure to test the heater, defroster and air conditioner (regardless of season), the radio, the locks, the horn, seat adjustments, all lights and seat belts. You should also inspect the tires (including the spare) and look under floor mats for rust.

Used Car Check Chart

Body

Sight down all body panels; check for waves, depressions and matching of all panels. Examine insides of trunk, inner rear and inner front fender panels, underside of entire car, and inspect for body fill, etc.	Quality of paint job, body work and evidence of prior accidents will surface here. Repaired body panels will also show, along with extent of rust and corrosion, as well as evidence of any liquid leakage under car.
Open and close all doors, hood and deck lid.	If doors open too easily or bind, car may have been in a major accident.

Suspension, Steering

Turn steering wheel both ways with car standing still.	Excessive steering wheel play may indicate worn or damaged steering gear. 2-3 inches is maximum.
During road test, find open area and do a series of figure-8 maneuvers.	Listen and feel for dead spots, clunks and squeals from the power steering pump or belt.
On same lot, release wheel completely in mid-turn.	Steering should center itself automatically. If not, box may be worn.
On open, clear road, remove hands from wheel at steady speed and continue driving.	If car abruptly or gradually wanders off its original path more than a few feet in either direction, front end and steering components may be worn or out of line.
Drive several miles over bumpy road surfaces.	Excessive noise, bouncing, jolts, stiffness and violent direction changes may show suspension problems.
Check tire tread wear pattern.	You should see about the same tread depth and wear patterns on all four tires. Lumps and flat spots on tread indicate bad balance and/or alignment.
Pull hard and fast with both hands at top and outside of front tires.	This test will reveal wear in ball joints, tie rod ends and front wheel bearings. If play is evident, the entire assembly should be checked.

Transmission

On stickshift cars, depress clutch pedal and put car in gear. Release to determine pedal position as clutch engages.	Normally a clutch should be adjusted to yield about 1-1½ inches of free play from stop to where throwout bearing begins to touch clutch fingers.
Take off slowly, noting clutch action, and stay in low gear, backing on and off the throttle.	Check for clutch slippage when fully engaged, listen for noises from gears, U-joints and rearend gears.

With automatic cars, start from dead stop, go through ranges manually and automatically, first slow, then fast, up to road speeds.	Listen and feel for smooth transition from gear to gear, no hesitation, no clunking, and beware of ratcheting noises and free-running engine.
Rock car slowly by going from Drive to Reverse.	Listen for slop and wear in universal joints and rear end.

Engine

Before starting, examine exterior of engine from all angles and views.	Check for signs of oil and water leakage, frayed belts, cracked hoses and non-milky coolant in radiator tank.
Start engine and let idle.	Listen for smoothness, no misses, hisses, surges or roughness, and check action and speed of starter.
Accelerate from stop to low-cruise speed; then lift foot from pedal entirely.	Knocking noises from engine when rapidly unloaded can mean bearing and/or piston wear problems.
Accelerate from a slow roll to 50 mph at full throttle.	There should be no hesitation, bucking, popping, missing or backfiring. If present, some tune-up, carburetor or valve work may be needed.
	Check rear of car for smoke to determine condition of rings, valve guides and carburetion system.

Brakes

Make several high-speed stops where road conditions permit.	Pedal action and feel should be identical through three to five stops without sponginess.
Before leaving lot, apply brakes and keep foot down firmly on pedal for 15 to 30 seconds.	If position of brake pedal changes or feel gets soft, there is a fluid leak.
Stop car rapidly from cruise with hands off wheel on open road.	Grabbing, pulling to one side, or grinding noises indicate unevenly worn, contaminated or poorly adjusted brake shoes.

SOURCE: *Hot Rod*, June 1976, p. 100. Reprinted with permission of the publisher.

Here are some further precautions:

1. If you're buying from a dealer, ask to see the odometer statement from the previous owner, which includes the name and address. The dealer is required by law to give you this information. Then call up the previous owner and ask about any mechanical or other problems with the car.

2. Never buy a used car without checking to see if the previous owner or owners failed to take the car back during any recall campaigns. The first step in doing this is to call the National Highway Traffic Safety Administration's toll-free hotline number (see Chapter 19). Give NHTSA the vehicle identification number and the make, model and year of the

car and ask if the car had ever been subject to a recall. If it was, contact a dealer for that make of car or the manufacturer's nearest zone office and have them find out whether or not the particular car was returned for inspection. If the car wasn't inspected, have it done and have any corrections made before you buy the car.

3.   Always buy a used car in broad daylight. Defects, particularly in the body, are easier to hide at night or in artificial light.

4.   Before going to a used car lot, check out the reputation of the dealer with the Better Business Bureau, local consumer protection agency and any local consumer group. Their phone numbers are in the appendixes.

5.   Don't put much faith in any used car dealer who gives you a warranty and doesn't have proper repair facilities. If a dealer says he has an agreement with a local garage to do his work, check out that garage before buying.

6.   Make the dealer fill in the disclosure statement and window sticker in Appendix M, marking off what systems and safety items are "OK" or "not OK" and giving the vehicle's previous use and terms of the warranty.

7.   Make sure any warranty is in writing and includes both parts and labor.

You can pick up additional hints on buying a used car from guides published periodically by *Consumer Reports* and *Consumer Guide*. Also:

Common Sense in Buying a Safe Used Car, U.S. Department of Transportation, free. Write Consumer Information Center, Pueblo, CO 81009.

What To/Not To Buy

To avoid repair problems, Consumers Union advises you to pass up the following four kinds of used cars: (1) those with power-operated gadgets like power windows and seats, because they're "trouble-prone," cost lots to fix and drive up the purchase price as well; (2) convertibles and pillarless hardtops, because they're "the cars most likely to develop rattles and squeaks"; (3) "muscle" cars with big V8 engines and racing stripes, because they've probably had a "hard life"; and (4) "orphans"— models no longer produced—because it's sometimes almost impossible to find parts for them.[27]

There are also specific makes and models you should stay away from if you don't want repair problems. To find out which ones they are as well as which models have the least repair problems, consult the April edition of *Consumer Reports* or the magazine's annual December buying-guide issue, which reprints the previous April's report. The magazine rates 15 areas of each car (16 if there's a manual transmission and clutch) as to frequency of repair on a scale from "much better than average" to "much worse than average." Among the cars receiving very bad repair marks in the April 1980 edition were the 1974–77 AMC Gremlin 6 and Audi 100, the 1977–79 Dodge Sportsman V8 and the 1976–79 Jeep Wagoneer Cherokee V8 (4WD). Among the cars with the very best repair records were the 1977–79 Honda Accord and Mazda GLC, the 1974–79 Mercedes-Benz 240O 4 (diesel) and 300D 5 (diesel) and the 1975–79 Toyota Celica, Corona and Corolla.

For additional help on good and bad used car buys, consult the various used car buying guides. Also, magazines like *Changing Times* and *Motor Trend* occasionally have articles on good used car buys.

One of the best potential bargains, according to most used car experts, is a two-year-old car with no more than 30,000 miles on it. They reason that it has taken its worse depreciation and still has 70% to 80% of its lifetime ahead of it.[28]

Whom to Buy From

There is evidence that you are better off buying a used car from a private seller than from a used car dealer. Pat Goss, a Washington, D.C., area mechanic, frequently inspects used cars for prospective purchasers. He says private sellers usually give prospective buyers an accurate description of their car's ills, whereas dealers typically don't disclose defects.[29] Private sellers also tend to give lower prices than dealers. The only drawback to buying a used car from an individual is that they rarely give warranties.

If you're in the market for a car four years old or less, it's best to buy it from a new car dealer's used car lot than from a used car dealer. You may pay a little more, but new car dealers generally display the cream of the crop that they get as trade-ins and wholesale the rest. New car dealers can also usually provide you with better service.

If you are going to buy from a dealer in just used cars, it might be a good idea—working on the old clout theory—to seek out a dealer who is a member of the National Independent Automobile Dealers Association. If anything goes wrong, you at least have an industry organization you can appeal to for help.

Another source of used cars is the rental car companies. The Hertz Corp., for example, sold more than 50,000 used cars from its rental fleet in 1979.[30] Hertz cars are usually between 9 and 17 months old with 15,000 to 25,000 miles on them.[31]

The disadvantage of buying a used car from a rental car company is that the car may have been driven by 60 people,[32] many of whom may have abused it. On the other hand, there are several advantages. Hertz claims that its cars have been given regular maintenance and washed after every rental. Also, you're given the car's service and maintenance record; you get a 12-month or 12,000-mile limited power train warranty; warranty repairs can be performed at locations throughout the country; the cars have a take-it-or-leave-it price tag so there's no haggling; and you get to borrow the car for eight hours and 50 miles to test-drive it and show it to your mechanic.[33]

To get an idea of how much to pay for a used car, consult one of the used car pricing guidebooks used by the industry. A loan officer at a bank or credit union will usually have one around. Among the more popular ones are the *Red Book Official Used Car Valuation,* the *N.A.D.A. Official Used-Car Guide,* the *Kelley Blue Book Market Record* and the *Black Book Official Used-Car Market Guide.*

Legislation Needed

Many of the problems encountered by consumers with used cars would be solved by the proposed Federal Trade Commission disclosure sticker. But the sticker will never be a reality unless the public pressures U.S. congressmen and senators (see Appendix L for addresses).

Actually, consumers would be better served if each state adopted the Wisconsin disclosure statement and window sticker, with one addition: The disclosure statement should be put on the window too. The Wisconsin law is tougher and it's much easier for state officials rather than federal officials to police used car dealers.

I propose these additional ideas for state or local legislation:

1.   Privately sold used cars should pass a safety inspection.

2.   A state agency should be set up to license and regulate used car dealers. About 16 states now do this.

3.   The sale of used cars "as is" should be prohibited, as is done in places like Kansas, Maryland, Massachusetts, Mississippi and West Virginia.[34]

4.   Warranties that require the buyer to split the repair costs should be outlawed, as in Maryland.[35]

5.   Used car dealers should be required to give power train warranties on certain cars that fall within specified age and price ranges. Puerto Rico, for example, requires power train warranties ranging from one month or 1,000 miles to three months or 3,000 miles if certain criteria are met. The one-month warranty is required if the car is three to six years behind the current model year and the sale price is over $800.[36]

6. Used car dealers should be required to repair a car under warranty within five days, excluding Saturdays, Sundays and holidays, unless parts are unavailable. If the dealer doesn't honor the warranty, a consumer should be able to rescind the contract, recover damages and collect reasonable attorney's fees and costs if he wins a breach of warranty suit in court. This is all part of Maine's Used Car Information Act.[37]

What to Do If Cheated

If you've been cheated by a used car dealer and live in one of the states listed below, there is a state agency which licenses used car dealers and may be able to resolve your complaint (see Appendix H):

California	Kentucky	Nevada	Rhode Island
Florida	Maryland	New York	Tennessee
Georgia	Michigan	Oklahoma	Washington
Hawaii	Nebraska	Pennsylvania	Wisconsin

If the agency is no help or if you live in another state, consult an agency listed in Appendix B.

If your problem is a used car bought from a new car dealer, you may be able to appeal to an AUTOCAP panel (see Appendix H). If you got taken by a member of the National Independent Automobile Dealers Association in California, Georgia, Oregon or Pennsylvania, complain to a UCCAP—Used Car Consumer Action Panel (see Appendix H). In other states, write the association's national headquarters (see Appendix I) and send a copy to your congressman and senators (see Appendix L).

PART TWO

*Getting the Better
of Mr. Badwrench*

14

Avoiding the New Car

Rip-off Blues

I hate to say this, but you've got to be almost a fool or a masochist to buy a new car—unless you have lots of money to burn.

First you must figure that the odds are about one in eleven that you're going to be put on the warranty merry-go-round.[1] Then you must realize that the odds are small that some government agency is going to come to your rescue. Nor will you be able to afford a long legal battle. Can you really afford to lose $5,000 or more of your savings or future earnings on such a poor gamble?

You should certainly stay away from any car that comes with a "limited" warranty. That leaves only American Motors cars, which *Consumer Reports* shows to have an average to much worse than average incidence of repair (the only exception among 1973 to 1977 AMC models is the 1977 Matador V8, which was rated better than average).[2]

I would suggest that until there are more stringent warranty laws or the attitudes of the auto companies change, either keep your old car and fix it up or buy a good late-model used car. By doing the latter, you'll save the brunt of the depreciation (Hertz Corp. figures a new car depreciates 31.5% after the first year and 57% after two years),[3] be able to get parts easier, and be able to have the car serviced by mechanics who've had time to become knowledgeable about it (remember, the newer your car, the less chance you'll be able to find someone who knows how to fix it). You'll also have a better idea of which car to buy based on how they've held up in service over a year or two.

MR. BADWRENCH

I truly believe that most people buy new cars on impulse or to soothe some psychological problem and not because they really need one. Robert P. Mallon, the Tacoma Ford dealer, says a psychologist friend told him new car buyers read more about the car they bought after they've bought it than before in order to rationalize their purchase.[4] Apparently the love affair with a new car doesn't last very long, for Hertz Corp. statistics show that the average domestic-make car is kept only 4.6 years.[5] If you're attracted to all that glitter and gadgetry, heed the words of Glen W. Gibson of Memphis. In a letter to *Motor Trend* magazine he describes that "new" car after you've owned it awhile:

"How often, after the 'new' wore off, did you reach over and caress the crushed velour upholstery, or push down that armrest or scan that overloaded instrument panel for some worthwhile information? How long has it been since you looked around the outside and admired that landau top, or the opera windows, the special wheel covers, the dual-accent body striping or the deluxe bumper group? I'll bet that the hood and the road in front of you are all that you've been aware of since you 'got used' to the car."[6]

Still not convinced? Then look at it this way: Why do you want to buy something you probably can't afford from people you most likely don't trust?

If You Must

If you still need to buy a new car, you can help yourself and humanity by not buying cars made by corporations which have a callous attitude toward death or are skinflints when it comes to honoring their warranties. "It has been my personal experience," says Mark R. Silber, a consumer-oriented attorney, "that the foreign manufacturers and importers have a higher regard for the consumer than do the domestics. In return I hold them in higher esteem, although it is still important to note that even the foreign manufacturers may require a lawsuit to be filed before they will take a car back."[7]

You should also read everything you can about the new cars *before* you buy. Perhaps the best source of information is the annual April car-buying issue of *Consumer Reports*. The magazine rates new cars as to their road handling, comfort and convenience, predicted repair incidence and gas mileage. Cars that deserve buyer preference are singled out. If April seems too long to wait—if you want to be the first in your neighborhood to buy that new model car—then wise up. You might enjoy the envy of the Joneses for a few days, but after that it may be all downhill. The earlier production models often have lots of bugs that need to be worked out, and replacement parts are often hard to come by because of the tremendous need for production parts at the beginning of the model run.

Next, choose your car with repairability as the most important objective. Far too many people make their choice of a new car based mainly on styling and are often sorry afterward. A survey of over 1,300 new car buyers in Pinellas and Pasco counties, Florida, revealed that one out of three thought body style the most important item in their buying decision.[8]

It's important to remember that each new car, aside from its original cost, has what I call a "screw factor" built into it. This includes extra money you'll have to spend sometime in the future because of poor bumper systems, monopoly parts prices, planned obsolescence, poor design hampering inspection and repair, unavailability of component parts and so on. Unfortunately, information on these repair costs is almost nonexistent.

It has been learned, however, that "small is beautiful." The U.S. Department of Transportation says diagnostic center studies show that owners of subcompacts expended 35% less per vehicle for their repairs than the owners of luxury cars, and 24% less than owners of full-size vehicles.[9]

The following free publications will help you figure out projected driving costs:

Cost of Owning and Operating Automobiles and Vans, published by the Federal Highway Administration. Write: Consumer Information Center, Pueblo, CO 81009.

Your Driving Costs. Write: American Automobile Association (see Appendix I).

Choosing a Dealer

Once you've decided which car you would like to buy, choose a dealer with service, not price, as the prime consideration. Lots of dealers—especially some that advertise heavily—can't possibly adequately service all the cars they sell. In fact, I doubt that the average dealer can. In 1979, the average domestic new car dealer sold 333 cars, up from about 98 cars per dealer in 1949.[10] That's an awful lot of cars to be responsible for servicing at one time.

You might be wise to pay an extra $50 or $100 for a car from a dealer who has a good service department and will go to bat for you in warranty disputes. A good way to test a dealership is to go down to the service department in the early morning and ask customers there how they're being treated. Don't buy a car at one dealership because it will give you a good deal and then expect to get warranty service at another dealership. Dealers often need the profits from new car sales to offset warranty losses, so it's usually "no sellee, no servee."

Another good test is to look in the telephone book and see if the dealer has his home telephone number listed. If it's not listed, it means that he's not interested in hearing from dissatisfied customers, so you should avoid buying a car from him.

You should also refuse to buy a car from any dealer who won't do the following:

1. Provide you with a detailed pre-delivery inspection sheet like the Datsun one in Appendix M, signed by the person who performed the inspection, attesting to the fact that he checked everything on the list and that everything is corrected to factory specifications.

2. Agree to give you copies of all warranty repair orders showing what work you requested or what symptoms you complained about.

3. Agree to give you invoices showing what warranty work was done and what parts were replaced.

4. Allow you to take the car, before you accept delivery, to a diagnostic center or to your own mechanic so that it can be properly inspected, and also through a car wash to check for leaks.

Buying the Car

After you've decided what car you want to buy and which dealer you want to buy it from, go into the dealership with a shopping list of exactly the options you want based on your transportation needs. Refuse to be talked into anything else. Just as people tend to make discretionary purchases like potato chips and cookies when they go into a supermarket without a shopping list, so do car buyers get talked into a lot of unnecessary options when they don't have a shopping list. At the car dealership, though, those discretionary purchases could add hundreds of dollars to your bill.

You must stand your ground. For dealers are interested not so much in selling you the base car, but in selling you options, financing and "after sale" gimmicks and getting their hands on your old car to sell. That's where the real money is. "The new car is actually a loss leader," says Raphael "Ray" Cohen, a former Dodge dealer who heads Independent Dealers Dedicated to Action, a militant dealers' group. He says dealers use the new car "as bait" to draw people in, sell them the profitable extras and get their old car. There is such a low profit on new cars that Mr. Cohen says a dealer can sell 1,700 new cars in a year and one-third fewer used cars and make just as much profit on the used cars.[11]

"After-Sale" Items

You really must be on your toes when the salesman tries to sell you "after-sale" items once you've agreed to buy the car. After-sale items are so profitable that an ad by Dana Corp. in a dealer trade journal boasts, "Today you can make almost as much profit on speed controls as you can on cars."[12]

One of the hottest-selling after-sale items is Polyglycoat, a petroleum-based sealant applied to the paint and chrome of cars. An advertisement for the product shows a snarling woman, reminiscent of the Wicked Witch in the *Wizard of Oz,* materializing herself in the midst of a storm and ripping a coat of paint off a rain-drenched car. The headline of the ad says, "Don't let Mother Nature rip you off!"

The headline should read, "Don't let your dealer rip you off," because that's exactly what he'll do if he talks you into buying this sealant. It's outrageously overpriced.

A Polyglycoat Corp. display chart at the 1978 National Automobile Dealers Association convention in San Francisco suggested selling the product for $150, even though, it said, the cost of the treatment to the dealer is only $20 and it will cost him only another $15 for labor to have it applied by hand. The only other expense noted by the display is a $25 commission to the new car salesman, bringing the total cost to the dealer up to $60 and giving him a tidy profit of $90. While this seems quite exorbitant, a Polyglycoat salesman told me that most dealers sell the treatment for more than $150 and make at least $100 for themselves after expenses.

Salesmen will typically ask you if you want Polyglycoat, Bodyglo, Ultra-Seal or some other sealant applied to your car. If you answer no, according to Mr. Cohen, they'll retort with something like "You mean you're going to spend $6,000 on this new car and you're not going to protect the finish?"[13]

There is some debate over whether these products are really necessary. *Money* magazine quoted a paint company spokesman as saying, "It's just a gimmick. It doesn't do any better than a good coat of wax."[14]

Another popular after-sale item is rustproofing, which is usually sold for $135 to $150, giving the dealer an outrageous 70% profit.[15] *Consumer Reports,* based on its 1977 annual questionnaire to readers, concluded, "We can find no reason to recommend rustproofing."[16] The Automobile Protection Association in Montreal said that of 308 motorists selected at random who answered its rustproofing questionnaire, more than 60% said they were dissatisfied with the rustproofing product purchased.[17] One of the biggest problems, according to the Ohio attorney general's office, is the refusal of rustproofing companies to honor their warranties. Consumers have been told that their warranties were invalid for such reasons as they waited too long to complain; the person who applied the stuff did a poor job; the damages weren't extensive enough; or they already had had free work done and only one claim was allowed under the warranty.[18] The Federal Trade Commission has targeted the rustproofing industry for investigation.

Consumer Reports doesn't recommend still another after-sale item: dealer-applied undercoating. The magazine says the rustproofing ability of undercoating is "questionable" and claims that sound-deadening packages, with strategically placed acoustical insulation, are better for keeping out road noises.[19]

Extended Service Contracts

Another after-sale gimmick is the increasingly popular extended service contract. Costing anywhere up to several hundred dollars, these contracts usually extend the warranty to three years or 36,000 miles on certain key components, such as the engine, transmission, differential gears, rear axle, intake manifold, torque converter, driveshaft, etc.

These contracts are potentially a bad deal for several reasons:

1. The companies offering them expect to make a profit. That means they've calculated that chances are you will lose money on the deal.

2. If you buy an American Motors car or purchase your car in Maine, Maryland, Massachusetts, Vermont, West Virginia or Kansas, you already have implied warranty protection for these items. Since it's reasonable for you to assume that these parts will last up to three years or 36,000 miles, there's a good chance, if anything goes wrong with them, that a judge would award you the repair cost.

3. The auto companies offering such coverage may not honor their service contracts any more than they honor their warranties. Also, some of the auto companies are forcing their dealers to use their extended service plans when independent companies might offer a better deal.

4. Many people have gotten burned with these contracts when the companies offering them went out of business.

5. The Federal Trade Commission has started an investigation of the whole service contract business, contending that "there is considerable potential for misleading or cheating customers with respect to contracts' scope of coverage, period of coverage and relative value compared to actuarial risks."[20]

6. If a design defect shows up in any of the parts covered, there's a chance the auto company involved will be pressured into making repairs free of charge.

7. Gregg Sutliff, a Harrisburg Chevrolet dealer, thinks service contracts are a big gyp. He says major mechanical problems rarely occur the first 50,000 miles when you take care of a car properly.[21]

You can get a good idea of the odds on something going wrong with many of the parts covered by the contracts by looking at the frequency of repair charts for past models in the April issue of *Consumer Reports*. One extended warranty firm said it found, based on ten or more claims, that Honda, Austin, Mercury, Chrysler and Oldsmobile models had the lowest average extended warranty costs and Jaguar and Saab had the highest.[22]

It's a good idea before signing an extended service contract to check out the company offering the warranty with your local or state consumer protection agency (see Appendix B) or your state insurance commission (see Appendix F).

Buying a Defect-Free Car

There *are* ways to buy a reasonably defect-free new car. One way is to become a U.S. senator. Cars ordered by such very important persons are frequently given special attention on the assembly line and gone over thoroughly before delivery. If you don't make it to the Senate, you can still buy a relatively defect-free car by being supercautious.

The precautions are slightly different depending on whether you order a car from the factory or buy a car from the dealer's stock.

Let's take buying a car from stock first. With a U.S.-built car, your initial precaution should be to find out from the invoice on what day the car was made. If it was made on Monday or Friday or the last workday before a holiday or the first workday after a holiday, pass it by. There is heavy absenteeism in the auto plants on these days and the usually sloppy standards for assembly are lowered even more.

Next, ask to see the pre-delivery inspection sheet on the car and make sure it was signed by the inspecting mechanic.

If you've gotten this far, visually inspect the car and make sure everything works—horn, air conditioner, etc. Then take the car for a road test. If you find nothing wrong so far, get a deal in writing but don't sign yet. The next step is to have the car thoroughly checked out by a diagnostic center or your own mechanic. This is absolutely essential. An independent expert might catch many things amiss, such as the front end out of alignment, improperly balanced wheels, doors out of alignment, paint imperfections, etc. Also take the car through a car wash to check for leaks.

If no defects are found, buy the car. However, if any defects *are* found, *do not buy the car until the defects have been corrected.* Many car buyers run into serious problems when they find a defect prior to delivery and are promised it will be fixed before they take possession or at the 1,000-mile checkup. Such promises are often part of the "lemon drop" scheme and the car never gets fixed.

Gene R. and Patricia Crook of Redding, California, present a classic example. In 1976 they took a Plymouth van for a test ride prior to purchasing it and noted a noise in the sliding door. The owner of the dealership assured them that the problem would be fixed before they took delivery if they bought the van. They signed the contract, picked up the vehicle four days later and went for another test drive. They heard the same noise. They were then assured it would be fixed at the first service appointment. However, after the third service appointment, it still hadn't been corrected. Then it rained for the first time since they owned the van and they discovered that the noisy door also had a bad leak. After several more trips to the service department, the leak was temporarily patched with stick-in rubber strips while nothing was done about the noise problem. The temporary patch came off after two days of sliding the door open and shut.

On the first anniversary of their purchase, with the door still not fixed, they got a card from Chrysler Corp. saying the company hoped it could continue to serve them now that their warranty had expired. They notified a state agency, which contacted the service department, which told the Crooks to bring their van back in for what was now the seventh time. Neither the noise nor the leak was fixed.

They talked once more to the owner of the dealership, who told them to make a service appointment. When they brought the van in, they were told it would cost them $75 to have the door fixed.[23]

If you've ordered a car from the factory instead of buying one from stock, take similar precautions and don't accept delivery until the car has been checked out and everything corrected. A major mistake made by people who order a car from the factory is not to road-test it before handing over the check and perhaps the old car. Such an omission can lead to disaster. Just ask Dr. and Mrs. Sam W. Banks of Sun City, Arizona, about what they went through over their Dodge Aspen. Mrs. Banks was impressed by the demonstrator model and says she was told by the salesman that her car would drive just as well. The car was put on order and the couple came to pick it up some three months later. They didn't test-drive the car before giving the salesman the payment check. Mrs. Banks drove the new car home and on the way discovered it made a loud "clunk" noise every time she depressed and released the accelerator and at other times as well. The salesman, when contacted, told Mrs. Banks the noise would go away in time. However, it didn't, and numerous trips to the service department failed to correct the problem. When the car had less than 500 miles on it, they considered trading it in, but dropped the idea when they learned they would have to take a $1,200 to $1,400 depreciation loss.[24] They later consulted a lawyer, who told them, ". . . I would . . . be concerned about the amount of time and money that you would have to invest in any litigation against Chrysler. It might be better for you to dispose of the Aspen and take your loss and buy another car. This might sound harsh but it may be the most practical answer."[25]

(Mechanics at Concord Dodge, the California dealership mentioned in Chapter 10, told investigators that Chrysler cars are in such bad shape when they come from the factory that it takes eight hours to prepare them as demonstrator models.[26] Meanwhile, buyers of the company's cars are lucky if the dealer spends two hours preparing them for delivery.)

If you don't have the car thoroughly inspected by an independent mechanic before taking delivery, at least take this precaution: Never pick up or pick out a new car at night or while it's raining, because you might miss some flaws.

Further Reading

Common Sense in Buying a New Car—an excellent pamphlet available free from: Consumer Information Center, Pueblo, CO 81009.

15

How to Get Hassle-Free

Auto Repairs

There *are* ways to take the trauma out of auto repairs without resorting to Valium. These ways may range from learning how to spot a Mr. Badwrench just by the questions he asks or doesn't ask to actually becoming part owner of a repair shop (it's not as farfetched an idea as you might think).

But let's start our search for hassle-free repairs by looking at how to choose a repair shop.

The general rule here is to go to an independent shop that doesn't advertise and is owned by a person who is on the premises and perhaps belongs to a trade organization.

Independents are best because, to paraphrase an old Gerber baby food slogan, auto repairs is their business—their only business. It's not a sideline to selling new cars or gasoline or tires or general merchandise.

The less a repair outfit advertises, probably the more you can trust it. For example, the University of Alabama diagnostic center project found that there were 14 major independent shops in Huntsville, 13 of which advertised in the yellow pages. The one that didn't bother to advertise, according to the center, was "the most reputable independent."[1] Especially avoid shops that advertise specials. "If the deal looks too good, you're going to get it in the rear," warns Douglas Laue, deputy chief of the California Bureau of Automotive Repair.[2]

You want to deal with a shop where the owner is on the premises and is the head mechanic because he's going to be more concerned about the quality of work and the shop's reputation than an absentee owner would be.

It's a good idea to deal with a shop that belongs to a trade organization because you can exert some peer pressure on the shop owner if anything goes wrong. Also, many trade groups do lobbying in Washington and the state capitals and are not anxious to have their images tarnished by irate consumers. If any shop belonging to a trade group does rip you off, complain to your state attorney general's office (see Appendix B) and the U.S. Senate and House consumer subcommittees (see Appendix L). Addresses of some national trade groups are in Appendix I. One trade group that has been highly praised for its consumer protection policies is the Independent Garagemen's Association in Texas. David F. Bragg, chief of the Consumer Protection Division of the Texas attorney general's office, says the organization's "dedication to eradicating fraud in the industry is unmatched."[3]

If you're in need of a specialty shop for work such as transmission, engine or radiator repair, besides looking for an independent shop that doesn't advertise, try to find one that does fleet work as well, perhaps for the city or county government.

The Checklist

Whatever type of repair shop you choose—independent, gas station, new car dealer, tire dealer, franchisee or chain outlet—you should consider these things before entrusting your car to a particular shop:

1. What kind of reputation does it have? Check with the Better Business Bureau, local consumer protection agency and any local consumer groups (see appendixes) and ask about the shop's complaint rate.

2. Has the shop precommitted itself to binding arbitration in case of a dispute? Many members of the Automotive Service Association in Texas have done so.

3. Will the shop give you a written estimate and agree to notify you before exceeding the estimate? This is the only safeguard you have against being shocked by a big repair bill when you come to pick up your car. An estimate form is provided in Appendix M. Make several photocopies and use one each time you get repairs.

4. Will the shop give you a copy of the repair order after you sign it? If not, repairs can be added to your order after you sign and there's no way you can prove you didn't authorize them.

5. Does the shop guarantee its work in writing? Unless your car is getting up in years, you should expect a 90-day or 4,000-mile written

guarantee on both parts and labor. One caveat: The better the guarantee, the greater the likelihood the shop will over-repair to protect itself.

6.   Will the shop give you back your old parts? Without your old parts, it's often hard to prove that a part was replaced unnecessarily.

7.   Will the shop, if it's not sure of what ails your car, test-drive it before and after repairs? A test drive before repairs can help pinpoint the problem, and a test drive afterward will tell if the problem has been corrected.

8.   Does the shop have proper equipment? A shop will usually do a better job if it has the proper equipment and people who know how to use it. However, this isn't always a truism. The Washington Center for the Study of Services gave top marks for equipment to dealers twice as often as to large independents, yet it found that customers were about 50% more likely to be satisfied with repairs performed by the independent shops than with those performed by dealers.[4]

9.   Is the mechanic who is to work on your car certified by the National Institute for Automotive Service Excellence?

10.   Does the shop pay its mechanics by the clock hour and charge by the clock hour?

Playing 20 Questions

It's sometimes possible to tell if a mechanic is going to rip you off merely by the questions he asks you or doesn't ask you. For in order to diagnose your car's troubles properly and avoid unnecessary repairs, it's often essential that a mechanic ask you logical questions.

Gerry Haddon, an automotive editor, thinks the lack of questioning is the reason that so many mechanics get tripped up by undercover car investigations. In an article directed at auto repairmen but also relevant to the general motoring public, he told mechanics, "Insist on getting the facts and you'll defeat the guy, if he's bent on making trouble. . . . Of more importance, you'll be better able to help the person if he's really just a car owner in trouble."

The first question a mechanic should ask you, according to Mr. Haddon, is: "When did you first notice the trouble?" Anyone doing an undercover operation would either have to evade the answer or lie. "There's no way any mechanic in his right mind would accept an explanation such as 'The engine just started missing,' " he said.

If someone gives such an answer, Mr. Haddon told mechanics that "you have to ask the follow-up questions: When did it start to miss? Has any work been done on the engine recently? Were any parts replaced? Could you examine a copy of the work order to determine if there's a connection between the miss and any recent service?"[5]

If the mechanic doesn't ask similar questions, either go elsewhere or take it upon yourself to give the mechanic a complete description of the problem—when it started, under what conditions it occurs and what recent work you've had done in the area. If you do this and also bring along a copy of all recent repair orders, you've got a much better chance of getting a correct diagnosis and repair. "The important thing is for the car owner to take the time to explain symptoms as precisely as possible to the mechanic," says Larry Pipes of the Automobile Club of Missouri.[6]

Thus, don't tell the mechanic you need a tune-up. Instead, tell him specifically that the car is hard to start in the morning, or whatever. Similarly, don't tell the mechanic you're having transmission problems, tell him you're having trouble shifting from second to third gear and when the trouble seems to occur.

You can get a free pamphlet entitled *Communicate with Your Mechanic and Save* by sending a self-addressed stamped envelope to Automotive Information Council, P.O. Box 273, Southfield, MI 48037. Also, the U.S. Government has a 13-page booklet entitled *Car Care and Service* which tells you how to recognize symptoms of common automotive problems and how to work with your mechanic. Send a check or money order for $1 to Consumer Information Center, Pueblo, CO 81009.

Other Precautions

You must take even more precautions when dealing with repair shops and mechanics to avoid being cheated. Here are a few to ponder:

1. When a shop recommends repairs, find out which repairs are absolutely necessary to solve an immediate problem and which are for preventive maintenance purposes. You should do this because shops often recommend repairs that may not be needed for many more miles. Sometimes this can save you money by avoiding an extra labor charge or a breakdown sometime in the future. However, insist that the mechanic give you the facts—the relative merits of replacing now vs. waiting— and let *you* make the decision.

2. Get more than one estimate and opinion, especially on major work. It could save you several hundred dollars.

3. Make sure the shop puts the symptoms you're complaining about on the estimate or repair order. That way, if the symptoms still exist after the repairs, you can prove your car wasn't repaired right. "Not knowing

the condition of the automobile before it was repaired, it is next to impossible to prove that the repair firm operated ethically or not," says the Better Business Division of the Greater Tampa Chamber of Commerce.[7] To be safe, type or write out the symptoms on a piece of paper and hand it to the repair shop, keeping a copy for yourself.

4. Never go into a repair shop and give carte blanche authority to do any repair necessary. Otherwise, you're just asking to get ripped off. Instead, ask the shop to check out the car and let you know what's wrong before proceeding with repairs. The wisdom of this approach was confirmed by the U.S. Department of Transportation's seven-city undercover car survey in 1979. Investigators went into 15 shops, said they had just bought the car and wanted the brakes checked out to see if they were OK. Only one of the shops ended up charging for unnecessary repairs. Investigators then went into 12 shops and gave the same story, but this time they authorized any brake repairs the shops thought necessary. Seven of the 12 shops sold them unnecessary repairs, with unneeded repairs at six of the shops ranging from $50 to $92.[8]

5. Mark your parts. Mechanics frequently tell you they've replaced parts when they really haven't. If you'd like to catch them red-handed at this, do what's recommended by Pat Gormley, a NIASE-certified repairman in the New York City area. He told a *Popular Science* interviewer: "Put a tick mark, with a carpenter's crayon or felt-tipped pen, on things like your alternator, battery, carburetor, master brake cylinder [and] front end components."[9] If your marked part is still on the car after it was supposed to have been replaced, not only will you have a good chance of getting your money back, but also you could send the mechanic to jail.

6. Don't leave your car for repairs early in the morning. Go later in the day when the shop isn't so busy and can spend more time diagnosing your car's ills.

7. If, after repairs, you're not satisfied with the job, complain nicely and don't be abusive. The nicer you are, the better your chance of getting an adjustment.

Always Pay by Credit Card

Always pay your auto repair bill with a credit card. If you've got it, flaunt it. The reason is twofold: (1) It will allow you, if there is a dispute over the bill, to escape a mechanic's lien on your car without having to shell out a cent; and (2) if repairs are done incompetently, fraudulently, unnecessarily or without authorization, you might be able to legally refuse to pay the credit card bill and put the burden on the shop to sue you if it wants the money. This is a far better position to be in than paying cash and then having to sue the shop if things are amiss.

The latter advantage is a result of a federal law, the Fair Credit Billing Act,[10] which allows credit card users to withhold payment for defective merchandise and services under certain conditions.

If the shop honoring the credit card doesn't also issue the credit card, there are two restrictions: (1) The amount of the purchase must exceed $50, and (2) the sale must take place in your home state or within 100 miles of your current address. This means, for example, that these restrictions apply if you pay your bill at a General Motors dealership or an independent shop with a Visa card or MasterCard.

There are no monetary or distance restrictions, however, if the same company that issued the credit card is offering the services. This would include using a Texaco credit card at a Texaco station or a Sears, Roebuck & Co. credit card at a Sears automotive service center. One other instance where there are no monetary or distance restrictions is when the creditor mailed you the advertisement for the particular goods or services you purchased.

The procedures for withholding payment from the credit card issuer will be discussed in Chapter 20.

Preventive Maintenance

Preventive maintenance can't be stressed enough in avoiding the auto repair rip-off. If you religiously follow the maintenance recommendations of your owner's manual—or, better yet, exceed them—you'll avoid lots of breakdowns, not only of your car but of your nervous system. Don't let the extended service intervals of the newer American cars lull you into a false sense of security. "The poor people that go by their printed schedule of maintenance," laments Anthony DeRosa of the Independent Garage Owners Association of Illinois. "It is going to cost them twice as much money."[11]

Consumer-minded mechanic Pat Goss recommends, regardless of what your owner's manual says, changing the oil every 90 days during the summer and every 2,000 miles or 60 days in the winter. You should also change the oil filter either each time or every other time you change the oil, he adds.[12] Following his advice will result in less engine wear and fewer engine problems.

Champion Spark Plug Co., in a 1975–76 survey, found that over 78% of the cars in the U.S. and Canada have undermaintained engines. The company says this is costing billions of dollars in unnecessary fuel bills, poor performance and poor air quality. Incorrect idle and timing was the most frequently neglected item; others included incorrect dwell settings, malfunctioning distributor components and worn spark plugs and plug wires.[13]

The most neglected maintenance chore, according to members of the Automotive Service Councils, Inc., is changing the transmission oil and filter and making necessary minor adjustments to the transmission. This is followed by failure to check battery cables, shock absorbers, headlight aiming, fan belts, radiator hoses and PCV valve.[14] If you buy your gas at self-service stations you should be especially conscious of your maintenance responsibilities. "When the car is not checked by an attendant week after week, things begin to wear out without the owner being aware of it," says the Car Care Council. "By the time the garage mechanic has a chance to see the car, the damage may already have been done."[15]

As mentioned earlier, another important part of preventive maintenance is replacing parts that aren't defective but will be with a little more use. John Goodman, former deputy director of the California Bureau of Automotive Repair, wonders how a person who complains about preventive maintenance repairs on their car "would feel about flying with an airplane [company] whose policy it was to send their airplanes to the maintenance hangar for a check-up only when one of its engines stops running."[16] Remember, when you get things fixed before they break down, you aren't at the mercy of the nearest repair shop and can shop around for the best price and quality.

For more information on preventive maintenance, there are several publications available.

The following two are available free at Shell dealers or by writing Shell Answer Books, P.O. Box 61609, Houston, TX 77208:

The Early Warning Book, Shell Answer Book No. 1. How to spot some car problems before they cost big money.

The Car Fix-Up Book, Shell Answer Book No. 10. Tells how to make your car look better and hold its value longer.

The following publications are available from the U.S. Government by writing Consumer Information Center, Pueblo, CO 81009:

Automotive Rust—Its Causes and Prevention. A free, 4-page fact sheet.

How to Save Gasoline . . . and Money. Free. Tells how to improve gas mileage through proper car maintenance.

Self-Service Gas Up and Go. Tells how to check the oil, tire pressure and fluid levels and to make other simple preventive checks to avoid future repairs. Send check or money order for 75 cents.

The Log Book

By law, private airplanes must carry log books where airplane mechanics must list all maintenance and repairs they have performed.

This is such a sensible idea that you should consider doing it for your car. Carry a log book in your car and list all maintenance and repairs and the date and mileage they were performed. This would give any mechanic an instant history of your car and would better enable him to fix it.

If that idea doesn't appeal to you, at least keep copies of all your repair orders in one place, preferably in some kind of folder, and keep a chart recording the date and mileage when particular maintenance duties were performed and are due to be performed. This is a common procedure in most fleet operations.

You can get a free "Maintenance Record File" by writing "100,000 Miles," Shell Oil Co., P.O. Box 61609, Houston, TX 77208.

Prepare for Emergencies

If you want to avoid expensive mechanical repairs and the body shop–insurance company rip-off, then learn how to handle your car properly in emergencies.

Many a person, for example, has ruined his car engine by driving after the oil pressure light has come on. In such cases, you're supposed to pull off the road and immediately turn off the ignition and not start your car again until you've added oil.[17] On the other hand, many motorists have needlessly gotten stuck by turning off the engine when the alternator light came on. When this happens, it's best to keep driving until you get to a garage or service station, while keeping a watchful eye on the temperature and oil pressure gauges. Once you turn off the engine, you might not be able to get the car started again.[18]

There are several free publications available which tell you how to handle car emergencies. The following can be obtained from the Consumer Information Center, Pueblo, CO 81009:

How to Deal with Motor Vehicle Emergencies. This 20-page booklet tells how to handle emergencies like overheating, brake or steering failure, blowouts and fire.

Battery Hazards. Tips on how to jump-start your car properly and what not to do around your battery.

Two can be obtained from Shell dealers or by writing Shell Answer Books, P.O. Box 61609, Houston, TX 77208:

The Breakdown Book, Shell Answer Book No. 2. Tells you things to carry in your car; how to safely change a tire, etc.

The Foul Weather Driving Book, Shell Answer Book No. 11. Gives safety tips on how to drive in rain, fog and snow and includes what to do if your car starts to hydroplane.

Auto Repair Classes

If you're not ready to give up owning a car and still don't want to be at the mercy of incompetent and corrupt auto repairmen, do as thousands have done and take a course in auto repairs. Even if you don't learn how to repair your car from such classes, you can at least learn how to talk intelligently to an auto mechanic so you don't get ripped off, and be able to do some of the simpler maintenance chores.

Many community colleges, YMCAs and even some new car dealers and independent repairmen offer adult education classes in auto mechanics. For example, in Houston, the Texas Public Interest Research Group sponsors a course on auto repairs and maintenance at the University of Houston, and the Automotive Service Association sponsors classes for women. In San Francisco, residents can take tuition-free auto mechanics classes through the San Francisco Community College District, or, for a negotiable fee, the San Francisco Auto Repair Center will teach you the basics in six weeks.

The do-it-yourself auto repair market is expected to grow dramatically in the coming years, increasing from $4.9 billion in 1976 to $14.1 billion in 1985.[19]

There are scores of books on the market for the do-it-yourself auto mechanic. The following three come out in annual editions: *Basic Car Care Illustrated* (Hearst Corp.), *Chilton's Easy Car Care* (Chilton Book Co.) and *Basic Auto Repair Manual* (Petersen Publishing Co.).

One of the better books for beginners is *Basic Automotive Troubleshooting* by Richard Bean (Petersen Publishing Co.). *Consumer Reports,* while finding a few omissions, called this a "generally well-written, down-to-earth book" with "lots of large, simple, extremely clear drawings that should help even a novice find the proper part in an engine or chassis."[20]

The federal government has two do-it-yourself books available: *The Backyard Mechanic—Volume I* and *The Backyard Mechanic—Volume II.* They're $1.60 each. Send a check or money order to Consumer Information Center, Pueblo, CO 81009.

Don't let lack of equipment or work space deter you from working on your own car. Many cities have fix-it-yourself garages that rent out work bays, supply tools and equipment and often offer technical help.

Co-op Garages

It *is* possible to own your own repair shop and fire any of the mechanics if they turn out to be Mr. Badwrenches. You could organize a cooperative auto repair garage or join one already in existence.

Unfortunately, co-op garages are a risky business and have failed almost everywhere. The chief reasons for failure seem to be bad management, undercapitalization, difficulty in hiring competent people, problems in getting co-op members to do volunteer work and too much unproductive mechanic time because of the lack of an adequate parts inventory.

In fact, there seems to be only one co-op garage in the country that has surmounted most of these problems: Cooperative Auto, Inc., in Ann Arbor, Michigan.

Co-Op Auto, as it's popularly called, in early 1981 had 1,729 members, a paid staff of 20, annual sales of $650,000,[21] and eight career-oriented mechanics with dealership experience and certification from the National Institute for Automotive Service Excellence.

Each of the mechanics specializes in particular cars (Fords, Japanese imports, etc.), which means members always deal with the same mechanic as long as they own a particular car. Each mechanic is responsible for giving estimates and making good on any work he has done wrong. They work on the flat rate system.

Beside repairing cars, Co-Op Auto also provides round-the-clock road service and towing, diagnostic inspections, free shuttle service, do-it-yourself facilities and auto repair classes.

The service department is open only Monday through Thursday from 7:30 a.m. to 6:30 p.m., with most work done by appointment, unless there's an emergency. The other three days of the week are devoted to do-it-yourselfers. For a nominal fee, members are given work space, tools and hoists. Roving mechanics are there to give assistance, and tutoring is available. Parts are often available, since the co-op keeps a large parts inventory. Classes on auto maintenance and repair are held periodically during weekday evenings.

A lifetime membership in the co-op costs $100 per household. Non-members can get their cars repaired at the garage, but they pay more ($30 a flat rate hour vs. $25 in 1981), aren't eligible for many of the services and can't vote for the board of directors.

David Friedrichs, president and general manager of the co-op, attributes part of his organization's success to the fact that board members come from four essential backgrounds: financial, legal, cooperative and consumer advisory.[22] He himself was chief executive of the North American Student Cooperative Organization and managed a YMCA.

217

Co-op garages may be a liberal-radical idea, but Raymond Paavo Arvio, an organizer of the Co-Operative Garage of Rockland County (West Nyack, New York), warns that you can't run a co-op garage solely on idealism. It requires conservative business practices, he says, adding, "You can't operate a business without money."[23]

The Rockland County garage is set up differently from the Ann Arbor one. The shop is open simultaneously for paid and do-it-yourself work, gives a parts discount and charges by the clock hour ($19.50 in 1978). The lifetime household membership fee is $50, and in 1978 there were about 352 members, not all of them active.[24]

Federal funds may be available from the National Bank for Consumer Cooperatives to set up co-op repair garages. If you are going to start one, I'd suggest that you begin with or perhaps concentrate solely on one manufacturer's cars to keep the parts problem to a minimum.

To contact the two co-ops—the only ones I know of in existence—see Appendix I.

VIMOs

Vehicle inspection/maintenance organizations, or VIMOs for short, would take the co-op idea in a different direction. These organizations, which do not yet exist, would charge participating vehicle owners an annual flat fee based on the age, make, model and use of the vehicle. The VIMO would then take complete responsibility for all maintenance and repairs provided that owners brought in their cars for required maintenance and possibly complete periodical diagnostic inspections.

"The VIMO concept," says a National Highway Traffic Safety Administration report, "eliminates the motivation for most of the problems currently causing consumer loss. VIMOs take away the profit motive for selling unneeded repairs (due to package deals or poor diagnosis) because the owner pays the same fee regardless of how many repairs are performed."

VIMOs, adds the report, "take out of the owners' hands most of the responsibility for decisions of when to perform repairs and preventive maintenance" and they maximize profits "by performing repairs and maintenance at correct intervals."[25]

NHTSA says federal funds could be made available to cover loan defaults and operating losses during the first three years of a VIMO's operation and to maintain a repair cost data bank. The agency figures that for a cost of $200 million annually, "almost entirely from the private sector," VIMOs could save consumers about $320 million annually.[26]

An additional benefit that NHTSA might not have considered is that

VIMOs, to maximize their profits, would tend to bring tremendous pressure on automobile manufacturers to recall cars which develop design defects after the warranty period has expired.

Employee Repair Shops

General Mills Inc. has an even more novel approach to the no-rip-off repair garage. The company has established a full-service garage for the use of its employees. It's located adjacent to the employee parking lot at the company's Minneapolis headquarters. Since the people who work at the garage are salaried General Mills employees, there is nothing questionable or unscrupulous about the operation. "If I'm not satisfied, I can go to management to bitch," says Ralph Ferrara, General Mills' manager of employee recreation.

The garage gives a 10% parts and service discount, has specials from time to time, sells gasoline cheaper than elsewhere, provides a free car-starting service in the winter if a car battery runs down while on the parking lot, offers shuttle service to satellite locations and has a car wash as well.

"I like it a lot," says Mr. Ferrara. "It's convenient. It's certainly economical."[27]

Repair Shop Rating Guides

Wouldn't it be wonderful if you could consult a guide that would tell you which repair shops in your area to patronize and which to avoid? Such a guide is a reality in the Washington, D.C., area and is a natural for the rest of the country.

In the summer of 1976, the Washington Center for the Study of Services put out a 136-page, $4.95 magazine called *Checkbook Cars*. It rated some 222 auto repair shops and included ratings as well of body shops, auto insurance companies, tire dealers and diagnostic centers.

The auto repair shops were graded on such criteria as their ability to fix cars right on the first try, having the car ready when promised, letting you know the cost early, courtesy and overall performance. To arrive at these grades, the Washington Center surveyed subscribers of *Consumer Reports* and had them report on their auto repair experiences. Only those shops which 10 or more people had dealt with were used in the report. The ratings for each category were then presented as percentages of those reporting.

Shops were also graded on their complaint rates at the Better Business Bureau and local consumer protection offices (average, higher than average, lower than average, etc.) and their responses to BBB complaints.

Significant differences were found among shops—even among dealers for the same line of car. For example, two Fiat dealers—Lachina's Imported Cars Sales and Service, Inc. in College Park, Maryland, and Manhattan Auto in Fairfax, Virginia—came out looking like day and night. Customers of Lachina's service department gave it high ratings, with 83% saying repairs were right the first time, whereas patrons of Manhattan's service department gave it very poor ratings. In fact, none of Manhattan's 14 customers surveyed had his car fixed right the first time. Also, while there were no complaints at the Better Business Bureau against Lachina's, Manhattan Auto had one of the highest complaint rates.[28]

Checkbook Cars also told how many mechanics each shop had and how many of those were NIASE-certified, rated the equipment and gave the following information for each shop: the hourly rate and whether it was based on flat rate or the clock, any miscellaneous charges, the shop's price index based on sample repair jobs, the guarantee, the types of repairs offered, the types of cars repaired, the hours for making repairs, the appointment policy, forms of payment generally accepted (Master Charge, American Express, etc.) and conveniences offered (rental cars, etc.).

The center has put out rating guides to other services as well, including health care, money (checking accounts, loans, etc.) and home maintenance (roofers, plumbers, etc.), and in 1978 and 1981 put out new ratings on auto repair shops.

Robert M. Krughoff, president of the center, says there appears to be no relation between quality and price. "We have found many excellent shops with low prices and many poor shops with high prices," he says.[29]

Mr. Krughoff, enthusiastic about his idea, is trying to convince Congress to set up grants so that organizations in communities across America can do the same thing. He figures for "less than $5 million" annually, "reliable evaluative data could be developed on all of the major auto repair shops serving the country's large and medium-size metropolitan areas, where half the country's population resides."[30] For less than $2 million more, he says, the ratings could also include TV and appliance repair shops and several types of home maintenance persons such as plumbers, roofers and heating/air conditioning contractors.[31]

The $5 million price tag, he adds, would include printing and distributing 200,000 free copies per year in each area and could be reduced if the reports were sold instead of given away. (The Washington Center gets more than 80% of its income from paid subscriptions and the rest from foundations.)[32]

	Sears, Roebuck & Co. West Lake Dr. (Mont. Mall) Bethesda, Md. 469-4267	Sears, Roebuck & Co. 11259 New Hampshire Ave. Silver Spring, Md. 593-2800	Tysons Auto Clinic 2053 Chain Bridge Rd. Vienna, Va. 893-3716	VOB Limited 4800 Hampden Lane Bethesda, Md. 656-3200
Number of customers who rated shop	20	17	11	29
"Overall Performance" (% of customers rating firm Superior)	25%	35%	73%	7%
"Overall Performance" (% of customers rating firm Adequate or Superior)	60%	82%	100%	54%
"Doing Work Properly on First Try" (% of customers rating firm Adequate or Superior)	65%	60%	100%	36%
"Starting and Completing Work Promptly" (% of customers rating firm Adequate or Superior)	35%	82%	100%	86%
"Letting You Know Cost Early" (% of customers rating firm Adequate or Superior)	80%	88%	100%	89%
"Keeping Costs Down" (% of customers rating firm Adequate or Superior)	65%	87%	91%	50%
Number of complaints on file at local government consumer affairs offices	3	5	0	19
From data reported to NIASE: number of NIASE certified mechanics/total number of mechanics	None on record	None on record	None on record	None on record
A.A.A. has approved (*)			*	
Firm's hourly labor rate	$18.50	$17	$16 to $20	$18
CHECKBOOK recommends for quality (√)	√	√	√	

An abbreviated version of a repair shop rating guide. From *Checkbook Update on Car Repair*, Summer 1978. Reprinted with permission of the publisher.

Mr. Krughoff thinks $5 million is "a bargain price" to pay for what he calls "an effective assault on a problem that is costing American consumers billions of dollars annually." He says the ratings alert consumers to the good shops and force lower-quality shops to either improve or lose business.[33] In San Francisco, the Bay Area Consumers' Checkbook, associated with Mr. Krughoff, was expected to debut in late-1981 with an auto repair/hospital emergency room rating guide.

Several organizations around the country, including the Cincinnati Experience, affiliated with the University of Cincinnati, are interested in the concept but don't have the money to completely carry it out.[34]

If no federal money is made available, city or county governments might consider publishing or helping to finance such rating guides.

For more information, contact Mr. Krughoff (see Appendix I).

A, B, C Shop Rating

A different approach would have the state government give each repair shop which does a minimum volume of business an annual letter rating, such as A, B, C, D, etc., in much the same manner as some states now rate restaurants as to health conditions. The ratings would be based on such criteria as complaints, price, equipment, mechanic competence and perhaps the results of undercover operations. Under the plan, each shop would be required to display its rating conspicuously and a book listing each shop's rating would be distributed statewide each year. About five states would be expected to adopt this program if federal funding were available. NHTSA estimates that such a program would return $8 to consumers for every dollar spent.[35]

In the following two chapters, we will look at two more ways of beating the auto repair rip-off: diagnostic centers which don't do repairs and AAA-approved repair shops.

16

Diagnostic Centers:

Big Brother Is Watching

You, Mr. Badwrench

Imagine being able to go into an auto repair shop knowing beforehand exactly what's wrong with your car, telling the repairman to fix only that and then being able to check up on him to make sure the repairs you requested were done and done right.

A pipe dream? Not for residents of St. Louis and Kansas City, Missouri, and a few other cities where there are auto diagnostic centers independent of repair shops. Indeed, such diagnostic centers offer such promise as aids in avoiding rip-offs, reducing pollution and cutting down on defect-caused accidents that they're being touted as the wave of the future and a cure-all for what ails the auto repair industry.

The University of Alabama's federally funded "Auto Check" diagnostic center project, which ran from March 19, 1975, to June 30, 1976, found that unnecessary repair costs dropped from 38 cents on the dollar at the beginning of the project to 24 cents on the dollar over the life of the project. Unnecessary engine repairs declined from 59 cents out of every dollar to 19 cents and brake repairs from 40 cents to 20 cents.[1]

Singled out by a project report as the most likely cause for the drop in unnecessary repairs was "a realization by the repair industry that the Auto Check participants would learn about the quality of the repair and that inadequate or unnecessary repairs would be brought to their customer's attention."[2]

Overall, at five federal demonstration project sites—Huntsville, Alabama; San Juan, Puerto Rico; Chattanooga, Tennessee; Tucson, Arizona; and Washington, D.C.—a tabulation of vehicles inspected after repairs showed that the incorrect repair rate dropped from about 30% during the first inspection circle to 20% in the second cycle.[3]

Federal officials estimate that a complete diagnostic inspection of your car, if done on an assembly-line basis, would cost about $15.[4] It would take less than a half hour, possibly even less than 20 minutes.[5] If you wanted only a certain component checked, such as your engine or transmission, the cost, of course, would be less.

To see how diagnostic centers unconnected to repair shops function, I paid a visit to such a center in San Francisco, which is operated by the California State Automobile Association—an AAA affiliate. The facility reminded me of a maternity ward in a hospital. A plate-glass window separated the reception room from one of the testing bays. People were pacing back and forth in the reception room waiting for their "babies" to be diagnosed. Through the window, the pacers could see their cars being tested for road speed, road horsepower, carburetion and ignition. Green wavy lines flashed on an oscilloscope. Every once in a while a technician in a white coat, looking every bit like a doctor, would come from the work area into the reception room to confer with the various pacers. I talked with one of those waiting.

"This is the only type of place for a woman like me to come," said Dorothy Fluallen of Oakland, who was there with her ailing 1970 Valiant Duster. "I feel more confident having something like this," she added. Ms. Fluallen had brought her car in because of an ominous noise in the engine. She was anxious to know not only what was wrong with the car, which had 67,000 miles on it, but whether it would pay her to fix it.

After her car had been put through its tests, one of the white-coated "auto doctors" came over. He presented her with a large sheet containing over 100 items which were checked off as either "satisfactory" or "not satisfactory." The sheet also listed specific defects. The "doctor" told her that the car needed a valve job, but that the knocking sound in the engine could be eliminated temporarily with a few minor adjustments. She was also informed that a bunch of minor repairs were needed and that her brakes had 5,000 miles left on them. All in all, the technician estimated the car could be put into shape for a "couple hundred dollars."

About 32 car owners a day use the San Francisco facility. Some, like Ms. Fluallen, go to find out exactly what's ailing their cars. Others typically go to have a new or used car tested before the warranty expires, to get a car checked out before a trip, or to see if there's anything wrong with a used car they're considering buying. Still others bring their cars in annually for a preventive maintenance check.[6]

Because the San Francisco facility isn't set up in assembly-line fashion, it takes about an hour to do an inspection. In early 1981, the charge to AAA members was $33 for most cars and $36 for hard-to-inspect cars. Nonmembers had to pay $38 and $41 respectively. There were also separate tests for engines ($20), emissions ($15.25) and speedometers ($6). The California State Automobile Association also operates a diagnostic center in San Jose and has mobile units which, in early 1981, did a 30-minute engine diagnosis for $20 and a complete under-the-hood maintenance inspection for $5.

The Automobile Club of Missouri has non-repair diagnostic clinics in St. Louis and Kansas City which operate a little differently. Four services are offered: a complete inspection ($32.50 for members and $42.50 for nonmembers in March 1981), system/component inspections (example: engines $25 for members and $32.50 for nonmembers), a recheck after repairs ($1) and an annual state safety inspection ($4.50). A $2 discount on the state inspection fee is given if a full diagnosis is done.

"Literally thousands of consumers . . . have been saved untold thousands of dollars by our service," says the auto club. "Case after case and time after time, we have proved that a nickel and dime part would solve a problem of a $250 repair estimate, made by those without the necessary knowledge or equipment."[7]

Diagnostic/Repair Shops

The diagnostic centers of the two auto clubs are among only a handful of such clinics in the United States which don't do repairs. There are perhaps thousands of others that do perform repairs, but, says Larry A. Pipes of the Automobile Club of Missouri, "Our experience has shown that neither the motoring public nor the automotive repair industry has much confidence in diagnostic clinics that also make repairs and sell parts and other related products."[8]

It seems that whenever undercover operations are conducted on diagnostic centers connected with repair shops, lots of unnecessary repairs are often recommended.

In one study, the Washington Center for the Study of Services in 1976 had a NIASE-certified mechanic rig a full-size 1971 car with a bad spark plug wire and a misaligned front end. The car was then taken through a diagnostic center which was part of the U.S. Government's demonstration project. The two defects were discovered, plus the need for new front side lights and engine and/or transmission mounts.

The car was then taken to seven diagnostic centers connected with repair shops. All found the faulty ignition wire, and those that included alignment in their diagnoses found that flaw as well. However, all seven discovered additional repairs needed that the government center had not. A Market Tire diagnostic center said the car needed $450 worth of repairs and might need another $49.48 worth. Included were $115 for a front brake job, $79.95 to rebuild the carburetor and $55 for shock absorbers. Another Market Tire diagnostic center said the car needed $142.35 worth of repairs and might need another $112.28 worth. A Shell station recommended $159.60 in repairs; a Nationwide Safti-Brake center, $84.30; a Montgomery Ward service center, $42, including $16 for all new ignition wires; and a Chevron and an Exxon station, between $64.60 and $68.50.

The Washington Center said the differences suggested one of three conclusions: "That some diagnosticians are more skilled and observant than others; that some are more prevention oriented than others (more inclined to act early before parts break down); or that some are simply over-selling to stir up business for their repair facilities."

Because of the last possibility, the center recommends that if you do get your car checked at such a center, make sure the staff understands "in no uncertain terms" that you'll be getting the repairs done elsewhere.[9]

To help ensure public confidence in worthy diagnostic clinics that *are* connected with repair shops, the Automobile Club of Southern California, since 1970, has had a program of giving approval to various diagnostic/repair centers. Criteria for approval include reputation, proper equipment, sufficient number of journeymen diagnosticians and mechanics, repair guarantees of 4,000 miles or three months and an agreement by the shop that the auto club has the right to act as final arbitrator in any dispute with a club member.[10]

A Nationwide System

"Diagnostic inspection," says the National Highway Traffic Safety Administration, "has the highest potential for benefit" of any other solution to the auto repair problem, "but the costs are substantial."[11]

NHTSA estimates that there could be mandatory diagnostic inspections —not connected with repair shops—in every state within six years at a cost of $1.8 billion annually. In return, consumers would save $3.3 billion a year, the agency says.[12]

Among the leading advocates of mandatory diagnostic inspections are the volunteers who fully participated in the five federal diagnostic center projects. Over 85% of them thought that mandatory diagnostic inspections were a good idea; 56% were so impressed that they "strongly agreed" with such mandatory inspections.[13]

One idea being considered in Washington is to have Congress enact legislation requiring each state to implement an approved diagnostic inspection program as a condition for receiving federal highway and safety grants. The states would be given the option of either building and operating the facilities themselves, building them and contracting out to have someone else run them, or contracting out to have private enterprise build and run them under state control. Under the proposal, a motorist, regardless of what is found wrong with his car, would be obligated to repair only those safety, emissions or fuel-economy-critical items which failed the inspection.[14]

According to NHTSA, it is "unlikely" that this plan will ever be brought to fruition, "unless there is substantial change in public attitude about auto repair, reasonable financing possibilities [are made available], or there is a nationwide mandatory emissions inspection program to which this remedy can be piggybacked."[15]

If no one salutes that idea, another possibility is to establish state, county or city diagnostic centers in densely populated areas which could be used on either a voluntary or mandatory basis.[16] In fact, the Dade County (Miami), Florida, Division of Consumer Protection wants to set up a consumer diagnostic center but hasn't been able to get the federal backing needed. (Victor Rothe of Hamilton Test Systems says such a diagnostic center in Dade County would need to charge only $10 to $15 in 1980 dollars for a full diagnostic inspection.)[17] Still another idea is to make federal subsidies available to auto clubs or other organizations or businesses to set up voluntary diagnostic inspection services.[18]

The Benefits

Diagnostic inspections not connected with repair shops have a long list of benefits. Let's look at the major ones:

1. *Better and more honest repairs at lower costs.* If you could go into a repair shop knowing exactly what is wrong with your car, you could eliminate faulty diagnosis and unnecessary repairs. And, knowing that the diagnostic center will be rechecking your car after repairs, no shop is likely to say it replaced a part when it didn't.

It's quite conceivable, according to all the studies I've seen, that repair costs could drop by a third with such a diagnostic system. In one study, a group of 100 General Services Administration vehicles were inspected by motor pool personnel using standard motor pool procedures. Another 100 vehicles were inspected at the Washington, D.C., diagnostic inspection demonstration project. The average repair cost of the motor-pool-inspected vehicles was $93.90 vs. $58.65 for the vehicles inspected by the diagnostic center.[19]

2. *Elimination of new car warranty problems.* Each new car should pass a diagnostic inspection before being sold. The diagnostic centers could also check out any problems that crop up during the warranty period and make sure the dealer fixed them correctly. Then too, cars could be inspected just before the end of the warranty period to catch any defects.

3. *Elimination of used car problems.* All used cars offered for sale should undergo diagnostic inspections. This would give potential buyers complete readouts on the condition of the cars. States could require that all safety and emissions problems be corrected before the cars could be sold.

4. *Aid in recalls and defect information.* The Automobile Club of Missouri says its diagnostic clinics have been instrumental in bringing about many factory recall campaigns, including the recall of 6.8 million Chevrolets in 1971 for engine mount problems.[20]

5. *Reduction of pollution and gas usage.* Cars involved in the federal demonstration projects showed an average 22% reduction in hydrocarbons and a 12% reduction in carbon monoxide over the life of the program.[21] Nationwide, it's projected that diagnostic inspections could reduce gasoline consumption by 1.8 billion gallons a year.[22]

6. *Reduction of accidents.* The Alabama diagnostic center project found that the accident rate of Huntsville vehicles inspected at the facility was "significantly lower" than that of vehicles not inspected.[23] For the five projects, the failure rate for having unsound brakes dropped from 34.9% during the first inspection cycle to 14.9% during the last inspection cycle.[24]

7. *Elimination of private garage state inspections.* This would bring more honesty and public support to periodic safety inspections.

8. *Preventive maintenance.* The diagnostic centers could help people decide what parts to replace before they fail.

9. *Aid to do-it-yourselfers.* The Alabama project found that 74% more car owners performed their own brake repairs when they were given diagnostic information.[25]

10. *Pressure on shops to keep their equipment properly calibrated.* By making rechecks after repairs, diagnostic centers can tell which equipment in which shops is out of calibration—something no one else seems to be checking up on. A 1978–79 study done for the Department of Transportation found that only 56% of auto test devices in repair shops give accurate readings. Not one of 36 dynamic wheel balancers tested was accurate. Also inaccurate were 94% of wheel alignment machines; 71% of ball joint testers; 70% to 80% of ammeters, ohmmeters and oscilloscopes; and 42% of tire pressure gauges.[26]

11. *Uncovering of problems that ordinary diagnostic equipment misses.* Mr. Pipes says the Missouri AAA diagnostic equipment is so

sophisticated that it "is providing us important information on the car the shop will not find with their hardware."[27]

12. *Informal mediation in disputes.* Personnel at the demonstration project centers occasionally took on the role of mediator in disputes between consumers and shops.[28] The Auto Club of Missouri, when rechecks show repairs haven't been done properly, calls up the shop and tries to resolve the problem.[29]

13. *Improved law enforcement.* Robert F. Leonard, prosecuting attorney for Genesee County (Flint), Michigan, says if diagnostic centers were plugged into district attorney offices, the nation's DAs would be prosecuting 1,000 auto repair shops a year instead of 100. He foresees the centers thoroughly checking out undercover cars before and after they're sent into repair shops.[30] This procedure has been used sucessfully by the Missouri attorney general's office in cooperation with the Auto Club of Missouri's St. Louis diagnostic center.

14. *Education of repairmen.* Diagnostic center personnel from the Auto Club of Missouri have, upon invitation, gone to a repair shop to show a mechanic how to repair a car properly.[31]

15. *Compilation of information on good and bad shops and cars.* Data on how often individual shops repair a car correctly could be put into a booklet and distributed. Also information on failure rates of various components on individual makes of cars could be distributed in booklet form. Mr. Rothe of Hamilton Test Systems says he can tell from the data collected from Arizona emissions inspections which manufacturers have lousy emissions systems and how much it would cost to fix them.[32]

Despite all these benefits, I'm not convinced that diagnostic centers are the cure-all some claim them to be—at least not for the present.

The major problem such centers seek to alleviate is the inability of most mechanics to diagnose malfunctions correctly. I would much rather see this shortcoming resolved by outlawing the flat rate pay system and spending money on a massive training/apprenticeship program for mechanics. As it now stands, a great many mechanics can't repair a car even after a diagnostic center has told them what's wrong with it.

The Plug-In Revolution

While the feasibility of diagnostic centers is being debated, the auto manufacturers are turning to "on-board" diagnostic systems as the answer to the service problem.

The "on-boards"—as the name implies—are part of the car and plug into special repair shop equipment, which, in turn, tells the mechanic where the problems are. They will be on most of the new generation of cars.

Unfortunately, not everyone is as enthusiastic about this new technology as the auto manufacturers are. "Diagnostic plug-in technology," says the Missouri AAA's Mr. Pipes, "is an unlikely solution for the foreseeable future. Few repair facilities can afford [the equipment that] is currently available because costs may be in the $10,000 to $60,000 range."[33]

Compounding the cost of the equipment is the fact that a different piece of diagnostic equipment is necessary for each make of car. This is because there is no standardization among plug-in units. "Unless something is done about it," says William A. Raftery, president of the Motor and Equipment Manufacturers Association, "we are faced with a situation where conceivably every make and model of vehicle will have a different type of diagnostic connection or umbilical cord."[34] Says repair shop owner Rick Marchitelli: "What is useful on a Volkswagen is of no use on a Chevrolet."[35]

Without standardization, new car dealers—since they generally repair only one line of car—will probably be the only repair facilities able to afford the proper diagnostic equipment to fit the on-board plugs. This might result not only in forcing you to go to dealers for repairs, but also in forcing independent shops out of business.

Other doubts about plug-in technology are expressed by *Motor Trend* magazine, which questions whether the dealers' diagnostic equipment will be any good. Volkswagen, according to the magazine, used on-board diagnostic equipment on its Beetle models but discontinued the system when it brought out the Rabbit largely because dealers were having so much trouble with their in-shop diagnostic equipment.[36]

Mr. Pipes has even more reasons why plug-ins aren't the answer to the service problem. For one thing, he says, they don't provide sufficient detail, such as whether it's the spark plugs that are bad or the spark plug wires. He also points out that there are still lots of parts which can't be plugged into, such as shock absorbers, brakes and steering components.[37]

(For my part, I'd rather see on-board lie detectors on cars. You could hook up the lie detector to the mechanic or service writer to see if he's telling the truth about the repairs he's recommended or done.)

Whatever their shortcomings, on-board diagnostic systems are here to stay, and so it's essential that the federal government standardize all the equipment. It's also necessary for the feds to create standards for non-plug-in diagnostic equipment. Mr. Pipes notes that there are seven or eight front end machines on the market which could all give different readings on the same car.[38] He also says there are at least six manufacturers of headlight aiming devices with "no commonality amongst that equipment."[39]

Non-repair Diagnostic Centers

It's scandalous that the federal government, after spending millions of dollars to set up five diagnostic centers for demonstration purposes, did not see to it that all five would continue to operate after the project was over. In fact, only the University of Alabama in Huntsville continued to do public diagnostic inspection, and even it stopped doing so in November 1980. That leaves only five diagnostic centers that don't do repairs that I know of in the whole U.S.: the four AAA centers and Auto Analysts Inc., a private firm in Denver. In case I have missed some, check the yellow pages of your telephone directory under "Automobile Diagnostic Service." The Connecticut Motor Club, an AAA affiliate, has a diagnostic center in Hamden, but the facility also does repairs.

17

The AAA to the Rescue

What is perhaps the best program to counter the auto repair rip-off involves no legislation and no tax money. It's the American Automobile Association's "Approved Auto Repair Services" program, which is operational in limited areas of the United States and Canada.

Under this scheme, the AA gives its approval to auto repair shops that meet its high standards and agree to abide by any decision the auto club makes when disputes arise between the shop and AAA members.

The plan, operational in such areas as Los Angeles, Washington, D.C., Houston, Miami and Milwaukee, is expected to spread in several years all across the United States.

The program has worked so successfully that mail surveys conducted from January through June 1980 found that 95% of those who had their cars repaired at approved facilities were satisfied with the quality of service and 96% said their car was ready when promised.[1]

Here are the criteria a shop must meet to get AAA approval:

1. *Good community reputation.* Questionnaires are sent to recent service customers picked at random, asking them to rate the shop on performance, efficiency, cleanliness and other matters. Data on the shop's reputation are also gathered from its Dun and Bradstreet report, the Better Business Bureau and consumer protection agencies.

2. *Staff qualifications.* The shop must have a mechanic certified by the National Institute for Automotive Service Excellence or its equivalent for each area of service it provides or agree to obtain such certification. In addition, a garage supervisor must be available during all service hours for member contact and quality control purposes and the facility must have a formal training system for keeping mechanics up to date.

3. *Consumer protection policy.* Along with letting the AAA be final arbitrator of all disputes, the shop must agree to give written estimates,

notify customers before exceeding the estimate by 10%, return replaced parts when requested, offer a 90-day/4,000-mile warranty on parts and workmanship and use only new parts unless authorized to use rebuilt or used parts.

4. *Minimum equipment.* Required, among other things, are an oscilloscope for engine tune-ups and a dynamic wheel balancer.

5. *Minimum services provided.* With the exception of Southern California, where full services must be offered, shops are obliged to provide the following five areas of service: engine tune-ups; minor engine repairs; tire, steering and suspension repairs; brake repairs; and electrical system repairs. If the facility offers major engine repairs, transmission repairs, heating and air conditioning service or a diagnostic lane, it must meet additional manpower and equipment requirements for each area.

6. *Customer service and appearance.* The shop must be clean, tidy and attractive inside and out. Also, waiting rooms must be comfortable and all staff members must be courteous and efficient.

Despite the tough requirements, there's often a long waiting list of garages seeking AAA approval. Repair shops see it as a way of enhancing their prestige and increasing their business.

D. James McDowell, AAA's managing director for automobile engineering and road services, says when complaints arise, the club doesn't concentrate on paperwork, but gets back to the member within one day and resolves all complaints within an average of six working days.[2] Another plus is that the AAA uses what it calls "technically qualified people" to investigate complaints.

If the shop doesn't abide by AAA's rules or refuses to accept the organization's decision in disputes, or if it engages in fraudulent or unethical practices, it can be bounced from the program.

To take advantage of the program, including the written estimate, guarantees and arbitration, you must be an AAA member and identify yourself as such before getting repairs done at an approved shop. See Appendix J for AAA clubs around the country which offer the program.

The British Way

While the American Automobile Association should be highly lauded for its approved repair shop program, the organization's overall auto repair protection activities are minimal when compared to what the Automobile Association (AA) in Great Britain offers its members.

The British AA, among other things, approves auto repair garages, handles consumer complaints, gives free legal advice on automotive matters, inspects used cars prior to purchase, conducts post-crash repair inspections, tests component parts on members' cars, handles new car warranty disputes, forces recalls, road tests and reports on new model cars, tests and reports on parts for the replacement market and runs a diagnostic center.

In fact, the AAA's approved repair shop program, which began in 1975, is based on a similar plan of the British Automobile Association which began in 1968.[3]

The English AA has a "spanner" (wrench) rating system whereby approved shops are permitted to use an AA sign with one, two or three spanners depending on such criteria as the size of the garage and the equipment and services offered. About 4,000 garages are in the program[4] vs. only 966 shops in the U.S. program as of December 31, 1980.[5]

Let's now take a closer look at some of the other consumer protection programs offered by the British organization:

1. *Complaint handling.* The AA receives about 40,000 complaints a year against auto repair shops—both in and out of the approved garage program—and finds that about 50% are wholly justified.[6] "Our success rate in resolving them is 97%," says AA spokesman Peter W. Rushton, "and that applies equally to warranty and other disputes."[7]

2. *Used car and after-accident repair checks.* The AA inspects for a fee about 40,000 cars a year for prospective purchasers and those whose cars have undergone crash repairs.[8] Pre-purchase inspection reports normally include a summary which recommends esssential repairs that should preferably be done by the seller and other desirable repairs which should be carried out at the discretion of the purchaser.[9] The used car inspections are very thorough and often take about two hours. The AA also has a program whereby garages selling used cars can have them inspected by the club. If all faults are rectified before a car is put on sale, it bears a sign, "AA technical services inspected."[10] On post-crash inspections, as mentioned earlier, the AA usually finds only about 20% of the cars wholly satisfactory.[11]

3. *Component testing.* If you've ever wanted to prove that there is a manufacturing defect in a particular component of your car or that a misrepaired part caused an accident, chances are you weren't able to because there was no expert handy to help you prove your case. The AA, since 1966, has had an engineering research unit which carries out, for a fair charge, material testing of failed components in support of members' complaints. A complete metallurgical examination is available in more serious cases. "The result of this work," says the association, "not only enables the technical advisers to successfully pursue members' complaints, but also helps the manufacturers in producing changes to design materials to avoid similar failures." The research unit also tests new automotive products to substantiate claims made by manufacturers.[12]

4. *Valuations.* If members want an honest opinion of how much a car is worth, the association will oblige for a fee.

5. *Road testing.* An engineer, for a price, will road-test a member's car to determine why it isn't running right.

6. *Free legal advice.* The AA hands out free legal advice to members on any legal problem arising out of the use and ownership of motor vehicles in the British Isles, including dealings with repair garages. Sometimes the club will even represent members in court free of charge.

7. *Seal of approval.* Since 1972, the association has awarded a seal of approval to manufacturers whose products have been rigorously tested by staff engineers and found to be satisfactory. Among the products that have received the AA's approval are Ziebart's rustproofing and Monroe Auto Equipment Co.'s shock absorbers.[13]

8. *Testing new cars.* The AA also performs some of the work that Consumers Union is known for in the U.S. It road-tests new model cars and issues reports on them. Manufacturers are notified if anything inherently wrong is found with the cars, and, as a result, modifications are often made.

9. *Diagnostic center.* A diagnostic center, which doesn't do repairs, has been operational in West Bromwich, near Birmingham, since 1972.

Another British motoring organization—the Royal Automobile Club—has some of the same programs as the Automobile Association, including some 1,500 approved general repair shops and about 450 approved body shops.[14] The RAC also handles consumer complaints against repair shops and says it is able to recover through arbitration about £12,000 (about $24,000) annually for members, half of which comes from nonapproved garages.[15]

Maps Are Not Enough

It's time that the American Automobile Association and its affiliates started providing *full* consumer protection services like their British counterpart, and not limit themselves to road service, maps, tour books, traffic information and the like.

The AAA, with over 18 million members representing over a fifth of the privately owned passenger cars in the U.S.,[16] surely has the power and the money to protect its members and the general public as well against the auto industry.

Although they don't publicize it, some AAA clubs, including the California State Automobile Association, which covers Northern California, will try to resolve members' complaints against auto repair shops.

MR. BADWRENCH

If you're a member of the AAA, you should demand that your particular affiliate adopt all the consumer protection services of the British AA. You should also protest the lack of consumer services to the AAA national office (see Appendix I).

PART THREE

*Getting Back at
Mr. Badwrench*

18

Squawking to Auto Repair

Shop Licensing and

Regulatory Authorities

Mr. R of Utica, Michigan, took his car to a repair shop because of a noise in the clutch. After paying $124 for repairs, he drove a few miles and—you guessed it—he heard the same noise as before.

He took the car back to get the repairs done right, but the shop denied it had botched the job and wanted another $175 for what it called "further necessary repairs."

In most states, our Mr. R would have been out of luck with no one to help him disprove the shop's claim. Fortunately, Michigan licenses and regulates auto repair shops. Mr. R simply dialed the toll-free number of the Bureau of Automotive Regulation—the state licensing authority—and asked for help.

The bureau contacted the garage and after much telephone negotiating got both the shop and Mr. R to agree to an inspection of the car by a bureau mechanic with his findings binding on both parties.

The bureau mechanic then disassembled the shop's repair work and found that the problem had been improperly diagnosed and not corrected. The manager agreed with this assessment and had the car repaired right at no additional cost to Mr. R.[1]

Licensing and regulatory control over auto repair shops, as this example shows, is absolutely essential if the consumer is to get an even break.

Licensing not only provides a government agency with authority to handle consumers' complaints, but also enables the government to get rid of shady operators and to deter reprehensible practices through its ability to suspend or revoke the licenses of shops.

As wonderful as shop licensing is, it's a reality in only five states, California, Connecticut, Hawaii, Michigan and New York; three cities, Chicago, Dallas and Washington, D.C.; and two counties—Montgomery and Prince George's counties in Maryland. (In addition, Rhode Island licenses body shops and St. Paul, Minnesota, licenses auto repair shops but can only take action for "misconduct.")

The chief reason why such licensing legislation has not been enacted elsewhere, according to a report by the U.S. Office of Consumer Affairs, is "industry opposition and its effective lobbying."[2] Major opposition usually comes from auto dealers, service station operators, auto manufacturers, oil companies, auto repair trade associations and sometimes mass merchandising chains.

Fortunately for consumers, the lobbyists have been somewhat less successful in defeating what are known as "disclosure laws" or "truth-in-auto-repair laws." These laws usually include your rights to get written estimates, to be notified if the estimate is to be exceeded, to have replaced parts returned to you and to get itemized repair bills stating whether parts installed were used, rebuilt or reconditioned.

These laws are in effect in the jurisdictions mentioned above that license all auto repair shops (with the exception of St. Paul) and in another 18 states, two counties and one city. The states are Alaska, Colorado, Florida, Idaho, Maine, Maryland, Massachusetts, Minnesota, Montana, Nevada, New Hampshire, New Jersey, Ohio, Pennsylvania, Utah, Virginia, Washington and Wisconsin. The counties are Broward and Dade in Florida, and the city is Minneapolis. (In addition, Oregon and Rhode Island have disclosure laws regarding body shops only.)

Your rights in each of these states, cities and counties are detailed in Appendix A, where you'll also find whom to contact if your rights have been violated.

To give you an idea of the merits of licensing auto repair shops, we'll now take an in-depth look at how it's working in California. After that, I'll suggest improvements for making a model auto repair licensing law which you should be lobbying for in your state or local community.

The California Way

Ever since the California Bureau of Automotive Repair began operations in 1972, telephone operators have been kept almost constantly busy during business hours answering calls on the agency's toll-free telephone number.

It's not an easy job. The bureau says people who call about auto repair rip-offs tend to be much more vehement in their anger than they might be over any other type of consumer problem. To some men, says Douglas Laue, deputy chief of the bureau, "it's almost like violating their daughter."[3]

The agency receives over 100,000 calls a year. However, most are either out of its jurisdiction (the bureau can do nothing about incompetence, nor can it do anything about new car warranty beefs or used car problems), are merely requests for information or don't pertain to auto repairs at all.[4]

As a result of some 19,000 auto repair complaints received in the 1979–80 fiscal year, the bureau issued 5,838 notices of violation of the state's Automotive Repair Act, and 58 civil, criminal, and administrative actions were taken.[5] Although the bureau isn't empowered to order restitution, it was able nonetheless to get consumers either adjustments, refunds or rework valued at $916,465 during the fiscal year.[6] That's not inconsequential, especially since the bureau doesn't operate on taxpayers' money. It gets its funds by charging each repair shop $50 a year for a license.

One of the major provisions of the state's Automotive Repair Act which the bureau enforces is that of mandatory written estimates. If a repair shop in California agrees to repair your car, it *must* give you a written estimate when you leave the car[7]—except under certain circumstances such as when you leave your car at the shop before it opens or when the shop must do some disassembling to find out the cause of the problem.[8] Even then you're protected. If you leave your car before opening time, the shop, after inspecting the car, has to prepare a written estimate and then contact you to get either written or oral authorization. If you give an oral authorization, the shop must put on the estimate the name of the person giving consent to repairs, the date, the time consent was given and the telephone number called, if any. If the shop can't give you an estimate right away because it must do some disassembling to find out the cause of the problem, the shop must follow strict guidelines. It must give you a written estimate for the cost of teardown, the cost of parts and labor to replace items that will be destroyed during the teardown (gaskets, seals, etc.) and the cost of reassembly in case you don't want recommended work done. The shop must also tell you beforehand if the car might not work the same after the teardown. Once the teardown is completed, the shop must prepare a written estimate, and, before proceeding with repairs, get your authorization in writing or orally in the manner described above.[9]

As an added measure of protection, California law provides that if the shop doesn't make out a written estimate authorized by you, you don't have to pay the repair bill.[10] This portion of the law has been upheld in at least two court decisions.[11] Also, if the shop goes over the estimate without your authorization, you need pay only the estimated price.[12] If a dispute arises, the burden of proof that the repairs were authorized is always on the repair shop and not on you.[13]

While many repair shop owners grumble about the estimate law, Robert N. Wiens, chief of the bureau, claims it "has been beneficial in attacking the root cause" of what he calls "the five-o'clock fury"[14]—the screaming that goes on when a motorist gets an unexpectedly high repair bill when he comes in at the end of the day to pick up his car.

Other key provisions of the California law are:

1. *Repair orders.* Shops must give you a copy of any document you sign as soon as you sign it.[15] This prevents the shop from adding items to your repair order that you didn't authorize.

2. *Invoice.* You must be given an itemized invoice after repairs are completed. The invoice must list all service work done, including warranty work, and all parts supplied with each part identified separately. The invoice must also inform you if any part installed was used, rebuilt or reconditioned or if any component system contains both new and used, rebuilt or reconditioned parts.[16]

3. *Return of parts.* Shops are required to return parts to you, but only if you ask for them at the time you agree to have the work done. Exempt are parts replaced under warranty or very heavy or very big parts. If you ask beforehand, the shop must let you inspect any large or heavy parts which don't have to be returned.[17]

Besides enforcing these consumer protection measures, the Bureau of Automotive Repair has the power to enact and enforce its own trade regulations. Two such regulations—one involving ball joints and the other transmissions—were mentioned in Chapter 3 and Chapter 5 respectively.

If any of the above laws or regulations are violated, the bureau is empowered to initiate proceedings which could result in the denial, suspension or revocation of a shop's license for doing business. Still other grounds for action against a shop's license are fraud, gross negligence, untrue statements, making false promises to induce someone to have his car repaired, having work done by someone other than the shop or its employees without a customer's knowledge or consent, and any willful departure or disregard of accepted trade standards for good and workmanlike repair.[18]

The laws relating to auto repairs are also enforceable by the state attorney general as well as by district attorneys and the Los Angeles city attorney. They, as a result, often bring civil or criminal charges against shops for violation of the laws. In fact, the bureau works very closely with these law enforcement officials and frequently supplies them with cars to use in undercover work. The bureau has a laboratory where cars are put into perfect shape with various parts marked and photographed. Then documented defects are introduced into the cars. The vehicles are then usually trailered within close range of a suspect shop and driven in by law enforcement agents posing as typical motorists. When repairs are finished, the cars are trailered back to the bureau's laboratory, where any unnecessary or fraudulent repairs are documented. Mr. Laue said in September 1978 that out of 136 undercover runs performed in the previous two years, 92 resulted in confirmed violations.[19] Such undercover runs are quite expensive, costing $1,500 to $1,800 per car,[20] but some of the money is recovered from shops caught violating the law. Besides incriminating corrupt shops, the undercover cars serve another useful purpose which justifies their expense: They strike fear into the hearts of many shop owners, who then refrain from ripping off customers.

Model Law

While California's system of auto repair regulation is good, it's far from ideal. I would suggest the following changes in the California program to come up with a model law that you should lobby for in your state, city or county:

FAST COMPLAINT RESOLUTION

One of my major criticisms of California's Bureau of Automotive Repair is the fact that the toll-free complaint line tries to average only four minutes per call,[21] and as a rule doesn't try to resolve complaints immediately. Instead, the agency sends those with legitimate-sounding beefs a complaint form to be mailed back. This loses a lot of people. For example, in the last half of 1980, 18,147 complaint forms were mailed out and only 9,824 were returned.[22] Mr. Laue figures it would cost an additional $750,000 in operating funds to be able to handle phone-in complaints without written forms.[23] That may seem like a lot of money, but it's only about 5 cents a year per licensed driver.[24]

The lack of a quick response to problems probably had a lot to do with the fact that only 60% of consumers surveyed from July to December 1980 were satisfied with the way the bureau handled their complaint.[25]

In contrast, the Michigan Bureau of Automotive Regulation tries to get the entire story from motorists when they call the toll-free phone number and then calls the shop to get its side of the story. Further investigation or mediation is often done by phone. "We don't believe in willy-nilly sending forms," says James D. Hunsucker, the bureau's administrative assistant, adding that most cases are wrapped up within a week and sometimes within hours. He cautions, however, that the ability to do this will diminish as the number of complaints increases.[26]

NEW AND USED CARS

In a state like California, it's senseless for three separate agencies to handle complaints about auto repair shops, new car warranties and used car repair problems. Since it usually requires mechanical knowledge to investigate and resolve all three types of complaints, one agency should handle all three, as is done in Connecticut.

AUTO INSURANCE COMPANIES

The auto repair bureau should also license auto insurance companies and regulate their repair-related activities.

LICENSING OF MECHANICS

See Chapter 8 for my specific suggestions.

LOCAL OPTION

All repair shops in the state should be required to be licensed, but individual counties or cities should be given the option of running their own licensing programs and having their own regulations as long as they are minimally as stringent as the state regulations.

George Rose, automotive investigator for the Montgomery County, Maryland, Office of Consumer Affairs, lists two major advantages of local licensing over state-run programs:

1. The staff knows many of the merchants personally. Thus, says Mr. Rose, if there's a complaint against a large dealership or repair shop, "I'll know the right person to talk to." He says he'll often direct the consumer to that Mr. Right, who isn't the owner, and the problem will be resolved.

2. There can be an immediate response to problems without what he calls "a lot of paperwork and red tape" associated with state-run programs. There are automotive specialists on Mr. Rose's staff who can check out the car the same day of the complaint to see if the complaint is valid. These specialists may test-drive the car or check out a part to see if it's defective. If the car is in a repair shop in a disassembled state and a dispute arises, a staffer can immediately go to the shop and see what the problem is. Mr. Rose's office also has a gas station under contract to check out the cars of those who register complaints.

Local licensing in Montgomery County has resulted in not only a homey complaint service for consumers, but a major deterrent to fraud as well. With local consumer protection people breathing down their backs, shops are reluctant to try anything unethical. Indeed, the Office of

Consumer Affairs, after nearly four years of licensing, found no fraud when it sent in undercover cars. Also in that time span, no shop lost its license and only one shop was suspended, and that was for two weeks. "Just the fact that someone can lose their license if they don't straighten out is a deterrent," says Mr. Rose.[27]

RESTITUTION

The licensing authority should be able to order a shop to refund money to a consumer as is allowed in Prince George's County, Maryland,[28] and some other jurisdictions.

FINES

As an added deterrent to abusing customers, the licensing authority should have the ability to level fines against shops as is the case in Connecticut,[29] Hawaii[30] and New York.[31]

BONDS

There are two ways bonds can be used to protect consumers. Prince George's County, Maryland, requires that each shop, as a precondition to being issued a license, must post a $2,000 bond with the county. The money can then be used by anyone who wins a court decision against the shop pertaining to services rendered or materials supplied if the shop doesn't pay up.[32] In Connecticut, after a shopowner has been found or convicted of making any false statement as to the condition of any vehicle repaired, he must post a $1,000 bond, which may be forfeited if further violations occur.[33]

FINANCING

I don't believe a licensing program should be financed by charging repair shops for licenses, because the expense could act as a deterrent to opening up new shops. Instead, the funds should come from vehicle license fees. The cost per car would be too low to put a dent in anyone's personal budget, and the savings from an adequately financed program would be enormous. A woman motorist was so ecstatic over what the Michigan Bureau of Automotive Regulation did for her that she wrote: "This is one department I don't mind my tax dollars going to. . . . I was so glad you could come to the 'rescue.' Yours is indeed a fine agency— particularly for [a] single woman like myself."[34] (Actually, the bureau operates on repair shop license fees.)

LABOR RATE

Regulations should be adopted, as discussed in Chapter 2, requiring disclosure of labor rates and methods of computation. Also flat rate manual price fixing should be outlawed.

MR. BADWRENCH

COMMISSIONS

It should be made illegal for any mechanic or service writer to receive a commission on labor or parts. As an alternative, shops should be required to disclose on a conspicuous sign whether service writers or mechanics are paid on a commission basis and details of the arrangement.

RETURN OF REPLACED PARTS

I would eliminate the provision contained in most disclosure laws that requires repair shops to return parts only when the customer asks in advance, and adopt the Michigan law, which requires that shops *must* give back all parts replaced, except those which are too heavy or large and those which must be sent back to the manufacturer or distributor as part of a warranty or exchange agreement. (The Michigan law also allows customers to inspect parts which can't be returned.)[35] "This provision of the law," says Mr. Hunsucker of the Michigan Bureau of Automotive Regulation, "has been an invaluable aid in the investigation of complaints and the disciplining of violators, since it is always preferable to build a case around physical evidence."[36] In short, having the old part handy is essential to proving it was replaced unnecessarily or fraudulently. I would add to the Michigan law a provision requiring shops to keep warranty and exchange parts for five business days after completion of repairs. This is the law in Minnesota[37] and discourages shops from replacing warranty and exchange parts unnecessarily.

WRITTEN ESTIMATES

California's mandatory written estimate law should be followed. Under most other "disclosure" laws, customers may waive their right to written estimates or are entitled to one only if the repair bill is expected to exceed a particular amount, like $15 or $25. Written estimates should be mandatory because they eliminate any misunderstandings and unexpectedly high repair bills, and where they aren't mandatory, shops often intimidate customers who ask for them.

SYMPTOMS

The written estimate or the repair order should include a description of the symptoms. This ensures that what you are complaining about is in writing, which could be very helpful if the symptoms continue to exist after repairs and you need proof that the repairs were not done correctly. This provision is contained in the estimate laws of Montgomery County, Maryland,[38] the District of Columbia[39] and Broward County, Florida.[40]

STORAGE AND OTHER CHARGES

Prior to taking possession of your car, shops should be required, as they are in Dallas,[41] to give you an itemized schedule of charges, including storage and towing fees as well as any other charges not included in the estimate. In addition, certain extraneous charges, such as "miscellaneous shop supplies," should be banned, as is done in Washington, D.C.[42]

COMPLETION DATE

Shops should be required to put the estimated completion date on the repair order. If the car is not ready by the estimated date due to the fault of the shop, you should be entitled to a free loaner car.

GUARANTEES

A major shortcoming of all the licensing and disclosure laws is that not enough attention is paid to guarantees. Ideally, I'd like to see mandatory guarantees for all parts and labor of three months or 3,000 miles except in cases where a car is so shot that repairs can't be guaranteed. As an alternative, shops should be required to post a conspicuous sign and state in bold lettering on the estimate and invoice exactly what the terms of the guarantee are or that there is no guarantee. A Berkeley, California, woman told me she was completely intimidated by a repair shop owner when she inquired about his guarantee. "You have my reputation," he snapped back. I would also make it the law that once a shop accepts your car for repair, it automatically guarantees that the recommended repairs will alleviate the symptoms you're complaining about. Florida is the only state I know of that requires a shop to state its guarantee, if any, on the estimate.[43]

PREVENTIVE MAINTENANCE

Shops should be forced to mark on the estimate those repairs to be performed and parts replaced as part of preventive maintenance. A "PM" notation could be used. The estimated useful life of parts to be replaced should also be put on the estimate or invoice. This will discourage throwing away usable parts before their time.

BINDING ARBITRATION

The licensing agency should have an arbitration service which could be used when both sides agree to abide by the decision of the arbitrator.

GARAGE RATING SYSTEM

The licensing authority should have the ability to rate repair garages as described in Chapter 15.

APPROVED SHOPS

The licensing agency should be able to do as the AAA has done and give its seal of approval to shops that do good work and agree to abide by the agency's decisions in disputes.

MR. BADWRENCH

INVOICE

A model invoice, in addition to what California requires, should have the brand name of parts installed and the name of the mechanic who performed each repair.

MECHANIC'S LIEN

Auto mechanics' ability to keep possession of your car if there is a dispute over the work should be outlawed. As an alternative, I would disallow, as Alaska does,[44] any shop from holding your car if you refuse to pay for any unauthorized repairs, including repairs that exceed the written estimate without your permission. I would also disallow a mechanic's lien on any repairs which failed to alleviate the symptoms described on the estimate. In addition, I would follow the lead of Florida and allow car owners to obtain a bond for release of the car and force the repair shop to sue in order to get its money—risking, if it loses, having to pay the consumer's legal fees and court costs.[45]

19

Getting Your New

Car Warranty Honored

Once new car warranty problems crop up and they're not corrected, you've got many roads to choose from to get restitution. However, before you do anything, first discuss the problem with the service manager, and if that doesn't help, then talk with the owner or general manager of the dealership. Many times problems aren't resolved at the dealership level because they don't come to the attention of those with the clout to do something about them.

If the dealership management is of no help, then get in touch with the auto company's nearest factory service representative. The addresses and phone numbers of representatives are probably in your owner's manual. Try not to bug the factory rep at the end of the month, since some of them work on monthly budgets. Also, don't hesitate to call the district rep even if your car has been out of warranty for a few years. There might be a secret warranty in effect which is available only to those who complain.

A Ford service executive gives these hints on dealing with factory reps: Be very polite; don't come on strong and don't threaten. Say that you have respect for the company but that your car doesn't meet your expectations for their product. Write down the name of the rep you're talking to and refer to him by name; if you're helped by the rep, call back and say thank you or write a thank-you letter—it will help you the next time you've got a complaint.

If the rep has rejected you, then sue (see Chapter 20) or choose one of the following alternatives.

MR. BADWRENCH

Dealer/Manufacturer Licensing Agencies

John W. Lambert of Sacramento, California, bought a 1974 American Motors Jeep Cherokee and soon afterward complained to the dealer about lack of power in the vehicle. The dealer denied that anything was wrong and refused to help. Then, shortly after the warranty expired, the transmission went out. Both American Motors and the dealer refused to fix or replace the transmission, claiming the vehicle was out of warranty.

Mr. Lambert, not accepting this, appealed to the California New Motor Vehicle Board, which licenses new car dealers and auto manufacturers.

The board staff called upon the California Bureau of Automotive Repair, which handles non-warranty auto repair complaints, to inspect the vehicle. The bureau had the Jeep's torque converter taken apart and discovered that a thrust washer designed to separate the converter forward body and the driven turbine had never been installed at the factory. This caused metal-to-metal grinding, sending fine metal particles throughout the torque converter and transmission and damaging the transmission, a bureau report said. The bureau also concluded that a definite loss of power would have resulted from the missing washer.

Armed with this documentation, the New Motor Vehicle Board filed a petition against American Motors and the dealer, accusing them of violating their written warranty and causing Mr. Lambert to suffer a loss through fraud or deceit. The petition required them to appear at a hearing which could lead to their licenses to do business in the state being either suspended or revoked. Prior to any hearing, however, American Motors relented and paid Mr. Lambert $424.92 to cover repairs.[1]

Such a case was unusual for the California New Motor Vehicle Board. Normally a dispute gets settled far before the petition stage. "The board approaches the majority of consumer complaints via the concept of amicable resolution of the problem," says A.E. Yodes, assistant executive secretary. "The board has been very successful in resolving consumer warranty complaints principally by opening lines of communication between either dealership or manufacturer and the consumer, with the board acting as third party uninvolved observer."[2]

California is not unique in having licensing authority over new car dealers which enables a state agency to handle new car warranty disputes. Some 19 other states have similar agencies.

This authority has been so successful where vigorously enforced that one could conclude that state licensing and de-licensing of dealers and auto companies could provide the best solution to the new car warranty problem.

"We've been getting excellent results," says Don Krohn, chief of the dealer section of Wisconsin's Division of Motor Vehicles. With licensing, he says, "we've got a definite handle."

While the primary focus of Wisconsin's dealer complaint section is on new and used car dealer sales practices, the agency can and does become involved in warranty disputes. When they receive a warranty complaint, a meeting is usually set up with the customer, the dealer and one of 12 field investigators. The investigator, usually a former state trooper, will inspect the car to determine if the complaint is bona fide and may check the dealer's records as well. If the problem is beyond the dealer's ability to handle, the complaint section will contact the auto company's district representative. If he doesn't cooperate, they'll talk to a zone official or someone in the main office of the auto company.[3]

The scope and enforcement of dealer-manufacturer licensing laws vary from state to state. Some state licensing agencies can help you get your car repaired or get restitution, while others, like Pennsylvania's Bureau of Professional and Occupational Affairs, can only take action against a dealer's license to do business. Several state agencies, like the California New Motor Vehicle Board and the Arkansas Motor Vehicle Commission, have the power to put an auto manufacturer out of business for not honoring its warranties. However, J.H. Burnside, executive director of the Arkansas commission, says he doubts he would ever deny, revoke or suspend General Motors' license for doing business in Arkansas. "Too many jobs are at stake," he says.[4]

In some states, like Texas, enforcement is lax and dealers control the licensing board. The Texas Motor Vehicle Commission had—at last look —a staff of only two responsible for the whole state.[5] The Texas Public Interest Research Group made a survey of those who complained to the commission during one month in 1977. It found that over a year after having filed complaints, 61% said their cars still hadn't been fixed. The research group said the commission, which decides issues by majority vote, is required by law to be composed of a majority of dealers and has never revoked a dealer's license.[6] Nevertheless, Texans can request a hearing before the commission if they are not satisfied with warranty performance.[7]

See Appendix H for contacting licensing authorities.

Arbitration

Arbitration, long used in management-labor disputes, is now being tried by some of the auto companies to resolve new car warranty disputes.

Ford, first with the concept, has set up Consumer Appeals Boards to cover California, Maryland, North Carolina, New Jersey, Oregon, South Carolina, Virginia, Washington and the District of Columbia. Decisions of the board—composed in each case of two dealers and three public members—are binding on both Ford Motor Co. and its dealers but not on consumers. Between September 1977 and December 31, 1980, the appeals boards decided 3,346 cases. About 40% favored customers, with awards ranging in value from $25 to $3,000. An additional 1,400 cases were resolved prior to board hearings.[8]

If you're having any type of servicing problem with a Ford, Lincoln or Mercury dealer in the areas covered by boards, first contact the Ford Parts and Service Division district office (see your owner's manual), and, if this office is not helpful, contact the appeals board at toll-free (800) 241-8450.

General Motors and Volkswagen are using a different approach. They have set up arbitration programs under the auspices of the Better Business Bureaus in, among other places, Minnesota, Pennsylvania and the Boston, Buffalo, Dallas, Detroit, Houston and San Francisco Bay areas. The programs involve only GM and VW and not their dealers and are limited to defect disputes for vehicles both in and out of warranty (the VW program is restricted to three years or 36,000 miles, whichever is first). A single arbitrator chosen from a pool of volunteers decides each case, and the decision is binding on both parties. Among the arbitrators in Minnesota have been a retired policewoman and the head of Hennepin County's consumer protection agency.

General Motors says that 76% of its cases are settled by mediation. Of 560 cases that went through arbitration by the end of 1980, about one-third favored the consumer to some degree.[9] GM was even forced to take back 13 cars by the end of 1979.[10]

For more information, contact a GM or VW service rep or your nearest Better Business Bureau office (see Appendix E).

Chrysler Corp., not to be outdone, has Customer Satisfaction Arbitration Boards covering the entire country. Each board consists of a Chrysler representative, a dealer, a public representative, a consumer advocate and an independent NIASE-certified mechanic. However, the Chrysler and dealer members don't vote, and a decision of the board is binding on Chrysler and its participating dealers but not on you. Only warranty disputes may be arbitrated. See participating Chrysler dealers for a special mail-in complaint brochure.

In addition to these programs, the Better Business Bureaus in Denver, Des Moines and Milwaukee have an "Autoline" program in which nine auto companies have precommitted themselves to binding arbitration to resolve defect complaints of cars both in and out of warranty. The companies are American Motors, BMW, GM, Jaguar Rover Triumph Inc.,

Nissan (Datsun), Renault, Toyota, Volkswagen and Volvo. Numerous dealers in the three cities have also precommitted themselves to arbitration of any complaint that involves sales or service.

AUTOCAP

If you want to avoid the frustration of getting tossed around by the dealer, the district service rep and the car company, you might consider letting AUTOCAP try its hand at settling the dispute. AUTOCAP stands for Automotive Consumer Action Panel. It was started in 1973 by the National Automobile Dealers Association in an attempt to have dealers clean up their own house.

Over 28 AUTOCAPs have been set up by statewide or local new car dealer associations for informal mediation of disputes between dealers and consumers. You should first try to resolve the problem with someone in authority at the dealership before contacting AUTOCAP (see Appendix H for addresses).

The AUTOCAP staff will contact the dealer, and, if necessary, the factory representative, and try to work out a solution. If you're still not satisfied, the dispute will be submitted to a panel consisting of dealer and public members. The panel members will review the case and give a decision as to what should be done.

In the past, this program had two major shortcomings: (1) Panels often consisted of more dealers than public members, and (2) the decision of the panel was not binding on dealers. Under new NADA rules, panels must have at least 50% public representation and decisions are binding on dealers but not on customers.

AUTOCAP still has one fatal flaw: It can do nothing about many warranty disputes where the problem is with the manufacturer and not the dealer. Only American Motors and the foreign automakers, with the exception of VW and Mercedes-Benz, have agreed to abide by AUTO-CAP decisions.

Written complaints to AUTOCAP should begin with what dealer the complaint is against; the nature of the complaint (warranty, service, new or used car purchase, etc.); the year, make, mileage and date of purchase of your vehicle; and a brief description of the problem and what you have done so far to resolve it.

Since AUTOCAP works basically on individual cases and doesn't stop unethical practices, complaints against dealers involving fraud or violation of laws should be filed with your local or state consumer protection agency (see Appendix B) so that others won't be victimized.

Writing the Auto Execs

If you haven't been able to solve the problem locally, you could try contacting the head of the auto company (see Appendix H for addresses and phone numbers). But don't expect the Big Cheese to understand your problem or to give you a fair hearing. In fact, don't even expect to get through to him. A survey for *Automotive Age* by the Power-Robertson research company showed that 56% of *dealers* surveyed felt that the top auto company management was too far removed to understand even *their* problems.[11] Also, Harry Sadler, a Toronto Chrysler dealer, was quoted by the *Wall Street Journal* as saying, "I can get an audience with His Holiness the Pope more easily than I can with Chrysler executives."[12]

While a letter to an auto executive might be an exercise in futility, you can make it worthwhile by sending copies to various government agencies and officials and to consumer organizations.

People who get such complaints often have to wade through dozens or even hundreds of them at a time, so I suggest that to make things easier on them and to help your cause as well, you type your letter or at least print it. Also have all the necessary information in capsule form at the top of the letter, including exactly what it is you want the executive to do, and then follow that up with details. Don't use abusive or threatening language, but do try to get across the message that if the problem isn't corrected you may have no alternative but to sue. If you know of others with the same problem, you might mention this fact and raise the possibility of a class action suit. A sample letter is given here.

Iva Gott Screwed
365 Consumer Blvd.
Caveat Emptor, NY 00000
Home: 777/777-7777
Work: 777/777-6666

May 2, 1982

Roger B. Smith, Chairman
General Motors Corp.
General Motors Building
Detroit, MI 48202

Dear Mr. Smith:

I am appealing to you for help with a warranty problem which your dealer and Chevrolet zone office have thus far refused to resolve. Here is the pertinent information:

Year, make and model of car: 1982 Chevy Citation
Vehicle identification number: 000000000000
Date purchased: February 2, 1982
Present mileage: 4,503
Description of problem: Engine conks out while driving
Remedy desired: Fix engine or refund purchase price
Dealer's name: Gotcha Motors
Address: 2700 Defect Lane
City, state, zip: Clunkersville, NY 00000
Telephone: 777/777-5555

(Describe problem in more detail here and tell what you've done to get it corrected.)

Sincerely,

Copies to:
National Highway Traffic Safety Administration
Federal Trade Commission
New York State Attorney General's Office
Center for Auto Safety
U.S. Congressman
U.S. Senators

Writing the Directors

If writing the head of the auto company doesn't work and you own an American car, you could try pressuring the car company's "outside" board of directors. Outside directors are those not involved in the day-to-day operations of the company. They're quite often bankers, financiers, industrialists, merchandisers and educators.

You may wish to write a personal letter to just one of the directors or to all of them giving your sob story and pleading for their help.

You might even find you have a little clout with one or more directors. For example, let's say you live in the Detroit area, have a warranty dispute with General Motors and also have an account at the National Bank of Detroit. You could write to Charles T. Fisher III, president of the bank and a GM director, requesting his help. You might even hint that you'll take your bank business elsewhere if he doesn't come through.

If you're a student, teacher or worker at the University of California at Berkeley, California Institute of Technology, State University of New York, University of Michigan, Wayne State University or the University of Wisconsin, there is an auto company director who is either an executive or teacher at your university. Ask for his help.

MR. BADWRENCH

Even your daily newspaper might have a connection with one of the auto company directors. The following three are all on the board of Ford Motor Co.: Franklin D. Murphy, chairman of the executive committee of Times-Mirror Co., publisher of the *Los Angeles Times* and *Newsday;* Marian Sulzberger Heiskell, former director of special activities and board member of the New York Times Co.; and Arjay Miller, former Ford president and a board member of the Washington Post Co. In addition, Jackson W. Tarver, publisher of the *Atlanta Constitution* and the *Atlanta Journal,* is a director of American Motors.

The names and addresses of selected outside directors of GM, Ford, Chrysler and American Motors are in Appendix H.

Get Your Car Recalled

If the auto company refuses to fix your car and the defects are in any way safety-related, you might be able to get your car fixed for free by forcing a recall campaign.

A few similar complaints about a particular car to the National Highway Traffic Safety Administration might start the ball rolling for an investigation. If you live in the continental U.S., except the District of Columbia, you can register your complaint by calling NHTSA's toll-free "hotline" number: (800) 424-9393. In the District of Columbia call 426-0123. Someone will answer the phone if you call between 8:30 a.m. and 5:00 p.m. Eastern Time, Monday through Friday. At all other times your call will be recorded and an operator will call you back. Be prepared to provide the year, make and model of your vehicle, the vehicle identification number (located in the upper left-hand corner of the dash in front of the driver's seat), a brief description of the problem and the mileage on your car. You can also call the hotline to find out if your particular car has been recalled. In such cases, be prepared to give just the year, make, model and VIN number of your vehicle.

If you live in Hawaii or Alaska you can report defects or get recall information by writing: Office of Defects Investigation, NHTSA, 400 7th St. S.W., Washington, DC 20590.

Canadians wishing to get their car recalled should contact:

Director
Road and Motor Vehicle Traffic Safety Branch
Department of Transport
Place de Ville
Ottawa K1A ON5
Tel: (613) 995-6663

I must warn you, however, that the recall approach may not solve your problems and may even add to them. Clarence Ditlow III, director of the Center for Auto Safety, says that you might have to wait up to six months after the recall is announced for your car to be repaired, and dealers may use the recall to sell you unneeded repairs.[13]

It usually takes a long time for recall work to be performed, because of a lack of parts availability or the dealers' reluctance to schedule unprofitable recall repairs.

A classic case is presented by a Chrysler Corp. recall because of defective carburetors that caused various models to stall—sometimes in traffic. The recall was announced in December 1977, and as late as May 24, 1978, many people in the Seattle area still couldn't get anyone to fix their cars and one dealer said he wasn't booking recalled cars until late September.[14] Meanwhile, a Woodbridge, Virginia, man who owned a car involved in the same recall was irate over the fact that when his wife took their 1976 Volare in for recall work she was talked into installing an excess carbon control valve for $139. He found out later that the part was worth anywhere from $2.95 to $12.60, could be installed in no more than 30 minutes and was possibly not even needed.[15]

It's obvious that if recalls are to be an effective way of forcing auto companies to fix defects, corrective legislation is needed. I suggest the following:

1. Auto companies should be required to pay dealers retail labor rates for doing recall checks or repairs and to pay the full price for any dealer administrative work involved. Dealers, in turn, should be required to do recall work before any other work.

2. The auto companies should be given a time limit to have recall parts available even if it means they have to close down their assembly lines.

3. People who paid to have a defect fixed prior to a recall should be fully reimbursed. As it now stands, they usually have to sue in small claims court to get their money back. Such a law would prevent a lot of foot dragging by the auto companies, which now figure that the longer they put off a recall the less it will cost them. This reimbursement problem was encountered by still another person involved in the Chrysler defective carburetor recall. Ms. M of Oxon Hill, Maryland, said she had her 1975 Dodge Dart serviced four times for the problem prior to the recall, costing her $117.55, and was upset that Chrysler refused to reimburse her.[16]

Federal Trade Commission

If you're having trouble getting your warranty honored or if your car is out of warranty and the auto company refuses to correct a design defect not involving safety, contact the FTC (see Appendix B and Chapter 22). The FTC can't help you with your individual complaint, but may use your letter and others like it as a basis for legal action against the auto company.

Environmental Protection Agency

If you've got defect or warranty problems with your emission control system, contact:

Director
Mobile Source Enforcement Division
U.S. Environmental Protection Agency
Washington, DC 20460

Center for Auto Safety

Besides telling NHTSA, the FTC or EPA about your defective car, also tell the Center for Auto Safety (see Appendix C). The center gets about 15,000 complaints a year from motorists and uses this information to pressure NHTSA into launching defect investigations and recalls and to publicize the failure of various auto companies to honor their warranties.

The center doesn't usually help people with their individual complaints, but rest assured it will use the information you provide to good advantage. The center will, however, give individual help to attorneys handling liability or warranty class action suits against auto or tire companies.

The center would also like to hear from you if you've been successful in fighting the auto companies and their dealers in court, by simply complaining or through some novel approach. Especially useful would be instances where you've been able to get some type of adjustment after your warranty expired. This could signify a secret warranty that thousands or even millions of others could benefit from if it were made public.

State Inspection Chiefs

If your new car was delivered to you with a safety defect as well as a state inspection sticker, report the dealer to the state inspection chief. He might order that the defect be fixed promptly and may even take away the dealership's privilege of inspecting its own cars. A list of state inspection chiefs is in Appendix G.

Publicizing Your Lemon

Don't be shy about your defective car and the reluctance of the auto company or dealer to do anything about it. Let as many people know as possible. Just the glare of bad publicity might make the auto company or dealer give in.

One of the more novel ideas in recent years was a "lemonstration." In 1978 about 50 irate owners of various makes of defective cars paraded their vehicles past a stream of auto dealerships along Route 1 between Stamford and Bridgeport, Connecticut. Vickie Huff, a Wilton, Connecticut, housewife, led the parade with a giant 200-pound lemon constructed of wood and cardboard atop her defective Dodge Aspen station wagon. She said several parts of her car, including the transmission, had not worked properly since she had bought the car nearly nine months earlier. Like the others in the parade, she had gotten the runaround when she complained. At the end of the parade, lemonade was served.[17]

There are many other ways to publicize your lemon besides a lemonstration. You could buy an ad in the newspaper. Broadway producer David Merrick put one on the bottom of page 1 of the *New York Times*. It read: "My Chrysler Imperial is a pile of junk. (signed) David Merrick."[18] A Long Beach, California, man, William Lanzone, Jr., succeeded in getting a new vehicle by painting messages on his Chevrolet Blazer announcing to the town that the car was a lemon and what dealer he had bought it from.[19] If your city has an annual auto show, you could take your defective car there and do what Steven Israeloff of Forest Hills, New York, did. He went to the International Auto Show at the New York Coliseum with a sign in the window of his Dodge Challenger reading, "4-sale. Please buy this car. It's a lemon and my Chrysler dealer won't fix it." He proceeded to tell a crowd all the problems he had with the car.[20]

You could also picket the dealer with signs telling about your lemon.

A young San Francisco area woman covered her car with plastic lemons and signs reading "lemon on wheels." She then parked the car in front of the dealer's showroom while she, her small sons and some sympathizers marched up and down the sidewalk. It took three days of picketing, but the dealer gave in and wrote her a refund check for over $4,000.[21] (When trying this tactic, make sure you don't block anyone from entering or leaving the dealership and be sure to call the news media to tell them what you're going to be doing.)

One good way to get a group together to fight a common problem—perhaps in a class action suit—is to put a notice up on a community signboard, like this one I spotted in a California supermarket: "CAR TROUBLE? If you have had crank trouble with your 1976 Buick Regal contact us. . . ."

Still another method of publicizing your problem is to order special license plates which say things like "LEMON," "BAD CAR" or "GM JUNK."

Keep Records

It's very important, in case you might have to file a warranty suit, to keep detailed records of your attempts to get warranty work done, whether successful or unsuccessful. Note the date, mileage, what you complained about and what repairs were performed. If your dealer doesn't supply this information, then you've got to do your own paperwork. Each time you take your car in for warranty repairs, follow it up with a letter to the dealer saying something like: "This is to confirm that I brought my Chevy Chevette to your service department on May 15, 1982, with 4,516 miles on the odometer, because paint was chipping on the left front fender and the car lacked power. I received the car back on May 16, 1982, with the problems not corrected."

It's also wise to take notes of any conversations you may have with dealer personnel or auto company representatives regarding warranty repairs and to immediately send such persons your written version of each conversation. For example, you might write to the service manager: "This is to confirm that on May 30, 1982, you said you would repair the oil leak on my Oldsmobile Cutlass if I brought the car in on June 7, 1982." Attorney Mark Silber suggests the following types of letter be sent to recalcitrant zone reps: "This will confirm you failed to return my call of yesterday's date"; "This will confirm our appointment for such and such a date"; "This will confirm you failed to keep our appointment of such and such a date"; "This will confirm I have called you 19 times and you have still not returned my calls."[22]

Save the Ads

When you buy a new car, save all the brochures about that car as well as the newspaper and magazine ads, and tape-record any radio and TV commercials for the car. These all create a warranty of sorts. If the car doesn't live up to the representations made, you've got yourself a good court case.

Further Reading

The Lemon Book by Ralph Nader, Clarence Ditlow and Joyce Kinnard, $7.95, Caroline House Publishers, Inc., 1980. Advice from the Center for Auto Safety on what best to do when your new car is a lemon.

Down Easter's Lemon Guide, an excellent guide to tactics for getting your warranty honored, with lots of capsulized success stories. Available for $1 from the Maine Bureau of Consumer Protection (see Appendix B).

20

How to Sue Mr. Badwrench Silly

and Other

Slick Legal Maneuvers

Have you ever wanted to squeeze the blood out of an auto repair shop for the frustration it caused you? Zina Zhadan, formerly of Santa Monica, California, did just that in what is possibly the greatest consumer auto repair victory in American history.

In 1977, a Los Angeles Superior Court jury awarded her $5,260 for the value of her car, which a dealer repair shop had taken on a mechanic's lien, and a whopping $90,000 in punitive and exemplary damages because of the hell the dealership put her through.

The story begins on Saturday, May 12, 1973, when Ms. Zhadan, then in her early 20s, couldn't start her 1967 230 SL Mercedes coupe. All she heard was a click and figured her battery was dead. Since she was flying to New York that night, she gave her roommate the car keys to take to Downtown L.A. Motors, a Mercedes dealership. Then on Monday Ms. Zhadan apparently called the dealership and told them to pick up the car. She testified that later she called the dealership four times from New York to find out what the problem was and each time was told that the car hadn't been diagnosed yet. She said she told the shop to store her car until she returned.

When Ms. Zhadan returned to the dealership, she was hit with a $1,957 repair bill and was reportedly shocked and reduced to tears.

In court, the dealership claimed that Ms. Zhadan had authorized—over the phone—a $300 to $500 repair job for a blown head gasket and a possible burned valve. Later, according to the dealership's testimony, she authorized an additional $1,500 for a new short block.

(The shop claimed it had complied with California's estimate law. The law, you may remember, requires that when an estimate is given over the phone, the shop must prepare a written estimate stating the name of the person giving consent to repairs, the date, the time and the phone number of the caller. Ms. Zhadan's lawyer, however, claimed that the dealership altered documents to make it appear this had been done.)

Instead of paying the bill, Ms. Zhadan found her car on the dealer's lot, and, using a spare set of keys, drove off. When she got to Santa Monica, the engine was steaming. She took the car to an independent Mercedes repair shop, which, according to the testimony of the proprietor, found that a radiator water circulating line from the reserve water tank had been welded shut. The proprietor also testified that he got a compression check reading of 120 to 150 pounds (165 is the norm); that in his opinion no valve job had been done despite Ms. Zhadan's being charged for one; that the wrong type of spark plugs had been installed; that the distributor was loose; that the thermostat was missing; that the timing was off; and that the air filter was dirty.

The shop owner freed the water line and did $90 worth of work. Ms. Zhadan then drove home and parked the car outside her apartment. The next morning it was missing. Downtown Motors, using its mechanic's lien power, had taken it.

A law firm filed suit on her behalf, but she had to drop the firm when it wanted $500 in legal fees which she didn't have. She then got David Glickman (no relation to the author), a top-notch Beverly Hills trial lawyer, to accept the case on a 40% contingency fee, meaning he would get 40% of her winnings.

Although she didn't have to pay legal fees, Ms. Zhadan was still stretched financially. She had to continue making monthly loan and insurance payments on her Mercedes, and she was forced to lease a Datsun and pay for that as well. Even with a second job, she fell behind in her credit obligations and ruined her credit rating.

The case first came to trial in mid-1975 when a jury awarded Ms. Zhadan the value of her car plus $175,000 in punitive damages. Downtown Motors appealed what it claimed was an excessive award. The state court of appeals agreed. However, instead of lowering the award, the court ordered a new trial, which resulted in the $90,000 punitive damages award. Attorney Glickman raised his contingency fee to 50% to handle the second trial. He says he spent about $7,500 out of his own pocket for court costs during the two trials and the appeal and spent some 400 hours on the case. He usually bills at $100 per hour.[1]

Attorney Glickman sees great potential for other lawyers in handling punitive damage auto repair cases on a contingency basis.[2] I agree.

State Recovery Laws

Few people realize it, but over 40 states have laws that sometimes entitle you, if you win certain private consumer suits, to get mandatory attorney's fees and costs; to get a minimum recovery, in some cases, of $25 to $500; and, in some instances, to get double or triple punitive damages. Let's take a look at such laws in Texas, Michigan and New Jersey:

TEXAS

Under the state's Deceptive Trade Practices and Consumer Protection Act, you have to prove one of the following to automatically get two times the amount of actual damages up to $1,000 plus attorney's fees and costs:

1. That the repair shop or business engaged in an unlawful deceptive trade practice, such as, but not limited to:

(a) Represented that work or services were performed on, or parts replaced in, goods when the work or services were not performed or the parts replaced.

(b) Knowingly made false or misleading statements of fact concerning the need for parts, replacement or repair service.

(c) Represented that goods were original or new when they were deteriorated, reconditioned, reclaimed, used or secondhand.

(d) Disparaged the goods, services or business of another by false or misleading representation of fact.

(e) Advertised goods or services with intent not to sell them as advertised.

(f) Advertised goods or services with intent not to supply a reasonable expectable public demand, unless the advertisements disclosed a limitation of quantity.

(g) Represented that goods or services were of a particular standard, quality or grade, or that goods were of a particular style or model, if they were of another.

2. There was a known breach of an express or implied warranty.

3. Any "unconscionable" action or course of action by any person.

4. Violation of the rules or regulations of the State Board of Insurance or Article 21.21 of the Texas Insurance Code, which pertains to unfair practices regarding auto insurance policies.

If it's found that the repair shop or business "knowingly" did any of the above, you could be awarded triple the actual damages.

Before you get any ideas of running down to the courthouse and filing suit without just cause, be forewarned that the act allows the other side to collect reasonable attorney's fees and court costs if the court finds your suit groundless and brought in bad faith or for the purposes of harassment.[3]

MICHIGAN

If a business engages in an unfair trade practice under the state's Consumer Protection Act, such as charging a grossly excessive price over what others charge, you're entitled, if you win a suit, to actual damages or $250, whichever is greater, and, at the court's discretion, to attorney's fees as well.[4] If an auto repair shop violates the state's Motor Vehicle Service and Repair Act or any regulation issued under it (see Appendix A), you're entitled to damages plus reasonable attorney's fees and costs. If there has been a "willful and flagrant" violation of the act, you're entitled to double the damages plus reasonable attorney's fees and costs.[5]

NEW JERSEY

You're entitled to threefold damages, reasonable attorney's fees, filing fees and reasonable costs of the suit if you successfully sue any commercial operation which, in connection with the sale or advertisement of any merchandise, engages in deception, fraud, false pretense, false promise, or misrepresentation or knowingly conceals, suppresses or omits any material fact with the intent that others will rely on such concealment, suppression or omission.[6]

Among the states in which attorney's fees are automatically awarded to consumers who win suits for unfair or deceptive trade practices, similar to those outlined for Texas, are Florida, Idaho, Louisiana, Maine, Mississippi and South Carolina.[7]

Contact your local or state consumer protection agency for details on such private action suits (see Appendix B).

New Cars—Rejecting Ownership

Mrs. Alfred J. Smith of New Jersey got her brand-new 1966 Chevrolet Biscayne only seven-tenths of a mile from the dealer's showroom when the car began stalling. After a little more than 1 mile away, the car couldn't be operated in "drive" gear. She telephoned her husband, who came and drove the car home in "low-low" gear. At home, Mr. Smith made two telephone calls: one to the bank to stop payment on the check for the car and the other to the dealer, saying he was rejecting the car.

The next day the dealership came and got the car. The dealer tried to soothe Mr. Smith by replacing the transmission, but he continued to reject the car. The dealer sued for the purchase price—less a $124 deposit Mr. Smith had put on the car—plus incidental damages. Mr. Smith countersued for the deposit plus incidental damages. The New Jersey Superior Court, in a landmark decision, ruled in Mr. Smith's favor and awarded him back his deposit. The court's decision, in part, said:

"Mr. Smith sought to purchase a new car. He assumed what every new car buyer has a right to assume and, indeed, has been led to assume by the high powered advertising techniques of the auto industry—that his new car, with the exception of very minor adjustments, would be mechanically new and factory furnished, operate perfectly, and be free of substantial defects. The vehicle delivered to Mr. Smith did not measure up to these representations."[8]

Mr. Smith's tactic of rejecting ownership is something you should seriously consider if a major defect crops up between taking delivery of your new car and getting it home. This puts the dealer, not you, on the defensive, since it's up to him to prove that the car conformed to what you bargained for. You might be able to use this ploy even after a day or two of using the car as long as you make no improvement to the car such as installing a tape deck or a CB radio. Such additions signify acceptance. The rejection must come prior to your having had a reasonable opportunity to inspect the car. In Mr. Smith's case, the court said the dealer's privilege of a "spin around the block" did not represent a "reasonable opportunity to inspect" the car.[9] It's also important to notify the dealer of your rejection as soon as you become aware that the car is defective.

Revoking Acceptance

Once you show signs of accepting a new car or give the dealer a chance to fix the defects, you can still get your money back or another car through a legal ploy known as "revocation of acceptance." However, in this case, the burden of proof is on you to show that there is a serious problem with the car that substantially impairs its value.

A person who successfully used this tactic was Angelo J. Asciolla of New Hampshire. He picked up his new $5,209 1973 Oldsmobile Delta 88 sedan on December 15, 1972, and the next day left for Wisconsin. A little more than three weeks later he found that he could no longer shift the gear lever either forward or backward. An Oldsmobile dealer in Wisconsin found deposits of ice in the transmission oil pan and 3 inches of water in the trunk wells plus considerable rust on the brake drums, exhaust pipe and other areas under the car. Also, the transmission oil filter was covered with ice and the forward clutch of the transmission at the pump hub had a split Teflon ring. Mr. Asciolla immediately notified his dealer in New Hampshire and General Motors as well that he wanted the car exchanged for a new one. They refused and instead offered him a new transmission. He turned that down and sued for his money back, contending he had no faith in the car. The court ruled that he was entitled only to a new transmission and consequential damages. He appealed. The New Hampshire Supreme Court agreed that his revocation of acceptance was justified and sent the case back to the lower court.[10] Finally, more than five years after the transmission problem occurred, he was awarded the cost of the car plus damages.[11]

Even if you've had your car for several months and allow the dealer to fix it, you can still revoke acceptance if the repairs are not to your satisfaction. Ronald Pavesi, a New Jersey schoolteacher, successfully did this.

He bought a new 1975 Ford on October 5, 1975, and didn't file suit until 17 months later. He had picked up the car at night and therefore didn't notice until the next day that some paint was chipped in front. He then demanded his money back or a new car. The dealer refused and got him to agree to repairs. The dealer's body shop manager noticed a slight difference in color between the front and rear ends and concluded the car as shipped by Ford had a replacement front end. The front end was then stripped down to the metal and repainted.

After several weeks, however, further chipping and peeling occurred. Mr. Pavesi again demanded recision of the sale, but the dealer talked him into giving the shop another chance to repair the car. This time the whole car was stripped and painted. It didn't work. By July 1976, paint could be peeled off by hand. Mr. Pavesi asked for his money back, less payment for his using the car, or a new vehicle. The dealer refused and this time sandblasted down to the metal and again repainted the whole car.

The paint adhered, but the sandblasting damaged other parts of the car, including the upholstery. For several months Mr. Pavesi tried to get an adjustment. He was offered credit toward a new car, but considered the offer inadequate.

He sued and won. A New Jersey Superior Court judge ruled he was entitled to the return of his purchase price plus interest, less 6½ cents for every mile he had used the car.[12]

Even if your car has no defects per se, you could still sue to revoke acceptance if the car fails to live up to its implied warranty of merchantability for a particular use. Retired Admiral J.D. Blitch won such a suit.

He purchased a 1976 Buick from a California dealer after telling the salesman he specifically wanted the car to tow a trailer. When it failed to do that to his satisfaction, he sued the dealer and General Motors. The judge awarded him the full cost of the car, to be paid by the dealer, plus $2,500 in attorney's fees and $7,500 in punitive damages to be paid by GM.[13]

Stop Sweatin'—Just Threaten

If you don't have the money or persistence to give up possession of your car while fighting in court for what could be several years, fear not. Sometimes even the threat of revoking acceptance can get results.

The Maine Bureau of Consumer Protection tells the story of Doris Pelletier of Waterville, Maine. While she was driving to work after a few days of owning her new 1977 car, the steering wheel suddenly locked. She took the car back to the dealer five times in the ensuing four weeks, but the problem wasn't corrected. After the steering wheel locked in traffic with her five children in the car, Mrs. Pelletier returned the car to the dealer, stripped off the license plates, canceled her insurance, told the bank she'd make no more payments until the dispute was settled and gave the dealer seven days to replace the car or return her purchase price. She threatened to hire an attorney if her demands weren't heeded. The day before she was to hire an attorney, the dealer succumbed and agreed to give her a brand-new replacement car. Mrs. Pelletier had to pay a little extra for added options, but she did get a new car.[14]

There is still more evidence that just threatening to get a lawyer will work. *Automotive Age,* a dealer-oriented magazine, reported in 1978 that out of 10 known cases in which consumers went to court to get a refund for a lemon, dealers lost nine. The magazine said that "the manufacturers and NADA [National Automobile Dealers Association] are in agreement—the best way for a dealer to handle a demand for a refund is to settle out of court, by fixing or replacing the car." A NADA attorney, according to the magazine, advises dealers faced with a warranty suit to give in, give a refund and try to recoup part of the loss by reselling the car as a used car.[15]

A 1980 court decision in New Jersey could give added impetus to your threats to sue. Acting under the Magnuson-Moss Warranty Act (see Chapter 10), which says a court "may" award attorney's fees in a successful warranty suit, state superior court judge David Furman ordered Ford Motor Co. to pay attorney Mark Silber $5,165 in attorney's fees. The judge also ruled that the dealer had to pay the car owner the $7,800 he had paid for a 1978 Mercury Marquis less an amount for depreciation and miles driven. The car owner had taken the car back to the dealer five or more times because of stalling or hesitation without the problem's being resolved.[16]

If you financed your car through the dealer, a threat to sue is likely to get action. That's because, as discussed in Chapter 10, you can legally stop car payments until the dispute is settled—as long as the warranty is still in effect.

Small Claims Courts

After a fire in his Chevrolet Impala, Charles Gegner of Chicago notified Allstate Insurance Co., his insurer, who authorized that the car be towed to a particular Chevrolet dealer. The dealer repaired the car in such a bad manner, according to Mr. Gegner, that it was almost impossible to keep the car running. Allstate refused to pay any more money, he said, and a company agent implied that he had intentionally set the fire.

Disgusted, Mr. Gegner sued Allstate in Cook County Pro-Se Court, which handles small claims up to $300 and where it's not necessary to have a lawyer. Allstate didn't even bother to contest the case and Mr. Gegner won a $126 settlement.[17]

Suing in small claims court, as Mr. Gegner did, is an ideal way of getting back the money that the automotive industry has gypped you out of—without going to the expense of hiring a lawyer. The amount of a small claims court suit can range from $150 all the way up to $3,000, depending on what state or locality you live in. Also, justice is speedy in such courts. While it might take a year or more for a case to be heard in regular court, it may take less than a month in small claims court. In Washington, D.C., for example, your case is likely to be heard within two weeks after you file suit.

While small claims courts differ somewhat in their names, filing fees and certain procedures, we can still get a rough idea of how the system works by looking at an imaginary case in California.

Let's say that your car is difficult to start and you take it to Joe Shade-tree's Garage. Joe does $100 worth of repairs, but you find, after paying the bill, that the car is not only still hard to start but has new problems. You return the car to Joe, and he says you need an extra $100 worth of work. Believing him to be not only incompetent but a shyster as well, you take your car to Honest Moe's Garage. Honest Moe immediately finds the problem, fixes it for $25 and then charges you another $50 to correct the botch job done by Joe Shadetree. You call up Joe and demand your $100 back plus the $50 it cost to correct his mistakes. Joe tells you to go lie down on the freeway.

You decide to sue. You look in the phone book under your county government listing and search for the heading "Courts." Under that, you find the municipal court or justice court for your area and under that the phone number of small claims court. You call and talk to the small claims clerk to find out what hours you can come in to file your claim (you must file in person in California). The clerk asks you if the party you're suing is located in the county. It is. This is important because generally, in California, if the company or person you are suing is located in a county other than where you live, you will have to file suit in that other county. A possible exception would be suing someone from another county who damaged your car while in your county.

You must also be 18 years or older to file suit in California. If you're under that age, a parent or guardian must file suit for you. You don't have to be a citizen of the United States in order to sue. If you don't speak English, the court may help you get an interpreter.

You now go off to see the clerk, and he gives you a form to fill out and requires that you pay a $2 filing fee. On the form, you must include the name and address of each person or company you are suing. If, for example, this had been an auto warranty case, you might sue both the dealer and the auto manufacturer. Be sure to fill out the full legal name of the company or companies you're suing or your suit may be no good. While the shop you're suing may be called Joe Shadetree's Garage, its legal name might be something completely different, like Shadetree Auto Repairs, Inc. The clerk can help you with this. (New York State in 1979 passed a precedent-setting law which requires companies to pay up even if you don't use their technically correct names.)[18]

You'll also have to fill out how much money you're suing for. You can sue only for money in small claims court. The maximum amount you can sue for in California is $750. If you're out more than that amount, you have a choice of either settling for $750 or hiring a lawyer and suing in regular court.

Once the form is filled out, the clerk will tell you on what date your trial is scheduled and will prepare an order to be served on Joe Shadetree's Garage. You can have the clerk send the order by certified mail at $2 per defendant or you can have a marshal, sheriff or constable serve the order at a slightly higher fee. You can also get anyone 18 or older not involved in your case to serve the order. If you would like someone to be a witness in your case and you're not sure he will show up voluntarily, you can ask the clerk to issue a subpoena to him. In your circumstances, you might want to subpoena Honest Moe to testify on your behalf. Honest Moe can demand a fee of $12 a day and 20 cents a mile, one-way, which you will have to pay if you lose. If you win, Joe Shadetree will have to pay the fee as part of the court costs.

Chances are your trial will be held within 40 days. On the trial date, bring with you all relevant documents, such as repair estimates and invoices from both shops. Also bring all witnesses with you.

If Joe Shadetree decides to settle out of court before the trial date, wait until you get the money in hand and then notify the clerk and arrange for a dismissal of the case.

If for some reason you can't be in court on the date of the trial, you must sign a statement asking the judge to postpone the trial. In case of emergency on the day of the trial, you can have someone go to the court for you and ask for a postponement.

California is one of the few states where neither side can have a lawyer at the trial (see Appendix K for the other states). You can, however, consult a lawyer beforehand for guidance.

There will probably be several cases scheduled the same day as yours, so you might have to wait an hour or more until your case is heard. When it comes time for your trial, you will testify first. Try to be as brief as possible, present all your evidence and call on your witnesses to support you. The judge may ask you questions. Joe Shadetree will then give his side of the story. Don't interrupt or argue. The judge, after hearing both sides, will usually make a decision right then, but he might want to think about it further and let you know his decision at a later date. If he sides with you, he might award you all you asked for or he might award you less.

If Joe Shadetree doesn't show up, the judge will still ask you to give your side of the story and will usually rule in your favor.

Once you've won, your next problem might be to collect. A 1976 survey of small claims court in the New York City borough of Queens found that 40% had recovered nothing after winning.[19] (New York State now allows you to collect, if the business doesn't pay after receiving notice, the amount you won, plus $100, plus a reasonable attorney's fee to continue pressure on the business to pay.)[20]

If Joe Shadetree refuses to pay you, you'll have to go back to the court clerk and take out a writ of execution, which directs a marshal, sheriff or constable to take control of an asset of his, such as a bank account or personal property. You will have to tell what bank the money is in or where his property is located. Once you do collect, you can force Joe Shadetree to pay all costs of trying to collect the money.

If you should lose the case, you can't appeal. However, if you win, Joe Shadetree has the right to appeal to a higher court.

A key question to ask yourself before filing a small claims court suit is whether it's going to be worth your time. You may have to take time off from work to file the suit as well as to appear in court. In an attempt to alleviate this problem, small claims courts in several California counties are now open on Saturdays, and, in Los Angeles at least, there is a night small claims court on Thursday nights. In New York City, small claims court is always held in the late afternoon or evening, and a New York State law mandates that small claims courts hold evening sessions unless it's certified that they're not needed.

See Appendix K for a state-by-state rundown of small claims court monetary limits. Pamphlets on small claims courts are available from many consumer protection agencies (see Appendix B), including the Pennsylvania Bureau of Consumer Protection and the New York City Department of Consumer Affairs.

Further Reading

Everybody's Guide to Small Claims Court by Ralph Warner, $6.95, Addison-Wesley Publishing Co., 1980.

Winning Small Claims Warranty Suits

There is evidence that small claims court is one of your best bets in a new car warranty dispute.

Harold C. Wright, a California lawyer who represents auto dealers, said dealers are losing a "substantial" amount of money in California small claims courts. "Given an equal position between dealer and purchaser," he said, "the court will routinely award judgment to the party least able to afford the loss. The merits of a small claims dispute may even be in favor of the dealer, but the court will still award judgment to the complaining purchaser if there is any way to do so legally."[21]

When considering the small claims approach to settling warranty disputes, remember that the judge can't order the dealer or manufacturer to fix your car. He can, however, award you the money it costs to fix your car. Therefore, it's first necessary either to have the car repaired by someone else and sue for the repair price or to get an estimate and sue for the estimate price.

An especially fertile area for a small claims court suit is premature rusting. The auto companies defend these cases by alleging that the rust is caused by the increased use of salt on the roads during wintertime. However, judges in Canada, at least, have frequently ruled that the auto companies, knowing the environmental conditions in which their vehicles will be used, have the obligation to build cars to withstand salt.

When suing over rust damage or almost anything that's of a technical nature, it's best to bring along an expert to testify on your behalf, such as a metallurgist or an auto repair instructor at a high school or community college. If you have to pay the expert for his services, simply add the cost to the amount of your suit.

Use Your Subpoena Power

You can often get an out-of-court settlement from an auto company—even in small claims court—by using your subpoena power.

Subpoena internal documents from the company relating to the defects in your car. These may include presentations at quality control meetings, communiqués and service information sent to regional or district offices and dealers, and computer printouts showing the percentage of cars that have your particular defect. Chances are that the auto company won't want to reveal any of this information and will try to settle with you out of court.

Another tactic is to subpoena people connected with your case, such as the district service representative, the service writer, the service manager, all mechanics who worked on your car and the owner of the dealership. The dealer and manufacturer may figure it's just not worth it to take up the productive time of so many people, so they'll settle with you before the date of the trial.

Getting Federal Information

In a warranty dispute, it's sometimes possible to obtain internal auto company documents that admit your car is defective without having to file suit. Once you're armed with these documents, the auto company will know you have the goods on it and will make you a settlement offer.

You do this through the Freedom of Information Act, which requires the executive branch of the federal government to send you, upon request, copies of practically anything in its files that isn't secret. It just so happens that the National Highway Traffic Safety Administration gets copies of auto company service bulletins and other communiqués sent to dealers about defects.

To get your hands on this information, write the head of NHTSA, putting "Freedom of Information Request" on the envelope, and asking for specific information about a specific car. Here's what such a letter should look like:

MR. BADWRENCH

Your name
Address
Phone number

Date

Raymond A. Peck, Jr., Administrator
NHTSA
400 7th St. S.W.
Washington, DC 20590

Dear Mr. Peck:

Pursuant to the Freedom of Information Act, 5 U.S.C. 552, I hereby request copies of any service bulletins, technical bulletins, service letters or other communiqués possessed by NHTSA that were sent by General Motors Corp. to its dealers regarding crankshaft problems with 1976 Buicks.

Sincerely,
(your signature)

Limited Class Action Suits

A highly effective way to get warranty disputes resolved is to get together with other people in your state who have the same problem and file a limited class action suit. Such a suit, as its name implies, is limited only to those filing the suit.

Not only does such a suit enable you to share attorney's fees, but there's a chance that the auto company involved—seeing that it's outnumbered—will wish to settle out of court if all those party to the suit will keep their mouths shut about what they know and how much of a settlement they got.

For example, it was learned in 1975 that a group of 39 owners of Ford cars in Michigan won an out-of-court settlement of $27,500 against Ford after filing a limited class action suit contending that the company's cars rusted prematurely.[22]

Withholding Credit Card Payments

If you paid for repairs or any other purchase by credit card and are dissatisfied, you are allowed under the Fair Credit Billing Act[23] to withhold payment from the credit card company if you meet the restrictions outlined in Chapter 15 and take the following actions:

1. You must give the shop a chance to correct the problem.

2. If the problem isn't corrected, you must send a letter to the merchant informing him that if he doesn't resolve the dispute within seven days you will withhold payment to the credit card issuer.

3. If the dispute still isn't resolved, you must then write a letter to the credit card company telling them you are withholding payment, how much and why, and include a copy of the letter you sent to the merchant.

You may withhold only the amount in dispute. For instance, if a mechanic performs two repairs, one good and one bad, you would have to pay for the good repair, but could withhold payment for the bad repair. If you are making minimum monthly payments to the credit card issuer, you don't have to pay for the portion that applies to the disputed repairs. Be sure to retain copies of the letters you send to the merchant and credit card company.

The next step is up to the merchant. He will either settle the dispute with you, forget about the debt or sue you—most likely in small claims court. (The latter is infinitely better than your having to sue the merchant to get your money back.)

Following are sample letters you could send to the merchant and credit card issuer. They are a variation of sample letters suggested in a pamphlet called *What to Do If You Think You Were Taken by an Auto Mechanic,* published by the Los Angeles County Bar Association and the Los Angeles City Attorney's Office.

(To shop)

Your name
Address
Phone number

Date

Shop operator
Name of shop
Address

Dear Mr. _____:

I had my car repaired at your shop on (date of repairs) and paid the bill with a (name of credit card), account number _____.

The car was not repaired properly, as it (give description of problem).

I hereby request that you fix my car properly at no additional cost to me within seven days or I will withhold payment to (name of credit card issuer) for (amount in dispute) as is my right under the Fair Credit Billing Act.

Sincerely,
(your signature)

MR. BADWRENCH

(To credit card issuer)

Your name
Address
Phone number

Date

Name of card issuer
Address

Dear sirs:

I had my car repaired at (name of shop and address) on (date), paying for the repairs with my (name of credit card), account number _____.

The repairs were improperly done, as (give description of problem).

In accordance with the Fair Credit Billing Act, I have made a good faith attempt to obtain satisfactory resolution of this dispute. I have notified the repair shop by letter (copy enclosed), but it has failed to fix my car correctly within a reasonable period of time.

I am therefore withholding payment of (amount) for the cost of the disputed repairs.

Sincerely,
(your signature)

Report any problems enforcing your rights to the Federal Trade Commission (see Appendix B).

21

Battling Mr. Badwrench

with Better Business Bureau

Binding Arbitration

If suing Mr. Badwrench presents too much of a hassle, you might consider, as an alternative, binding arbitration offered by over 111 local Better Business Bureau offices.

The advantages over going to court are many: It's entirely free to you; you don't have to leave your home to initiate proceedings; your case is usually heard at a time convenient to you; independent automotive experts are sometimes made available as neutral witnesses; an independent testing laboratory may be used to inspect car parts at no cost to you; the businessman who enters into arbitration with you can't appeal if you win; the proceedings are completely private; the company you're complaining against doesn't even necessarily have to be located in your state; disputes are sometimes settled faster than by going to court; you needn't have a lawyer, and, if the other side has a lawyer and you don't, you needn't worry about the lawyer's scoring legal points against you because rules of law don't apply at arbitration hearings.

However, there are some disadvantages to arbitration compared to going to court. Dean W. Determan, vice-president of the Council of Better Business Bureaus, Inc., and originator of the arbitration program, says you're better off going to court under the following circumstances: If there is a dispute where your rights under state or federal law have been abused; if product liability is involved; if you want public exposure of a particular company or problem; if you want to set a precedent in a test case; and if you would like to get damages beyond the amount in dispute.[1]

Here's the way the arbitration system works:

1. You are expected to try to resolve the problem yourself with the repair shop, auto company, used car dealer, insurance company, etc.

2. If you fail to get satisfaction, contact one of the BBB offices listed in Appendix E.

3. The BBB will try to resolve the case informally.

4. If the mediation is unsatisfactory, you can ask for arbitration.

But there's one hitch. Unless the company you are complaining against has signed a precommitment with the BBB to turn over all complaints to arbitration, you must get the other side to agree to arbitrate. Among those precommitted to arbitration are members of the Hartford County (Connecticut) Auto Body Council.

5. If you and the businessman or corporation agree to arbitrate, both of you must sign an agreement that the decision of the arbitrator will be binding.

6. The bureau will send you and the other party a list of five arbitrators with a short biographical sketch of each. The arbitrators, who volunteer their services, have no connection with the BBB and come from all walks of life, including housewives, retirees, lawyers, ministers, educators and even former judges. In Kansas, Peoria and Baton Rouge, arbitrators are exclusively lawyers. You and your adversary both look over the list of arbitrators, cross out any you definitely don't want and then rank the rest in order of preference—one, two and three. "The consumer is fast to cross off lawyers," says Mr. Determan, a former U.S. Justice Department civil rights attorney. "I think we lawyers have a bad reputation."[2] The BBB takes the two lists of selections and chooses the person ranked highest by both to be the arbitrator. Three arbitrators are used in Georgia, where state law requires it, and in Kansas, where the state bar association demands it. Sometimes three arbitrators are used elsewhere as well if a lot of money is involved, say $1,000 or more. In such cases, each party selects one arbitrator from a list of five, and the two selected pick the third arbitrator. A majority vote decides a case. On the same form used to select the arbitrators, you and the other party select what day of the week and time is most acceptable to you for a hearing.

7. The arbitrator will then set a hearing date and time and so inform both parties. If need be, witnesses and documents can be subpoenaed. If necessary, you, the businessman, the arbitrator and an independent expert obtained by the BBB may inspect the car prior to the hearing, or the hearing itself could be held at a repair garage. In North Carolina, the North Carolina Stock Car Drivers Association supplies experts. At least two bureaus have local dealerships volunteer their top mechanics to inspect cars, with the mechanics not knowing the parties involved in the

dispute. Still other bureaus use auto mechanic instructors at local schools. However, not all bureaus have mechanical experts available.

8. An informal hearing will be held, often at BBB headquarters, with both sides presenting their stories, witnesses and documentation. Either side may have a lawyer present. You can, if you wish, have a mechanic of your choice argue your case for you. Hearings have even been held via a telephone conference hookup. In one such case, a motorist in Washington State was in a mountain ski area when the engine of his car developed trouble. A mechanic there made repairs. However, when the motorist drove further down the mountain, his car developed engine troubles again, which required work to be done by another mechanic. The motorist complained that the first mechanic misrepaired his car. He and the first mechanic then agreed to binding arbitration, and the BBB sent an independent expert to review both repair jobs. A conference call was held between the motorist, who was in Seattle; the expert and the repairman, who were in the mountains; and the arbitrator, a former judge, who was on an island in Puget Sound. The expert said the engine trouble which developed further down the mountain was unrelated to the original trouble, and therefore the arbitrator ruled that the first mechanic wasn't responsible.

9. The arbitrator will listen to both sides and then make a decision right there or take a few days to decide. He or she may give you all, part or nothing of what you want or could order the work to be redone in case of faulty repairs—something a small claims court judge can't do.

The whole procedure from the time of the complaint to the decision of the arbitrator takes, on average, 18 days and at the most 45 days, according to an in-depth study of six bureaus. One case was even settled within one day. A man complained to the Seattle BBB that a mechanic was demanding payment for work that he didn't request and that, in his opinion, wasn't needed. Furthermore, he said, the mechanic was keeping his car pending payment, and if he didn't get his car back he would lose his job. An arbitration hearing was set for 8:00 a.m. the next morning, and by 11:00 a.m. the arbitrator had canceled the debt and the man had his car.

The decision of the arbitrator is binding by state courts unless it's found, perhaps, that the arbitrator was in cahoots with one of the parties or was not totally impartial. (Not all states will enforce arbitration decisions if, as part of the purchase contract, you had to agree to put disputes to arbitration.)[3] If the businessman doesn't pay up, the courts can enforce the judgment.

Auto repair cases are the most prevalent type arbitrated, constituting at one time some 23% of all cases. How often do motorists win? That depends, according to Mr. Determan, on whether the BBB tries to mediate the dispute before it goes to arbitration. Businessmen who think they might lose in arbitration often settle during mediation. In the case of franchised new car dealers, he says, if the BBB does mediate and there isn't a settlement, the dealer will most often win in arbitration. Consumers get a mediated adjustment in 82% of the cases involving dealers.[4]

Despite the charm of the BBB arbitration program, many in the consumer movement are still skeptical. Most consumer activists frankly don't trust the Better Business Bureau, which has built up a reputation over the years as being anti-consumer and ineffectual in resolving disputes.

Mr. Determan is well aware of the BBB's tarnished image among consumer activists and contends that he is trying to pull the organization out of the 19th century with this program.[5]

Also cautious about the program are government consumer protection people. They're afraid, because the proceedings are private, that instances of fraud or repeated rip-offs by the same repair shop or companies will go undetected. For this reason, they advise you, if you do complain to the Better Business Bureau, to contact them as well (their addresses and phone numbers are in Appendix B). Some consumer protection agencies even have their own arbitration programs. One such program, involving the Maryland attorney general's office, is discussed in the next chapter. There are also other dispute resolution programs in many communities.

It's also wise to do a reverse on the consumer protection agencies' request and make sure you register a complaint with the BBB at the same time you complain to the government. This will help forewarn others who call the BBB to find out the reputation of a particular company.

The addresses and phone numbers of Better Business Bureau offices in the United States and Canada are in Appendix E.

22

Complaining to Government

Consumer Protection Agencies

A 1976 study conducted for the U.S. Office of Consumer Affairs discovered that over 45% of those interviewed were not familiar with their local consumer protection agencies and 41.5% were not familiar with the U.S. Office of Consumer Affairs.[1]

Those ignorant of the U.S. consumer agency aren't missing much, but those who are unfamiliar with their local consumer protection agencies should know that such agencies can be very helpful in resolving auto repair complaints. To help you contact a consumer protection agency, I've included in Appendix B a list of the addresses and phone numbers of several hundred of them.

Here I would like to highlight some of the better state, county and city consumer protection programs involving auto repairs—aside from those mentioned in Chapter 18—and give you a brief description of federal consumer protection agencies that deal with automotive matters.

District Attorneys

Some 42 district attorney offices are part of a national program to zero in on auto repair frauds and other so-called white-collar crimes. The program, called the Economic Crime Project, once boasted over 60 DA's offices, but many dropped out after federal funding was withdrawn at the end of 1980. The project is now financed by local communities and coordinated by the Philadelphia district attorney's office.

While most of the district attorneys in the program will help you only if fraud or violations of state laws are involved, some DAs have made their offices available to handle and/or mediate certain types of auto repair complaints regardless of whether fraud is involved or not. These include DA offices in Philadelphia; Denver; San Francisco; Westchester County, New York; and Pima County (Tucson), Arizona. Let's look at two such programs.

Philadelphia

Here the auto industry is actually assisting the DA's office in prosecuting corrupt shops and resolving consumer complaints. The concept originated when Richard Silva, president of Cottman Transmission System, Inc., approached the district attorney's office because he was getting complaints against one of his franchisees and was finding it difficult to do anything to the franchise holder in civil court. He wanted the DA's office to prosecute the franchisee, and so it was agreed that Cottman would set up an undercover car and the DA's office would handle the investigation. It worked. They got a successful prosecution, when, prior to that, the district attorney's office had a history of botching transmission investigations.[2]

With such good results, a permanent "watchdog committee" of industry members was set up to assist the DA, and it helped bring about many successful prosecutions for auto repair fraud.

In 1977, the committee expanded its duties and made its expertise available to help consumers in civil cases as well. The system, now known as AUTOTAP—Automobile Technical Advisory Panel—works in this way:

If you have a complaint against an auto repair shop, contact the district attorney's economic crime unit (see Appendix B).

Your complaint, minus the name of the repair shop, will be turned over to the AUTOTAP panel. If the panel members think there's fraud involved, they may help set up an undercover car—without knowing which repair shop they're investigating. If the panel members determine that fraud isn't involved but the mechanic or shop erred, they will try to get the shop to make amends. If the shop refuses, the panel will supply expert testimony on your behalf in small claims court. Michael M. Mustokoff, ex-chief of the unit, says he knows of no case where the judge has found contrary to the panel's opinion.[3] Robert J. Sussman, former director of the Economic Crime Project, says what often happens in court cases is that the mechanic gives the judge some technical "mumbo jumbo" which the consumer is not technically knowledgeable enough to refute, and thus the consumer loses the case. "This gives the citizen some mumbo jumbo to fight back with," he says.[4]

The fact that 30% of private criminal complaints reported to the Philadelphia DA's office involve auto repair fraud[5] indicates how badly a program like this is needed.

Westchester County, New York

The district attorney's office here is working closely with an AUTOCAP panel set up by the Greater New York, Long Island & Westchester Auto Dealers Association. The panel, which is not a watchdog committee as is AUTOTAP, is made up of new car dealers' representatives and consumers.

If you have a complaint against a dealer belonging to the association, contact the frauds bureau of the DA's office (see Appendix B).

If a crime is involved, the DA's office will handle the case itself. Otherwise, the complaint will be referred to the AUTOCAP staff, which will refer it to the dealer or auto manufacturer or both. If the complaint isn't resolved in 10 days, it's turned over to the AUTOCAP panel. If the panel decides against the dealer, the dealer must abide by the decision. In cases where the auto manufacturer is at fault, pressure is put on the auto company to settle the dispute. Arthur L. DelNegro, Jr., former chief of the DA's fraud bureau, says the program is not only "reducing some of the pressure between the manufacturer and the dealer," but is also responsible for getting the manufacturer to resolve complaints in certain cases where it might have refused before.[6]

State Consumer Agencies

"Most state agencies," according to Albert H. Kramer, director of the Federal Trade Commission's Bureau of Consumer Protection, "do not have the power to handle complaints about unsatisfactory [auto] repair unless fraud is involved."[7]

One of the exceptions to Mr. Kramer's statement is the Maryland attorney general's office, which provides a binding arbitration service for consumers and businessmen. Auto repairs, according to Gilbert "Gibby" Birnbach, director of the program, "is our major source of arbitration."[8]

Here's the way it works: You write or call the consumer protection division of the attorney general's office (see Appendix B) and one of the investigators in the office will call the repair shop and try to mediate the dispute. If mediation is unsuccessful, you and the businessman must sign and return a form showing your agreement to accept the decision of the arbitrator. Once the forms are returned, the director appoints an arbitrator from either a panel of lawyers or the attorney general's staff, or he might appoint himself.

He then sets the date and place of hearing. Hearings have been held all over the state and at such varied places as the director's office, the bedroom of a sick farmer and a firehouse.

The arbitration is entirely free, and both parties can have legal counsel if they wish. After the hearing, the arbitrator has 30 days to hand down a decision. The major advantage over Better Business Bureau arbitration is that if the businessman doesn't abide by the decision of the arbitrator, he'll have the attorney general's office breathing down his neck.

If you live in a state other than Maryland and file a complaint with a consumer protection agency that doesn't involve fraud, you might ask if the agency could arrange for binding arbitration if it is unable to resolve the problem.

Police Departments

One of the more unusual and most successful organizations involved in combating auto repair fraud is the City of Los Angeles' police department. The department has had an auto fraud section for many years and was one of the pioneers in the use of undercover cars to nab corrupt shops. Robert Reed, officer in charge of the section, says an average of 40 auto repair shops a year are prosecuted and the conviction rate is 98%.[9] See Appendix B for how to contact the unit.

Federal Consumer Protection Agencies

If you want to resolve your particular auto repair complaint against a national company, don't waste your time contacting the U.S. Government's main consumer affairs agency. It's more than likely that if you write to the Office of Consumer Affairs in the Department of Health and Human Services, you'll be referred to a state or local agency. I suggest, therefore, that you write to the U.S. agency (see Appendix B), not to get your particular complaint resolved, but to suggest legislation or needed federal action or to point out the corrupt activities of a national company. Send a copy to the President of the United States, White House, 1600 Pennsylvania Ave. N.W., Washington, DC 20500.

In Canada, the Department of Consumer and Corporate Affairs (see Appendix B), which says auto repairs accounted for 17% of its inquiries in 1977,[10] is also disinterested in receiving auto repair complaints and suggests instead that provincial consumer protection agencies be contacted.

Federal Trade Commission

The Federal Trade Commission, which is supposed to protect consumers and honest businessmen from anti-competitive, unfair and deceptive business practices, is *not* a complaint-handling agency. It can't help you with your individual problems. What it can do, however, is use your complaint as a basis for taking antitrust action, issuing industry-wide trade regulations or citing a particular company for illegal or unethical practices. From my observations of the way the commission works, I think it would be best, instead of sending a complaint letter, to send a petition requesting that the commission take a particular course of action. While you can send a petition with just your name on it, it's much more effective if you get a lot of people to sign it or get an organization to endorse it, such as a labor union, a consumer group, a service club, etc. Here are two brief examples of how a petition might be worded:

BEFORE THE FEDERAL TRADE COMMISSION

PETITION

We, the undersigned, hereby petition the Federal Trade Commission to take antitrust action against Ford Motor Co. for fixing prices of retail repair work.

(You could then explain that Ford forces its dealers to use its flat rate manuals when computing retail labor charges and cite personal examples of how this resulted in having to pay for more hours of labor than were actually consumed.)

BEFORE THE FEDERAL TRADE COMMISSION

PETITION

I, the undersigned, petition the Federal Trade Commission to force AAMCO Transmissions, Inc., and its franchisees to reveal to all customers, prior to disassembling their transmissions, the cost of having their transmissions rebuilt or replaced.

(You could then explain that an AAMCO shop refused to give you a price for repairs until after your transmission was disassembled and you were trapped.)

To contact the FTC, see Appendix B. Send a copy of your petition to Public Citizen Litigation (see Appendix C).

23

Prodding and Picketing:

Getting Help from

Consumer Activist Groups

Maclean's magazine, the Canadian equivalent of *Time* and *Newsweek,* gave the Automobile Protection Association (APA) perhaps its greatest compliment when it labeled the organization "a major pain in the neck to the automobile industry."[1]

Indeed, the Montreal-based association comes close to being an ideal auto repair consumer activist organization, one that Americans would do well to emulate.

APA bills itself as a nonprofit, public-interest, consumer corporation founded in 1971 "to bring the powers of honest lawyers, mechanics and journalists to the aid of motorists victimized by fraud or mechanic incompetency."[2]

It's a complaint-handling membership organization with annual dues—the last I heard—of $15. For this the motorist gets, among other things, support in settling claims, legal assistance, a list of "honest and crooked garages," free auto repair inspections, mechanic and insurance consulting, new and used car purchasing consulting and a consumer bulletin.

Every complaint against a repair shop goes through a mechanic committee to judge if it's legitimate. If it is and the repair shop or dealer or whoever doesn't make amends, a publicity committee exposes the dishonesty as a warning to the public and a legal committee uses "ordinary laws in extraordinary ways" to resolve the dispute.[3]

According to the association, "if a proven case of fraud exists in a franchised gas station, or incompetency is found within a well-known new car dealership, the APA takes the complaint through its three regular committees. If the garage or car dealer ignores the APA's demands for justice, a form of consumer corporate Jiu-Jitsu is used by the Association. The APA may organize a boycott, press conference, picketing, or bring legal action all at once or spread the activities over several days."[4]

Among its better achievements, the Automobile Protection Association helped to develop a national Canadian anti-rust code for new cars and forced Ford Motor Co. of Canada to voluntarily compensate owners of prematurely rusting cars.[5]

In 1977, the Ministry of Consumer and Corporate Affairs gave the organization a $45,000 grant for its consumer help and representation activities. Minister Warren Allmand said the APA was "synonymous with efficient protection in the field of motor vehicle problems."[6]

Canadians in need of help and those wishing to start a similar organization in America should see Appendix C for APA's address.

Automobile Owners Action Council

The closest thing in the U.S. to the Automobile Protection Association is the nonprofit Automobile Owners Action Council (AOAC) in Washington, D.C.

AOAC is the only complaint-handling consumer activist organization that I know of in the United States devoted exclusively to automobiles, including sales, repairs, warranties, insurance and financing.

Aid from the Action Council, however, doesn't come cheap. In order to be helped, you've got to become a full member, which costs $25 a year. But, contends Archie G. Richardson, Jr., president of AOAC, "that $25 is well worth it," considering the money members get back, the frustration they avoid by not trying to fight alone and the fact that it would cost them much more to hire a lawyer.[7]

He gives the example of Amy Isaac of Washington, D.C. She purchased a new 1974 Subaru DL with a one-year, no-mileage-limitation warranty. Over three years and eight months later, with some 37,343 miles on the odometer, the car blew a head gasket and then overheated, causing major engine damage. On October 10, 1977, she got a repair bill for $674.82, including $441.80 for parts.

Ms. Isaac paid the bill but contended the blown head gasket was a design defect and wanted Subaru to reimburse her. But she got nowhere on her own. On November 2, 1977, she appealed to the Action Council for help. Mr. Richardson said he talked to several Subaru dealers who told him that there were an inordinate number of head gasket failures on Subarus, which usually occurred after the expiration of the warranty and prior to 50,000 miles. Mr. Richardson, on November 30, 1977, wrote to M.L. Rausenberger, national customer relations manager of Subaru. He asked that Subaru reimburse Ms. Isaac only the $441.30 she had paid for parts.

He got a letter back from Mr. Rausenberger, dated December 22, 1977, saying: "The useful life of any gasket is variable, but we feel that leaks after almost four years of service cannot be considered the responsibility of Subaru." Mr. Rausenberger also said the car would have cost only $150 to $200 to repair had Ms. Isaac had it towed after the gasket blew instead of driving it.

While most consumers would have given up at this point, Mr. Richardson didn't. He called Mr. Rausenberger and bugged him. Eventually, on February 3, 1978, Subaru sent a check to Ms. Isaac for $335.[8]

AOAC makes great use of small claims courts, especially for getting settlements out of the auto manufacturers. In one case, Mr. Richardson helped a consumer file suit in District of Columbia small claims court against American Motors for the maximum $750. Included in the suit was a "motion for protective order" asking American Motors to answer all sorts of questions. Mr. Richardson figured the questions would be so time-consuming to answer and some of the answers would be so embarrassing to the company if they were made public that AMC would settle out of court. Indeed they did, for $375. "What we try to do is make it expensive for them," Mr. Richardson says.[9]

AOAC members, in addition to being helped with specific problems for their $25, also get voting privileges, a quarterly newsletter and other Action Council publications, discounts on new and used cars and repair work, and personalized counseling when buying a car or obtaining auto insurance or car repairs. There are also $10-per-year supporting members and $100-per-year organizational members. Supporting members get the newsletter and AOAC publications plus the right to vote. However, they have to pay another another $15 if they want help with complaints. The newsletter reports on fair and competent dealerships and repair shops, and gives advice on pitfalls.

Mr. Richardson got started in the consumer activist business in 1970 after becoming radicalized when he couldn't buy parts for his Cortina, which had been discontinued by Ford. He organized the Cortina Owners Action Committee, which, in 1973, evolved into Automobile Owners Action Council.

Although Mr. Richardson has long dreamed of building AOAC into a national complaint-handling organization, lack of funds keeps him confined mainly to the Washington, D.C., metropolitan area. This, however, hasn't stopped the organization from becoming involved in national automotive issues. AOAC, for example, was instrumental in getting General Motors to expand its warranty coverage of 1974 and 1975 model Vega engines that failed because of overheating.[10] One of the council's tactics was to organize a well-publicized bash-in at which owners and former owners of Vegas pickaxed and sledgehammered a lemon-colored Vega donated by a used car dealer.[11] The organization also once picketed a Chevrolet dealership which was adding an outrageous 25% "shop supplies" charge to its labor bill. As a result, the dealership reduced the charge to a somewhat less outrageous 15%.[12]

AOAC also gets into the national limelight by virtue of the fact that it is in the nation's capital. Mr. Richardson has been called upon to testify before Congress.

If you want to join AOAC or want information on how you can start a similar organization, the council's address is in Appendix C under District of Columbia.

Senior Citizen Power

Members of the American Association of Retired Persons (AARP) and other "senior citizens" are eligible to be helped with automobile and other consumer problems by AARP's National Consumer Assistance Center (see Appendix C). Although understaffed and swamped with complaints, the center says it won't turn you down if you come to it for help. They've got a WATS line to call anywhere in the country on your behalf.

By mentioning that AARP has 11.5 million members, the assistance center can put lots of pressure on national concerns like auto manufacturers, oil companies and auto insurance companies to resolve complaints.

Ralph Nader

Although Ralph Nader is the nation's top consumer crusader, he has done practically nothing about America's number one consumer problem: the $20 billion-a-year auto repair rip-off.

The only consumer advocacy agency under his bureaucratic umbrella that comes close to fighting the auto repair industry is the Center for Auto Safety, which he helped start, but which is now independent of him. As explained in Chapter 19, the center is involved almost solely with the issues of vehicle and tire safety and new car warranties.

Mr. Nader's staff usually sends all complaints related to automobiles to the Center for Auto Safety, which generally pays no attention to them if they don't relate to the organization's primary focus.

The only other Nader-related organization remotely involved with auto repairs is Public Citizen Litigation, which is interested in the price-fixing implications of auto repair flat rate manuals, but has been lackluster in doing anything about it.

If you want to write to Mr. Nader (see Appendix C), I suggest that you urge him to start using some of the money he gets from speaking engagements to set up a Center for Auto Repair Reform. Such a center could attack all the outrageous practices outlined in this book through lawsuits; lobbying on the national, state and local levels; publicizing outrages; and criticizing government agencies that don't do their jobs. The organization could also be a resource center on the auto repair industry to help lawyers, legislators, consumer groups, government officials and journalists. Then too, it could keep track of national auto repair companies and coordinate local and statewide organizations run on the order of the Automobile Protection Association in Montreal.

Organizing a Consumer Group

If you would like to start a consumer group, you can get help from the state and local organizing project of the Consumer Federation of America (see Appendix C).

The federation has a case study called "How to Form a Consumer Complaint Group," which is available for 75 cents. It also has newsletters, bibliographies and files of experts on various consumer issues.

See Appendix C for a list of local and state consumer activist organizations.

24

Calling on the Power

of the Press

Never underestimate the power of the press.

Newspapers and radio and television stations have helped many motorists get justice from repair shops, dealers, auto manufacturers, auto insurance companies and the like.

Over 200 newspapers have reader service columns, usually called "Action Line," which may be able to help if you've been gypped. The newspaper might even print your complaint, mentioning the name of the business that's giving you trouble.

In addition, over 35 radio and television stations are connected with a national organization called Call for Action, Inc., which will either help resolve your problem or tell you who to contact in your community.

Let's now take a closer look at both Action Line and Call for Action.

Action Line

I wish I could be optimistic about Action Line as a tactic, but I'm not. Several Action Line editors report that trying to help auto repair victims is strictly slow lane. "It's the toughest area in which to correct a complaint," says Robert McNight, editor of the *Cleveland Press* Action Line.

For one thing, it's hard to prove a rip-off in cases where a consumer complains that he was quoted a price of $50 for repairs and then got socked with a $200 repair bill. On new car warranty repairs, Mr. McNight says, the dealer usually refers him to the auto company zone office. But the zone people "are very hard to do business with; they don't answer their phones; they don't return calls . . . 90% of the time they rule in favor of the dealer."

Is there a better place for Cleveland area motorists to get help? According to Mr. McNight, "none of them seem to do any better than we do" with the possible exception of the Ohio attorney general's office. "The Better Business Bureaus don't do a damn," he says.[1]

Andy Bruno, Action Line editor at the *San Jose* (California) *Mercury*, says he's "more successful with the larger firms," like dealerships, AAMCO, Sears and Ward, than with small shops. The reason is that with small shops, the consumer has already argued with the owner and gotten nowhere, which is where he usually gets. But with the big repair outfits, consumers have usually argued only with an underling at the clerk level. Thus, says Mr. Bruno, he can often contact someone at the supervisory level who will then help the consumer.[2]

Despite many failures, Action Lines *have* scored many impressive victories for consumers. For instance, the *Oakland* (California) *Tribune/East Bay Today* Action Line helped a local resident get a critical part for a new 1981 Ford Escort. The month-old car was involved in an accident and hadn't been fully repaired seven weeks later for lack of a metric nut— a part of the steering mechanism. The person wrote to Ford Motor Co., but got no reply. The newspaper got the Ford dealer, who was making the repairs and also making money by renting the reader a car, to order the part on a "critical basis." It arrived in a week. The newspaper also printed the reader's criticism of Ford: "It is incomprehensible to me that an automobile can be so strongly advertised, then when bought, cannot be repaired."[3]

A list of Action Lines and addresses of newspapers carrying them can be found in the *Editor & Publisher International Yearbook*, available at many libraries.

Call for Action

Call for Action is a nonprofit franchise organization that provides radio and television stations with volunteers to help the public with practically any problem imaginable, including auto repair rip-offs, discrimination, emergency housing, etc. Stations pay for office, telephone and materials expenses and offer other support in exchange for a guarantee of exclusivity in their market area. With a few exceptions, volunteers are on duty to answer phones only a few hours a day, usually between 11:00 a.m. and 1:00 p.m. weekdays. All calls are kept confidential.

At radio station WTOP in Washington, D.C., about 50% of all

consumer-type calls involve automobiles. There are some 35 volunteers who take turns working in the office, which is open from 10:00 a.m. to 2:00 p.m. Although calls are accepted only between 11:00 a.m. and 1:00 p.m., the other two hours are taken up with making calls to help people or following up on cases to make sure they've been resolved. "We don't just drop a case," says Shirley Rooker, director of the station's Call for Action. "We follow up on it."

On automobile complaints, volunteers will either try to mediate the dispute or refer callers to other organizations which might be able to help, such as government consumer affairs offices, AUTOCAP or consumer activist groups. "Between all these things we hope to get a resolution," she says. Ms. Rooker figures, however, that when she and her volunteers try to do the mediating they have "a little more clout" because they're calling or writing the businessman from a radio station. "If put on an official [radio station] letterhead, it gets more attention than if a private citizen writes," she says. If the complaint involves a business in another city or state, Ms. Rooker says her staff might have Call for Action in that area contact the business or they might write the businessman themselves.

Often, according to Ms. Rooker, the problem is just one of faulty communications between the consumer and the businessman. "People get so mad that they lose the ability to communicate," she says.[4]

WTOP, besides paying the office expenses of Call for Action, also gives the organization air time. There are spot announcements about community services available, an occasional success story is aired about someone helped by the organization, and Ms. Rooker does an interview show on the station. In addition, the station sometimes does news stories on tips provided by Call for Action volunteers.

Call for Action phone numbers are in Appendix D.

25

Turning the Political Screws

Although auto repair has been the nation's top consumer problem for over a decade and is getting worse every year, the politicians and bureaucrats in Washington and most of the state capitals have their collective heads in the sand, hoping the problem will somehow go away by itself.

Let's face it: The auto repair problem will not go away and you'll continue to be cheated out of dollar after dollar after dollar until *you* and millions like you begin channeling your frustrations against the automotive industry into organized political activity.

I believe that auto repair is a potentially explosive political issue, testing whether government will be run by the people and for the people, or by and for selfish and immoral special interest groups. It shouldn't be hard to rally a cross section of Americans in support of the legislation and tough law enforcement recommended in this book. After all, auto repair is a problem that adversely affects young and old, men and women, poor and rich, black and white, Catholic and Jew and even those both for and against such issues as abortion and nuclear power. In other words, it's an issue which cuts across normal political boundaries.

Michigan exemplifies what can be accomplished by organized citizens and politicians who use auto repairs as a campaign issue.

In the early 1970s, a group calling itself the Michigan Citizens Lobby approached State Representative Earl Nelson with a proposal for licensing of auto repair shops and auto mechanics. Nelson introduced a licensing bill in the state legislature and led the fight to get it passed. The measure passed the state house of representatives, but a state senate committee attempted to water it down. Nelson ran for the senate seat held by the chairman of that committee, using auto repairs and lack of leadership as campaign issues. Feeling the heat, the committee chairman acquiesced to tough auto repair legislation, although it was too late to help him politically. Mr. Nelson defeated him at the polls.

The Role of the Feds

Certainly some of the auto repair problem could be resolved at the state or local level, particularly by licensing and strenuously regulating auto repair shops, auto mechanics, new and used car dealers, auto manufacturers and auto insurance companies. But that doesn't leave the federal government off the hook. While many in Washington contend that auto repair really isn't a problem that can be resolved by the federal government, I believe the feds could clean up 85% of the mess if only the bureaucrats and legislators did what they were getting paid to do.

The types of repair shops which are causing the most trouble all have connections with national companies and are therefore a federal law enforcement problem. These include franchised auto dealers, mass merchandisers, tire company stores, franchised auto repair outlets and franchised gas stations, particularly those near Interstate highways.

It's also within the federal government's province to clean up the whole new car warranty problem; to outlaw flat rate manual price fixing and the paying of mechanics for warranty work via a flat rate commission; to begin a massive mechanic recruitment and apprenticeship program; to give tax breaks to shops which hire apprentices; to set minimum requirements for pre-delivery inspections; to force auto insurance companies to deal fairly with body shops and consumers over crash repairs; to make tire companies give fair prorated cash adjustments; to require auto companies to put inexpensive and effective bumpers on their cars; to outlaw secret warranties; to reduce the number of car models, frequency of styling changes and incompatibility of parts between models; to force the auto companies to design with repair in mind; to issue comparative repair and maintenance cost information on new cars; to ensure that the auto companies give all repair shops necessary servicing information; to do something about the unavailability and high prices of many parts; to keep track of all crash parts prices and blow the whistle on excessive increases; to force the auto companies to sell crash parts directly to wholesalers and independents; to set up a national system of diagnostic centers not connected with repair shops; to make all diagnostic plug-in units compatible; to create standards for diagnostic equipment; to provide loans or funds for setting up vehicle inspection maintenance organizations, co-op garages and repair shop rating guides; to provide management expertise to small repair shops so that they can become more efficient; to undertake a crash program to improve the reading and mathematical abilities of potential mechanics; to issue acceptable trade standards regarding tune-ups, transmission rebuilding and ball joints; to imprison corporate executives who knowingly sell dangerously defective products; etc.

Who's in Charge?

Looking over the federal government's meager efforts to reform auto repairs, it's strikingly evident that no one is in charge. I have found that the staffs of the two congressional subcommittees that have been responsible for auto repair reform have little understanding of the situation.

In 1978, many days of auto repair hearings were held by the Subcommittee for Consumers of the U.S. Senate Committee on Commerce, Science and Transportation and by the Subcommittee on Consumer Protection and Finance of the House Committee on Interstate and Foreign Commerce. Yet neither subcommittee explored the flat rate commission pay system or the widespread price fixing of auto repairs. Nor did they have the Labor Department testify as to what it was doing about the mechanic shortage and incompetence problems. Aside from that, few tough questions were asked of industry witnesses. The only legislation introduced as a result of the hearings was related solely to auto warranties.

On the federal bureaucracy front, the Federal Trade Commission, the National Highway Traffic Safety Administration, the U.S. Office of Consumer Affairs, the Department of Energy and the Environmental Protection Agency have formed a committee to coordinate federal auto repair efforts. But the main three members are procrastinating, ineffective organizations that are more a part of the problem than the solution. Also, it's unbelievable that the Labor Department was not made a full member of the committee.

The Federal Trade Commission, as I've pointed out time and again in this book, has failed to do anything about the auto repair problem. If your local police fought street crime as vigorously as the FTC fights corporate and business crime, you wouldn't be able to step out of your front door without being mugged. An April 1978 commission report reveals that although automobiles accounted for the most complaints it received regarding consumer products, automobile-related matters took up approximately only 5.2% of the FTC's program resources.[1] Many businessmen squawk that the commission is doing too much regulating; the truth is that it's not doing enough in the right places.

Meanwhile, the National Highway Traffic Safety Administration took 10 years to come up with a tire grading standard and six years to put into effect a minimum property-loss standard for bumpers, and, after over eight years, has still not come up with operating cost disclosures for new cars. NHTSA has had a poor track record just meeting its original purpose for existence—regulating the safety of automobiles—and yet Congress has been foolishly saddling the agency with responsibility for auto repair reform. Auto repair has such low priority at NHTSA that former agency administrator Joan Claybrook didn't even show up at a major consumer-government-industry auto repair conference held in 1980. Her aides said she was too busy with auto safety work to attend.

As for the U.S. Office of Consumer Affairs, it has been less than vigorous in protecting auto owners. For example, it took federal consumer affairs officials 1½ years after their counterparts in Canada got the auto companies to voluntarily extend rust warranties to publicly scold the car makers for not offering extended rust warranties in the U.S.

It's time that the White House set up a special office to coordinate the entire federal government's auto repair reform effort and prod agencies which aren't doing their job. Such an office could also be a resource center to help states, cities and counties handle auto repair problems.

Why More Regulation?

Here I am advocating more regulation at a time when the public is complaining that its tax money goes to support more and bigger bureaucracies and businessmen are complaining that regulations are driving up prices. Have I gone bananas?

The answer is no. We're talking about a $20 billion annual loss to consumers. And if Congress allocated wisely $55 million a year—just one day's rip-off—for auto repair reform, much of the problem could be alleviated, saving consumers billions of dollars a year. Also, more than 750,000 jobs could be created.

While the auto companies have loudly claimed that regulations drive up car prices, I think it's largely propaganda. The social and monetary benefits from federal safety, emissions and fuel economy regulations have been enormous. It's estimated that safety regulations saved 50,000 to 60,000 lives between 1966 and 1977.[2] The air you breathe is much cleaner than it would have been without regulations, and NHTSA contends that federal fuel savings rules will save the average buyer of a 1980 car $1,700 in gasoline bills (computed at $1.25 a gallon).[3]

The added regulatory costs are actually not that significant when compared to other costs of a new car. For example, General Motors spent about $333 a car in 1978 for needless annual styling changes,[4] the U.S. auto companies spent $55 per vehicle in 1977 for advertising,[5] the average

1977 new car buyer spent $900 for comfort and convenience options like air conditioning and vinyl roofs,[6] and many new car dealers extract hundreds of dollars from consumers for grossly overpriced and questionably needed "after-sale" items.

Write the Politicians

The auto repair problem can best be attacked by citizens banded together in a common effort, but individuals can make their weight felt as well. If you're tired of being ripped off, sit down and write letters to politicians, telling them specific legislation you want passed and the agencies you'd like to see pushed into action. It's up to you.

See Appendix L for addresses of U.S. Labor and Justice Department officials; U.S. senators and congressmen; and various congressional committees, including the Senate Subcommittee for Consumers and the House Subcommittee on Telecommunications, Consumer Protection and Finance, which have jurisdiction over auto repair matters.

Addresses of governors and individual members of the state legislatures may be found in *Elective Officials and the Legislatures,* published annually by the Council of State Governments and available in many libraries.

Appendixes

Appendix A

State, City and County

Auto Repair Laws

and Enforcement Agencies

Alaska[1]

Written estimates are required upon request. The shop can't go over the estimate without your approval. Parts, except warranty or exchange parts, must be returned to you if you so request at the time the repair order is taken. The shop must provide you with an invoice detailing costs of all parts and labor and identifying parts as new, used, rebuilt or reconditioned. The shop can't hold your car if you refuse to pay for any unauthorized repairs, including repairs that exceed the written estimate without your permission. No shop may misrepresent, even by implication, the cost of repairs authorized by you; the terms or conditions of a warranty or service agreement; that repairs have been made when they haven't been; or that your vehicle is in a dangerous condition or that its continued use will be hazardous to either persons or the vehicle. The shop may not collect or attempt to collect for repairs not authorized, which have not been made or which the shop knew or reasonably ought to have known were unnecessary. No shop which is a warrantor or a party to a warranty or service agreement may refuse to repair your vehicle in accordance with the terms and conditions of the warranty or service agreement. No shop may alter your vehicle with intent to create a condition requiring repairs. No shop can charge you for making an estimate unless it tells you the amount of the charge beforehand, or, if that can't be determined, the basis on which the charge will be calculated. If you don't authorize repairs above the original estimate, the shop must return your vehicle in at least as good condition as it was delivered. If you give oral authorization to exceed a written estimate, the shop must specify on the repair order or invoice the newly authorized repairs and estimated cost plus the date, the time of authorization and the person and telephone number called. Report violations to the Consumer Protection Section of the attorney general's office (see Appendix B).

California

See Chapter 18 for explanation of the state licensing and disclosure laws. Contact:

> Robert N. Wiens, Chief
> Bureau of Automotive Repair
> 3116 Bradshaw Rd.
> Sacramento, CA 95827
> (916) 366-5131
> Toll-free complaint no.: (800) 952-5210

You can also register complaints in person at one of the six district offices:

3116 Bradshaw Rd.	20 Harold Ave.	3374 East Shields
Sacramento, CA 95827	San Jose, CA 95117	Room 14
(916) 366-5023	(408) 277-1860	Fresno, CA 93726
		(209) 445-5015
107 South Broadway	28 Civic Center Plaza	1350 Front St.
Room 8019	Room 360	Room 3050
Los Angeles, CA 90012	Santa Ana, CA 92701	San Diego, CA 92101
(213) 620-5347	(714) 558-4008	(714) 237-7295

Complaints of auto repair fraud can also be handled by your local district attorney, or, in the city of Los Angeles, by the auto fraud unit of the police department. See Appendix B for addresses and phone numbers.

Colorado[2]

Written estimates are required if the shop agrees to do repairs expected to cost over $75, unless you waive the right in writing or are given an oral estimate. If the shop gives an oral estimate, it must record in writing, along with the estimated cost, the date, time, manner of consent and telephone number called to get consent. Estimates must include the expected completion date and storage charges which shall accrue if the car is not picked up within three days after completion of repairs, exclusive of weekends and legal holidays. If an estimate can't be given without some disassembly, the shop must give you the cost of reassembly in the event you do not elect to have repairs done. If disassembly is expected to prevent the restoration of a particular unit to its former condition, the shop must inform you of this. The estimate can't be exceeded by $10 or 10%, whichever is less, without your consent. If the estimate is thus exceeded without your consent, you need not pay any more and the shop is not entitled to a lien on the excess amount. The shop must also notify you of any change in the expected completion date. Your consent must be obtained before any used, reconditioned or rebuilt parts are installed. Invoices must include the following: an itemized list of parts, including which are new, used, rebuilt or reconditioned; the cost of each part; the amount charged for labor; the name or identification of each mechanic who performed each repair, and identification of any repairs subcontracted to another repair garage (designation of mechanics, parts or labor is not required if such repairs are customarily done and billed on a flat rate price basis and agreed upon by you or if such flat rates are conspicuously posted by the shop or otherwise made available to you prior to rendering the estimate). Shops must return replaced parts, except body shop repair parts and parts that the garage must return under a warranty or exchange arrangement, if you so request at the time of consenting to repairs. Prohibited practices, except for clerical errors or omissions, include willfully charging for repairs which have not been authorized, representing that repairs are necessary when such is not a fact and known not to be a fact, representing that repairs have been performed which is untrue and known to be untrue and representing that your vehicle or a part is in dangerous condition when such is not a fact and known not to be a fact. In any civil action taken against a repair shop for violation of these disclosure provisions or prohibited practices, you are entitled to damages of not less than $50 and the court may award you reasonable attorney's fees and costs. However, you must first demand damages from the shop at least 10 days prior to filing suit, exclusive of weekends and legal holidays. You must also file suit within one year of an alleged violation. Report violations to the chief of the Consumer Protection Act in the attorney general's office (see Appendix B).

Connecticut[3]

Licenses auto repair shops. Licenses can be suspended or revoked for incomplete or improper work or for making any false statement as to the condition of any motor vehicle repaired. Shops may be fined up to $1,000 for violations and be forced to post a $1,000 bond, which may be forfeited for further violations. You are entitled to a written estimate if the repairs are to cost $50 or more. You may waive this right only in writing, and, in such cases, must give the shop a dollar amount not be exceeded without your authorization. If you so request, you must be given a written estimate for repairs expected to cost under $50. If a shop can't give you a written estimate when you deliver the car, it must notify you of the estimate and get your written or oral authorization. The shop can't exceed the written estimate or the maximum you allow without your authorization. A shop can have a claim against a vehicle only for repairs which were actually performed and authorized. Prior to repairing your car, the shop must note in writing the specific repairs you request or a brief description of the nature of the problem. Invoices must separately itemize all labor and parts, state if any used parts were installed and state any warranty on parts and labor. Upon your request when the work order is taken or before the vehicle is returned to you, the shop must give you all replaced parts, except those normally sold on an exchange basis or subject to a warranty. Such unreturned parts must be made available for your inspection. Shops must post a sign where repair orders are taken stating (1) the hourly charge for labor; (2) the conditions, if any, under which the shop may impose charges for storage and the amount of such charges; and (3) the charge, if any, for a diagnosis. A shop must complete repairs the same business day the car is delivered unless (1) you are informed when you bring in the vehicle that repairs will not be completed that day; (2) you consent to a later completion day; or (3) the shop makes a reasonable effort to inform you as soon as it knows that repairs can't be completed that day. Complaints should be made to:

Edward L. Simmons, Director
Department of Motor Vehicles
60 State St.
Wethersfield, CT 06109
(203) 566-5820
Toll-free complaint no.: 1 (800) 842-2220

District of Columbia[4]

Licenses auto repair shops and "supervisory inspectors" for each category of repair a shop engages in. The Board of Consumer Goods Repair Services—made up of two industry members and three public members—has the power to deny, suspend, revoke or refuse to renew any license. Written estimates are required unless you waive the right. The estimate must include all malfunctions as described by you, the promised completion date, a notation by the repair shop owner or supervisory inspector of all repairs required to correct the malfunctions you've described and a general description and cost of the parts and labor required to perform the authorized repairs. Further authorization is needed to exceed the estimate by 20% on repairs costing $300 or less and 10% for repairs costing more than $300. Replaced parts must be returned to you in the container in which new parts were packed unless you expressly waive the right or the parts are heavy or must be returned under a warranty or exchange arrangement. Invoice requirements include an itemization of labor and parts; disclosure of any parts which were used, rebuilt or reconditioned; identification of each repairman who had a hand in each repair; identification of any subcontractor; and a statement describing the exact nature of the warranty. No miscellaneous charges such as "shop supplies" or "shop materials" are allowed. If authorized repairs are not completed by the promised completion date—due to either the inability, unwillingness or failure of the repair shop or your unwillingness to accept an increase in the cost of repairs beyond the allowable percentage—you have the right to a prompt return of your car with all parts properly reassembled and in a condition which is in no way inferior to the condition of the car when you brought it in for repair. In such circumstances, the shop can't charge you more than what's specified in the written estimate. Any shop that subcontracts work is held responsible for that work. Prohibited conduct includes knowingly making untrue or misleading statements, false or misleading advertising, failure to give you a copy of any document you sign just after you sign it, dishonesty, fraud, deceit, gross negligence, making false promises to induce you to authorize repairs or maintenance and exhibiting a persistent pattern of conduct which departs from or disregards accepted trade standards. Complaints against shops, including complaints about new car warranty work and supervisory inspectors, should be directed to the D.C. Office of Consumer Affairs (see Appendix B).

Florida[5]

Special Broward County and Dade County laws are summarized after the general discussion here. If the cost of repair work is to exceed $50, the shop must give you a written form giving you the following three choices: (1) a written estimate; (2) a waiver of a written estimate; or (3) waiver of a written estimate as long as the repair costs do not exceed a particular amount, in which case the shop may not exceed the amount designated without your consent. The shop can't exceed the written estimate by more than $10 or 10%, whichever is greater, without your authorization. The estimate must include the proposed work completion date; a general description of the customer's problem or request for repair or service; the charge for making the estimate, or if that can't be determined, the basis on which the charge will be calculated; a statement indicating what, if anything, in connection with the repair work is guaranteed, and the time and mileage period for which the guarantee is effective; a statement allowing the customer to indicate whether replaced parts should be saved for inspection or return; and a statement indicating the daily charge for storage, which can begin only three work days after you've been notified that repairs have been completed. No shop can impose or threaten to impose a clearly excessive charge in relation to work involved in making the estimate. If you cancel repairs after being advised that they can't be done for the original estimate, the shop must "expeditiously" reassemble your vehicle the way it was originally unless you waive such reassembly or the reassembled vehicle would be unsafe. After such cancellation, the shop can charge you for the cost of teardown, the cost of parts and labor to replace items that were destroyed in the teardown and the cost to reassemble the component or vehicle—but only if you were notified of these possible costs in the estimate prior to the beginning of the diagnostic work. Upon your request made at the time of authorized repairs, you're entitled to inspect all parts removed from your vehicle and to keep those not involved in a warranty arrangement or exchange parts program with a manufacturer, supplier or distributor. Shops must supply invoices which include a statement indicating what was done to correct the problem or a description of the service provided; an itemized description of all labor, parts and merchandise supplied with costs thereof; indication of which parts were replaced under a shop or manufacturer's warranty; a statement identifying any replacement part that is used, rebuilt or reconditioned; and a statement indicating what, if anything, is guaranteed and the time and mileage period for which the guarantee is effective. If a shop has given you a written estimate and is holding your vehicle under a mechanic's lien while a dispute is on, you may get back possession of the vehicle by obtaining a cash or surety bond, payable to the person claiming the lien, in the circuit court where the disputed transaction occurred. The bond must be in the amount stated on the invoice plus accrued storage charges, if any, less any amount on the invoice paid by you to the shop. The shop will have 60 days to sue you to recover the bond, after which time the bond will be discharged. If the shop sues, the winning party may be entitled to damages plus court costs and reasonable attorney's fees. Report violations to the Consumer Protection and Fair Trade Practices Bureau of the Florida Department of Legal Affairs (see Appendix B).

BROWARD COUNTY[6]

Free written estimates are required for work judged to cost $25 or more unless you waive the right in writing. Estimates must include a general description of your complaint and requested repairs; a notation by the shop if it won't guarantee that requested repairs will remedy the complaint; total cost of parts, labor and incidental services; a notation as to whether new, rebuilt or used parts are to be installed; and any charges for release of your car in the event it is not repaired. The shop can't go over the estimate by $10 or 10%, whichever is less, without your approval. Replaced parts, except those which must be returned under a warranty or exchange agreement or for which there is no charge, must be returned to you if you request them at the time the work order is taken. Shops can't charge you for storage unless they notify you three working days in advance and can't charge more than $2 per day for the first ten days and $4 per day thereafter. Invoices must itemize all parts and services and denote whether parts were used or rebuilt. (If the repair bill is in dispute and the shop won't let you have your car, you can go to Room 380 of the county courthouse and post a cash or surety bond in the amount of the disputed bill and then get your car.) Report violations to the director of the county's Consumer Affairs Division (see Appendix B).

DADE COUNTY[7]

Written estimates are required, unless waived, if the repairs are to exceed $15. Estimates must include an itemized list of parts; whether new or used parts will be used; and charges for labor, incidental services, making the estimate (if any) and to release your vehicle if it isn't repaired. The shop can't go over the estimate by $10 or 10%, whichever is less, without your approval. If you refuse to authorize further repairs, the shop must return your car in the same condition as it was when you brought it in and charge you no more than the written estimate. The shop must notify you three work days in advance if it is to charge you storage fees and can charge you no more than $1 per day for the first 10 days and $2 per day thereafter. All parts and labor must be itemized on invoices and any used parts must be noted. Report violations to the county's Consumer Protection Division (see Appendix B).

Hawaii[8]

Hawaii has required repair shops to be licensed since January 1, 1976. In addition, mechanics who had less than two years of experience prior to that date or who failed to register by that date also must be licensed. The Motor Vehicle Repair Industry Board has the power to fine or suspend, revoke or refuse to renew the license of both shops and mechanics for any violation of state law or board regulations. State law requires a fine of $75 for the first offense, $150 for the second offense and $300 to $1,000 for subsequent offenses. In lieu of or in addition to a fine, the board can require a shop or mechanic to make restitution to a customer. You must be given a written estimate unless you waive the privilege in writing. The shop is allowed, without your authorization, to go 15% over the estimate if the estimated price is less than $100 and 10% over if the estimated price is over $100. You have the right to a copy of any document you sign as soon as you sign it. You must be given an itemized statement following repairs, including warranty repairs, of all work done and parts replaced, with the shop telling you whether any parts were used, rebuilt or reconditioned. You are entitled to the return of replaced parts if requested at the time the work order is taken with the exception of large or weighty parts and warranty parts that must be returned to a manufacturer or distributor. Prohibited practices include knowingly making untrue or misleading statements, fraud, gross negligence, disregard of accepted trade standards for good and workmanlike repair, making false promises to induce you to authorize repairs and having work subcontracted without your knowledge unless you could not reasonably have been notified. Complaints against shops or mechanics can be registered with the Department of Regulatory Agencies office on each island or by contacting:

George Muramaru, Executive Secretary
Motor Vehicle Repair Industry Board
Professional & Vocational Licensing Division
Department of Regulatory Agencies
P.O. Box 3469
Honolulu, HI 96801
(808) 548-4100

Idaho[9]

A shop doesn't have to give you an estimate. However, you may put a ceiling on the authorized costs of any repair and the shop may not exceed the price without obtaining your oral or written consent. If an estimate is given, the shop can't go over the estimate without your consent if the additional repairs will "unreasonably or substantially" increase the original estimated price. It is illegal for a shop to unreasonably or substantially understate or misstate any estimated costs. The shop must, upon your request, return or allow inspection of replaced parts. A shop can't keep, for reuse or resale, replaced parts you request unless such retention was made known prior to performing any repairs or the shop is able to demonstrate it made a bona fide reduction in consideration for keeping the parts or the replacement was made under a warranty. Upon your request, the shop must give you an itemized bill showing (1) the labor charge, designating the number of hours and the rate per hour (such designation need not be used if a customary flat rate charge is made or if there is a minimum charge); (2) each part and material, designating whether parts are used or rebuilt; (3) miscellaneous charges, designating the reason for the charge and its basis of calculation. Outlawed practices include (1) representing that repairs are necessary when they aren't or that repairs have been made when they haven't been or that a car is in a dangerous condition when it isn't so; (2) performing unnecessary repairs; and (3) filing a lien if you have tendered payment in full or in accordance with the contract authorizing repairs. Report violations to the Consumer Protection Division of the attorney general's office (see Appendix B).

Illinois

CHICAGO[10]

Auto repair shops are licensed and licenses can be revoked by the mayor for violating the city's motor vehicle repair shop ordinance. Shops can also be fined upon conviction of violating the ordinance. Shops must give you a written estimate unless you voluntarily waive the right without coercion. The shop can't exceed the estimate by 10% or $15, whichever is less, without your consent. Replaced parts must be returned to you, except those that must be returned under a warranty or exchange agreement, if you make the request at the time the work order is taken. The invoice must include a description of all work done, including warranty work; all parts supplied, including the name of the manufacturer (or any distributor giving a warranty of 90 days or more and/or 3,000 miles); the total price for parts and labor; if any parts were used, rebuilt or reconditioned; and if a part of a component system is composed of new and used, rebuilt or reconditioned parts. All repair work and parts used must be warranted for 90 days and/or 3,000 miles unless a statement appears on the estimate and invoice to the effect that the work performed and parts replaced are not warranted for that period. If repair work or parts are subject to a warranty, the shop must give you the warranty in writing. Prohibited practices include knowingly making false or misleading statements, failing to give you a copy of any document requiring your signature as soon as you sign the document, fraud, gross negligence and unfair or deceptive practices. Report troubles to the commissioner of consumer services (see Appendix B).

Maine[11]

You have the right, before repairs begin, to have the shop put in writing a monetary limit on authorized repairs. You are not liable for any charges above the limit without your oral or written authorization. You have the right, upon request, to inspect any replaced parts and also to their return unless they must be returned to a manufacturer or distributor under a bona fide warranty or exchange arrangement. A shop isn't allowed to install used, reconditioned or rebuilt parts unless you agree beforehand. The shop must post a sign where it is reasonable that you'll see it, telling you, among other things, the charge per hour, or, if it applies, that the flat rate charges will be explained to you if you ask. Report violations to the Consumer and Antitrust Division of the attorney general's office (see Appendix B).

Maryland[12]

Montgomery County and Prince George's County laws are summarized after the general discussion here. Written estimates are required, upon request, if the repairs are to exceed $50. The shop must get your approval to go 10% over the estimate. The shop must return replaced parts unless they are to be returned to the manufacturer or distributor under a warranty agreement or if they are disposed of with your consent. Written estimates must include the estimated completion date, and shops are expected to adhere to the date unless delays are caused by an act of God, strike, unexpected illness or unexpected shortage of labor or parts. You must be given an invoice which includes all work done, including warranty work, and all parts supplied with it clearly stated if any parts are used, rebuilt or reconditioned. Report violations to the Consumer Protection Division of the attorney general's office (see Appendix B).

MONTGOMERY COUNTY[13]

Licenses of auto repair shops can be revoked or suspended after a hearing before the director of the Department of Environmental Protection, the county's licensing agency. You're entitled to a written estimate only upon request and only if the estimate exceeds $25. The estimate statement must include the labor charges and method of computation; the cost of each part and whether it will be used or rebuilt; your description of the problems and any specific repair you request; incidental service charges; any charges for making the estimate or for the release of your vehicle in case it's not repaired; and any express warranty on parts or workmanship. The shop must get your approval to go over the written or oral estimate by 10%. The invoice must tell you whether labor has been charged by the clock hour or flat rate hour, and the time spent on each repair if charges are by the clock hour, and must itemize all parts supplied or work performed except if the total bill is under $15. The invoice must also state whether any used or rebuilt parts were supplied, the brand name and part number of all parts installed (except where there is a warranty of 90 days or more) and the name, initials or identifying number of the mechanic who worked on the car. No shop can charge for miscellaneous shop supplies unless you were informed of such charges prior to the repairs. Upon your request, the shop must give you an estimated completion date in writing or put in writing that such a date is undeterminable. The shop will not incur any liability if a delay is caused by an act of God, strike, unexpected illness or unexpected shortage of labor or parts. The shop must return to you all replaced parts except those which must be returned to a manufacturer or distributor under a warranty agreement or those which are disposed of with your oral or written consent. Prohibited practices include gross negligence, repeated false and misleading statements and advertisements and knowingly charging for parts or services not furnished or performed. Report complaints to the county's Office of Consumer Affairs (see Appendix B).

PRINCE GEORGE'S COUNTY[14]

The county's Consumer Protection Commission has the power to intercede in disputes involving both regular and warranty repairs, to order restitution, to issue cease and desist orders to shops and to require the county Department of Licenses and Permits to conduct a hearing to deny, suspend or revoke a repair shop's license. As a precondition to being issued a license, each shop must post a $2,000 bond with the county which any person who is awarded a final judgment from any court of competent jurisdiction which involves services rendered or materials supplied can use, if necessary, to recover money, damages, or both. Repair shops must give you, upon request, a written estimate for parts and labor which can't be exceeded by 10% without your approval. Also upon your written request prior to repairs, the shop has to retain all replaced parts for your inspection and give you any replaced parts, except those that must be returned to a manufacturer or distributor under a warranty agreement. The invoice must show all work performed, including warranty work, with all labor and parts itemized; all parts replaced must be designated on the invoice as new, used, rebuilt or reconditioned; and the terms and conditions of all warranties and guarantees must be attached to the invoice. Direct complaints to the county's Consumer Protection Commission (see Appendix B).

Massachusetts[15]

You must be given a written estimate unless you sign a waiver. If the shop can't give you a written estimate immediately, it can get your oral approval and, in such cases, must record the date, time, name of employee placing the call, the name and number of person called and the exact work approved. Estimates must include a breakdown of parts and labor unless combined charges are posted where they may be readily seen. You must give your approval for the estimate to be exceeded by $10. Before commencing repairs, the shop must record in writing the specific repair you request, or, if you don't request specific repairs, a brief description of the problem. The shop must give you a copy of any document you sign. The work must be completed the same day your car is brought in unless you are informed of and consent to a further delay or there are unforeseen circumstances beyond the shop's control. The invoice must break down parts and labor charges and indicate if any parts are used, rebuilt or reconditioned (flat rate charges must be broken down unless clearly posted). You can't be charged for storage, estimates or diagnosis unless you have previously agreed to such charges or there is a sign posted indicating the conditions under which such charges are imposed. You may inspect all parts replaced and keep those which don't have to be returned to the manufacturer under a warranty or similar arrangement. Repair shops must correct promptly at no charge any work not performed in a good workmanlike manner in accordance with accepted trade standards. Prohibited practices include knowingly making false statements, saying repairs are necessary or desirable when they're not, trying to make you believe your vehicle is in a dangerous condition when it is not and that repairs have been performed when such is not a fact. Direct complaints to the Consumer Protection Division of the attorney general's office (see Appendix B).

Michigan[16]

Auto repair shops and mechanics are licensed. The secretary of state or anyone he designates can deny, suspend, or revoke a shop's license, a mechanic's certification or a mechanic's trainee permit after opportunity of a hearing. Offenses include engaging in unfair or deceptive practices, making untrue statements, violating the Motor Vehicle Service and Repair Act or any regulations issued under it, making unnecessary or unauthorized repairs, refusing to honor warranties made by the repair facility and getting you to sign a blank repair order. The state also has the power to mediate disputes. You may request a written estimate for repairs under $20 but shops must give you a written estimate for repairs over $20 unless you waive the estimate in writing. The shop is allowed to go over the estimate by $10 or 10%, whichever is less, without your written or verbal consent. Shops must give back all parts replaced, except those which are too heavy or large and those that must be sent back to the manufacturer or distributor as a result of warranty work or as part of an exchange agreement. When parts can't be returned, you are entitled to inspect them. Upon completion of repairs, the shop must furnish you with a statement detailing the repairs requested by you; the repairs authorized by you; the repairs needed as determined by the shop; an itemized list of the cost of parts and labor; and identification of all parts replaced, designating whether they are new, used, rebuilt or reconditioned. The shop owner or his designee must also certify that the repairs were completed properly or else give a detailed explanation of why repairs were unable to be properly performed. If a shop willfully and flagrantly violates the above rules, you are entitled, upon winning a court case, to recover double the damages plus reasonable attorney's fees and costs. Report anything that bugs you about an auto repair shop or mechanic to:

Marvin Goldstein, Director
Bureau of Automotive Regulation
Department of State
Mutual Building
208 N. Capitol
Lansing, MI 48918
(517) 373-9064
Toll-free complaint no.: (800) 292-4204

Minnesota[17]

Special Minneapolis and St. Paul ordinances are summarized following the general discussion here. Written estimates are required, on request, if the repairs are to be more than $100 and less than $2,000. The shop may not charge for the estimate unless it informs you beforehand and tells you the basis on which the charge will be calculated. A shop may not exceed the written estimate by more than 10% unless it receives authorization from you and provides you with a revised written estimate. If you refuse to authorize additional repairs over the original estimate, the shop must return your vehicle "as close as possible to its former condition" and release it to you upon payment of charges for repairs actually performed and not more than 10% in excess of the original estimate. If a shop gives you an estimate over the telephone, upon your request and meeting the above monetary criteria, it must make a written estimate and note on it the date, time, telephone number called and the name of the person authorizing repairs. Invoices must contain an itemization for parts, materials, labor, tax and any other other charges; a notation specifying which parts, if any, are used, rebuilt or reconditioned if that information is known by the shop; and a statement of any charge for a service call or for making an estimate. A shop can't keep your car if you refuse to pay for (1) unauthorized repairs, service calls or estimates; (2) charges for service calls or estimates which exceed prior agreement; or (3) charges which exceed by more than 10% those authorized. Any keeping of your car under these circumstances could entitle you to consequential damages, reasonable attorney's fees and punitive damages not to exceed three times the total charge. Upon your request, prior to the start of repairs, the shop must return all replaced parts except those that must be returned to the manufacturer, distributor or other person under a warranty or exchange agreement or as necessary for pending litigation. You must be given a chance to examine warranty or exchange parts for five business days after completion of repairs. Violations should be reported to the Minnesota Office of Consumer Services (see Appendix B).

MINNEAPOLIS[18]

Written estimates are required upon request if the repairs are to total $35 or more. If repairs are to be under $35 you can still request that an estimate be given if and when it's determined that the bill will go over $35. Estimates must include a detailed description of the parts (brand name and whether new, used, rebuilt or reconditioned), labor, incidental services, any charge for release of your car should it not be repaired and any charges for making the estimate. Your authorization must be given before the estimate can be exceeded by 10%. Replaced parts must be returned to you unless they are too large to be easily moved, must be returned to the manufacturer if you wish to take advantage of a parts warranty or can be rebuilt and the repairman will purchase them from you for that purpose. Invoices must itemize all services performed and parts supplied and tell whether any parts are used or rebuilt. Report violations to Consumer Affairs Division of the Department of Licenses and Consumer Services (see Appendix B).

ST. PAUL[19]

Auto repair shops must be licensed, and the City Council has the power to revoke such licenses for "misconduct." Prohibited practices include making false statements in an effort to deceive or mislead you, misrepresenting the characteristics of goods or services and falsely stating that repairs are needed. Complaints should be directed to:

> Joseph F. Carchedi, License Inspector
> Division of License and Permit Administration
> City of St. Paul
> 209 City Hall
> St. Paul, MN 55102
> (612) 298-5056

Montana[20]

You must be given, upon request, a written estimate if the repairs are expected to be over $50. The estimate must include the price for labor and for parts, any storage charges and the approximate date of completion. The shop must get your consent to exceed the estimate by 10% or $25, whichever is greater. Replaced parts must be returned to you upon your request at the time the work order is taken except large or weighty parts or parts that must be returned under a warranty or parts exchange arrangement. The invoice must describe all service work done and parts supplied, except for warranty work, and state whether used, rebuilt or reconditioned parts were used (except parts that have been manufactured and carry a new part warranty). Prohibited practices include misrepresenting that repairs have been made or that your vehicle is in a dangerous condition, knowingly making statements which are deceptive or misleading and making false promises to persuade you to authorize repairs. Report violations to the Consumer Affairs Division of the Department of Business Regulation (see Appendix B).

Nevada[21]

You must be given a written estimate for parts and labor unless you sign a waiver. If a diagnosis must be done prior to giving an estimate, you must be given an estimate for the cost of the diagnosis and the cost of disassembling and reassembling your car in case you don't authorize the repairs. The shop must get your permission to exceed the written estimate by 20% or $40, whichever is less. If you elect not to authorize further repairs, the shop can begin charging you for storage if you don't take possession of your car within 24 hours after notification. You are entitled to the return of replaced parts except those parts which must be returned by the shop under a warranty or exchange arrangement. Prohibited practices include representing that goods are new when they aren't and making false or misleading statements concerning the price of goods or services. Report violations to the Consumer Affairs Division of the Department of Commerce (see Appendix B).

New Hampshire[22]

You must be given a written estimate, upon request, which includes an itemization of the work to be performed, an estimated price for labor and parts and the estimated completion date. The shop can't exceed the estimate by 10% without your permission. The shop isn't liable if the estimated completion date is exceeded because of an act of God, strike, unexpected illness or shortage of labor or parts, or your unavailability to give permission to perform additional work. All parts must be returned to you if you so request prior to the work being performed except parts which must be returned under a warranty or exchange agreement. The invoice must include an itemization of all parts over 50 cents, the number of hours of labor charged, the cost of labor, notation of any subcontracted work, a statement as to whether the repairs are guaranteed or not, the terms of any guarantee and indication of any parts which are used, rebuilt or reconditioned. Report problems to the Consumer Protection and Antitrust Division of the attorney general's office (see Appendix B).

New Jersey[23]

Unless you waive the right, the shop must give you a written estimate showing one of the following: (1) a "not-to-exceed" price; (2) a detailed breakdown of necessary parts and labor; or (3) a price for a specific repair such as a "valve job." In lieu of a written estimate, the shop must give you an oral estimate. The shop can't exceed the estimate without your permission. The shop must give you a copy of any document you sign when you sign it. Upon your request prior to repairs beginning, shops must return all replaced parts except those which are impractical to return because of size or weight or those which must be returned to a manufacturer or distributor under a warranty or exchange agreement. Invoices must itemize parts and labor, and state whether parts are new, used, rebuilt or reconditioned, and include all guarantees and their terms. The shop can't use a fictitious price for prorating guarantee adjustments. Report violations to Department of Law and Public Safety, Division of Consumer Affairs (see Appendix B).

New York[24]

Auto repair shops are licensed by the Department of Motor Vehicles. The department has the power to suspend, revoke or refuse to renew the license of any shop and/or fine any shop for up to $350 per violation or order restitution if the case is not in litigation. Such actions can be taken if a shop engages in fraud or deception or violates any laws or regulations. Complaints are handled only for repairs done within the previous 90 days. Written estimates are required only upon your request. If you do request an estimate, you are entitled to be told in writing the cost of anticipated repairs, the completion date, the charge for reassembly of any parts disassembled for inspection and any service charge to be imposed. The estimate must also indicate the hourly labor charge and whether it is computed by clock hours or flat rate hours. If computed by flat rate, the manual used must be specified and you have the right to see the relevant time rates in the manual upon request. No charge may be made which exceeds the written estimate without your authorization. You are entitled to the return of replaced parts, excluding warranty and exchange parts, only if you ask for them in writing in a timely manner. Invoices must include, among other things, an itemized list of all parts supplied and labor performed, a notation indicating any parts that are used, rebuilt or reconditioned and the terms and time limit of any guarantee. Shops must post a sign telling how their labor charge is computed (clock hours and/or flat rate) and their labor rate per hour. To complain about an auto repair shop, either call one of the following numbers between 7:30 a.m. and 4:30 p.m. or write the address below:

Albany: (518) 474-8943
All others: (800) 342-3823, -24, -25

Department of Motor Vehicles
Division of Vehicle Safety
1st Floor, Core 1
Swan Street Bldg.
Empire State Plaza
Albany, NY 12228

Ohio[25]

Written estimates are mandatory when repairs are anticipated to exceed $25. You must authorize any repairs that exceed the written estimate by 10%. Estimates must include the cost of repair, the basis upon which the charge will be made, the expected completion date, any charge for reassembling parts disassembled for inspection and any service charge to be imposed. No shop can charge you for repairs you haven't authorized. The shop must give you all replaced parts except those that are to be rebuilt or sold by the supplier, provided such intended reuse is made known to you prior to being given the original estimate. Invoices must be itemized and include a list of parts with a statement whether they are new, used or rebuilt; the number of hours of labor charged (except for fiat rate prices); and the name of the mechanic performing the service. Prohibited practices include representing repairs have been made when it isn't so, untruthfully representing that your car is in a dangerous condition and materially understating or misstating the estimated cost of repair services. Report violations to the Consumer Frauds and Crimes Section of the attorney general's office (see Appendix B).

Oregon[26]

Law applies only to body shops. Shop must, upon your request, give you a written estimate for parts and labor. The estimate can't be exceeded without your authorization. Invoices must describe all service work done and parts replaced and reveal if any used parts were supplied or if any component system was composed of new and used parts. Prohibited practices include installing used parts or component systems containing new and used parts when new parts or component systems were to be installed; adding the cost of repairs not actually to be performed to any repair estimate; and charging for repairs not performed. Contact the Consumer Services Division of the Department of Commerce to report violations (see Appendix B).

Pennsylvania[27]

Repair shops must, when possible, record in writing and give to you a copy of the specific repairs you request, or, if you have no specific request, a brief description of your car's problems. Repairs must be authorized by you in writing. The price to be charged for repairs must also be authorized by you or displayed in a clear and conspicuous manner on the premises. If the exact nature of the repairs needed are unknown when you deliver your car for repairs, you must be so informed and given the opportunity to select one of the following three options: (1) No repairs can be performed until you are notified of the exact nature of the repairs to be performed plus the total price to be charged and you give your permission orally or in writing to proceed; (2) repairs can be initiated without your authorization but cannot, unless you are notified, exceed a price specified in advance by you; or (3) the shop can do any repairs without limitation of price provided you are informed of the hourly labor rate prior to the start of repairs. Upon request before repairs commence, you have the right to have any parts replaced returned to you with the exception of parts which must be returned to the manufacturer or someone else under the terms of a warranty or rebuilding arrangement. The shop must tell you before beginning repairs whether any part installed will be new, used, reconditioned or rebuilt; the conditions under which it can charge you for storage and the amount of the storage charges; and the price, if any, for the estimate or diagnosis. The shop must complete repairs within 24 hours after you deliver the car unless you're informed of and consent to a delay. Shops must remedy promptly, at no charge to you, any repair or maintenance service "not performed in a skilled and workmanlike manner" provided you promptly complain or bring the matter to the attention of the repair shop. You must be given an invoice for all repairs and maintenance, including warranty work, which contains an itemized list of service performed; a list of parts supplied by name or number; the price charged for each part and the total parts charge; a notation of any parts that were used, reconditioned or rebuilt; and the labor charge, including the number of hours and the price charged for each hour (labor and parts needn't be itemized if there is a single charge for a particular service which is included in a schedule of charges posted in a clear and conspicuous manner on the premises or otherwise disclosed to you at the time you delivered the car to the shop). No other charges are permitted unless clearly and conspicuously disclosed to you prior to the start of repairs. The shop must give you, at no charge, a copy of any document in which legal obligations are imposed on you. Report violations to the Bureau of Consumer Protection of the attorney general's office (see Appendix B).

Rhode Island[28]

Licenses and regulates body shops only. A shop's license can be denied, suspended or revoked for defrauding a customer, dismantling a car without your authorization, refusing to surrender your car to you after payment of the proper charges for towing and work done, indulging in any unconscionable practice, willfully failing to perform work as contracted for, failing to comply with industry safety standards and failing to comply with laws and regulations pertaining to auto body shops. Contact:

> Thomas Caldarone, Jr., Director
> Automobile Body Repair Shop Commission
> Department of Business Regulation
> 100 North Main St.
> Providence, RI 02903
> (401) 277-2449

Texas

DALLAS[29]

Repair shops are licensed. The city government has the power to revoke or refuse to renew licenses on several grounds, including two convictions within a two-year period of the shop or for violating the motor vehicle repair ordinance. Charges for violations are usually brought in municipal court, where the shops, upon conviction, can be fined from $50 to $200. However, if more than $200 is involved, felony theft charges are brought in state district court, where convictions can bring up to $5,000 in fines and 10 years imprisonment. Shops must give a written or oral estimate of total charges and an estimated completion time unless the job is $15 or less. The estimate can't be exceeded by more than 10% or $10, whichever is greater, without further authorization. If the estimate or further authorization is given over the phone, the shop must record in writing on the work order or invoice the date, time, name of person doing the authorizing and the telephone number called, together with an itemized list of the estimated cost of both parts and labor or additional parts and labor. Shops, prior to taking custody of your car, must supply you with a written itemized schedule of charges including the charges for making an estimate, the cost for release of your car in a disassembled and reassembled state if not repaired, storage charges, towing charges and an itemized list of all other charges other than those included in the estimate. If repairs are to be subcontracted, you must be informed of that fact before handing over custody of your car. You must be given a copy of any document which requires your signature. All parts, except those which must be returned under warranty or exchange agreements, must be returned to you if you so request at the time the estimate is given. If the shop gives you a warranty on repairs, it must disclose to you in writing, among other things, the nature and extent of the warranty, including a description of parts or services included or excluded; the duration of the warranty; all conditions and limitations, and the manner in which the warrantor will fulfill the warranty, such as repair, replacement or refund. Shops must give you an itemized invoice of parts and services and state if parts are used, rebuilt or reconditioned. New car warranty disputes can be handled as well as regular repair disputes. Prohibited practices include intentionally making repairs which are not bona fide or necessary and representing work was done or parts replaced when such is not true. All complaints should go to the city's Department of Consumer Affairs (see Appendix B).

Utah[30]

Written estimates must be given, upon your request, for repairs exceeding $25. The estimate must include the basis upon which you will be charged, the expected completion date, any charges for reassembling parts and any storage charges. The shop may not exceed the written estimate by 10% (excluding taxes) without getting your authorization. Replaced parts must be returned to you unless you waive the right in writing or if the parts are to be rebuilt, returned to the factory under a warranty agreement or if return is impractical due to size, weight or similar factors. The invoice must describe all parts replaced and state whether any used parts were supplied, and must include the name or identification of the mechanic who performed the repairs. Prohibited practices include representing repairs are necessary when they're not, representing repairs have been made when it's not true, telling you that your car is in a dangerous condition when it's not the case and intentionally understating or misstating the estimated cost of repairs. If violations occur, contact the Consumer Protection Division of the attorney general's office (see Appendix B).

Virginia[31]

You're entitled to a written estimate between 10:00 a.m. and 4:00 p.m., upon request, if the repairs are to be more than $25. The estimate shall include the cost of labor, the cost of parts, a description of the work or problem as described or authorized by you and the estimated completion time. Your authorization must be received to go over the estimate by more than 10% or to extend the completion time. A shop may charge you for a written estimate and related diagnostic work if it lets you know of such charges in writing before giving you an estimate or by disclosing the charges on a sign conspicuously posted at the entrance of the facility. The shop must offer to return all replaced parts except warranty, core charge or trade-in parts that must be returned to a manufacturer or distributor unless, on the latter two, you agree to pay the core or trade-in charge. You must be given a written invoice, even for warranty work, indicating separately the charge for labor and for parts except for work done on an advertised single price basis. The invoice must also include identification of those parts provided under warranty and those not and those parts which are used, rebuilt or reconditioned. The shop will not be liable if a delay in the estimated completion date is caused by an act of God, an unexpected shortage of labor or parts or other causes beyond the control of the shop. Complaints should be made to the Virginia Office of Consumer Affairs (see Appendix B).

Washington[32]

Unless you waive the right, you are entitled to a written estimate if the price is expected to exceed $50. If you do request an estimate, you can choose to have the shop contact you for further authorization if the repairs exceed the estimate by more than 10% or you can name your own limit. Replaced parts, except those covered by a manufacturer's warranty, must be returned to you if you so request at the time your work order is taken. The invoice must contain all work done and parts replaced, including warranty repairs, and a statement if any parts are used, rebuilt or reconditioned. Shops cannot place a lien on your car for the following charges: (1) unauthorized work done or parts replaced that are not part of the written estimate, (2) undisclosed used, rebuilt or reconditioned parts used in the repairs, and (3) any parts, except warranty parts, which the shop refuses to return to you. Report violations to the Consumer Protection and Antitrust Division of the attorney general's office (see Appendix B).

Wisconsin[33]

The shop must give you a copy of the repair order describing the repairs to be performed if the repairs may exceed $25 unless there's no face-to-face contact between you and a shop representative. When repairs are to exceed $25 and there's face-to-face contact, the shop has a choice of giving you a price quotation on the repair order which you must take advantage of within five days or a choice of the following: (1) a written estimate which can't be exceeded without your authorization, (2) a written estimate with an okay to proceed with repairs up to an amount you specify, or (3) a chance to waive the right to an estimate. A shop can't charge you for a price quotation or estimate unless it informs you of the price, if any, beforehand, nor can the shop in making the quotation or estimate hit you with a charge that is "clearly excessive in relation to the work involved." The shop must inform you orally or in writing at the time the work order is taken that you are entitled to a return of replaced parts if you request them at that time, except for parts which must be returned to the manufacturer because of a warranty or exchange agreement (this doesn't apply if there's no face-to-face contact between you and a shop representative). The invoice must contain an itemized description of all labor, parts and merchandise supplied, including warranty parts; a statement of any warranty on parts or labor; identification of any parts which are used, rebuilt or reconditioned; the identity of each person performing repairs, including the name of any shop retained as a subcontractor; the total price or separate total prices for parts and labor; and the actual time required to complete repairs if units of time are stated as being based on flat rate time. Shops are prohibited from misrepresenting the terms of any warranty or service agreement, the repairs necessary, that repairs have been made or that a motor vehicle is in a dangerous condition. No shop can collect or attempt to collect for repairs not authorized, which have not been made or which the shop knew or reasonably ought to have known were unnecessary. No shop which is a warrantor or party to a service agreement can refuse to honor the warranty or service agreement. A shop can't keep your car if you refuse to pay for unauthorized repairs as long as you pay for the authorized repairs. Shops can't alter your car with the intent to create a condition requiring repairs. Report violations to the Bureau of Consumer Protection in the Department of Agriculture (see Appendix B).

Updating

To keep up to date on the latest auto repair legislation, get yourself on the mailing list of the Government Affairs Department, Automotive Parts and Accessories Association, 1025 Connecticut Avenue N.W., Washington, DC 20036. The organization issues an annual pamphlet on state auto repair laws and regulations and keeps current with state auto repair legislation.

Appendix B

Federal, State, Local

and Provincial Consumer

Protection Agencies

1. Federal

Chairman
Federal Trade Commission
Washington, DC 20580
(202) 523-3711

Director
Office of Consumer Affairs
Dept. of Health and Human Services
621 Reporters Bldg.
7th and D Sts.
Washington, DC 20201
(202) 755-8820

Director, Communications Service
Consumer and Corporate Affairs Canada
Place du Portage, Phase 1
Hull, PQ K1A OC9
(819) 997-2938

2. State and Local

ALABAMA
Attorney General's Office
of Consumer Protection
560 S. McDonough
Montgomery, AL 36104
(205) 832-5936
800-392-5658

ALASKA
Consumer Protection
Section
Office of Attorney
General
1049 W. 5th St., Suite 101
Anchorage, AK 99501
(907) 279-0428

BRANCH OFFICES
State Court Office
Building
604 Barnette, Room 228
Fairbanks, AK 99707
(907) 456-8588

Pouch K, Room 1568
NBA Bldg.,
217 2nd St.
Juneau, AK 99811
(907) 465-3692

ARIZONA
Economic Protection
Division
Office of Attorney General
1700 W. Washington
Phoenix, AZ 85007
(602) 255-3702

BRANCH OFFICE
402 W. Congress,
Suite 315
100 N. Stone Ave.,
Suite 1004
Tucson, AZ 85701
(602) 628-5501

COUNTY OFFICES

COCHISE COUNTY
Cochise County
Attorney's Office
P.O. Drawer CA
Bisbee, AZ 85603
(602) 432-5703

MARICOPA COUNTY
White Collar Crime
Division
County Attorney's Office
101 W. Jefferson
Phoenix, AZ 85003
(602) 261-5831

PIMA COUNTY
Consumer Protection/
Economic Crime Unit
Pima County Attorney's
Office
111 W. Congress, 9th
Floor
Tucson, AZ 85701
(602) 792-8668

YUMA COUNTY
Yuma County Attorney's
Office
P.O. Box 1048
Yuma, AZ 85364
(602) 782-4534, ext. 55

CITY OFFICES

PHOENIX
Mayor's Citizens
Assistance Office
251 West Washington
Phoenix, AZ 85003
(602) 262-7777

TUCSON
Public Affairs Division
Tucson City Attorney's
Office
P.O. Box 27210
Tucson, AZ 85726
(602) 791-4886

CALIFORNIA
California Department
of Consumer Affairs
1021 O St.
Sacramento, CA 95814
(916) 445-0660

BRANCH OFFICES
107 S. Broadway, Room
8020
Los Angeles, CA 90012
(213) 620-4360

66 Bovet Rd., Suite 3113
San Mateo, CA 94402
(415) 573-2978

Public Inquiry Unit
Office of Attorney
General
555 Capitol Mall
Sacramento, CA 95814
(916) 322-3360

COUNTY OFFICES
ALAMEDA COUNTY
Consumer Fraud
Division
District Attorney's
Office
24405 Amador St.
Hayward, CA 94544
(415) 881-6150

CONTRA COSTA COUNTY

District Attorney's
Office
Special Operations
Division
P.O. Box 670
725 Court St.
Martinez, CA 94553
(415) 372-4500, ext.
4620

DEL NORTE COUNTY

Division of Consumer
Affairs
2650 Washington Blvd.
Crescent City, CA
95531
(707) 464-2716 or
3756

FRESNO COUNTY

Department of Weights,
Measures and
Consumer Protection
4535 E. Hamilton Ave.
Fresno, CA 93702
(209) 453-5904

Consumer Fraud
Division
District Attorney's
Office
Courthouse
1100 Van Ness Ave.
Fresno, CA 93721
(209) 488-3141

KERN COUNTY

Deputy District
Attorney
Consumer Unit
1215 Truxton Ave.
Bakersfield, CA 93301
(805) 861-2421

LOS ANGELES COUNTY

Consumer and
Environment
Protection Division
District Attorney's
Office
540 Hall of Records
320 W. Temple
Los Angeles, CA 90012
(213) 974-3970

Department of
Consumer Affairs
500 W. Temple St.
Room B-96
Los Angeles, CA 90012
(213) 974-1452

MADERA COUNTY

Consumer Protection
Unit
Madera County
Weights and
Measures
902 N. Gateway Dr.
Madera, CA 93637
(209) 674-4641

MARIN COUNTY

Consumer Protection
Div.
District Attorney's
Office
Hall of Justice, Room
180
San Rafael, CA 94903
(415) 499-6482

MENDOCINO COUNTY

District Attorney's
Office
Consumer Unit
P.O. Box 1000
Ukiah, CA 95482
(707) 468-4211

MONTEREY COUNTY

Consumer Affairs Dept.
Monterey County
1220 Natividad Rd.
Salinas, CA 93906
(408) 758-3859

NAPA COUNTY

Deputy District
Attorney
Consumer Affairs
Division
1125 3rd St.
Napa, CA 94558
(707) 253-4427

ORANGE COUNTY

Major Fraud and
Economic Crime Unit
District Attorney's
Office
P.O. Box 808
700 Civic Center Dr.
West
Santa Ana, CA 92702
(714) 834-3600

Office of Consumer
Affairs
511 N. Sycamore St.
Santa Ana, CA 92701
(714) 834-6100

RIVERSIDE COUNTY

Economic Crime
Division
District Attorney's
Office
P.O. Box 1148
Riverside, CA 92502
(714) 787-6372

SACRAMENTO COUNTY

District Attorney's
Fraud Division
P.O. Box 749
Sacramento, CA 95804
(916) 440-6823

SAN DIEGO COUNTY

Consumer Fraud
Division
District Attorney's
Office
P.O. Box X-1011
San Diego, CA 92112
(714) 236-2474

SAN FRANCISCO COUNTY

Consumer Fraud
Economic Crime Unit
District Attorney's
Office
880 Bryant St., Room
320
San Francisco, CA
94103
(415) 553-1821

SAN JOAQUIN COUNTY

Consumer Affairs &
Education
San Joaquin County
2065 East 8th St.
Stockton, CA 95206
(209) 944-2379

SAN LUIS OBISPO COUNTY

Consumer Unit
District Attorney's
Office
302 Courthouse Annex
San Luis Obispo, CA
93408
(805) 549-5800

SAN MATEO COUNTY

Consumer Fraud Unit
District Attorney's
Office
Hall of Justice and
Records
Redwood City, CA
94063
(415) 363-4656

SANTA BARBARA COUNTY

District Attorney's
Office
Consumer Business Law
Section
118 E. Figueroa
Santa Barbara, CA
93101
(805) 963-6173

SANTA CLARA COUNTY

Department of
Consumer Affairs
1553 Berger Dr.
San Jose, CA 95112
(408) 299-4211

Consumer Fraud Unit
District Attorney's
Office
70 W. Hedding St.,
West Wing
San Jose, CA 95110
(408) 275-9651

SANTA CRUZ COUNTY

Office of District
Attorney
Division of Consumer
Affairs
County Building
701 Ocean St., Room
240
Santa Cruz, CA 95060
(408) 425-2054

Consumer Protection
Unit
District Attorney's
Office
P.O. Box 1159
701 Ocean St.
Santa Cruz, CA 95061
(408) 425-2071

SOLANO COUNTY

District Attorney's
Office
Consumer Fraud Unit
600 Union Ave.
Fairfield, CA 94533
(707) 429-6451

STANISLAUS COUNTY

Office of Consumer
Affairs
1100 H St.
Modesto, CA 95353
(209) 523-7707

District Attorney's
Office
Consumer Fraud Unit
P.O. Box 442
Modesto, CA 95353
(209) 577-0570

VENTURA COUNTY

Department of Weights
and Measures
800 S. Victoria Ave.
Ventura, CA 93009
(805) 654-2446

Consumer Fraud
Economic Crime Unit
District Attorney's
Office
800 S. Victoria Ave.
Ventura, CA 93009
(805) 654-3110

YOLO COUNTY

District Attorney's
Office
Consumer Fraud
Division
P.O. Box 446
Davis, CA 95617
(916) 758-4840

CITY OFFICES

CHICO

Chico Consumer
 Protection Agency
Box 3371
Chico, CA 95926
(916) 345-7088

LOS ANGELES

Consumer Protection
 Section
Assistant City Attorney
1700 City Hall East
200 N. Main St.
Los Angeles, CA 90012
(213) 485-4515

Auto Fraud Division
Los Angeles Police
 Dept.
150 North Los Angeles
 St.
Los Angeles, CA 90012
(213) 485-2121

SAN DIEGO

Consumer Protection
 Unit
City Attorney's Office
202 C St.
City Administration Bldg.
San Diego, CA 92101
(714) 236-6007

SANTA MONICA

City Attorney's Office
Consumer Division
1685 Main St.
Santa Monica, CA
 90401
(213) 393-9975

COLORADO

Unit Chief
Consumer Protection
 Act
Office of Attorney
 General
1525 Sherman St., 3rd
 Floor
Denver, CO 80203
(303) 866-3611

COUNTY OFFICES

ARCHULETA, LAPLATA AND SAN JUAN COUNTIES

District Attorney's
 Consumer Office
P.O. Drawer 3455
Durango, CO 81301
(303) 247-8850

ADAMS, ARAPAHOE, DENVER AND JEFFERSON COUNTIES

Metro District
 Attorney's Consumer
 Office
625 South Broadway
Denver, CO 80209
(303) 777-3072

BOULDER COUNTY

District Attorney's
 Consumer Office
P.O. Box 471
Boulder, CO 80306
(303) 441-3700

EL PASO AND TELLER COUNTIES

District Attorney's
 Consumer Office
27 E. Vermijo, Suite 413
County Office Building
Colorado Springs, CO
 80903
(303) 471-5861

LARIMER COUNTY

District Attorney's
 Consumer Office
Rocky Mountain Bank
 Building
P.O. Box 1969
Fort Collins, CO 80522
(303) 221-7000

PUEBLO COUNTY

District Attorney's Office
Consumer Affairs
Courthouse
10th and Main Sts.
Pueblo, CO 81003
(303) 544-0075

WELD COUNTY

District Attorney's
 Consumer Office
P.O. Box 1167
Greeley, CO 80632
(303) 356-4000, ext.
 706, 707

CONNECTICUT

Department of
 Consumer Protection
State Office Building
165 Capitol Ave.
Hartford, CT 06115
(203) 566-4999
800-842-2649

CITY OFFICE

Office of Consumer
 Protection
City Hall
Dekoven Drive
Middletown, CT 06457
(203) 347-4671, ext.
 216

DELAWARE
Consumer Affairs
Division
Department of
Community Affairs
and Economic
Development
820 N. French St., 4th
Floor
Wilmington, DE 19801
(302) 571-3250

Assistant Attorney
General
Consumer Protection
Department of Justice
820 N. French St.
Wilmington, DE 19801
(302) 571-2500

DISTRICT OF COLUMBIA
D.C. Office of
Consumer Protection
1424 K St. N.W.
Washington, DC 20005
(202) 727-1158

FLORIDA
Division of
Consumer Services
110 Mayo Building
Tallahassee, FL 32301
(904) 488-2221
800-342-2176

Consumer Protection
and Fair Trade
Practices Bureau
Department of Legal
Affairs
State Capitol
Tallahassee, FL 32301
(904) 488-8916

BRANCH OFFICES
Dade County Regional
Service Center
401 N.W. 2nd Ave.,
Suite 820
Miami, FL 33128
(305) 377-5441

1313 Tampa St., 8th
Floor
Park Trammell
Tampa, FL 33602
(813) 272-2670

COUNTY OFFICES
BREVARD COUNTY
Consumer Fraud
Division
State Attorney's Office
County Courthouse
400 South St.
Titusville, FL 32780
(305) 269-8401

BROWARD COUNTY
Consumer Affairs
Division
236 S.E. 1st Ave., 6th
Floor
Fort Lauderdale, FL
33301
(305) 765-5306

DADE COUNTY
Consumer Protection
Division
Metro Dade County
140 W. Flagler St., 16th
Floor
Miami, FL 33130
(305) 579-4222

BRANCH OFFICES
South Dade
Government Center
10750 S.W. 211th St.
Miami, FL 33189
(305) 232-1810, ext.
285

Consumer Fraud
Division
Office of State Attorney
1351 N.W. 12th St.
Miami, FL 33125
(305) 547-5200

Consumer Advocate
Metropolitan Dade Co.
44 W. Flagler St., 23rd
Floor
Miami, FL 33130
(305) 579-4206

MANATEE, SARASOTA,
DESOTO COUNTIES
Consumer Fraud
Division
Office of State Attorney
2070 Main St.
Sarasota, FL 33577
(813) 955-0918

DUVAL COUNTY
Division of Consumer
Affairs
Department of Human
Resources
614 City Hall
Jacksonville, FL 32202
(904) 633-3429, 3940

HILLSBOROUGH COUNTY
Hillsborough Co.
Department of
Consumer Affairs
305 N. Morgan St.,
Suite 707
Tampa, FL 33602
(813) 272-6750

PALM BEACH COUNTY
Department of
    Consumer Affairs
324 Daytura St.
West Palm Beach, FL
    33401
(305) 837-2670

Economic Crime Unit
Office of State Attorney
P.O. Drawer 2905
West Palm Beach, FL
    33402
(305) 837-2391

PINELLAS COUNTY
Office of Consumer
    Affairs
Office of State Attorney
801 West Bay Dr.,
    Suite 601
Largo, FL 33540
(813) 448-3801

SEMINOLE COUNTY
Consumer Fraud
    Division
Office of State Attorney
149 Seminole County
    Courthouse
Stanford, FL 32771
(305) 322-7534

CITY OFFICES

Consumer Affairs
    Committee
1080 N.W. 47th Ave.
Lauderhill, FL 33313
(305) 584-9521

Board of Consumer
    Affairs
City of Tamarac
5811 N.W. 88th Ave.
Tamarac, FL 33321
(305) 722-5900, ext.
    26

GEORGIA
Governor's Office of
    Consumer Affairs
225 Peachtree St., NE
Suite 400
Atlanta, GA 30303
(404) 656-4900
800-282-4900

Attorney General for
    Deceptive Practices
Office of Attorney
    General
132 State Judicial
    Building
Atlanta, GA 30334
(404) 656-3391

CITY OFFICE

Office of Consumer
    Affairs
City Hall
Memorial Dr. Annex
121 Memorial Dr., S.W.
Atlanta, GA 30303
(404) 658-6704

HAWAII
Director of Consumer
    Protection
Dept. of Regulatory
    Agencies
P.O. Box 3767
Honolulu, HI 96812
(808) 548-2540

IDAHO
Attorney General's
    Office
Consumer Protection
    Division
State Capitol
Boise, ID 83720
(208) 384-2400
800-632-5937

ILLINOIS
Consumer Advocate
    Office
Governor's Information
    Agency
160 N. LaSalle St.,
    Room 2010
Chicago, IL 60601
(312) 793-2754

Consumer Fraud
    Section
Office of Attorney
    General
228 N. LaSalle St.,
    Room 1242
Chicago, IL 60601
(312) 793-3580

BRANCH OFFICES

228 N. LaSalle,
    Room 1242
(312) 537-8984

1104 N. Ashland Ave.
Chicago, IL 60622
(312) 793-3583

4750 N. Broadway,
    Room 216
Chicago, IL 60640
(312) 769-3742

7906 S. Cottage Grove
Chicago, IL 60619
(312) 488-2600

1104 N. Ashland
Chicago, IL 60622
(312) 793-5638

800 Lee Street
Des Plaines, IL 60016
(312) 824-4200 (Sat.
    only)

P.O. Box 752
71 N. Ottawa St.
Joliet, IL 60434
(815) 722-0433

6101 Capulina
Morton Grove, IL
60053
(312) 965-4658 (Sat.
only)

163 Lakehurst
Waukegan, IL 60085
(312) 473-3302 (Sat.
only)

5127 Oakton St.
Skokie, IL 60065
(312) 674-2522

1339 W. Irving Park Rd.
Bensenville, IL 60106
(312) 595-2374

1616 N. Arlington Hts. Rd.
Arlington Hts. IL 60004
(312) 259-7730 (Wed.
only)

403 W. Galena Blvd.,
Rm. 203
Aurora, IL 60506
(312) 892-4341 (Thur.
only)

500 South Second St.
Springfield, IL 62706
(217) 782-9011

103 S. Washington,
Suite 12
Carbondale, IL 62901
(618) 457-7831

818 Martin Luther
King Dr.
St. Louis, IL 62201
(618) 874-2238

500 Main St.
Peoria, IL 61602
(309) 671-3191

1800 3rd Ave., Room 220
Rock Island, IL 61201
(309) 788-7623

401 W. State St., Suite 301
Rockford, IL 61101
(815) 968-1881

COUNTY OFFICES

COOK COUNTY

Consumer Fraud
Division
Office of State's
Attorney
Rm. 303, Daley Center
Chicago, IL 60602
(312) 443-8425

MADISON COUNTY

Office of State's
Attorney
103 Purcell St., 3rd
Floor
Edwardsville, IL 62025
(618) 692-4550

ROCK ISLAND COUNTY

Office of State's
Attorney
Courthouse
Rock Island, IL 61201
(309) 786-4451

CITY OFFICE

CHICAGO

Department of
Consumer Services
121 N. LaSalle St.,
Room 808
Chicago, IL 60602
(312) 744-4090

INDIANA

Consumer Protection
Division
Office of Attorney
General
215 State House
Indianapolis, IN 46204
(317) 232-6330

COUNTY OFFICES

LAKE COUNTY

Prosecuting Attorney
2293 N. Main St.
Crown Point, IN 46307
(219) 738-9055

MARION COUNTY

Prosecuting Attorney
560 City-County
Building
Indianapolis, IN 46204
(317) 633-3522

VANDERBURG COUNTY

Prosecuting Attorney
Civic Center Complex—
Courts Bldg.
Evansville, IN 47708
(812) 426-5150

CITY OFFICE

GARY

Office of Consumer
Affairs
Annex East
1100 Massachusetts
Gary, IN 46407
(219) 944-6475

IOWA

Consumer Protection
Division
Office of Attorney
General
1300 E. Walnut
Des Moines, IA 50319
(515) 281-5926

Citizens' Aid
Ombudsman
515 E. 12th St.
Des Moines, IA 50319
(515) 281-3592

KANSAS
Consumer Protection
Division
Office of Attorney
General
Kansas Judicial Center
301 W. 10th, 2nd Floor
Topeka, KS 66612
(913) 296-3751

COUNTY OFFICES
JOHNSON COUNTY
District Attorney's
Office
Consumer Fraud
Division
Johnson County
Courthouse, Box 728
Olathe, KS 66061
(913) 782-5000, ext.
318

SEDGWICK COUNTY
Consumer Fraud and
Economic Crime
Division
District Attorney's
Office
Sedgwick County
Courthouse
Wichita, KS 67203
(316) 268-7921

SHAWNEE COUNTY
Assistant District
Attorney for
Consumer Affairs
Rm. 212, Shawnee County
Courthouse
Topeka, KS 66603
(913) 295-4340

CITY OFFICES
KANSAS CITY
Department of
Consumer Affairs
701 N. 7th St., Room
969
Kansas City, KS 66101
(913) 371-2000, ext.
230 or 231

TOPEKA
Consumer Protection
Division
City Attorney's Office
215 E. 7th St.
Topeka, KS 66603
(913) 295-3883

KENTUCKY
Deputy Attorney
General
Consumer Protection
Division
Executive Building
209 St. Clair St.
Frankfort, KY 40601
(502) 564-6607
800-372-2960

COUNTY OFFICE
JEFFERSON COUNTY
Consumer Protection
Department
208 S. Fifth St., Rm.
401
Louisville, KY 40202
(502) 581-6280

CITY OFFICES
Consumer Affairs
Commission
101 E. 4th St.
Owensboro, KY 42301
(502) 684-7251

LOUISIANA
Governor's Office of
Consumer Protection
P.O. Box 44091
2610 A Wooddale Blvd.
Baton Rouge, LA 70804
(504) 925-4401
800-272-9868

Consumer Protection
Section
Office of Attorney
General
1885 Wooddale Blvd.,
Suite 1208
Baton Rouge, LA 70806
(504) 925-4181

BRANCH OFFICE
234 Loyola Ave., 7th
Floor
New Orleans, LA 70112
(504) 568-5575

COUNTY OFFICES
EAST BATON ROUGE
PARISH
Consumer Protection
Center
304 Old Courthouse
Building
P.O. Box 1471
215 St. Louis Ave.
Baton Rouge, LA 70821
(504) 389-3451

JEFFERSON PARISH
Consumer Protection
and Commercial
Fraud Division
District Attorney's
Office
New Courthouse
Annex, 5th Floor
Gretna, LA 70053
(504) 368-1020

Appendix B

MAINE
Assistant Attorney
General
Consumer and Antitrust
Division
505 State Office
Building
Augusta, ME 04333
(207) 289-3716

MARYLAND
Consumer Protection
Division
Office of Attorney
General
26 S. Calvert St., 8th Floor
Baltimore, MD 21202
(301) 659-4250

BRANCH OFFICES

METRO BRANCH OFFICE
5112 Berwyn Rd., 3rd
Floor
College Park, MD
20740
(301) 474-3500

COUNTY OFFICES

ANNE ARUNDEL COUNTY
Board of Consumer
Affairs
Arundel Center
Annapolis, MD 21401
(301) 841-6750, ext.
7300 (in Baltimore)
(202) 261-8250, ext.
7300 (in
Washington, DC)

BALTIMORE COUNTY
Assistant State
Attorney
Major Fraud Unit
309 Court House
Baltimore, MD 21202
(301) 396-4997 (major
cases)

HOWARD COUNTY
Howard County Office
of Consumer Affairs
Carroll Building
3450 Courthouse Dr.
Ellicott City, MD 21043
(301) 992-2176

MONTGOMERY COUNTY
Office of Consumer
Affairs
611 Rockville Pike
Rockville, MD 20852
(301) 279-1776

PRINCE GEORGE'S COUNTY
Consumer Protection
Commission
1142 County
Administration
Building
Upper Marlboro, MD
20772
(301) 952-4700

MASSACHUSETTS
Executive Office of
Consumer Affairs
John W. McCormack
Building
One Ashburton Place,
Room 1411
Boston, MA 02108
(617) 727-7755

Self-Help Consumer
Information Office
John W. McCormack
Building
One Ashburton Place,
Room 1411
Boston, MA 02108
(617) 727-7780

Consumer Protection
Division
Department of Attorney
General
One Ashburton Place,
19th Floor
Boston, MA 02108
(617) 727-8400

BRANCH OFFICES
20 Maple St.
Springfield, MA 01103
(413) 785-1951

COUNTY OFFICES

HAMPSHIRE COUNTY
Consumer Protection
Agency
District Attorney's
Office
Courthouse
Northampton, MA
01060
(413) 584-1597

FRANKLIN COUNTY
Consumer Protection
Agency
District Attorney's
Office
Courthouse
Greenfield, MA 01301
(413) 774-5102

HAMPDEN COUNTY
Consumer Action
Center
721 State St.
Springfield, MA 01109
(413) 737-4376

CITY OFFICES

BOSTON

Mayor's Office of
Consumer Affairs and
Licensing
Rm. 703, City Hall
1 City Hall Square
Boston, MA 02201
(617) 725-3320

FITCHBURG

Central Massachusetts
Legal Services, Inc.
435 Main St.
Fitchburg, MA 01420
(617) 345-1946

LOWELL

Community Team Work
Consumer Division
167 Dutton St.
Lowell, MA 01852
(617) 459-0551

MICHIGAN

Assistant Attorney
General
Consumer Protection
Division
690 Law Building
Lansing, MI 48913
(517) 373-1140

Michigan Consumers
Council
414 Hollister Building
106 N. Allegan St.
Lansing, MI 48933
(517) 373-0947

COUNTY OFFICES

BAY COUNTY

Prosecuting Attorney
Consumer Protection
Unit
Bay County Building
Bay City, MI 48706
(517) 893-3594

GENESEE COUNTY

Prosecuting Attorney
Consumer Affairs Division
South Center Rd.
Burton, MI 48529
(313) 257-3161

MACOMB COUNTY

Consumer Fraud Unit
Office of Prosecuting
Attorney
Macomb Court
Building, 6th Floor
Mt. Clemens, MI 48043
(313) 469-5600

WASHTENAW COUNTY

Consumer Protection
Division
Office of Prosecuting
Attorney
120 Catherine St.
P.O. Box 8645
Ann Arbor, MI 48107
(313) 994-2420

WAYNE COUNTY

Consumer Protection
Agency
Office of Prosecuting
Attorney
Murphy Hall of Justice
1200 6th St.
Detroit, MI 48226
(313) 256-2519

CITY OFFICES

Consumer Affairs
Commission
4500 Maple
Dearborn, MI 48126
(313) 943-2143, 2285

City Consumer Affairs
Department
1600 Cadillac Tower
Detroit, MI 48226
(313) 224-3508

MINNESOTA

Assistant Attorney
General
Consumer Protection
Division
117 University Ave.,
2nd Floor
St. Paul, MN 55155
(612) 296-3353

Office of Consumer
Services
7th and Roberts Sts.
St. Paul, MN 55101
(612) 296-4512
(612) 296-2331
(complaints)

BRANCH OFFICE

604 Alworth Building
Duluth, MN 55802
(218) 723-4891

COUNTY OFFICE

HENNEPIN COUNTY

Assistant County
Attorney
Citizen Protection and
Economic Crime
Division
C 2100 Government
Center
Minneapolis, MN
55487
(612) 348-8105, 4528

CITY OFFICE

MINNEAPOLIS

Consumer Affairs
Division
Department of Licenses
and Consumer
Services
101 A City Hall
Minneapolis, MN
55415
(612) 348-2080

MISSISSIPPI
Consumer Protection
Division
Office of Attorney
General
Justice Building, P.O.
Box 220
Jackson, MS 39205
(601) 354-7130

Consumer Protection
Division
Department of
Agriculture and
Commerce
High and President Sts.
P.O. Box 1609
Jackson, MS 39205
(601) 354-6258

MISSOURI
Consumer Protection
Division
Office of Attorney
General
Supreme Court Building
P.O. Box 899
Jefferson City, MO
65102
(314) 751-3321

BRANCH OFFICES

Wainwright State Office
Bldg.
Suite 1323
St. Louis, MO 63101
111 N. 7th, Suite 903
(314) 444-6815

431 Missouri Office Bldg.
615 E 13th St.
Kansas City, MO 64106
(816) 274-6686

Missouri Consumer
Information Center
(MCIC)
P.O. Box 1157
Jefferson City, MO
65102
(314) 751-4996

MONTANA
Consumer Affairs
Division
Department of Commerce
1424 9th Ave.
Helena, MT 59620
(406) 449-3163

COUNTY OFFICE
Missoula County
Attorney
County Courthouse
200 W. Broadway
Missoula, MT 59801
(406) 721-5700

NEBRASKA
Consumer Protection
Division
Department of Justice
605 S. 14th
Lincoln, NE 68509
(402) 471-2682

COUNTY OFFICE

DOUGLAS COUNTY

Consumer Fraud
Division
County Attorney's
Office
909 Omaha-Douglas
Civic Center
Omaha, NE 68183
(402) 444-7625

NEVADA
Deputy Attorney
General
Consumer Affairs
Division
2501 E. Sahara Ave.
3rd Floor
Las Vegas, NV 89158
(702) 386-5293

Consumer Affairs
Division
Department of
Commerce
2501 E. Sahara Ave.
Las Vegas, NV 89158
(702) 386-5293

BRANCH OFFICE

201 Nye Building
Capitol Complex
Carson City, NV 89710
(702) 885-4340

COUNTY OFFICE

WASHOE COUNTY

Consumer Protection
Division
District Attorney's
Office
P.O. Box 11130
Reno, NV 89520
(702) 785-5652

NEW HAMPSHIRE
Consumer Protection
Antitrust Division
Office of Attorney
  General
State House Annex
Concord, NH 03301
(603) 271-3641

NEW JERSEY
Division of Consumer
  Affairs
Department of Law and
  Public Safety
1100 Raymond
  Boulevard, Room 504
Newark, NJ 07102
(201) 648-4010

COUNTY OFFICES

ATLANTIC COUNTY
Office of Consumer
  Affairs
1601 Atlantic Ave.
Atlantic City, NJ 08401
(609) 345-6700, ext.
  475

BERGEN COUNTY
Office of Consumer
  Affairs
355 Main St.
Hackensack, NJ 07601
(201) 646-2650

BURLINGTON COUNTY
Office of Consumer
  Affairs
54 Grant St.
Mt. Holly, NJ 08060
(609) 261-5054

CAMDEN COUNTY
Office of Consumer
  Affairs
600 Market St.
Camden County
  Admin. Building
Camden, NJ 08101
(609) 757-8387

CUMBERLAND COUNTY
Department of Weights
  and Measures and
  Consumer Protection
788 E. Commerce St.
Bridgeton, NJ 08302
(609) 451-8000, ext.
  369, 370

HUDSON COUNTY
Office of Consumer
  Affairs
County Courthouse
595 Newark Ave.
Jersey City, NJ 07306
(201) 792-3737, ext.
  252

HUNTERDON COUNTY
Office of Consumer
  Affairs
P.O. Box 198, Califon
Lebanon, NJ 07830
(201) 832-5621

MERCER COUNTY
Division of Consumer
  Affairs
County Administration
  Building
640 S. Broad St.
Trenton, NJ 08650
(609) 989-6671

MIDDLESEX COUNTY
Office of Consumer
  Affairs
841 Georges Rd.
North Brunswick, NJ
  08902
(201) 745-2787

MONMOUTH COUNTY
Office of Consumer
  Affairs
Hall of Records
Main St.
Freehold, NJ 07728
(201) 431-7900

MORRIS COUNTY
Office of Consumer
  Affairs
Morris County
  Administration
  Building
Courthouse
  Washington St.
Morristown, NJ 07960
(201) 285-2811

OCEAN COUNTY
Department of
  Consumer Affairs
Ocean County
  Administration Bldg.
101 Hooper Ave.
C.N. 2191
Toms River, NJ 08753
(201) 929-2105

PASSAIC COUNTY
Consumer Affairs
  Division
Administration Building
309 Pennsylvania Ave.
Paterson, NJ 07503
(201) 881-4549

SOMERSET COUNTY
Department of
  Consumer Affairs
County Administration
  Building
Somerville, NJ 08876
(201) 725-4700, ext.
  306

UNION COUNTY
Division of Consumer
Affairs
300 North Ave. East
P.O. Box 186
Westfield, NJ 07091
(201) 233-0502

CITY OFFICES

Consumer Protection
Board
Borough Hall
Fort Lee, NJ 07024
(201) 947-4148

Division of Consumer
Protection
125 Ellison Street,
2nd Floor
Paterson, NJ 07503
(201) 881-3700, 3703

NEW MEXICO
Consumer and
Economic Crime
Division
Office of Attorney
General
P.O. Drawer 1508
Santa Fe, NM 87501
(505) 982-6000

COUNTY OFFICES

BERNALILLO COUNTY
Consumer Affairs
Division
District Attorney's
Office
415 Tijeras
Albuquerque, NM
87102
(505) 848-1200

NEW YORK
Consumer Protection
Board
99 Washington Ave.
Albany, NY 12210
(518) 474-8583

BRANCH OFFICES

Two World Trade
Center
25th Floor
New York, NY 10047
(212) 488-5666

Consumer Frauds and
Protection Bureau
Dept. of Law
Office of Attorney
General
Two World Trade
Center
New York, NY 10047
(212) 488-7450

STATE OFFICE
State Capitol
Albany, NY 12224
(518) 474-5481

BRANCH OFFICES

100 Genesee St., Suite 23
Auburn, NY 13021
(315) 253-9765

38 Riverside Drive
Binghampton, NY
13905
(607) 773-7823

65 Court St.
Buffalo, NY 14202
(716) 842-4396

State Office Building
Veterans Memorial
Highway
Hauppauge, NY 11788
(516) 979-5190

48 Cornelia St.
Plattsburgh, NY 12901
(518) 563-8012

16 Main St. E., Suite 900
Reynolds Arcade
Rochester, NY 14614
(716) 454-4540

333 E. Washington St.
Syracuse, NY 13202
(315) 473-8430

40 Garden St.
Poughkeepsie, NY
12601
(914) 452-7744, 7760

207 Genesee St., Box
528
Utica, NY 13501
(315) 797-6120

317 Washington St.
Watertown, NY 13601
(315) 782-0100

COUNTY OFFICES

ERIE COUNTY
Consumer Fraud
Bureau
District Attorney's
Office
25 Delaware Ave.
Buffalo, NY 14202
(716) 855-2424

Consumer Protection
Committee
95 Franklin St.
Buffalo, NY 14202
(716) 846-6690

KINGS COUNTY
Consumer Frauds and
Economic Crimes
Bureau
Municipal Building
210 Joralemon St.
Brooklyn, NY 11201
(212) 834-5000

NASSAU COUNTY
Office of Consumer
Affairs
160 Old Country Rd.
Mineola, NY 11501
(516) 535-3100

Commercial Frauds
Bureau
310 Old Country Rd.
Mineola, NY 11501
(516) 535-3000

Office of Consumer
Affairs
County Office Building
800 Park Ave.
Utica, NY 13501
(315) 798-5601

Office of Consumer
Affairs
County Civic Center
421 Montgomery St.
Syracuse, NY 13202
(315) 425-3479

Department of Weights
and Measures and
Consumer Affairs
99 Main St.
Orange County
Courthouse Annex
Goshen, NY 10924
(914) 294-5151, ext.
162

District Attorney's
Office of Consumer
Affairs
County Government
Center
Goshen, NY 10924
(914) 294-5471

Department of
Consumer Affairs
206 County Office
Building
Carmel, NY 10512
(914) 225-3641, ext.
215

Citizens Affairs
1600 7th Ave.
Troy, NY 12180
(518) 270-5444

Office of Consumer
Protection
County Office Building
18 New Hampstead Rd.
New City, NY 10956
(914) 425-5280

Department of Weights
and Measures and
Consumer Affairs
19 E. Morris St.
Bath, NY 14810
(607) 776-4949

Department of
Consumer Affairs
Suffolk County Center
Veterans Memorial
Highway
Hauppauge, Long
Island, NY 11787
(516) 979-3100

Consumer Fraud
Bureau
285 Wall St.
Kingston, NY 12401
(914) 331-2926

Director of Weights and
Measures and
Consumer Protection
Municipal Center
Lake George, NY 12845
(518) 792-9951, ext.
264

Frauds Bureau
District Attorney's
Office
111 Grove St.
County Courthouse
White Plains, NY 10601
(914) 682-2160

Office of Consumer
Affairs
County Office Building
White Plains, NY 10601
(914) 682-3300

CITY OFFICES

Babylon Consumer
Protection Board
200 E. Sunrise Highway
Lindenhurst, NY 11757
(516) 957-3021

Colonie Consumer
Protection Agency
Memorial Town Hall
Newtonville, NY 12128
(518) 783-2790

Consumer Affairs
Bureau
Town of Cortlandt
Municipal Building
Croton–on–Hudson,
NY 10520
(914) 739-7900
(Mon.–Fri.: 9:00 a.m.
to Noon)

Greenburgh Consumer
Board
Town of Greenburgh
P.O. Box 205
Elmsford, NY 10523
(914) 693-7808

HUNTINGTON
Consumer Protection
Board
Town Hall, 180 Main St.
Huntington, NY 11743
(516) 351-3007, 3013

MT. VERNON
Office of Consumer
Affairs
City Hall, Rm. 11,
Office of Consumer
Protection
Mt. Vernon, NY 10550
(914) 668-2200, ext.
201

NEW ROCHELLE
Consumer Affairs Office
City Hall
White Plains, NY 10811
(914) 632-2021, ext.
218

NEW YORK CITY
Department of
Consumer Affairs
80 Lafayette St.
New York, NY 10013
(212) 566-5456

NEIGHBORHOOD OFFICES

BROOKLYN
209 Joralemon St.
Brooklyn, NY 11201
(212) 596-4780

QUEENS
120–55 Queens
Boulevard
Room 203
Kew Gardens, NY
11424
(212) 261-2922, 2923

BRONX
Consumer Complaint
Center
1932 Arthur Ave.
Bronx, NY 10457
(212) 299-1400

EAST HARLEM
227 E. 116th St.
New York, NY 10029
(212) 348-0600

STATEN ISLAND
Staten Island Borough
Hall
Staten Island, NY 10301
(212) 390-5154
(212) 390-5155

ORANGEBURG
Consumer Protection
Board
Town of Orangeburg
26 Orangeburg Rd.
Orangeburg, NY 10962
(914) 359-5100

OSWEGO
Office of Consumer
Affairs
104 City Hall, Rm. 103
Oswego, NY 13126
(315) 342-2410

RAMAPO
Consumer Protection
Board
Ramapo Town Hall,
Route 59
Suffern, NY 10901
(914) 357-5100, ext.
57

SCHENECTADY
Bureau of Consumer
Protection
Rm. 22, City Hall
Jay St.
Schenectady, NY 12305
(518) 382-5061

SYRACUSE
Consumer Affairs Office
Rm. 419, City Hall
Syracuse, NY 13202
(315) 473-3240

YONKERS
Office of Consumer
Protection
City Hall, Rm. 316
Yonkers, NY 10701
(914) 965-0707
(914) 963-3980

NORTH CAROLINA
Office of Attorney
General
Consumer Protection
Division
Justice Building, P.O.
Box 629
Raleigh, NC 27602
(919) 733-7741

NORTH DAKOTA
Assistant Attorney
General's Office
Consumer Fraud
Division
State Capitol Building
Bismarck, ND 58505
(701) 224-3404
800-472-2600

QUAD COUNTY
Quad Counties
Community Action
Agency
27½ S. Third
Grand Forks, ND 58201
(701) 746-5431

OHIO
Assistant Attorney
General's Office
Consumer Frauds and
Crimes Section
30 E. Broad St.
Columbus, OH 43215
(614) 466-8831
1-800-282-0515

COUNTY OFFICES

GREENE COUNTY
Consumer Protection
and Education Office
194 E. Church St.
Xenia, OH 45385
(513) 376-1351

LAKE COUNTY
Consumer Protection
Division
Office of Prosecuting
Attorney
Lake County
Courthouse
47 N. Park Place
Painesville, OH 44077
(216) 352-6281

MAHONING COUNTY
Consumer Fraud
Division
County Prosecutor's
Office
County Courthouse
120 Market St.
Youngstown, OH 44502
(216) 747-2000

MONTGOMERY COUNTY
Assistant Prosecuting
Attorney
Fraud Section
County Courts Building
41 N. Perry
Dayton, OH 45422
(513) 228-5126

PORTAGE COUNTY
County Prosecutor's
Office
Consumer Protection
Division
247 S. Chestnut St.
Ravenna, OH 44266
(216) 296-4593

SUMMIT COUNTY
Assistant Prosecuting
Attorney
Bureau of
Investigations
53 E. Center St.
Akron, OH 44308
(216) 379-5230

CITY OFFICES

AKRON
Division of Weights
and Measures and
Consumer Protection
1420 Triplett Boulevard
Akron, OH 44306
(216) 375-2878

CANTON
City Sealer and
Commissioner of
Consumer Protection
919 Walnut Ave., N.E.
Canton, OH 44704
(216) 489-3065

CINCINNATI
Consumer Protection
Division
City Solicitor's Office
236 City Hall
Cincinnati, OH 45202
(513) 352-3971

CLEVELAND
Office of Consumer
Affairs
119 City Hall
601 Lakeside Ave.
Cleveland, OH 44114
(216) 664-3200

COLUMBUS
Director of Community
Services
50 West Gay St., 3rd
Floor
Columbus, OH 43215
(614) 222-8350

DAYTON
Consumer Advocate
Division of Consumer
Services
7 E. 4th St., Room 824
Dayton, OH 45402
(513) 225-5048

TOLEDO
Consumer Protection
Agency
151 N. Michigan Ave.
Toledo, OH 43624
(419) 247-6191

YOUNGSTOWN
Division of Consumer
Affairs
Mill Creek Community
Center
496 Glenwood Ave.
Youngstown, OH 44502
(216) 747-3561

OKLAHOMA
Assistant Attorney
General for
Consumer Protection
112 State Capitol
Building
Oklahoma City, OK
73105
(405) 521-3921

Appendix B

OREGON
Consumer Protection
    Division
Office of Attorney
    General
520 S.W. Yamhill St.
Portland, OR 97204
(503) 229-5522

Consumer Services
    Division
Department of
    Commerce
Labor and Industries
    Building
Salem, Oregon 97310
(503) 378-4320

PENNSYLVANIA
Bureau of Consumer
    Protection
Office of Attorney General
Strawberry Square,
    15th Floor
Harrisburg, PA 17120
(717) 787-9707

BRANCH OFFICES
27 N. 7th St., 1st Floor
Allentown, PA 18102
(215) 821-6690

919 State St., Room
    203
Erie, PA 16501
(814) 871-4371

333 Market St., 19th Floor
Harrisburg, PA 17101
(717) 787-7109

1405 Locust St., Suite
    825
Philadelphia, PA 19102
(215) 238-6475

300 Liberty Ave., Room
    1405
Pittsburgh, PA 15222
(412) 565-5135

507 Linden St., 1st Floor
Scranton, PA 18503
(717) 961-4913

Office of Consumer
    Advocate
Department of Justice
Strawberry Square, 14th
    Floor
Harrisburg, PA 17127
(717) 783-5048

COUNTY OFFICES

ALLEGHENY COUNTY
Bureau of Consumer
    Affairs
320 Jones Law Annex
311 Ross St.
Pittsburgh, PA 15219
(412) 355-5402

ARMSTRONG COUNTY
Armstrong Consumer
    Protection
Community Action
    Agency
125 Queen St.
Kittanning, PA 16201
(412) 548-8696

BUCKS COUNTY
Bucks County
    Department of
    Consumer Protection
Administration Annex
Broad and Union Sts.
Doylestown, PA 18901
(215) 348-7442

CARBON COUNTY
Carbon County Action
    Committee
Consumer Referral
    Service
61 Broadway
Jim Thorpe, PA 18229
(717) 325-3678

CUMBERLAND COUNTY
Bureau of Consumer
    Affairs
114 N. Hanover St.
Carlisle, PA 17013
(717) 249-1133, ext.
    251, 252

DELAWARE COUNTY
Office of Consumer
    Affairs
Toal Building
2nd and Orange Sts.
Media, PA 19063
(215) 891-2430

LANCASTER COUNTY
Consumer Protection
    Commission
Lancaster County
    Courthouse
Lancaster, PA 17602
(717) 299-7921

MONTGOMERY COUNTY
Consumer Affairs
    Department
County Courthouse
Norristown, PA 19404
(215) 278-3565

WESTMORELAND COUNTY
Bureau of Consumer
    Affairs
911 S. Main St.
P.O. Box Q
Greensburg, PA 15601
(412) 836-6170

YORK COUNTY
York County Consumer
    Protection Office
Courthouse
28 E. Market St.
York, PA 17401
(717) 848-3301

CITY OFFICES

Mayor's Office of
Consumer Services
143 City Hall
Philadelphia, PA 19107
(215) 686-6205

Economic Crime Unit
District Attorney's
Office
Centre Square W.
16th and Market Sts.
24th Floor
Philadelphia, PA 19102
(215) 686-8030

PUERTO RICO
Department of
Consumer Affairs
Minillas Station
Torre Norte Building
De Diego Ave., Stop 22
P.O. Box 41059
Santurce, PR 00940
(809) 726-6090

RHODE ISLAND
Public Protection
Consumer Unit
Department of Attorney
General
72 Pine St.
Providence, RI 02903
(401) 277-3163

SOUTH CAROLINA
Office of Citizens
Service
Governor's Office
P.O. Box 11450
Columbia, SC 29211
(803) 758-3261

Department of
Consumer Affairs
2221 Devine St.
Columbia, SC 29250
(803) 758-2040
800-922-1594

Assistant Attorney
General for
Consumer Protection
Rembert Dennis Bldg.
P.O. Box 11549
Columbia, SC 29211
(803) 758-3040

State Ombudsman
Office of Executive
Policy and Program
1205 Pendleton St., 4th
Floor
Columbia, SC 29201
(803) 758-2249

SOUTH DAKOTA
Attorney General's
Office
Division of
Consumer Protection
Insurance Building
Pierre, SD 57501
(605) 773-3215

TENNESSEE
Division of Consumer
Affairs
Department of
Agriculture
Ellington Agriculture
Center
Box 40627, Melrose
Station
Nashville, TN 37204
(615) 741-1461
800-342-8385

Assistant Attorney
General for
Consumer Protection
450 James Robertson
Parkway
Nashville, TN 37219
(615) 741-1671

TEXAS
Consumer Protection
and Antitrust
Division
Office of Attorney
General
P.O. Box 12548,
Capitol Station
Austin, TX 78711
(512) 475-3288

BRANCH OFFICES

4309 N. 10th, Suite B
McAllen, TX 78501
(512) 682-4547

1607 Main St., Suite 1400
Dallas, TX 75201
(214) 742-8944

4824 Alberta Ave.
Suite 160
El Paso, TX 79905
(915) 533-3484

312 County Office
Building
806 Broadway
Lubbock, TX 79401
(806) 747-5238

200 Main Plaza, Suite
400
San Antonio, TX 78205
(512) 225-4191

1220 Dallas Ave., Suite
202
Houston, TX 77002
(713) 650-0666

DALLAS COUNTY

Consumer Fraud
Division
Special Crime Division
2700 Stemmons
Expressway
500 Stemmons Tower
East
Dallas, TX 75207
(214) 630-6300

EL PASO, CULBERSON
AND HUDSPETH
COUNTIES

Consumer Protection
Division
Office of Attorney
General
El Paso County Annex
Building
4824 Alberta St., Suite
160
El Paso, TX 79905
(915) 533-3484

HARRIS COUNTY

Consumer Fraud
Division
Office of District
Attorney
201 Fannin
Houston, TX 77002
(713) 221-5836

TARRANT COUNTY

Assistant District Attorney
Economic Crimes
200 W. Belknap St.
Fort Worth, TX 76102
(817) 334-1261

TRAVIS COUNTY

Consumer Affairs Office
624 B
N. Pleasant Valley Rd.
Austin, TX 78702
(512) 474-6554

WALLER, AUSTIN AND
FAYETTE COUNTIES

District Attorney's
Office
County Courthouse,
Box 171
Hempstead, TX 77445
(713) 826-3335

CITY OFFICES

Department of
Consumer Affairs
1FN 7500 Marilla
Dallas, TX 75201
(214) 670-4433

FORT WORTH

Office of Consumer
Affairs
Weights and Measures
1800 University Dr.
Room 208
Fort Worth, TX 76107
(817) 870-7570

UTAH

Division of Consumer
Affairs
Utah Trade Commission
Department of Business
Regulation
330 E. Fourth S.
Salt Lake City, UT
84111
(801) 533-6441

Consumer Protection
Unit
Office of Attorney
General
236 State Capitol
Salt Lake City, UT
84114
(801) 533-5261

VERMONT

Consumer Protection
Division
Office of Attorney
General
109 State St.
Montpelier, VT 05602
(802) 828-3171
800-642-5149

VIRGINIA

Attorney General's
Office
Division of Consumer
Counsel
11 S. 12th St., Suite 308
Richmond, VA 23219
(804) 786-4075

Consumer Council
Department of
Agriculture and
Consumer Services
Washington Bldg.
1100 Bank St.
Richmond, VA 23219
(804) 786-2042
800-552-9963

BRANCH OFFICE

Four Seasons Office Bldg.
3016 Williams Dr.
Fairfax, VA 22031
(703) 573-1286

COUNTY OFFICES

ARLINGTON COUNTY

Office of Consumer
Affairs
2049 15th St., North
Arlington, VA 22201
(703) 558-2142

FAIRFAX COUNTY

Department of
Consumer Affairs
4031 University Dr.
Fairfax, VA 22030
(703) 691-3214

PRINCE WILLIAM COUNTY

Office of Consumer
Affairs
Garfield Administration
Bldg.
15960 Cardinal Dr.
Woodbridge, VA 22191
(703) 221-4156

CITY OFFICES

ALEXANDRIA

Office of Consumer
Affairs
P.O. Box 178
City Hall
Alexandria, VA 22313
(703) 838-4350, 4351,
4353

NORFOLK

Division of Consumer
Protection
Rm. 804, City Hall
Building
Norfolk, VA 23501
(804) 441-2823

ROANOKE

Citizens Request for
Services
Consumer Protection
Rm. 353, Municipal
Building
215 Church Ave., S.W.
Roanoke, VA 24011
(703) 981-2583

VIRGINIA BEACH

Division of Consumer
Protection
City Hall
Virginia Beach, VA
23456
(804) 427-4421

WASHINGTON

Attorney General's
Office
Consumer Protection
and Antitrust
Division
1366 Dexter Horton
Building
Seattle, WA 98104
(206) 464-7744
800-552-0700

BRANCH OFFICES

Temple of Justice
Olympia, WA 98504
(206) 753-6210

960 Paulsen Professional
Building
Spokane, WA 99201
(509) 456-3123

949 Market St. Suite 380
Tacoma, WA 98402
(206) 593-2904

COUNTY OFFICE

KING COUNTY

Prosecuting Attorney's
Office
Fraud Division
E531 King County
Courthouse
Seattle, WA 98104
(206) 583-2200

CITY OFFICES

EVERETT

Weights and Measures
Department
City Hall
3002 Wetmore Ave.
Everett, WA 98201
(206) 259-8845

SEATTLE

Department of Licenses
and Consumer Affairs
102 Municipal Building
Seattle, WA 98104
(206) 625-2536
(206) 625-2712
(Complaint Line)

WEST VIRGINIA

Consumer Protection
Division
Office of Attorney
General
3412 Staunton Ave.,
S.E.
Charleston, WV 25304
(304) 348-8986

CITY OFFICE

Consumer Protection
Department
P.O. Box 2749
Charleston, WV
25330
(304) 348-8173

WISCONSIN

Office of Consumer
Protection
123 W. Washington Ave.
P.O. Box 7856
Madison, WI 53707
(608) 266-1852

BRANCH OFFICE

State Office Building
819 N. 6th St., Room
520
Milwaukee, WI 53203
(414) 224-1867

Division of Consumer
Protection
Department of
Agriculture, Trade
and Consumer
Protection
P.O. Box 8911
Madison, WI 53708
(608) 266-9837
800-362-3020

BRANCH OFFICES

1727 Loring Ave.
Altoona, WI 54720
(715) 836-2861

1181 A Western Ave.
Green Bay, WI 54303
(414) 497-4210

10320 W. Silver Spring
Dr.
Milwaukee, WI 53225
(414) 257-8962

COUNTY OFFICES

KENOSHA COUNTY

Consumer Investigator
912 56th St.
Kenosha, WI 53140
(414) 656-6480

MARATHON COUNTY

District Attorney's
Office
Marathon County
Court House
Wausau, WI 54401
(715) 842-0471

MILWAUKEE COUNTY

District Attorney's
Office
Consumer Fraud Unit
821 W. State St.
Room 412
Milwaukee, WI 53233
(414) 278-4792

PORTAGE COUNTY

District Attorney's
Office
Consumer Fraud Unit
Portage County
Court House
Stevens Point, WI
54481
(715) 346-3393

RACINE COUNTY

District Attorney's
Office
Consumer Fraud
Division
Racine County Sheriff
Office
1717 Wisconsin Ave.
Racine, WI 53403
(414) 636-3125

WYOMING

Consumer Protection
Division
Attorney General's
Office
123 Capitol Building
Cheyenne, WY 82002
(307) 777-7841

3.   Canadian Provincial

ALBERTA
Consumer Credit
Dept. of Consumer and Corporate
Affairs
10065 Jasper Ave.
Edmonton, Alta. T5J 3B1
(403) 427-5210

BRITISH COLUMBIA
Consumer Education and Information
Branch
Ministry of Consumer and Corp.
Affairs
940 Blanchard St.
Victoria, B.C. V8W 3E6
(604) 387-1251

CONSUMER CENTERS

Kamloops:	(604) 374-5676
Prince George:	(604) 562-9331
Vancouver:	(604) 666-6971
Victoria:	(604) 388-3341

MANITOBA
Consumers' Bureau
307 Kennedy St.
Winnipeg, Man. R3C OV8
(204) 956-2040
(1-800) 262-8844

NEW BRUNSWICK
Consumer and Corporate Services
Department of Justice
348 King St.
P.O. Box 6000
Fredericton, N.B. E3B 5H1
(506) 453-2682

NEWFOUNDLAND
Consumer Affairs Division
Elizabeth Towers, Elizabeth Ave.
St. John's, Nfld. A1C 5T7
(709) 737-2591

NORTHWEST TERRITORIES
Consumer Services
Dept. of Justice and Public Services
Yellowknife, N.T. X1A 2L9
(403) 873-7406

NOVA SCOTIA
Consumer Services Bureau
Dept. of Consumer Affairs
5151 Terminal Rd.
P.O. Box 998
Halifax, N.S. B3J 2X3
(902) 424-4690

ONTARIO
Consumer Advisory Services Bureau
555 Yonge St., 8th Floor
Toronto, Ont. M7A 2H6
(416) 963-0321

PRINCE EDWARD ISLAND
Director of Consumer Services
Dept. of Community Affairs
Box 2000
Queen, P.E.I. C1A 7N8
(902) 892-5321

QUEBEC
Office de la protection du
  consommateur
6 rue de l'université
Quebec, P.Q. G1R 5G8
(418) 643-1467

REGIONAL BUREAUS

Quebec:	(418) 643-1467
Montreal:	(514) 255-0344
Outaouais:	(819) 770-9004
Bas St.-Laurent:	(418) 724-6692
Laurentides-Lanaudière:	
	(514) 432-3110
Côte-Nord:	(418) 968-8581
Abitibi-Temiscamingue:	
	(819) 762-2355
Estrie:	(819) 566-4266
Mauricie Bois-France:	
	(819) 374-2424
Saguenay-Lac St.-Jean:	
	(418) 547-5741
Montreal-Rive Sud:	
	(514) 463-1888
Gaspesie-Iles de la Madeleine:	
	(418) 368-4141

SASKATCHEWAN
Communication and Extension Branch
Consumer and Commercial Affairs
1871 Smith St.
Regina, Sask. S4P 3V7
(306) 565-5577

YUKON
Consumer Affairs Officer
Dept. of Consumer and Corp. Affairs
Box 2703
Whitehorse, Y.T. Y1A 2C6
(403) 667-5212

Appendix C

Consumer Activist Organizations

1. National

National Consumer Assistance Center
American Assn. of Retired Persons
1909 K St. N.W.
Washington, DC 20049
(202) 872-4700

Phil Edmonston, President
Automobile Protection Assn.
292 Boul. St. Joseph O.
Montreal, Que. H2V 2N7
(514) 273-1733
  Branch:
  255 Argyle
  Ottawa, Ont. K2P 1B8
  (613) 235-9941

Clarence M. Ditlow III
Executive Director
Center for Auto Safety
1223 Dupont Circle Bldg.
Washington, DC 20036
(202) 659-1126

Consumer Federation of America
1314 14 St. N.W.
Washington, DC 20005
(202) 387-6121

Consumers' Assn. of Canada
2660 S. Vale Crescent, Level 3
Ottawa, Ont. K1B 5C4
(613) 733-9450

National Insurance Consumer
  Organization
344 Commerce St.
Alexandria, VA 23314
(703) 549-8050

Public Citizen Litigation Group
2000 P St. N.W.
Washington, DC 20036
(202) 785-3704

Ralph Nader
c/o Center for the Study of
  Responsive Law
Box 19367
Washington, DC 20036
(202) 387-8030

2. State and Local

The following are involved in complaint resolution or lobbying or both. Some, as noted, are for low-income or elderly persons only.

ALASKA
Kenai Peninsular Consumer Council
P.O. Box 2940
Kenai, AK 99611
(907) 283-7838

ARIZONA
Arizona Consumers Council
P.O. Box 1288
Phoenix, AZ 85001
(602) 265-9625

CALIFORNIA
Consumer Federation of California
621 South Virgil Ave.
Los Angeles, CA 90005
(213) 736-1316

Consumer Fraud Action
2512 South Central
Los Angeles, CA 90011
(213) 232-4917
  (low income)

Consumer Action
1417 Irving
San Francisco, CA 94115
(415) 922-3500

Consumers United of Palo Alto, Inc.
P.O. Box 311
Palo Alto, CA 94301
(415) 325-1924

Oakland/Alameda County Consumer
  Council
4538 East 14th St.
Oakland, CA 94601
(415) 261-6522

Consumers Aid of Shasta Inc.
P.O. Box 4684
Redding, CA 96099
(916) 243-3031

Consumer Protection Project
308 Westwood Plaza, UCLA
Los Angeles, CA 90024
(213) 825-2820

Pasadena Community and Consumer
  Action Center
1020 N. Fair Oaks
Pasadena, CA 91103
(213) 794-7194

COLORADO
Colorado League for Consumer
  Protection
8230 West Sixteenth Place
Lakewood, CO 80215
(303) 233-5891

CONNECTICUT
Connecticut Citizen Action Group
Box 6390
130 Washington St.
Hartford, CT 06106
(203) 527-7191

DISTRICT OF COLUMBIA
Archie G. Richardson, Jr., President
Automobile Owners Action Council
1025 Vermont Ave., N.W., Suite 750
Washington, DC 20005
(202) 638-5550

D.C. Consumers Assn.
440 Emerson St. N.W.
Washington, DC 20011
(202) 882-2230

Consumer Protection Center
George Washington Univ.
2000 H St. N.W. Suite 100
100 Bacon Hall
Washington, DC 20052
(202) 676-7585

Neighborhood Legal Services
1337 H St. N.E.
Washington, DC 20002
(202) 399-6431
  (low-income)

FLORIDA
Florida Consumer's Federation
Box 2206
West Palm Beach, FL 33402
(305) 832-6077

GEORGIA
Price Neighborhood Service Center
215 Lakewood Ave., S.W.
Atlanta, GA 30315
(404) 624-1281
  (low-income)

IDAHO
Idaho Consumer Affairs, Inc.
106 North Sixth St.
Boise, ID 83702
(208) 343-3554

Idaho Legal Aid Services, Inc.
P.O. Box 973
Lewiston, ID 83501
(208) 743-1556
  (low-income)

ILLINOIS
Village of Skokie Consumer Affairs
  Commission
5127 Oakton St.
Skokie, IL 60077
(312) 673-0550 or 676-0863

Chicago Consumer Coalition
5516 South Cornell
Chicago, IL 60637
(312) 955-0197

Fenton Action Consumer Team
Fenton High School
1000 West Green St.
Bensenville, IL 60106
(312) 766-2500

INDIANA
Consumer Center
730 East Washington St.
Fort Wayne, IN 46802
(219) 422-7630

IOWA
Iowa Consumers League
Box 189
102½ N. Franklin St.
Corydon, IA 50060
(515) 872-2329

KANSAS
Consumer Assistance Center
217 Seth Child Rd.
Manhattan, KS 66502
(913) 776-9294
(800) 432-2703
  (for elderly)

Consumer Relations Board
Kansas State University
Student Government Services
Manhattan, KS 66506
(913) 532-6541

Consumer United Program
8410 West Highway 54
Wichita, KS 67209
(316) 722-4251

KENTUCKY
Consumer Advisory Council
Rm. 116, Capitol Bldg.
Frankfort, KY 40601
(502) 564-2200

LOUISIANA
Louisiana Consumers' League
P.O. Box 52882
Baton Rouge, LA 70152
(504) 581-9322

MAINE
Northeast Combat
189 Exchange St.
Bangor, ME 04401
(207) 947-3331

MARYLAND
Maryland Citizens Consumer Council
Box 34526
Bethesda, MD 20034
(301) 249-7042

MASSACHUSETTS
Association of Massachusetts
  Consumers
Boston College Economics
  Department
140 Commonwealth Ave.
Chestnut Hill, MA 02167
(617) 969-0100

MICHIGAN
Consumer Research Advisory Council
2990 East Grand Blvd.
Detroit, MI 48202
(313) 871-2087

Michigan Citizens Lobby
19111 West 10 Mile Rd., Ste. 206
Southfield, MI 48075
(313) 356-1250

Michigan Consumers Council
414 Hollister Bldg.
106 W. Allegan St.
Lansing, MI 48933
(517) 373-0947

MISSISSIPPI
Mississippi Consumers' Assn.
375 Culley Dr.
Jackson, MS 39206
(601) 362-6643

MONTANA
Montana Legal Services Assn.
Neighborhood Facilities Bldg.
201 S. Last Chance Gulch, Rm. 212
Helena, MT 59601
(406) 442-4510
  (low-income)

NEW JERSEY
Consumers League of New Jersey
20 Church St.
Montclair, NJ 07042
(201) 744-6449

Essex–Newark Legal Services Project
18 Rector St.
Newark, NJ 07102
(201) 624-4500
  (low-income)

NEW YORK
New York Consumer Assembly
989 Ave. of the Americas
New York, NY 10018
(212) 594-6020

Consumer Action
St. U. College, Room 302
1300 Elmwood
Buffalo, NY 14222
(716) 881-6154

Niagara Frontier Consumers Assn.
2912 Delaware Ave.
Buffalo, NY 14217
(716) 881-6154

OHIO
Ohio Consumer Assn.
Box 1559
Columbus, OH 43216
(614) 227-6344

Cleveland Consumer Action
445 The Arcade
Cleveland, OH 44114
(216) 687-0525

Consumer League of Ohio
1365 Ontario, Rm. 513
Cleveland, OH 44114
(216) 621-1175

Consumer Protection Assn.
3134 Euclid Ave.
Cleveland, OH 44115
(216) 881-3434
  (low-income)

Appendix C

OKLAHOMA
Consumer Action Council
361 Student Union
Oklahoma State University
Stillwater, OK 74074
(405) 624-7523

Legal Aid Society of Western
  Oklahoma, Inc.
1000 Court Plaza
2228 Robert S. Kerr Ave.
Oklahoma City, OK 73102
(405) 272-9461
  (low-income)

PENNSYLVANIA
Pennsylvania League for Consumer
  Protection
P.O. Box 948
Harrisburg, PA 17108
(717) 233-5704

Pennsylvania Consumers Board
Houston Hall, 1st Floor
3417 Spruce St.
Philadelphia, PA 19104
(215) 243-6000

Consumers Education and
  Protective Assn.
6048 Ogontz Ave.
Philadelphia, PA 19141
(215) 424-1441

Alliance for Consumer Protection
Public Works Bldg.
Route 51
Fallston, PA 15066
(412) 728-5700, ext. 422

RHODE ISLAND
Rhode Island Consumers' Council
365 Broadway
Providence, RI 02909
(401) 277-2764

TEXAS
Texas Consumers Assn.
500 W. 13 St.
Austin, TX 78701
(512) 477-1882

VIRGINIA
Virginia Citizens Consumer Council
Box 777
Springfield, VA 22150
(703) 370-2030

  BRANCH OFFICES
  Roanoke: (703) 345-6781
  Tidewater: (804) 424-5186

WASHINGTON
Seattle Consumer Action Network
312 Lowman Bldg.
107 Cherry St.
Seattle, WA 98114
(206) 623-6650

Citizens Action
P.O. Box 159
Bellingham, WA 98227
(206) 734-5121

WISCONSIN
Concerned Consumers League
614 West National Ave.
Milwaukee, WI 53204
(414) 645-1808

Center for Consumer Affairs
University Extension
929 North Sixth St.
Milwaukee, WI 53203
(414) 224-4177

Appendix D

Call for Action Stations

Altoona, PA: WFBG, (814) 944-9336

Atlanta, GA: WSB, (404) 873-1980

Baltimore, MD: WBAL,
(301) 366-5900

Boston, MA: WBZ, (617) 787-2300

Buffalo, NY: WIVB-TV,
(716) 874-1700

Chicago, IL: WIND, (312) 644-0560

Cleveland, OH: WJKW-TV,
(216) 578-0700

Columbus, OH: WBNS-TV,
(614) 463-9494

Decatur, IL: WDZ, (217) 428-1050

Denver, CO: KLZ, (303) 759-2285

Detroit, MI: WJR, (313) 873-8700

Durham, NC: WRAL-TV,
(919) 688-9306

Ft. Wayne, IN: WOWO,
(219) 424-3030

Kansas City, KS: KCMO,
(913) 576-7700

Long Island, NY: WGSM,
(516) 423-1400

Los Angeles, CA: KFWB,
(213) 461-4366

Memphis, TN: WDIA,
(901) 278-6316

Miami, FL: WCIX-TV,
(305) 371-6566

New Bedford, MA: WBSM,
(617) 997-3349

New Haven, CT: WELI,
(203) 281-1011

New York, NY: WMCA,
(212) 586-6666

Oklahoma City, OK: KOCO–TV,
(405) 232-2755

Orlando, FL: WDBO,
(305) 841-8181

Philadelphia, PA: KYW,
(215) 925-1060

Providence, RI: WEAN,
(401) 277-7621

Raleigh, NC: WRAL-TV,
(919) 832-7578

St. Louis, MO: KMOX,
(314) 421-1975

San Diego, CA: KGTV,
(714) 263-2294

Syracuse, NY: WHEN,
(315) 457-6116

Utica, NY: WTLB, (315) 797-0120

Washington, DC: WTOP,
(202) 686-8225

Youngstown, OH: WFMJ,
(216) 744-5155

Appendix E

Better Business Bureau Offices

BIRMINGHAM, AL 35203
  2026 Second Ave. N., Suite 2303
  (205) 323-6127
HUNTSVILLE, AL 35804
  102 Clinton Ave., W.
  Terry Hutchens Building, Suite 512
  P.O. Box 382
  (205) 533-1640
MOBILE, AL 36602
  307 Van Antwerp Building
  (205) 433-5494

ARIZONA
PHOENIX, AZ 85013
  4428 N. 12th St.
  (602) 264-1721
TUCSON, AZ 85701
  100 E. Alameda St., Suite 403
  Inq. (602) 622-7651
  Comp. 622-7654

ARKANSAS
LITTLE ROCK, AR 72204
  1216 South University
  (501) 664-7274

CALIFORNIA
BAKERSFIELD, CA 93301
  705 Eighteenth St.
  (805) 322-2074
COLTON, CA 92324
  1265 North La Cadena
  (714) 825-7280
FRESNO, CA 93721
  413 T.W. Patterson Building
  (209) 268-6424
LOS ANGELES, CA 90005
  639 South New Hampshire Ave.,
  3rd Floor
  (213) 383-0992
OAKLAND, CA 94612
  360 22nd St., El Dorado Building
  (415) 839-5900
PALM DESERT, CA 92260
  74–273½ Highway 111
  (714) 346-2014
SACRAMENTO, CA 95814
  1401 21st St., Suite 305
  (916) 443-6843
SALINAS, CA 93901
  20 West Gabilan St., Suite 3
  (408) 757-2022

SAN DIEGO, CA 92105
4310 Orange Ave.
(714) 283-3927
SAN FRANCISCO, CA 94109
2740 Van Ness Ave., #210
(415) 775-3300
SAN JOSE, CA 95155
P.O. Box 8110
(408) 298-5880
SAN MATEO, CA 94401
20 North San Mateo Dr.,
P.O. Box 294
(415) 347-1251, 52, 53
SANTA BARBARA, CA 93102
P.O. Box 746
(805) 963-8657
STOCKTON, CA 95202
1111 North Center St.
(209) 948-4880
TUSTIN, CA 92680
17662 Irvine Blvd., Suite 15
Inq. (714) 544-5842
Comp. 544-6942

COLORADO
COLORADO SPRINGS, CO 80903
524 South Cascade
(303) 636-1155
DENVER, CO 80204
841 Delaware St.
(303) 629-1036

CONNECTICUT
FAIRFIELD, CT 06430
P.O. Box 1410
(203) 368-6538
HARTFORD, CT 06103
250 Constitution Plaza
(203) 247-8700
NEW HAVEN, CT 06501
35 Elm St., P.O. Box 2015
(203) 787-5788

DELAWARE
MILFORD, DE 19963
20 South Walnut St., P.O. Box 300
(302) 856-6969

WILMINGTON, DE 19807
1901-B West Eleventh St.,
P.O. Box 4085
(302) 652-3833

DISTRICT OF COLUMBIA
WASHINGTON, D.C. 20005
1334 G St., N.W., Prudential Bldg.,
6th Floor
(202) 393-8000

FLORIDA
MIAMI, FL 33138
8600 NE 2nd Ave.
(305) 757-3446
WEST PALM BEACH, FL 33409
3015 Exchange Ct.
(305) 686-2200

GEORGIA
ATLANTA, GA 30335
212 Healey Building,
57 Forsyth St., N.W.
(404) 688-4910
AUGUSTA, GA 30903
P.O. Box 2085
(404) 722-1574
COLUMBUS, GA 31907
Cross Country Plaza Office Building,
Suite 260, P.O. Box 6889
(404) 568-3030, 31
SAVANNAH, GA 31405
6822 Abercorn
(912) 354-7521

HAWAII
HONOLULU, HI 96813
677 Ala Moana Blvd., Suite 614
(808) 531-8131, 32, 33
KAHULUI, HI 96732
P.O. Box 311
(808) 877-4000

IDAHO
BOISE, ID 83702
Idaho Building, Suite 324
(208) 342-4649

ILLINOIS
CHICAGO, IL 60601
  35 East Wacker Dr.
  Inq. (312) 346-3868
  Comp. 346-3313
PEORIA, IL 61602
  109 S.W. Jefferson St., Suite 305
  (309) 673-5194

INDIANA
ELKHART, IN 46515
  118 South Second St., P.O. Box 405
  (219) 293-5731
FORT WAYNE, IN 46802
  716 South Barr St.
  (219) 423-4433
GARY, IN 46408
  2500 West Ridge Rd.,
  Calumet Township
  (219) 980-1511
INDIANAPOLIS, IN 46205
  300 East Fall Creek Blvd., Suite 501
  (317) 923-1593
MARION, IN 46952
  204 Iroquois Building
  (317) 668-8954
MUNCIE, IN 47306
  Ball State Univ. BBB,
  Whitinger Bldg., Rm. 160
  (317) 285-6375
SOUTH BEND, IN 46601
  230 West Jefferson Blvd.
  (219) 234-0183
TERRE HAUTE, IN 47801
  105 S. Third St.
  (812) 234-7749

IOWA
DAVENPORT, IA 52801
  619 Kahl Building
  (319) 322-0782
DES MOINES, IA 50309
  234 Insurance Exchange Building
  (515) 243-8137
SIOUX CITY, IA 51101
  Benson Bldg., Suite 645,
  7th & Douglas Sts.
  (712) 252-4501

KANSAS
TOPEKA, KS 66607
  501 Jefferson, Suite 24
  (913) 232-0454
WICHITA, KS 67202
  300 Kaufman Bldg.
  (316) 263-3146

KENTUCKY
LEXINGTON, KY 40505
  1523 North Limestone
  (606) 252-4492
LOUISVILLE, KY 40203
  844 S. Fourth St.
  (502) 583-6546

LOUISIANA
BATON ROUGE, LA 70806
  2055 Wooddale Blvd.
  (504) 926-3010
HOUMA, LA 70361
  300 Bond St., Box 9129
  (504) 868-3456
LAFAYETTE, LA 70502
  804 Jefferson St., P.O. Box 3651
  (318) 234-8341
LAKE CHARLES, LA 70602
  1413 Ryan St., Suite C,
  P.O. Box 1681
  (318) 433-1633
MONROE, LA 71201
  141 De Siard St., 141 ONB Bldg.,
  Suite 503
  (318) 387-4600
NEW ORLEANS, LA 70130
  301 Camp St., Suite 403
  (504) 581-6222
SHREVEPORT, LA 71101
  320 Milam St.
  (318) 221-8352
  [Texarkana residents call
  (214) 792-7691]

MARYLAND
BALTIMORE, MD 21201
  401 North Howard St.
  (301) 685-6986

BETHESDA, MD 20084
6917 Arlington Rd.
(301) 656-7000

MASSACHUSETTS
BOSTON, MA 02111
150 Tremont St.
(617) 482-9151
HYANNIS, MA 02601
The Federal Bldg., Suite 1,
78 North St.
(617) 771-3022
LAWRENCE, MA 01840
316 Essex St.
(617) 687-7666
NEW BEDFORD, MA 02740
908 Purchase St.
(617) 999-6060
SPRINGFIELD, MA 01103
293 Bridge St., Suite 324
(413) 734-3114
WORCESTER, MA 01601
32 Franklin St., P.O. Box 379
(617) 755-2548

MICHIGAN
DETROIT, MI 48226
150 Michigan Ave.
(313) 962-7566
GRAND RAPIDS, MI 49503
1 Peoples Building
(616) 774-8236
Holland/Zeeland (616) 772-6063
Muskegon (616) 722-0707

MINNESOTA
ST. PAUL, MN 55104
1745 University Ave.
(612) 646-4631

MISSISSIPPI
JACKSON, MS 39205
P.O. Box 2090
(601) 948-4732

MISSOURI
KANSAS CITY, MO 64106
906 Grand Ave.
(816) 421-7800
ST. LOUIS, MO 63102
Mansion House Center,
440 N. Fourth St.
(314) 241-3100
SPRINGFIELD, MO 65808
P.O. Box 4331
Holland Bldg., Park Central
(417) 862-9231

NEBRASKA
LINCOLN, NE 68504
719 North 48th St.
(402) 467-5261
OMAHA, NE 68102
417 Farnam Building,
1613 Farnam St.
(402) 346-3033

NEVADA
LAS VEGAS, NV 89104
1829 East Charleston Blvd.,
Suite 103
(702) 382-7141
RENO, NV 89505
372-A Casazza Dr., P.O. Box 2932
(702) 322-0657

NEW HAMPSHIRE
CONCORD, NH 03301
1 Pillsbury St.
(603) 224-1991

NEW JERSEY
COLLINGSWOOD, NJ 08108
836 Haddon Ave., P.O. Box 303
(609) 854-8467
CRANBURY, NJ 08512
Rte. 130 South River Rd
Mercer County
(609) 586-1464
(Monmouth County 536-6306)
(Middlesex, Somerset and
Hunterdon Counties 297-5000)

NEWARK, NJ 07102
34 Park Place
(201) 643-3025
PARAMUS, NJ 07652
2 Forest Ave.
(201) 845-4044
TOMS RIVER, NJ 08753
1721 Route 37 East
(201) 270-5577

NEW MEXICO
ALBUQUERQUE, NM 87110
2921 Carlisle, N.E.
(505) 884-0500
FARMINGTON, NM 87401
1206 East 20th St., Suite 4
(505) 325-1136
SANTA FE, NM 87501
227 East Palace Ave., Suite C
(505) 988-3648

NEW YORK
BUFFALO, NY 14203
775 Main St.
(716) 856-7180
NEW YORK, NY 10010
257 Park Ave. South
Inq. & Comp. (212) 533-6200
Other 533-7500
NEW YORK, NY 10010
257 Park Ave. South (Harlem)
(212) 749-7106
ROCHESTER, NY 14604
1122 Sibley Tower Bldg.
(716) 546-6776
SYRACUSE, NY 13202
Suite 512, University Bldg.
120 East Washington St.
(315) 479-6635
UTICA, NY 13501
209 Elizabeth St.
(315) 724-3129
WESTBURY, NY 11590
435 Old Country Rd.
(516) 334-7662

WHITE PLAINS, NY 10601
158 Westchester Ave.
(914) 428-1230, 31
120 E. Main, Wappinger Falls,
12590
(914) 297-6550

NORTH CAROLINA
ASHEVILLE, NC 28801
29½ Page Ave.
(704) 253-2392
CHARLOTTE, NC 28202
Commerce Center, Suite 1300
(704) 332-7152
GREENSBORO, NC 27410
3608 West Friendly Ave.,
(919) 852-4240, 41, 42
RESEARCH TRIANGLE PARK, NC
27709
100 Park Dr. Building, Suite 203,
P.O. Box 12033
(919) 549-8221
WINSTON-SALEM, NC 27101
914 First Union National Bank Bldg.
(919) 725-8348

OHIO
AKRON, OH 44308
P.O. Box F 596
(216) 253-4590
CANTON, OH 44702
500 Cleveland Ave., North
(216) 454-9401
CINCINNATI, OH 45202
26 East Sixth St.
(513) 421-3015
CLEVELAND, OH 44115
1720 Keith Building
(216) 241-7678
COLUMBUS, OH 43215
527 S. High St.
(614) 221-6336
DAYTON, OH 45402
15 East Fourth St., Suite 209
(513) 222-5825
TOLEDO, OH 43604
214 Board of Trade Building
(419) 241-6276

YOUNGSTOWN, OH 44503
903 Mahoning Bank Building,
(Mailing: P.O. Box 1495, 44501)
(216) 744-3111

OKLAHOMA
OKLAHOMA CITY, OK 73102
606 N. Dewey
(405) 239-6081
TULSA, OK 74145
4833 South Sheridan, Suite 412
(918) 664-1266

OREGON
PORTLAND, OR 97204
623 Corbett Building
(503) 226-3981

PENNSYLVANIA
BETHLEHEM, PA 18018
528 North New St.,
Dodson Building
(215) 866-8780
LANCASTER, PA 17602
53 N. Duke St.
(717) 291-1151
(Toll Free, York Co. Resident
846-2700)
PHILADELPHIA, PA 19107
1218 Chestnut St.
(215) 574-3600
PITTSBURGH, PA 15222
610 Smithfield St.
(412) 456-2700
SCRANTON, PA 18503
Brooks Bldg., 5th Floor
(717) 342-9129

PUERTO RICO
SAN JUAN, PUERTO RICO 00910
P.O. Box BBB,
Fernandez Juncos Station
(809) 724-7474
Cable: BEBUSBU

RHODE ISLAND
PROVIDENCE, RI 02903
248 Weybosset St.
(401) 272-9800

TENNESSEE
CHATTANOOGA, TN 37402
716 James Building, 735 Broad St.
(615) 266-6144
KNOXVILLE, TN 37917
P.O. Box 3608
(615) 522-2139
MEMPHIS, TN 38104
1835 Union, Suite 202, Box 41406
(901) 272-9641
NASHVILLE, TN 37201
506 Nashville City Bank Building
(615) 254-5872

TEXAS
ABILENE, TX 79604
465 Cypress Duffy Bldg., Box 3275
(915) 677-8071
AMARILLO, TX 79101
518 Amarillo Building
(806) 374-3735
AUSTIN, TX 78701
American Bank Tower, Suite 720
(512) 476-6943
BEAUMONT, TX 77704
P.O. Box 2988
(713) 835-5348
BRYAN, TX 77801
202 Varisco Building
(713) 823-8148
CORPUS CHRISTI, TX 78401
109 N. Chaparral, Suite 101
(512) 888-5555
DALLAS, TX 75201
1511 Bryan St.
(214) 747-8891
EL PASO, TX 79902
2501 North Mesa St., Suite 301
(915) 533-2431
FORT WORTH, TX 76102
709 Sinclair Building,
106 West 5th St.
(817) 332-7585

HOUSTON, TX 77008
  P.O. Box 7499
  (713) 868-9500
LUBBOCK, TX 79408
  1015 15th St., P.O. Box 1178
  (806) 763-0459
MIDLAND, TX 79701
  Air Terminal Building,
  P.O. Box 6006
  (915) 563-1880
  Comp. 563-1882
SAN ANGELO, TX 76903
  224 W. Beauregard
  (915) 653-2318
SAN ANTONIO, TX 78205
  406 West Market St., Suite 301
  (512) 225-5833
WACO, TX 76710
  608 New Rd., P.O. Box 7203
  (817) 772-7530
WICHITA FALLS, TX 76301
  First National Bank Bldg., Suite 600
  (817) 723-5526

UTAH
PROVO, UT 84601
  40 North 100 East
  (801) 377-2611
SALT LAKE CITY, UT 84115
  1588 South Main
  (801) 487-4656

VIRGINIA
NORFOLK, VA 23514
  First & Merchants Bank Building,
  Suite 620
  300 Main St., E., P.O. Box 3548
  (804) 627-5651
  Peninsula area 851-9101
RICHMOND, VA 23230
  4020 West Broad St.
  (804) 355-7902
ROANOKE, VA 24011
  646 A Crystal Tower,
  145 West Campbell Ave., SW
  (703) 342-3455

WASHINGTON
SEATTLE, WA 98121
  2332 Sixth Ave.
  (206) 622-8066, 67-69
SPOKANE, WA 99201
  N. 214 Wall
  (509) 747-1155
TACOMA, WA 98402
  950 Pacific Ave.
  (206) 383-5561
YAKIMA, WA 98907
  P.O. Box 1584,
  424 Washington Mutual Bldg.
  (509) 248-1326

WISCONSIN
MILWAUKEE, WI 53203
  740 North Plankinton Ave.
  (414) 273-1600

CANADA
  ALBERTA
CALGARY, ALBERTA T2P 1G6
  630 8th Ave., SW, Suite 404
  (403) 269-3905
EDMONTON, ALBERTA T5N 3W6
  600 Guardian Building,
  10240 124th St.
  (403) 482-2341
  [Grande Prairie, Alberta (Open
  8:30 to 4:30) (403) 532-7778]
  Red Deer, Alberta (403) 343-3280

BRITISH COLUMBIA
VANCOUVER, BC V6B 1S3
  100 West Pender St., 12th Floor
  (604) 682-2711
VICTORIA, BC V8W 1A7
  P.O. Box M-37, 635 Humboldt St.
  (604) 386-6348

MANITOBA
WINNIPEG, MANITOBA R3B 2K3
  365 Hargrave St., Room 204
  (204) 942-7166

MONCTON, NB E1C 8P2
Box 1002, 331 Elmwood Dr.,
Suite 2
(506) 854-3330

NEWFOUNDLAND
ST. JOHN'S, NEWFOUNDLAND
A1C 5K4
P.O. Box 516, 2 Adelaide St.
(709) 722-2222

NOVA SCOTIA
HALIFAX, NOVA SCOTIA B3J 3B7
P.O. Box 2124, 1722 Granville St.
(902) 422-6581

ONTARIO
HAMILTON, ONTARIO L8N 1L4
170 Jackson St., East
(416) 526-1119
KITCHENER, ONTARIO N2H 2R1
58 Scott St.
(519) 579-3080

OTTAWA, ONTARIO K1P 5N2
71 Bank St., Suite 503
(613) 237-4856
TORONTO, ONTARIO M4W 3K6
321 Bloor St., East, Suite 901
(416) 961-0088
WINDSOR, ONTARIO N9A 5K6
500 Riverside Dr. West
(519) 258-7222

QUEBEC
MONTREAL, PQ H3A 1V4
2055 Peel St., Suite 460
(514) 286-9281
QUEBEC CITY, PQ G1R 1K2
475 Rue Richelieu
(418) 523-2555

SASKATCHEWAN
REGINA, SASKATCHEWAN,
S4P 2C4
1942 Hamilton St., Suite 3
(306) 352-7601

Appendix F

State Insurance Commissions

Commissioner of
  Insurance
64 N. Union St., Rm. 453
Montgomery, AL 36130
(205) 832-6140

Director of Insurance
Pouch D
Juneau, AK 99811
(907) 465-2515

Director of Insurance
1601 West Jefferson
Phoenix, AZ 85007
(602) 255-4862

Consumer Affairs
  Coordinator
Department of
  Insurance
12th and University
Little Rock, AR 72204
(501) 371-1811

Insurance Commissioner
600 S. Commonwealth
Los Angeles, CA 90005
(213) 736-2572

Commissioner of
  Insurance
106 State Office
  Building
Denver, CO 80203
(303) 866-3201

Insurance Commissioner
425 State Office
  Building
(Mailing: 165 Capital
  Ave., Rm. 425)
Hartford, CT 06115
(203) 566-5275

Insurance Commissioner
21 The Green
Dover, DE 19901
(302) 736-4251

Superintendent of
  Insurance
614 H St., N.W.,
  Suite 512
Washington, DC 20001
(202) 727-1273

Insurance Commissioner
State Capitol
Tallahassee, FL 32301
(904) 488-3440

Insurance Commissioner
238 State Capitol
Atlanta, GA 30334
(404) 656-2056

Insurance Commissioner
P.O. Box 3614
Honolulu, HI 96811
(808) 548-7505

Director of Insurance
700 West State St.
Boise, ID 83720
(208) 334-2250

Director
Department of
  Insurance
320 W. Washington St.
Springfield, IL 62767
(217) 782-4395

Deputy Commissioner
  and Director
Consumer Services
  Division
Department of
  Insurance
509 State Office
  Building
Indianapolis, IN 46204
(317) 232-2385

Commissioner of
Insurance
Lucas State Office
Building
Des Moines, IA 50319
(515) 281-5705

Commissioner of
Insurance
State Office Building
Topeka, KS 66612
(913) 296-3071
800-432-2484

Insurance Commissioner
151 Elkhorn Court
Frankfort, KY 40601
(502) 564-3630

Commissioner of
Insurance
P.O. Box 44214
Baton Rouge, LA
70804
(504) 342-5328

Superintendent of
Insurance
Department of Business
Regulation
Bureau of Insurance
State House Station 34
Augusta, ME 04330
(207) 289-3101

Insurance Commissioner
One S. Calvert St.
Baltimore, MD 21202
(301) 659-6300

Commissioner of
Insurance
100 Cambridge St.
Boston, MA 02202
(617) 727-3333

Commissioner of
Insurance
P.O. Box 30220
Lansing, MI 48909
(517) 373-0240

Commissioner of
Insurance
Metro Square Building
St. Paul, MN 55101
(612) 296-6907

Commissioner of
Insurance
P.O. Box 79
Jackson, MS 39205
(601) 354-7711

Division of Insurance
515 E. High St.
P.O. Box 690
Jefferson City, MO
65101
(314) 751-4126

Commissioner of
Insurance
Mitchell Building
Helena, MT 59601
(406) 449-2040

Director of Insurance
301 Centennial Mall
South
P.O. Box 94699
Lincoln, NE 68509
(402) 471-2201, ext.
238

Insurance Commissioner
Nye Building
201 S. Fall St.
Carson City, NV 89710
(702) 885-4270

Insurance Commissioner
169 Manchester
Concord, NH 03301
(603) 271-2261

Division of Consumer
Services
Department of
Insurance
201 E. State St.
Trenton, NJ 08625
(609) 292-5374

Superintendent of
Insurance
P.O. Drawer 1269
Santa Fe, NM 87501
(505) 827-2451

Consumer Services
Bureau
State Insurance
Department
Two World Trade
Center
New York, NY 10047
(212) 488-4005

Consumer Complaint
Bureau
State Insurance
Department
Agency Bldg. 1
Albany, NY 12257
(518) 474-4556

Consumer Liaison
Department of
Insurance
P.O. Box 26387
Raleigh, NC 27611
(919) 733-2032

Commissioner of
Insurance
Capitol Building,
5th Floor
Bismarck, ND 58505
(701) 224-2444

Director of Insurance
2100 Stella Court
Columbus, OH 43215
(614) 466-3584
1-800-282-4658

Insurance Commissioner
408 Will Rogers
Memorial Building
Oklahoma City, OK
73105
(405) 521-2828

Insurance Commissioner
158 12th St., NE
Salem, OR 97310
(503) 378-4271

Policy Holders Service
and Protection
Department of
Insurance
Strawberry Square,
13th Floor
Harrisburg, PA 17120
(717) 787-2317

Commissioner of
Insurance
P.O. Box 3508
San Juan, PR 00904
(809) 724-6565

Insurance Commissioner
100 N. Main St.
Providence, RI 02903
(401) 277-2223

Market Conduct
Division
Department of
Insurance
P.O. Box 4067
Columbia, SC 29240
(803) 758-2876

Director of Insurance
Insurance Building
Pierre, SD 57501
(605) 773-3563

Commissioner of
Insurance
114 State Office
Building
Nashville, TN 37219
(615) 741-2241

Commissioner of
Insurance
1110 San Jacinto
Boulevard
Austin, TX 78786
(512) 475-2273

Commissioner of
Insurance
326 S. 500 E.
Salt Lake City, UT
84102
(801) 533-5611

Commissioner of
Banking and
Insurance
120 State St.
State Office Building
Montpelier, VT 05602
(802) 828-3301

Commissioner of
Insurance
700 Jefferson Building
Richmond, VA 23209
(804) 786-3741

Insurance Commissioner
Insurance Building
Mail Stop AQ21
Olympia, WA 98504
(206) 753-7301

Insurance Commissioner
2100 Washington St., E.
Charleston, WV 25305
(304) 348-3386

Commissioner of
Insurance
P.O. Box 7873
Madison, WI 53707
(608) 266-3585

Insurance Commissioner
2424 Pioneer
Cheyenne, WY 82001
(307) 777-7401

Appendix G

State Auto Inspection Chiefs

ARKANSAS
Capt. Wilbur Hileman
P.O. Box 4005
Little Rock, AR 72214
(501) 371-2235

COLORADO
Frank Manshiem, Supervisor
Motor Vehicle Division
140 W. Sixth Ave.
Denver, CO 80204
(303) 866-3422

DELAWARE
T. Marvel Everett
Registration Section
Motor Vehicle Division
P.O. Box 698
Highway Administration Bldg.
Dover, DE 19901
(302) 736-4458

DISTRICT OF COLUMBIA
Noel K. Dawson, Chief Control
   Division
Department of Motor Vehicles
301 C St., N.W.
Washington, DC 20001
(202) 727-6680

FLORIDA
Maj. C. P. Reynolds, Commander
   Florida Highway Patrol Troop M
Neil Kirkman Building
Tallahassee, FL 32304
(904) 488-8518

GEORGIA
Capt. Paul W. Nagent
Georgia State Patrol
P.O. Box 1456
Atlanta, GA 30371
(404) 656-6072

HAWAII
Lawrence Hirohata
Vehicle Equipment Safety Specialist
State Dept. of Transportation
Motor Vehicle Safety Office
79 South Nemitz Hwy.
Honolulu, HI 96813
(808) 548-5755

INDIANA
Walter H. Frick, Director
Dept. of Traffic Safety
100 Senate Ave., Rm. 801
Indianapolis, IN 46204
(317) 232-1297

IOWA
Dennis Ehlert, Director
  Office of Safety Programs
Dept. of Transportation
Lucas State Office Bldg.
Des Moines, IA 50319
(515) 281-5254

LOUISIANA
Lt. Leon "Bucky" Millet, Supervisor
Louisiana State Police
265 S. Foster Dr.
Baton Rouge, LA 70806
(504) 292-8200

MARYLAND
Capt. Bruce E. Diehl, Chief
Automotive Safety Enforcement
  Division
Maryland State Police
6601 Ritchie Hwy., N.E.
Glen Burnie, MD 21061
(301) 486-3101, ext. 390

MASSACHUSETTS
Ernest Sabatino, Supervisor
100 Nashua St.
Boston, MA 02114
(617) 727-3825

MISSISSIPPI
James Able, Director
Motor Vehicle Inspection Bureau
P.O. Box 958
Jackson, MS 39205
(601) 982-1212

MISSOURI
Lt. L. A. Webb, Director
Vehicle Inspection Division
Missouri State Highway Patrol
1510 E. Elm St.
(Mailing: Box 568, 65102)
Jefferson City, MO 65101
(314) 751-3313

NEBRASKA
Keith Kennedy, Administrator
Mtr. Veh. Inspec.
Department of Motor Vehicle
State Building
Lincoln, NE 68509
(402) 471-2281

NEW HAMPSHIRE
Tom Power, Director
Division of Motor Vehicles
James H. Hayes Safety Building
Hazen Drive
Concord, NH 03301
(603) 271-2251

NEW JERSEY
James Grandgean, Chief
Bureau of Vehicle Inspection
Division of Motor Vehicles
25 S. Montgomery Street
Trenton, NJ 08666
(609) 292-4538

NEW MEXICO
C. H. Garcia, Chief
Mtr. Veh. Inspection
Dept. of Motor Vehicles
Manuel Lujan Sr. Bldg.
Santa Fe, NM 87503
(505) 827-2936

NEW YORK
Bernard Schiff, Director Operations
Department of Motor Vehicles
Swan St. Building
Empire State Plaza
Albany, NY 12228
(518) 474-0861

NORTH CAROLINA
J. G. Wilson, Director
Enforcement & Theft Section
Division of Motor Vehicles
1100 New Bern Ave.
Raleigh, NC 27697
(919) 733-7872

OKLAHOMA
Lt. Jim Snider
Vehicle Inspection Division
Oklahoma Highway Patrol
3600 N. Eastern
P.O. Box 11415, 73136
Oklahoma City, OK 73111
(405) 424-4011, ext. 2289

PENNSYLVANIA
Cathy G. Phillips, Manager
Vehicle Safety Div.
Bureau of Traffic Safety
1200 Transportation & Safety
  Building, Room 407
Harrisburg, PA 17123
(717) 787-2895

RHODE ISLAND
Alfred Massarone
Investigator & Inspection Div.
Automotive Emission Safety Div.
1310 Pontiac Ave.
Cranston, RI 02920
(401) 277-2983

SOUTH CAROLINA
W. H. Kay, Chief
Motor Vehicle Inspection
Motor Vehicle Division
P.O. Box 1498
Columbia, SC 29216
(803) 758-2109

SOUTH DAKOTA
Jerry Baum, Director
  Division of Highway Patrol
Dept. of Public Safety
118 W. Capitol
Pierre, SD 57501
(605) 773-3105

TEXAS
Maurice Beckham, Chief
  Inspection and Planning Division
Department of Public Safety
P.O. Box 4087
5805 North Lamar
Austin, TX 78773
(512) 465-2000, ext. 224

UTAH
Lt. Howard Cooper
Utah Highway Patrol
Safety Inspection Div.
313 State Office Building
Salt Lake City, UT 84114
(801) 533-4925

VERMONT
George Paquette, Director
Field Services
Department of Motor Vehicles
State Office Building
120 State St.
Montpelier, VT 05603
(802) 828-2121, ext. 66

VIRGINIA
Capt. R. M. Terry, Safety Officer
Department of State Police
P.O. Box 27472
Richmond, VA 23261
(804) 323-2000

WEST VIRGINIA
Lt. G. D. Hill, Director
Dept. of Public Safety
725 Jefferson Road
South Charleston, WV 25309
(304) 348-2365

Appendix H

New and Used Car Dealer Licensing Agencies; Auto Company Executives and "Outside" Directors; AUTOCAPs; UCCAPs

1. New and Used Car Dealer Licensing Agencies

All the agencies listed here license new car dealers except those marked "UO," which license used car dealers only. A "U" means that the agency licenses both new and used car dealers. The authority of licensing agencies in Washington, D.C., Dallas, Texas, and Prince George's County, Maryland, extends only to new car warranty repairs. Almost all other licensing agencies can handle any type of complaint against a dealer.

ARKANSAS
J. H. Burnside, Executive Secretary
Arkansas Motor Vehicle Commission
2020 W. Third, Suite 2B
Little Rock, AR 72205
(501) 371-1428

CALIFORNIA
Sam W. Jennings, Executive Secretary
New Motor Vehicle Board
1401 21 St., Ste. 407
Sacramento, CA 95814
(916) 445-1888

"UO"
Department of Motor Vehicles
Division of Compliance
2570 24th St.
P.O. Box 689
Sacramento, CA 95803
(You're asked to either send in a written complaint or call your local DMV office.)

COLORADO
Larry Dyslin, Director
Colorado Dealer Licensing Board
140 W. 6th Ave.
Denver, CO 80204
(303) 866-2677

CONNECTICUT
"U"
Dealers and Repairers Division
Department of Motor Vehicles
　(See Appendix A)

DISTRICT OF COLUMBIA
D.C. Office of Consumer Affairs
　(See Appendix B)

FLORIDA
"U"
Department of Highway Safety and
　Motor Vehicles
Division of Motor Vehicles
Neil Kirkman Bldg.
Tallahassee, FL 32201
　(Complaints should be in writing
　only, although you may lodge a
　complaint by phone with local
　offices of the Division of Motor
　Vehicles)

GEORGIA
"UO"
Mr. Les Maddern, Exec. Dir.
Georgia State Board of Registration
　of Used Car Dealers
166 Pryor St. S.W.
Atlanta, GA 30303
(404) 656-3929

HAWAII
"U"
George Muramaru
Executive Secretary
Motor Vehicle Industry Licensing
　Board
Department of Regulatory Agencies
P.O. Box 3469
Honolulu, HI 96801
(808) 548-4100

INDIANA
Dealer Division
Bureau of Motor Vehicles
402 State Office Building
Indianapolis, IN 46204
(317) 232-2798

KENTUCKY
"U"
William Debord, Assistant Director
Department of Transportation
Division of Motor Carriers
State Office Building
Frankfort, KY 40622
(502) 564-3750

LOUISIANA
Louisiana Motor Vehicle Commission
234 Loyola Ave., Ste. 609
New Orleans, LA 70112
(504) 568-5282

MARYLAND
"U"
George W. Osenburg, Chief
　Investigator
Dealer Licensing Section
Motor Vehicle Administration
6601 Ritchie Hwy., N.E.
Glen Burnie, MD 21061
(301) 768-7536 to 7538

PRINCE GEORGE'S COUNTY
Consumer Protection Commission
　(See Appendix B)

MICHIGAN
"U"
Dept. of State
Dealer Div.
Bur. of Automotive Regulation
208 N. Capitol
Lansing, MI 48918
(517) 373-9080
　or
(for new car dealer repair only)
Bureau of Automotive Regulation
　(See Appendix A)

MISSISSIPPI
Alton E. McKey, Director
Mississippi Motor Vehicle Commission
P.O. Box 1212
Jackson, MS 39205
(601) 354-7472

NEBRASKA
"U"
Larry Kelley, Executive Secretary
Motor Vehicle Industry Licensing
 Board
P.O. Box 94697
Lincoln, NB 68509
(402) 471-2148

NEVADA
"U"
Dorothy Scott, Supervisor
Vehicle Compliance and Enforcement
 Section
Department of Motor Vehicles
555 Wright Way
Carson City, NV 89711
(702) 885-5396

NEW YORK
"U"
Department of Motor Vehicles
Consumer and Facility Services
Empire State Plaza
Albany, NY 12228
Telephones: See Appendix A

NORTH CAROLINA
"U"
 (New and used car dealers are
 licensed by the Division of Motor
 Vehicles, Department of Transporta-
 tion. However, complaints should
 be directed to:)
Consumer Protection Division
Office of Attorney General
 (See Appendix B)

OKLAHOMA
H. Mead Norton, Executive Director
Oklahoma Motor Vehicle Commission
333 Northwestfield
Oklahoma City, OK 73102
(405) 521-2375

PENNSYLVANIA
Bureau of Professional and
 Occupational Affairs
ATTN: Complaints Office
Transportation and Safety Bldg.,
 Room 618
Harrisburg, PA 17120
(717) 783-3650

RHODE ISLAND
"U"
John Cardarelli, Executive Secretary
Dealers License Commission
345 Harris Ave.
Providence, RI 02909
(401) 277-2422

TENNESSEE
"U"
E. B. Noles, Director
Motor Vehicle Commission
502 Doctors Bldg.
Nashville, TN 37219
(615) 741-2711

TEXAS
Russell Harding, Executive Director
Texas Motor Vehicle Commission
P.O. Box 2293
Austin, TX 78768
(512) 476-3587

CITY OF DALLAS
Department of Consumer Affairs
 (See Appendix B)

WASHINGTON
"U"
Bob Hayter, Administrator
Dealer and Manufacturer Control
 Division
Department of Licensing
Highway-Licenses Bldg.
Olympia, WA 98504
(206) 753-6954 (call between
 8:00 a.m.–10:00 a.m.)

District Offices:

Kennewick	(509) 545-2363
Seattle	(206) 545-6750
Spokane	(509) 456-4118
Tacoma	(206) 593-2995
Vancouver	(206) 696-6038
Yakima	(509) 575-2777

WISCONSIN
"U"
Don Krohn, Chief
Dealer Section
Division of Motor Vehicles
P.O. Box 7909
Madison, WI 53707
(608) 266-1425

2. Auto Company Executives

Joseph R. Dent
Chief Executive Officer
ALFA ROMEO, INC.
250 Sylvan Ave.
Englewood Cliffs, NJ 07632
(201) 871-1234

Tetsuo Chino, President
AMERICAN HONDA MOTOR CO.
 INC.
100 W. Alondra Blvd.
Gardena, CA 90247
(213) 327-8280

M. Tsukamoto, President
CANADIAN HONDA MOTOR LTD.
255 Hutchings Street
Winnepeg, Man. R2X 2R4

Yukio Itagaki, President
AMERICAN ISUZU MOTORS INC.
2300 Pellissier Pl.
Whittier, CA 90601
(213) 949-0611

Gerald C. Meyers, Chairman
AMERICAN MOTORS CORP.
27777 Franklin Rd.
Southfield, MI 48034
(313) 827-1000

Maurice Fertey, President
AMERICAN MOTORS CANADA
 LTD.
3500 Kennedy Rd. S.
Brampton, Ont. L6V 2M3

Morris L. Hallowell IV, President
ASTON MARTIN LAGONDA, INC.
14 Weyman Ave.
New Rochelle, NY 10805
(914) 576-3202

John A. Cook, President
BMW OF NORTH AMERICA, INC.
Montvale, NJ 07645
(201) 573-2000

BRITISH LEYLAND: See Jaguar
 Rover Triumph Inc.

David R. Markin, Chairman
CHECKER MOTORS CORP.
2016 N. Pitcher
Kalamazoo, MI 49007
(616) 343-6121

Lee A. Iacocca, Chairman
CHRYSLER CORP.
P.O. Box 1919
Detroit, MI 48288
(313) 956-5252

Donald H. Lander, President
CHRYSLER CANADA LTD.
2199 Chrysler Centre
Windsor, Ont. N9A 4H6

Pierre Lemaire, President
CITROEN CARS CORP.
31 Garland Way
Lyndhurst, NJ 07071
(201) 438-9300

DATSUN: See Nissan

John Z. De Lorean, Chairman
DE LOREAN MOTOR CO.
280 Park Ave.
New York, NY 10017
(212) 889-8900

Claudio Ferrari, President
FIAT MOTORS OF NORTH
   AMERICA, INC.
155 Chestnut Ridge Rd.
Montvale, NJ 07645
(201) 573-3700

Philip Caldwell, Chairman
FORD MOTOR CO.
The American Road
Dearborn, MI 48121
(313) 322-3000

Roy F. Bennett, President
FORD MOTOR CO. OF CANADA
   LTD.
Knight Lane at Hwy. 122
Oakville, Ont. L6J 5E4

Louis E. Lataif, General Manager
Ford Division
Ford Motor Co.
300 Renaissance Center
Detroit, MI 48243
(313) 568-7500

J. A. Capolongo, General Manager
Ford Truck & Recreation Products
   Operations
2000 Rotunda Dr.
Dearborn, MI 48121
(313) 323-2365

Gordon B. MacKenzie, Gen. Mgr.
Lincoln-Mercury Division
300 Renaissance Center
Detroit, MI 48243
(313) 568-3306

Roger B. Smith, Chairman
GENERAL MOTORS CORP.
General Motors Bldg.
3044 West Grand Blvd.
Detroit, MI 48202
(313) 556-5000

J. R. Rinehart, President
GENERAL MOTORS OF CANADA
   LTD.
215 William St. E.
Oshawa, Ont. L1G 1K7

Lloyd E. Reuss
General Manager
Buick Motor Division
General Motors Corp.
902 E. Hamilton Ave.
Flint, MI 48550
(313) 766-5000

Edward C. Kennard
General Manager
Cadillac Motor Car Division
2860 Clark Ave.
Detroit, MI 48232
(313) 556-6000

Robert D. Lund
General Manager
Chevrolet Motor Division
General Motors Corp.
General Motors Bldg.
30007 Van Dyck
Warren, MI 48090
(313) 556-5000

Robert W. Truxell
General Manager
GMC Truck & Coach Division
General Motors Corp.
660 S. Blvd. East
Pontiac, MI 48053
(313) 857-5000

Robert J. Cook
General Manager
Oldsmobile Division
General Motors Corp.
920 Townsend St.
Lansing, MI 48921
(517) 373-5000

William E. Hoglund
General Manager
Pontiac Motor Division
General Motors Corp.
1 Pontiac Plaza
P.O. Box 910
Pontiac, MI 48053
(313) 857-5000

HONDA: See American Honda

Archie R. McCardell, Chairman
INTERNATIONAL HARVESTER
 CO.
401 N. Michigan Ave.
Chicago, IL 60611
(312) 836-2000

ISUZU: See American Isuzu

Graham W. Whitehead, President
JAGUAR ROVER TRIUMPH INC.
600 Willow Tree Rd.
Leonia, NJ 07605
(201) 461-7300

E. J. Mackie, President
JAGUAR ROVER TRIUMPH
 CANADA
8 Indell Lane
Bramalea, Ont. LT6 4H3
(416) 792-9400

George A. Garbutt, President
MASERATI AUTOMOBILES INC.
1501 Caton Ave.
Baltimore, MD 21227
(301) 646-3630

Toru Ogawa, President
MAZDA MOTORS OF AMERICA
 (CENTRAL) INC.
3040 E. Ana St.
Compton, CA 90221
(213) 537-2332

Hiroyuki Uchida, President
MAZDA MOTORS OF CANADA
 LTD.
55 Milner Ave.
Agincourt, Ont. M1S 3P6

Walter Bodack, President
MERCEDES-BENZ OF NORTH
 AMERICA, INC.
One Mercedes Dr.
Montvale, NJ 07645
(201) 573-0600

MERCEDES-BENZ OF CANADA
 LTD.
849 Eglinton Ave. E.
Toronto, Ont. M4G 2L5

Tetsuo Arakawa, President
NISSAN MOTOR CORP. IN U.S.A.
18501 S. Figueroa St.
Carson, CA 90247
(213) 532-3111

Y. Kawana, Executive Vice President
NISSAN AUTOMOBILE CO.
 CANADA LTD.
480 Audley Blvd.
P.O. Box 2501
New Westminster, BC V3L 5A1

Pierre Lemaire, President
PEUGEOT MOTORS OF AMERICA,
    INC.
One Peugeot Plaza
Lyndhurst, NJ 07071
(201) 935-8400

Pierre Gazarian, General Manager
RENAULT USA, INC.
499 Park Ave.
New York, NY 10022
(212) 980-8500

Bernard Hanon, President
AUTOMOBILES RENAULT
    CANADA
1305 Boul. Marie-Victorin
St. Bruno de Montareille, P.Q. J3V 4P7

George W. Lewis, President
ROLLS-ROYCE MOTORS INC.
P.O. Box 476
Lyndhurst, NJ 07071
(201) 460-9600

Norman Miller, President
ROLLS-ROYCE CANADA LTD.
3870 Griffith Street
St. Laurent, P.Q. H4T 1A7

Robert J. Sinclair, President
SAAB-SCANIA OF AMERICA, INC.
Saab Drive
Orange, CT 06477
(203) 795-5671

Harvey Lamm, President
SUBARU OF AMERICA, INC.
7040 Central Hwy.
Pennsauken, NJ 08109
(609) 665-3344

Isao Makino, President
TOYOTA MOTOR SALES, U.S.A.,
    INC.
2055 W. 190th St.
Torrance, CA 90504
(213) 532-5010

James W. McLernon, President
VOLKSWAGEN OF AMERICA,
    INC.
27621 Parkview Blvd.
Warren, MI 48092
(313) 574-3300

B. R. Rubess, President
VOLKSWAGEN CANADA INC.
1940 Eglinton Ave. East
Scarborough, Ont. M1L 2M2

Bjorn Ahlstrom, President
VOLVO OF AMERICA CORP.
Rockleigh, NJ 07647
(201) 768-7300

Bjorn Ahlstrom, President
VOLVO CANADA LTD.
175 Gordon Baker Rd.
Willowdale, Ont. M2H 2N7

3.   Auto Company "Outside" Directors (Partial Listing)

AMERICAN MOTORS CORP.
Edward L. Cushman
Executive Vice President
Wayne State University
David Mackenzie Hall
Detroit, MI 48202

Stephen A. Girard, President
Kaiser Industries Corp.
300 Lakeside Dr.
Oakland, CA 94666

Patricia Shontz Longe, Professor
Graduate School of Business
   Administration
University of Michigan
Ann Arbor, MI 48104

Felix Rohatyn, Partner
Lazard Freres & Co.
One Rockefeller Plaza
New York, NY 10021

Andrew G. C. Sage II
Managing Director
Lehman Brothers Kuhn Loeb Inc.
One William St.
New York, NY 10004

Jackson W. Tarver, Publisher
Atlanta Newspapers
72 Marietta St.
Atlanta, GA 30303

Kenneth J. Whalen
Executive Vice President
American Telephone & Telegraph Co.
295 N. Maple Ave.
Basking Ridge, NJ 07920

CHRYSLER CORP.

Anthony J. A. Bryan, Chairman
Copperweld Corp.
Two Oliver Plaza
Pittsburgh, PA 15222

John H. Coleman, President
J.H.C. Associates Ltd.
P.O. Box 14
Royal Bank Plaza
Toronto, Ontario M5J 2J1

Albert Jean de Grandpre, Chairman
Bell Canada
1050 Beaver Hall Hill
Montreal, Que. H3C 3G4

J. Richardson Dilworth
Rockefeller Family & Associates
30 Rockefeller Plaza
New York, NY 10020

Douglas A. Fraser, President
United Auto Workers
8000 E. Jefferson Ave.
Detroit, MI 48214

William R. Hewlett
Chairman, Executive Committee
Hewlett-Packard Co.
1501 Page Mill Rd.
Palo Alto, CA 94304

Tom Killefer, Chairman
United States Trust Co. of New York
45 Wall Street
New York, NY 10005

Robert B. Semple, Chairman
BASF Wyandotte Corp.
P.O. Box 111
Wyandotte, MI 48192

FORD MOTOR CO.

George F. Bennett, President
State Street Investment Corp.
225 Franklin St.
Boston, MA 02110

Carter L. Burgess, Chairman
Foreign Policy Association
205 Lexington Ave.
New York, NY 10016

John B. Connally
First City National Bank Bldg.
Houston, TX 77002

Joseph F. Cullman III, Chairman
Executive Committee
Philip Morris Inc.
100 Park Ave.
New York, NY 10017

Marian Sulzberger Heiskell
870 UN Plaza
New York, NY 10017

Arjay Miller
225 Mountain Home Rd.
Woodside, CA 94062

Franklin D. Murphy, Chairman,
  Executive Committee
Times-Mirror Co.
Times Mirror Sq.
Los Angeles, CA 90053

Kenneth H. Olsen, President
Digital Equipment Corp.
146 Main St.
Maynard, MA 01754

Clifton R. Wharton Jr.
Chancellor
State University of New York
99 Washington Ave.
Albany, NY 12210

GENERAL MOTORS CORP.

Mrs. Anne L. Armstrong
Armstrong Ranch
Armstrong, TX 78338

Catherine B. Cleary
Adjunct Professor
School of Business Administration
University of Wisconsin
735 N. Water St.
Milwaukee, WI 53202

James H. Evans, Chairman
Union Pacific Corp.
345 Park Ave.
New York, NY 10022

Walter A. Fallon, Chairman
Eastman Kodak Co.
343 State St.
Rochester, NY 14650

Charles T. Fisher III, President
National Bank of Detroit
Woodward at Fort
Detroit, MI 48232

Dr. Marvin L. Goldberger, President
California Institute of Technology
Pasadena, CA 91125

Robert S. Hatfield
Continental Group, Inc.
1 Harbor Plaza
Stamford, CT 06902

John J. Horan, Chairman
Merck & Co., Inc.
P.O. Box 2000
Rahway, NJ 07065

William Earle McLaughlin
The Royal Bank of Canada
1 Place Ville Marie
Montreal, Que. H3C 3A9

Edmund T. Pratt Jr., Chairman
Pfizer Inc.
235 E. 42nd St.
New York, NY 10017

Leon H. Sullivan, Pastor
Zion Baptist Church
Broad & Venango
Philadelphia, PA 19401

Charles H. Townes, Professor
Department of Physics
University of California
Berkeley, CA 94720

4. AUTOCAPS

Those with an (s) beside the name are statewide organizations. All others are local. To complain against dealers not connected with an AUTOCAP, contact the National Automobile Dealers Association (see Appendix I).

ARIZONA
Arizona Auto Dealers Assn. (s)
P.O. Box 5438
Phoenix, AZ 85010
(602) 252-2386

CALIFORNIA
San Diego County Motor Car Dealers
Assn.
2333 Camino Del Rio South
Suite 265
San Diego, CA 92108
(714) 296-3175

Motor Car Dealers Assn. of Southern
California
5757 W. Century Blvd.
Los Angeles, CA 90045
(213) 776-6144
1-800-252-9488

COLORADO
Metro Denver Auto Dealers Assn.
517 East 16th Ave.
Denver, CO 80203
(303) 831-1722

CONNECTICUT
Connecticut Auto Trades Assn. (s)
18 N. Main St.
West Hartford, CT 06107
(203) 521-8970

DISTRICT OF COLUMBIA
Automotive Trade Assn. of National
Capital Area
4330 East-West Hwy., Suite 218
Bethesda, MD 20814
(301) 657-3200

FLORIDA
Better Business Bureau
8600 N.E. Second Ave.
Miami, FL 33138
(305) 522-AUTO (Dade & Monroe
Counties)
(305) 758-AUTO (Broward County)

Better Business Bureau
3015 Exchange Court
West Palm Beach, FL 33409
(305) 686-6168 (Palm Beach
County)
(305) 272-4445 (Boca Raton &
Delray)

GEORGIA
Georgia Auto Dealers Assn. (s)
1380 West Paces Ferry Rd., Suite 230
Atlanta, GA 30327
(404) 237-1658

KENTUCKY
Kentucky Auto Dealers Assn. (s)
123 Walnut St.
P.O. Box 498
Frankfort, KY 40602
(502) 695-3310

MAINE
Maine Automobile Dealers Assn. (s)
P.O. Box 2667
Augusta, ME 04330
(207) 623-3882

MARYLAND
See District of Columbia

MASSACHUSETTS
Massachusetts State Auto Dealers
Assn. (s)
59 Temple Place, Room 505
Boston, MA 02111
(617) 451-1048

MICHIGAN
Michigan Automobile Dealers Assn. *
1500 Kendale Blvd.
P.O. Box 860
East Lansing, MI 48823
(517) 351-7800
1-800-292-1923
  * Covers all counties except
    Macomb, Oakland and Wayne

NEW MEXICO
New Mexico Automobile & Truck
 Dealers Assn. (s)
510 Second St. N.W., Suite 202
Albuquerque, NM 87102
(505) 243-1002

NEW YORK
Capital District AUTOCAP
90 State St.
Albany, NY 12207
(518) 438-0645

Broome County Auto Dealers
 Council, Inc.
P.O. Box 1057
Binghamton, NY 13902
(607) 723-7127

Westchester Auto Dealers Assn.
One Hanson Pl., Room 1212
Brooklyn, NY 11243
(212) 783-2900

Rochester Auto Dealers Assn.
179 Lake Ave.
Rochester, NY 14608
(716) 458-7150

Jefferson County AUTOCAP
P.O. Box 884
Watertown, NY 13601
(315) 782-1600

Niagara Frontier Auto Dealers Assn.
1144 Wehrle Dr.
Williamsville, NY 14221
(716) 631-8510

NORTH DAKOTA
North Dakota Auto Dealers Assn. (s)
1325 23 St. South
Box 2524
Fargo, ND 58108
(701) 293-6822

OHIO
Cleveland Auto Dealers Assn.
1367 East 6th, Suite 300
Cleveland, OH 44114
(216) 241-2880

OREGON
Oregon Auto Dealers Assn. (s)
P.O. Box 14460
Portland, OR 97214
(503) 233-5044

PENNSYLVANIA
PADA, Inc.
2807 North Front St.
Harrisburg, PA 17110
(717) 238-2581

SOUTH CAROLINA
South Carolina Automobile & Truck
 Dealers Assn. (s)
1517 Laurel St.
Columbia, SC 29201
(803) 254-4040

TENNESSEE
Chattanooga Automotive Trades
 Assn., Inc.
P.O. Box 8791
Chattanooga, TN 37411
(615) 894-3287

Nashville AUTOCAP
P.O. Box 40023
Nashville, TN 37204
(615) 269-4948

TEXAS
Texas Auto Dealers Assn. (s)
P.O. Box Drawer 1028
1108 Lavaca
Austin, TX 78767
(512) 476-2686

VIRGINIA
(see also District of Columbia)

Virginia Automobile Dealers Assn. (s)
1800 W. Grace
Richmond, VA 23220
(804) 359-3578

WASHINGTON
Washington State AUTOCAP (s)
King County Auto Dealers Assn.
2024 8th Ave.
Seattle, WA 98121
(206) 623-2034
1-800-552-0746

5.   Used Car Consumer Action Panels (UCCAPs)

GEORGIA
UCCAP
Georgia Independent Automobile
    Dealers Assn.
200 Wendell Court, Suite 207
(Mailing: P.O. Box 43303, 30315)
Atlanta, GA 30036
(404) 941-4814

PENNSYLVANIA
UCCAP
Pennsylvania Independent Automobile
    Dealers Assn.
1919 N. Front St.
Harrisburg, PA 17102
(717) 238-9002

OREGON
UCCAP
Oregon Independent Automobile
    Dealers Assn.
1095 25th St., S.E.
Salem, OR 97301
(503) 362-6839

Appendix I

National and Regional Auto Repair Chain and Franchise Companies; Automotive Organizations

1. Chain and Franchise Companies

AAMCO
Robert Morgan, President
AAMCO Transmissions, Inc.
408 E. Fourth St.
Bridgeport, PA 19405
(215) 277-4000
(You can call collect if you have a
   complaint)

ACC-U-TUNE
Acc-U-Tune
2510 Old Middlefield Way
Mountain View, CA 94043
(415) 968-8863

AUTO LUBE
Auto Lube, Inc.
6220 Pacific Avenue
Stockton, CA 95207
(209) 957-1155

AUTO OIL CHANGERS
K. Kennepohl, President
Auto Oil Changers
525 E. Pacific Coast Hwy.
Long Beach, CA 90806
(213) 591-1141

AUTO SPECIALTIES
(see National Auto Service Centers)

AUTOCARE SERVICE CENTERS
Autocare, Inc.
817 Remsen Ave.
Brooklyn, NY 11236
(212) 346-2600

BRAKE WORLD
Brake and Alignment Supply Corp.
7700 N.W. 27th Ave.
Miami, FL 33147
(305) 836-4434

BRAKE-O
Bill King, President
Bill King's Brake-O
(Mailing: Box 829)
4101 Lindberg
Addison, TX 75001
(214) 387-4900

BUGHAUS
Fred A. Sawyer, President
Bughaus Inc.
100 Brainard Rd.
Hartford, CT 06114
(203) 522-1251

CAR DOCTOR
Car Doctor Int'l Marketing, Inc.
333 N. Black Canyon
Phoenix, AZ 85009
(602) 264-2444

CAR-MATIC
W. W. Vail, President
Car-Matic Systems, Inc.
3111 Virginia Beach Blvd.
(Mailing: P.O. Box 12466)
Norfolk, VA 23502
(804) 627-2979

CAR-X
J. Tate Hale, President
Car-X Service Systems, Inc.
444 N. Michigan Ave., Suite 800
Chicago, IL 60611
(312) 836-1500

CARCOA AUTO PAINTING
Carcoa Inc.
7012 Owensmouth Ave.
Canoga Park, CA 91304
(213) 883-4141

COOL-AIDE
Cool-Aide Auto Service Centers, Inc.
7425 W. Chester Pike
Upper Darby, PA 19082
(215) 352-4600

COTTMAN
Michael Ambrose, President
Cottman Transmission Systems, Inc.
575 Virginia Drive
Fort Washington, PA 19034
(215) 643-5152
Toll-free: (800) 523-8910

DIAMOND QUALITY TRANSMISSIONS
Al Gold, President
Diamond Quality Transmission
  Centers
P.O. Box 6147
Philadelphia, PA 19115
(215) 742-8333

DR. NICK'S
Dr. Nick's Transmissions
150 Broadhollow Rd.
Melville, NY 11747
(516) 549-3661

DRIVE LINE
L. D. Wilson, President
Drive Line Service, Inc.
P.O. Box 1326
1309 Tradewinds Circle
West Sacramento, CA 95691
(916) 371-8117

EARL SCHEIB
Earl Scheib, President
Earl Scheib, Inc.
8737 Wilshire Blvd.
Beverly Hills, CA 90211
(213) 652-4880

EAST COAST RADIATOR
C. Hindermyer, Proprietor
East Coast Radiator Franchises, Inc.
1403 W. Shelthan Ave.
Elkins Park, PA 19126
(215) 635-7150

ECONO LUBE
Econo Lube N'Tune Inc.
4911 Birch Street
Newport, CA 92660
(714) 851-2259

FIRESTONE
John J. Nevin, President
The Firestone Tire & Rubber Co.
1200 Firestone Parkway
Akron, OH 44317
(216) 379-7000
Toll-free: (800) 321-9638

GIBRALTAR TRANSMISSIONS
Dennis A. Ballen, President
Gibraltar Transmission Corp.
127 Dupont St.
Plainview, NY 11803
(516) 482-6930

GOODRICH
John D. Ong, Chairman
The B F Goodrich Co.
500 S. Main St.
Akron, OH 44318
(216) 374-2000

GOODYEAR
Charles J. Pilliod, Jr., Chairman
The Goodyear Tire & Rubber Co.
1144 East Market St.
Akron, OH 44316
(216) 794-2121

GRAND AUTO
Irving Krantzman, President
Grand Auto, Inc.
7200 Edgewater Dr.
Oakland, CA 94621
(415) 568-6500

GREASE MONKEY
Grease Monkey International, Inc.
811 Lincoln St., Suite 500
Denver, CO 80203
(303) 839-1222

INTERSTATE
Interstate Automatic Transmission
    Co., Inc.
29200 Vassar Ave.
Livonia, MI 48152
(313) 478-9206

JIFFY LUBE
W. J. Hindman, President
Jiffy Lube International, Inc.
6666 Security Blvd.
Baltimore, MD 21207
(301) 298-8200

K MART
Bernard Fauber, Chairman
K mart Corp.
3100 W. Big Beaver
Troy, MI 48084
(313) 643-1000

KELLY-SPRINGFIELD
A. W. Dunn, President
The Kelly-Springfield Tire Co.
Kelly Road
Cumberland, MD 21502
(301) 777-6000

KORVETTES
C. Herline, Chairman
Korvettes, Inc.
1293 Broadway
New York, NY 10001
(212) 971-8000

LEE MYLES
Charles George, President
Lee Myles Associates Corp.
325 Sylvan Ave.
Englewood Cliffs, NJ 07632
(201) 568-2200
Toll-free: (800) 631-1699

LUBE PIT STOP
Lube Pit Stop
9025 Owensmouth
Canoga Park, CA 91304
(213) 341-0178

LUBE WAGON
The Lube Wagon
9430 Mission Blvd.
Riverside, CA 92509
(714) 685-8540

MAACO
Anthony A. Martino, President
MAACO Enterprises, Inc.
381 Brooks Road
King of Prussia, PA 19406
(215) 265-6606

MACY'S
Edward Finkelstein, Chairman
R. H. Macy & Co., Inc.
151 W. 34th St.
New York, NY 10001
(212) 695-4400

MAD HATTER
Fred Vaccaro, Proprietor
Mad Hatter Mufflers International
1700 Clearwater Largo Road
Clearwater, FL 33516
(813) 581-9032

MAJOR MUFFLER
Nathan Shapiro, President
Major Muffler Center
630 Third Ave.
New York, NY 10017
(212) 697-0300

MARKET TIRE
Irwin Monsein, President
Market Tire Co.
5481 Randolph Rd.
Rockville, MD 50852
(301) 770-5600

MARSHALL FIELD
Mr. Rudolph Hirsch, President
Marshall Field
111 N. State St.
Chicago, IL 60690
(312) 781-1000

MEINEKE
Harold Nedell, President
Meineke Discount Muffler Shops, Inc.
12013 Wilcrest
Houston, TX 77301
(713) 879-1811
Toll-free: (800) 867-5472

MERCHANT'S TIRE
W. Caton Merchant, Jr., President
Merchant's Tire Co., Inc.
9073 Euclid Ave.
Manassas, VA 22110
(703) 631-0477

MIDAS MUFFLER
R. P. de Camara, President
Midas International Corp.
222 S. Riverside Plaza
Chicago, IL 60606
(312) 648-5600

MING AUTO BEAUTY CENTERS
Ming of America, Inc.
4121 W. 83rd St.
Prairie Village, KS 66208
(913) 648-4303

MINIT LUBE
Arctic Circle, Inc.
150 E. Ninth South
Salt Lake City, UT 84110
(801) 521-6100

MIRACLE AUTO PAINTING
Multiple Allied Services
800 Airport Blvd., Suite 310
Burlingame, CA 94040
(415) 579-0460

MONTGOMERY WARD
Edward S. Donnell, Chairman
Montgomery Ward & Co., Inc.
One Montgomery Ward Plaza
Chicago, IL 60671
(312) 467-2000

MR. QUICK LUBE
Mr. Quick Lube
1515 Brooks Road East
Memphis, TN 38116
(901) 345-6590

MR TRANSMISSION
Joseph R. Dockery, President
Mr Transmission Inc.
400 Harding Industrial Dr.
Nashville, TN 37211
(615) 833-5030

MUFFLER WAGON
The Muffler Wagon
9430 Mission Blvd.
Riverside, CA 92509
(714) 685-8540

MUFFLERMAN
Mufflerman International Inc.
806 Mason Ave.
Daytona Beach, FL 32014
(904) 255-8318

NATIONWIDE BRAKE
David Lawson, President
Nationwide Brake & Alignment
    Centers, Inc.
5481 Randolph Rd.
Rockville, MD 20852
(301) 770-5481

NO-KORRODE RUSTPROOFING
No-Korrode Rustproofing &
    Refinishing Org.
4609 Bayard St.
Pittsburgh, PA 15213
(412) 683-1841

PAINTMASTER
Paintmasters Auto Painting and
    Body Work, Inc.
713 Losstrand Lane
Rockville, MD 20850
(301) 424-1475

J.C. PENNEY
Donald V. Seibert, Chairman
J. C. Penney Co., Inc.
1301 Ave. of the Americas
New York, NY 10019
(212) 957-4321

POLY-GUARD RUSTPROOFING
Poly-Oleum Corp.
16135 Harper Ave.
Detroit, MI 48224
(313) 882-4600

PRECISION TRANSMISSION
Curtis Butcher, President
Precision Transmission
2040 State Rd. 109 South
Anderson, IN 46013
(317) 649-9283

PRECISION TUNE
Precision Tune
3329 West Mockingbird Lane
Dallas, TX 75235
(214) 352-8067

THE RADMAN
Steven R. White, President
Radman, Inc.
17100 Southfield Rd.
Allen Park, MI 48101
(313) 388-8800

ROV-A-TUNE
Rov-A-Tune
434 E. Bernhard
Hazel Park, MI 48030
(313) 541-2210

RUSTMASTER
(see Paintmaster)

SCOTTI MUFFLER
Scotti Muffler Centers, Inc.
5959 E. Rosedale
Ft. Worth, TX 76112
(817) 451-0753

SEARS
E. R. Telling, Chairman
Sears, Roebuck and Co.
Sears Tower
Chicago, IL 60684
(312) 875-2500

STOP AND GO
Bou-Faro Co.
274 Broadway
Pawtucket, RI 02860
(401) 724-8180

TIDY CAR
Tidy Car Inc.
1051 Clinton
Buffalo, NY 14206
(716) 856-2826

TOP TUNE
Top Tune Service Center
1107 Brookhurst St.
Anaheim, CA 92801
(714) 991-5260

TUFF-KOTE DINOL
William F. Widger, President
Tuff-Kote Dinol, Inc.
13650 E. Ten Mile Road
Warren, MI 48089
(313) 776-5000

TUFFY SERVICE CENTERS
Tuffy Service Centers, Inc.
5462 State Street
Saginaw, MI 48603
(517) 792-4040

TUNE KING
J. Stewart Bell, President
Tune King International, Inc.
315 Glenbrook Center
1140 N.W. 63rd
Oklahoma City, OK 73116
(405) 848-6014

TUNE-UP CLINIC
Al Massey, President
Tune-Up Clinic, Inc.
2675 Cumberland Parkway, Suite 240
Atlanta, GA 30339
(404) 432-5900

TUNEUP MASTERS
Andy Granatelli, Chairman
Tuneup Masters
21031 Ventura Blvd.
Woodland Hills, CA 91364
(213) 999-5600

TUNEX
Gordon Jiles, President
Tunex, Inc.
556 E. 2100 South
Salt Lake City, UT 84106
(801) 486-8133

WESTERN AUTO
Western Auto Supply Co.
2107 Grand Ave.
Kansas City, MO 64108
(816) 421-6700

WOOLCO
Edward F. Gibbons, Chairman
F. W. Woolworth Co.
Woolworth Bldg.
New York, NY 10279
(212) 553-2000

ZAYRE
Sumner L. Feldberg, Chairman
Zayre Corp.
Framingham, MA 01701
(617) 620-5000

ZEEGARD CAR CONDITIONING
(see Ziebart)

ZIEBART RUSTPROOFING
D. W. Janssan, President
Ziebart Rustproofing Co.
P.O. Box 1290
1290 East Maple Rd.
Troy, MI 48099
(313) 588-4100

2. Automotive Organizations

J. B. Creal, President
American Automobile Assn.
8111 Gatehouse Rd.
Falls Church, VA 22047
(703) 222-6332

Gene Lewis, Executive Director
National Business Office
Automatic Transmission Rebuilders
  Assn.
6663 Ventura Blvd., Suite B
Ventura, CA 93003
(805) 656-ATRA

J. W. Nerlinger, President
Automotive Service Industry Assn.
444 N. Michigan Ave.
Chicago, IL 60601
(312) 836-1300

George W. Merwin III, President
Automotive Service Councils, Inc.
188 Industrial Dr., Suite 112
Elmhurst, IL 60126
(312) 530-2330

John Kushnerick, President
Chilton Co.
201 King of Prussia Rd.
Radnor, PA 19089
(215) 964-4000

Gene Brown, President
Cooperative Auto, Inc.
2232 S. Industrial Hwy.
Ann Arbor, MI 48104
(313) 769-0220

Cooperative Garage of Rockland
  County
West Nyack, NY 10994
(914) 358-9452

Dr. William Haddon, Jr., President
Insurance Institute for Highway Safety
Watergate Six-Hundred
Washington, DC 20037
(202) 333-0770

Frank E. McCarthy, Executive V.P.
National Automobile Dealers Assn.
8400 Westpark Dr.
McLean, VA 22102
(703) 821-7000

Stanley A. Rodman, Executive
  Director
National Automotive Radiator
  Service Assn.
(Mailing: P.O. Box 567
Lansdale, PA 19446)
1744 Sumneytown Pike
Kulpsville, PA 19943
(215) 368-6766

Dan C. Ray II, Executive Director
National Independent Automobile
  Dealers Assn.
3700 National Drive, Suite 208
Raleigh, NC 27612
(919) 781-2350

Herbert Fuhrman, President
National Institute for Automotive
  Service Excellence
1825 K St. N.W.
Washington, DC 20006
(202) 833-9646

Philip P. Friedlander, Jr.,
  Executive V.P.
National Tire Dealers &
  Retreaders Assn.
1343 L St. N.W.
Washington, DC 20005
(202) 638-6650

Robert M. Krughoff, President
Washington Center for the Study
  of Services
1518 K St. N.W., Suite 406
Washington, DC 20005
(202) 347-9612

Appendix J

Locations of AAA Approved

Repair Shop Program

At the end of 1980, the following AAA clubs had Approved Repair Shops:

Northeastern Region: Maine Automobile Association, New Hampshire Division, Automobile Club of Vermont, Massachusetts Division, Automobile Club of Merrimack Valley, Bancroft Automobile Club, Automobile Club of Hartford, and the Automobile Club of Rhode Island.

Mid-Atlantic Region: Automobile Club of Maryland, Blue Grass Automobile Club, and the Potomac Division.

Southeastern Region: St. Petersburg Motor Club, and the East Florida Division.

Northcentral Region: Wisconsin Division, Minnesota State Automobile Association, Ohio Motorists Association, and the Ohio Automobile Club.

Southcentral Region: Texas Division, Arizona Automobile Association, and the Southwest Motor Club.

Southwestern Region: Automobile Club of Southern California.

The following clubs were expected to be in the program during 1981:

Automobile Club of Washington	New Jersey (5 clubs)
Automobile Club of Oregon	Hoosier Motor Club
Inland Motor Club	Delaware Motor Club
Pennsylvania Federation (38 clubs)	Austin Automobile Club
	Duluth Automobile Club

Clubs likely to join the program after 1981 include:

Automobile Club of Western N.Y.	Cornhusker Motor Club
Automobile Club of Rochester	Automobile Club of Oklahoma
Chicago Motor Club	Oklahoma Division
New Mexico Division	Automobile Club of Minneapolis
Tuscarawas County Auto. Club	Tri-County Automobile Club

Appendix K

Highlights of State

Small Claims Court Laws

1. State Small Claims Court Limits

Here are the monetary limits for small claims courts. The figures are from a 1978 study except for more current data on Massachusetts, Michigan, North Dakota and Pennsylvania.

Alabama, $500; *Alaska*, $1,000; *Arizona*, $999.99; *Arkansas*, $300 ($100 if personal); *California*, $750; *Colorado*, $500; *Connecticut*, $750; *Delaware*, $1,500; *District of Columbia*, $750; *Florida*, $2,500 (attorney required if over $1,500); *Georgia*, $300 ($200 in justice of the peace court); *Hawaii*, $300; *Idaho*, $500; *Illinois*, $1,000 ($300 in Cook County); *Indiana*, $3,000; *Iowa*, $1,000; *Kansas*, $300; *Kentucky*, $500; *Louisiana*, $300; *Maine*, $500; *Maryland*, $500; *Massachusetts*, $750; *Michigan*, $600; *Minnesota*, $1,000 ($500 in Minneapolis and St. Paul); *Missouri*, $500; *Montana*, $1,500; *Nebraska*, $500; *Nevada*, $300; *New Hampshire*, $500; *New Jersey*, $500; *New Mexico*, $2,000; *New York*, $1,000; *North Carolina*, $500; *North Dakota*, $1,000 ($500 in justice court); *Ohio*, $300; *Oklahoma*, $600; *Oregon*, $500; *Pennsylvania*, $2,000 (Philadelphia, $1,000); *Rhode Island*, $300; *South Carolina*, $200 to $3,000; *South Dakota*, $1,000; *Tennessee*, $3,000; *Texas*, $150 ($200 for wages); *Utah*, $200; *Vermont*, $200; *Virginia*, $5,000; *Washington*, $300; *West Virginia*, $1,500; *Wisconsin*, $500; *Wyoming*, $200.

Source: John C. Ruhnka and Steven Weller, *Small Claims Courts: A National Examination*, National Center for State Courts, 1978.

2. States Where Attorneys Are Excluded from Small Claims Court

California, Colorado, Idaho, Illinois (Cook County only), *Kansas, Michigan* (except Detroit), *Minnesota* (except Minneapolis–St. Paul), *Montana* (if you don't have an attorney, the other side can't use one), *Nebraska, Oregon* (unless the judge consents to have lawyers), *Washington.*

Source: Same as above.

Appendix L

Federal Legislators and Officials

1. Legislators

You can write your two U.S. senators and your congressman thusly:

Hon. (senator's name)
U.S. Senate
Washington, DC 20510

Hon. (congressman's name)
U.S. House of Representatives
Washington, DC 20515

Copies of your letters should be sent to the two subcommittees most involved in auto repair:

Chairman
Subcommittee for Consumers
Committee on Commerce,
  Science and Transportation
U.S. Senate
Washington, DC 20510
(202) 224-4768

Chairman
Subcommittee on Telecommunications,
  Consumer Protection and Finance
Committee on Energy and Commerce
B331 Rayburn Bldg.
Washington, DC 20515
(202) 225-9304

The committees responsible for antitrust and price-fixing legislation are:

Chairman
Committee on the Judiciary
U.S. Senate
2226 Dirksen Office Bldg.
Washington, DC 20510

Chairman
Committee on the Judiciary
U.S. House of Representatives
2137 Rayburn Bldg.
Washington, DC 20515

The committees that can do something about mechanic incompetency are:

Chairman
Committee on Labor and Human
  Resources
U.S. Senate
4230 Dirksen Office Bldg.
Washington, DC 20510

Chairman
Committee on Education and Labor
U.S. House of Representatives
2181 Rayburn Bldg.
Washington, DC 20515

2. Officials

William Baxter
Assistant Attorney General
Antitrust Division
U.S. Justice Dept.
Room 3109
Washington, DC 20530
(202) 633-2401

Raymond J. Donovan
Secretary of Labor
Room S2018
200 Constitution Ave. N.W.
Washington, DC 20210
(202) 523-8271

Appendix M

California Transmission Regulation;

Datsun Pre-delivery Inspection

Record; Wisconsin Disclosure

Statement and Window Sticker

for Used Cars; Auto Repair

Estimate Form

California Transmission Regulation

An automatic transmission shall be described by a word such as "rebuilt," "remanufactured," "reconditioned," or "overhauled," or by any expression of like meaning, only if the following work has been done since the transmission was last used:

(1) All internal and external parts, including case and housing, have been thoroughly cleaned and inspected.

(2) The valve body has been disassembled and thoroughly cleaned and inspected.

(3) All front and intermediate bands have been replaced with new or relined bands.

(4) All the following parts have been replaced with new parts:
  (A) friction plates
  (B) internal and external seals
  (C) metal sealing rings that are used in rotating applications
  (D) gaskets
  (E) organic media disposable type filters (if the transmission is so equipped)

(5) All impaired, defective, or substantially worn parts not mentioned above have been restored to a sound condition or replaced with new, rebuilt, or unimpaired parts. All measuring and adjusting of such parts have been performed as necessary.

(Note: These minimum requirements, according to the regulation, are not to be used to promote the sale of "rebuilt" automatic transmissions when a less costly repair is desired by the customer. Any repair shop that represents to customers that the regulation requires the rebuilding of automatic transmissions is subject to disciplinary action.)

1981.5 PRE-DELIVERY INSPECTION RECORD

DEALER NAME	DEALER CODE	VEHICLE ID. NO.	ENGINE NO.	MM	DD	YY
				PDI Completion Date		

We at Nissan are proud of our Datsun vehicles. They are built to the highest engineering and production quality standards. To maintain the good performance and economy features built into Datsun products, owners have found it wise to return to their dealer for service and maintenance. Datsun service people are the "Little Things Experts," and you will find that their attention will make your Datsun ownership a long and satisfying experience.

1. EXTERIOR CHECKS – CORRECT AS NECESSARY
- ☐ Tires: Inflation pressure, condition, balance weight
- ☐ Torque of wheel lug nuts: Passenger cars 58-72 ft.lbs. (8-10 kg-m); Pickup Truck 81-108 ft.lbs. (12-15 kg-m)
- ☐ Install wheel covers and outside rear view mirror
- ☐ Primary/secondary hood latch operation and mounting bolt torque
- ☐ Hood, door, trunk/tailgate/hatch, sunroof, windows, locks: Operation/alignment

2. INTERIOR CHECKS – VISUALLY CHECK & CORRECT AS NECESSARY
- ☐ Seat belt operation
- ☐ Windshield wipers, washers and fluid level
- ☐ Headlight aim, high and low beams, quick flash switch and lane changer
- ☐ Parking, side clearance, license plate lights
- ☐ Install clock/voltmeter fuse or turn on extended storage switch
- ☐ Hazard warning lights
- ☐ Back-up lights
- ☐ Dash, dome and courtesy lights
- ☐ Indicator warning lights and sound
- ☐ All accessories
- ☐ Spare tire mounting and pressure
- ☐ Installation of jack, tools, and tire inflator (if applicable)
- ☐ Glove box: Operation and owner's literature

3. UNDERBODY CHECKS – VISUALLY INSPECT AND CORRECT AS NECESSARY
- ☐ Oil, brake, fuel and cooling lines (Auto. Trans.) for leaks
- ☐ Transmission/transfer case: leaks and fluid level
- ☐ Steering gear box: leaks
- ☐ Differential: leaks and oil level
- ☐ Shock absorbers: leaks

CHECK FOR PROPER ASSEMBLY & TIGHTEN AS NECESSARY
- ☐ Underbody mounting bolts
- ☐ Steering linkage, suspension
- ☐ Drive shaft and differential mounting nuts/bolts
- ☐ Exhaust system and shielding
- ☐ 280ZX: Remove front spring spacers and windshield caution label

4. UNDERHOOD CHECKS – CORRECT AS NECESSARY
- ☐ Steering box fluid level
- ☐ Power steering fluid level (if applicable)
- ☐ Brake and clutch master cylinders fluid level
- ☐ Engine oil level
- ☐ Automatic transmission fluid level
- ☐ Radiator coolant level; also check all clamps and hoses for leaks
- ☐ Battery: clamps, state of charge (specific gravity), electrolyte level and charge indicator
- ☐ Tension of all belts
- ☐ Fuel filter for leaks, water or dirt
- ☐ Fuel clamps and hoses for leaks
- ☐ EFI equipped models: torque all fuel line clamps to 9-13 in.lbs
- ☐ Spark plug condition
- ☐ Air conditioning charge and compressor clutch operation

UNDERHOOD CHECKS (Cont'd.)
- ☐ Exhaust gas sensor operation (if applicable)
- ☐ Check ignition timing
- ☐ Check idle speed
- ☐ Check adjustment & operation of throttle valve switch (if applicable)
- ☐ Glow plug and clamps (D)
- ☐ Accelerator cable for proper attachment and operation (D)
- ☐ Diesel pump controller (SD), linkage and governor hose (SD)

5. ROAD TEST – CHECK OPERATION & CORRECT AS NECESSARY
- ☐ Instruments and gauges
- ☐ Service and parking brakes
- ☐ Standard transmission, transfer case, and clutch
- ☐ Automatic transmission: shift patterns, kickdown, park position and inhibitor switch
- ☐ Steering for wheel return, tracking, pull and free play
- ☐ Engine performance during all driving conditions (carburetor linkage)
- ☐ Heater / defroster
- ☐ Windshield wipers and washers
- ☐ Horn
- ☐ A.S.C.D. operation (if applicable)
- ☐ Glow plug system operation (D)

6. APPEARANCE & FINAL CHECKS – CORRECT AS NECESSARY
- ☐ All decals and identification numbers
- ☐ Remove protective covering (seats, bumpers)
- ☐ Visual check for smoke during no-load acceleration (D)
- ☐ Check match marks on injection pump and front plate (D)
- ☐ Wash car, check for water leaks

I certify that I have personally checked and corrected to factory specifications the items indicated on this check list to make Datsun ownership more enjoyable.

Pre-Delivery Technician _____ *Date* _____

- ☐ Review document package with owner
- ☐ Explain maintenance schedule and performance warranty
- ☐ Demonstrate accessories
- ☐ Demonstrate headlight dimmer

The owner of this new Datsun has been briefed on the items listed above, our service department business hours, and the person he can contact to make appointments for his maintenance services

Service Manager _____ *Date* _____

Delivered By _____ *Date* _____

It was explained to me that it is important to follow the maintenance schedule as my part of the team effort required to keep my new Datsun performing efficiently.

Customer _____

OWNER'S NAME — CITY — ADDRESS — STATE — ZIP — Key Numbers — Dealer Stock No. — Trim and Paint — Trans. Number — In Service Date

KEY: D = All Diesel
SD = SD22 only
LD = LD 28 only

Subject to.audit any time for two years after the delivery of the vehicle.

Form S-61-S/1-81   **WHITE** – DEALER COPY   **CANARY** – CUSTOMER COPY   NISSAN MOTOR CORPORATION IN U.S.A.

DISCLOSURE STATEMENT FOR USED MOTOR VEHICLES

Original — Dealer Retain
Duplicate — Customer Copy

DEALERSHIP	VEHICLE STOCK NO.	YEAR — MAKE
	IDENTIFICATION NUMBER	
	AUTHORIZED DEALER INSPECTION AGENT	DATE

"I have exercised reasonable diligence in inspecting this vehicle, including at least a review of my repair records, the prior owner's disclosure, a walk-around and interior inspection, an under-hood inspection, an under-vehicle inspection, and a test drive. On the basis of such inspection, I declare the apparent existing condition to be as indicated in the boxes below."

Disclosure of general condition as required by MVD 24.03(5)

YES NO **FRAME & BODY**
☐ ☐ Apparent cracks or corrective welds on frame
☐ ☐ Dogtracks - bent or twisted frame
☐ ☐ Inoperative doors

ENGINE
☐ ☐ Known or visible oil leakage, excluding normal seepage
☐ ☐ Cracked block or head
☐ ☐ Belts missing or inoperable
☐ ☐ Knocks or misses
☐ ☐ Abnormal visible exhaust discharge

TRANSMISSION & DRIVE SHAFT
☐ ☐ Improper fluid level or visible leakage, excluding normal seepage
☐ ☐ Cracked or damaged case, which is visible
☐ ☐ Abnormal noise or vibration
☐ ☐ Improper shifting into or functioning in all gears
☐ ☐ Manual clutch slips or chatters

DIFFERENTIAL
☐ ☐ Improper fluid level or visible leakage, excluding normal seepage
☐ ☐ Cracked or damaged housing, which is visible
☐ ☐ Abnormal noise or vibration

COOLING SYSTEM
☐ ☐ Improper fluid level or visible leakage
☐ ☐ Leaky radiator
☐ ☐ Improperly functioning water pump
☐ ☐ Inadequate antifreeze strength for season of year

ELECTRICAL SYSTEM
☐ ☐ Improper fluid level or visible leakage of battery
☐ ☐ Battery fails to start engine
☐ ☐ Improperly functioning alternator, generator, or starter

FUEL SYSTEM
☐ ☐ Visible leakage

ACCESSORIES - INOPERATIVE
☐ ☐ Gauges and warning devices
☐ ☐ Radio
☐ ☐ Heater & Defroster
☐ ☐ Air Conditioner
☐ ☐ Dash Lights
☐ ☐ Windows

Explain probable cause for malfunction or defect on all items marked "Yes".

Disclosure of safety equipment defects as required by MVD 24.03(6)(a) 2.

ALL REQUIRED safety equipment items below, except those marked "Not OK", are in legal operating condition. If the dealer does not correct all such defects prior to delivery of the vehicle to the retail purchaser, the required warning statement must be made on the contract, the vehicle must be towed or hauled, the title application shall be marked "THIS VEHICLE MAY NOT BE LEGALLY OPERATED ON WISCONSIN HIGHWAYS AND NO REGISTRATION WILL BE ISSUED" and sent by the dealer to the Division of Motor Vehicles on behalf of the purchaser.

NOT
OK OK
☐ ☐ Headlamp and Aim
☐ ☐ Parking Lamps
☐ ☐ Directional Lamps
☐ ☐ Flashing Warning Lamps
☐ ☐ Sidemarker Lamps and Reflectors
☐ ☐ Tail Lamps
☐ ☐ Back Up Lamps
☐ ☐ Brake Lamps
☐ ☐ License Plate Lamp
☐ ☐ Steering and Suspension
☐ ☐ Front Bumper and Fenders
☐ ☐ Hood and Trunk Latches
☐ ☐ Emission System
☐ ☐ Door Latches
☐ ☐ Tires
☐ ☐ Exhaust and Fuel System
☐ ☐ Rear Bumper and Fenders
☐ ☐ Rear Suspension
☐ ☐ Windshield
☐ ☐ Other Windows
☐ ☐ Windshield Wipers
☐ ☐ Horn
☐ ☐ Mirror
☐ ☐ Speed Indicator
☐ ☐ Odometer
☐ ☐ Restraining Devices and Seats
☐ ☐ Service Brake
☐ ☐ Parking Brake
☐ ☐ Floor and Trunk Pans

Explain all items marked "Not OK".

USED VEHICLE WINDOW STICKER

Model Year 19 _____ Make _____

Identification Number _____

Engine Type _____ Transmission _____

Stock # _____ Asking Price $_____

VEHICLE USE: This vehicle previously was used as a

☐ Privately driven vehicle | ☐ Taxi-driven
☐ Leased vehicle | ☐ Company vehicle
☐ Rental vehicle | ☐ Demonstrator
☐ Municipal owned | ☐ Executive driven
☐ Police vehicle | ☐ Driver education vehicle
☐ Public vehicle | ☐ Flood damaged vehicle

ODOMETER: The Odometer Reading at time of trade-in or purchase
was _____ miles which is <u>corroborated by</u>
ODOMETER READING
<u>the prior owners statement</u> and is (CHECK ONE)

☐ the actual mileage   ☐ not known to be the actual mileage

☐ Known to be inaccurate and known actual mileage was

_____ miles.

Name, address and mileage (odometer) statement of prior owner
available upon request.

This vehicle is for sale:
☐ With limited warranty as follows: _____

_____

Ask salesperson to see copy of warranty.

☐ AS IS. No warranty, express or implied.

**EXCEPT FOR ANY MANUFACTURER'S OR OTHER EXPRESS
WARRANTY WHICH EXISTS ON THIS VEHICLE, THE ENTIRE
RISK AS TO THE QUALITY AND PERFORMANCE OF THE
VEHICLE IS WITH THE BUYER, AND SHOULD THE VEHICLE
PROVE DEFECTIVE FOLLOWING THE PURCHASE, THE BUYER
WILL ASSUME THE ENTIRE COST OF ALL SERVICING AND
REPAIR.**

☐ Service agreement available, ask salesperson for details.

☐ Mechanical Breakdown Insurance available — ask sales
person for details.   WATDASI #4 10/78

AUTO REPAIR ESTIMATE

Date _____

Name _____

Address _____

City _____ State _____ Zip _____

Phone _____ car _____ year _____

Mileage _____ Mfrs. No. _____ License _____

Rate per hour $_____ Based on clock hour _____ flat rate hour _____

Name of flat rate manual _____

Date and time promised _____

Symptoms _____

_____

_____

Labor Recommended   Est. Cost

_____

_____

_____

_____

Parts Recommended   n   u   r   Est. Cost
                               e   s   e
                               w   e   b
                                    d   t

_____

_____

_____

_____

Total Estimate _____

Guaranty _____

I believe, to the best of my ability, that the above repairs are necessary to correct the malfunction(s) of the above car. I agree to do only those repairs on this estimate form unless authorized by the customer to do additional work. I further agree not to exceed the estimated cost of repairs without getting authorization from the customer.

Signed _____

Name (printed) _____

Title _____

Shop name _____

Notes

Chapter 1

1. Robert Hodierne and Marti Stewart, "Auto repair: it's Russian roulette," *Wilmington Evening Journal,* July 26, 1973, p. 1.
2. "The auto repair go-round," Part I, WMAL-TV, telecast October 29, 1973.
3. Hearings before the Subcommittee for Consumers of the Committee on Commerce, Science and Transportation, United States Senate, Ninety-fifth Congress, Second Session, *National Traffic and Motor Vehicle Information and Cost Savings Authorizations of 1979 and 1980,* March 21, 22, and 23, 1978, p. 7.
4. National Institute for Automotive Service Excellence, *Automobile Mechanic Data,* April 1980.
5. *Ibid.* and National Institute for Automotive Service Excellence, *Excelsior,* August 1980, p. 3. There were 522,032 mechanics working on consumer vehicles in 1980 out of which 28,000 passed all tests.
6. Letter to U.S. Senator Wendell H. Ford, December 13, 1977.
7. Telephone interview with Ann Barnes, U.S. Office of Consumer Affairs, May 21, 1979.
8. Letter from James E. Dodds, legal intern, Consumer Protection Division, Texas attorney general's office, to U.S. Senator Wendell Ford, December 21, 1977.
9. Letter from Robert S. Tongren, chief of the Consumer Frauds and Crimes Section, Ohio attorney general's office, to U.S. Senator Wendell Ford, February 3, 1978.
10. Rod Cockshutt, "N.C. bill to penalize car repair rip-offs," *Columbia* (S.C.) *State,* May 13, 1979.
11. *Washington Post,* August 13, 1978, p. A16.
12. Letter from Robert N. Hilgendorf, director of the Consumer and Economic Crimes Division of the New Mexico attorney general's office, to U.S. Senator Wendell Ford.
13. *Ibid.*
14. Illinois Legislative Investigating Commission, *Auto Repair Abuses,* June 1975, p. 5.
15. *Ibid.,* p. xii.
16. *Op. cit.,* note 3 above, p. 128.
17. Norris and Ross McWhirter, *Guinness Book of World Records* (New York: Sterling Publishing Co., Inc., 1978), p. 401.

18. This figure was arrived at by taking the car population of 99,903,594 as of July 1, 1977 (source: R.L. Polk & Co.; *Automotive News*, July 3, 1978, p. 28), and dividing it into $13 billion.

19. *Op. cit.*, note 3 above, p. 129.

20. Federal Trade Commission, *Staff Report on the Used Motor Vehicle Industry*, December 1975, p. 40.

21. Hearings before the Subcommittee on Consumer Protection and Finance of the Committee on Interstate and Foreign Commerce, House of Representatives, Ninety-fifth Congress, Second Session, *Auto Repair*, September 14, 20, 21, 25, October 19, and December 4, 1978, p. 6.

22. *Ibid.*

23. *Ibid.*, p. 262 (service station statistics).

24. Sentry Insurance, *Consumerism at the Crossroads*, 1977, p. 13 (Harris poll).

25. *U.S. News and World Report*, February 20, 1978, p. 17.

26. *Money*, December 1978, p. 59.

27. *Roper Reports*, Summary of 78–10, issued late December 1978, Question No. 44.

28. *Op. cit.*, note 3 above, p. 113.

29. Johnson Center for Environmental and Energy Studies, University of Alabama in Huntsville, *Survey of Automotive Repair Practices*, draft report, prepared for the Office of the Secretary of Transportation, Division of Consumer Affairs, May 7, 1979.

30. Patricia Hinsberg, "Service groups blast DOT repair survey," *Automotive News*, May 28, 1979, p. 50.

31. Telephone interview with Judy Anderson, WTVF-TV, November 9, 1978.

32. Colorado Public Interest Research Group, *An Investigation of Market Conditions of the Auto Repair Industry*, December 1977.

33. *Chicago Tribune*, June 20, 1976, p. 1.

34. Bernard J. Schroer and J.F. Peters, *An Evaluation of Vehicle Repair Costs for Auto Check Participants*, University of Alabama in Huntsville, February 1, 1977 (Contract No. DOT–HS–5–01056), pp. 1 & 2.

35. U.S. Department of Commerce, Bureau of the Census, *Statistical Abstract of the United States: 1979*, p. 650.

36. *Congressional Quarterly Weekly Report*, November 22, 1980, p. 3406.

37. *Business Week*, November 3, 1980, p. 42.

38. *U.S. News & World Report*, March 8, 1971, p. 32.

Chapter 2

1. Telephone interview with Raymond T. Bonner, San Francisco district attorney's office, March 1978.

2. Washington Center for the Study of Services, *Checkbook Cars*, Summer 1976, pp. 30–76.

3. Telephone interview with S. Chandler Visher, San Francisco district attorney's office, June 25, 1979.

4. Telephone interview, March 1978.

5. *Op. cit.*, note 1 above.

6. *California* v. *Auto Pacific Corp.*, Statement of Facts; Memorandum of Points and Authorities in Support of Temporary Restraining Order and Preliminary Injunction, Superior Court, San Francisco, March 1, 1978, Case No. 734815.

7. William Endicott, " 'Flat-rate' billing for car repairs under challenge," *Los Angeles Times*, March 2, 1978, p. 1.

8. *Op. cit.*, note 6 above.

9. *San Francisco Chronicle*, July 16, 1980, p. 2.

10. Letter of June 15, 1977.

11. Martin H. Bury, *The Automobile Dealer* (Haverford, Pa: Philpenn Publishing Co., 1974), p. 97.
12. *Chilton's 1981 Labor Guide and Parts Manual,* p. 795.
13. Alan Flores at seminar on *Shop Trak,* 2:00–3:15 p.m., February 20, 1978.
14. *Op. cit.,* note 12 above, p. 426.
15. Prepared statement to the Subcommittee on Consumer Protection and Finance of the Committee on Interstate and Foreign Commerce, House of Representatives, September 20, 1978.
16. John A. Russell, "New York gears for flat-rate battle," *Automotive News,* November 10, 1980, p. 26.
17. *Op. cit.,* note 12 above, p. 383.
18. Wisconsin Attorney General's Office, *Nine-Week Random Sample of Flat Rate Hours v. Clock Hours.* 1974.
19. *Op. cit.,* note 12 above.
20. Mo Mehlsak, "Warranty administration," *Automotive Age,* June 1979, p. 63.
21. Interview, April 26, 1978.
22. *Op. cit.,* note 11 above, pp. 96–97.
23. Tom Peterson, "The other side of auto repair," *Newsday,* July 21, 1974, p. 5.
24. Glenn C. Garrett, "The mechanics of an industry rip-off," *Los Angeles Times,* July 18, 1977, Part II, p. 7.
25. Booz Allen Applied Research, Inc., *Maintainability and Repairability of Vehicles In Use,* Final Report, June 1971, Vol. 1, p. iii–19.
26. James A. Mateyka, David W. Weiss and Lloyd Emery, *Automobile Maintainability by Design,* presented at Sympo-72, Los Angeles Maintainability Association, Los Angeles, May 20, 1972.
27. Telephone interview, July 15, 1978.
28. *Op. cit.,* note 23 above.
29. *Op. cit.,* note 21 above.
30. Telephone interview, May 4, 1978.
31. Letter of November 10, 1975.
32. *Automotive Age,* August 1977, p. 40B.
33. Celia A. Maloney, Tom Alderman and Nat Williams, *Illinois Consumers' Auto Repair Inquiry,* Illinois Consumer Advocate Office, Office of the Governor, 1974.
34. *Op. cit.,* note 21 above.
35. Illinois Legislative Investigating Commission, *Auto Repair Abuses,* June 1975, p. xii.
36. Letter to U.S. Senator J. Glenn Beall, Jr., July 28, 1975.
37. Gerry Haddon, "Car repairs the greatest bargain on earth," *Motor Age,* February 1969, pp. 112–113.
38. Letter from C.W. Mackenzie, executive director, National Automobile Radiator Service Association, to the Federal Trade Commission, December 27, 1976. FTC File No. 683 7090.
39. Letter from Joseph W. Shea, Federal Trade Commission secretary, to C.W. Mackenzie. FTC File No. 683 7090.
40. Memorandum from Kenneth James, attorney, Bureau of Competition, to Bureau of Consumer Protection, December 15, 1977. FTC File No. CH6–0054.
41. Letter of June 5, 1978.
42. *Op. cit.,* note 40 above.
43. Regulations of the Commissioner of Motor Vehicles, New York State, Section 82.7 (c).
44. *Ibid.,* Section 82.8 (a) and (b).
45. *Motor Parts and Time Guide,* 1978, p. 786.
46. *Chilton's Labor Guide and Parts Manual,* 1976, p. 826.

Notes

Chapter 3

1. Wendell A. Cook, *Repair Industry Response to Diagnostic Inspection Projects*, paper presented at Congress of Society of Automotive Engineers, Inc., February 27–March 3, 1978, Technical Paper Series No. 780030, p. 17.

2. Joseph Ralph Pisani, *Automobile Repair: A Study of Consumer and Repair Shop Attitudes Toward the Industry, the Performance of Repair Work and Regulation*, doctoral thesis, University of Maryland, November 15, 1972, pp. 231 and 181–182.

3. Bernard J. Schroer, William F. Peyston and J.F. Peters, *An Evaluation of Component Repair Costs for Auto Check Participants*, Kenneth E. Johnson Environmental and Energy Center, University of Alabama in Huntsville, Contract No. DOT–HS–5–01056, May 31, 1977, p. 31. (While six chains are listed as Chains A through F, Chain C is not a national chain and is therefore not included here).

4. *Ibid.*, p. 23.

5. *Ibid.*, p. 13.

6. *Ibid.*, p. 23.

7. Center for Environmental and Energy Studies, University of Alabama in Huntsville, *An Evaluation of Vehicle Repair Costs for Auto Check Participants*, Contract No. DOT–HS–5–01056, February 1, 1977, p. 20.

8. From signed statement, August 27, 1973.

9. Office of the District Attorney, County of Santa Barbara, Bureau of Investigation, Investigation Report Re: Goodyear Tire & Rubber Co., March 29, 1973.

10. State of Michigan, Department of Attorney General, in the matter of K mart Corporation, Notice of Intended Action, File No. 77–1029–CPA, September 22, 1977.

11. *Lansing State Journal*, December 29, 1977.

12. State of Michigan, Department of Attorney General, in the matter of K-Mart Corporation, Assurance of Discontinuance, File No. 78–1004–CPA, August 23, 1978.

13. Telephone interview with John Davis, deputy district attorney, Alameda County, March 14, 1978.

14. *California* v. *S.S. Kresge Company*, Complaint for Injunction, Civil Penalties, Restitution and Other Relief, Superior Court of the State of California, County of Alameda, No. 457435–8, November 21, 1974.

15. *California* v. *S.S. Kresge Company*, Agreement of Compromise and Settlement, Superior Court of the State of California, County of Alameda, No. 457435–8, February 24, 1976.

16. *California* v. *K-Mart Enterprises of California, Inc.*, Complaint for Injunction, Civil Penalties and Other Relief, in the Superior Court of the State of California, in and for the County of Sacramento, No. 264231, November 24, 1976.

17. *California* v. *K-Mart Enterprises of California*, Agreement for Dismissal with Prejudice, in the Superior Court of the State of California, in and for the County of Sacramento, No. 264231, December 11, 1978.

18. News Release, California Bureau of Automotive Repair, "Orange County settles with K mart auto repair facilities," undated, and telephone interview with Robert N. Wiens, chief of the Bureau of Automotive Repair, February 6, 1981.

19. Telephone interview with Shirley Katt, consumer protection analyst, Washoe County district attorney's office, February 1981, and *Nevada* v. *K mart Corp.*, in the Second Judicial District Court of the State of Nevada in and for the County of Washoe, Stipulation for Entry of Judgment, No. 81–360, Dept No. 2, January 14, 1981.

20. Letter to author from Mark A. Vining, director, Consumer Fraud and Economic Crime Division, Sedgwick County district attorney's office, March 3, 1981.

21. Telephone interview, April 11, 1978.

22. Telephone interview, March 14, 1978.

23. *Ibid.*

24. *Op. cit.*, note 21 above.

25. *California* v. *Sears, Roebuck & Co.*, Stipulation, in the Superior Court of the State of California, in and for the County of Orange, Case No. 26–77–61, April 29, 1977.

26. From transcript of program aired on KHOU-TV, November 6, 1975, 6:00 p.m.; and Tom Kennedy, "Sears, Roebuck and Co. found guilty of deception," *Houston Post*, April 3, 1976.

27. News release, State of Vermont, Office of the Attorney General, "Attorney general sues Sears," December 9, 1977, and in Re: Sears, Roebuck and Co., State of Vermont, Washington County Superior Court, Assurance of Discontinuance, May 3, 1978.

28. News release, Montgomery County Office of Consumer Affairs, "Sears signs agreement over alleged unnecessary auto repairs," January 28, 1981; case summaries, and In Re: Sears, Roebuck and Co., Assurance of Discontinuance, Office of Consumer Affairs, Montgomery County, Maryland, January 1981.

29. Nevada against Sears Roebuck & Co. and Bruce Williams, Criminal Complaint, in the Justice's Court of Reno Township in and for the County of Washoe, Case No. CF80–60A/CF80–76, October 21, 1980.

30. National Association of Consumer Agency Administrators, *News*, December 1980, p. 3.

31. *California* v. *Goodyear Tire and Rubber Co.*, Complaint for Civil Penalties, Injunction and Other Relief, Superior Court of the State of California, for the County of Santa Barbara, S.C. No. 99310.

32. Press release information, Santa Barbara County district attorney's office.

33. *Caveat Emptor*, June 1973, p. 24.

34. *Missouri* v. *Goodyear Tire & Rubber Co.*, Petition for Injunction and Court Orders, in the Circuit Court of the County of St. Louis, State of Missouri, Cause No. 373047, Division No. 10.

35. Telephone interview, April 19, 1978.

36. *Missouri* v. *Goodyear Tire & Rubber Co.*, Decision and Order, in the Circuit Court of the County of St. Louis, State of Missouri, Cause No. 373047, Division No. 10, September 23, 1975.

37. *Consumer Reports*, January 1979, p. 38. See also: In the matter of Goodyear Tire & Rubber Co., Stipulation for Special Order, State of Wisconsin, Department of Agriculture, Trade & Consumer Protection, Docket No. 1372, June 22, 1978.

38. *Kansas* v. *Goodyear Tire & Rubber Co.*, Petition for Civil Penalties, Injunction, and Other Relief, in the Eighteenth Judicial District, District Court, Sedgwick County, Kansas, Civil Department, Case No. 78C727.

39. *Kansas* v. *Goodyear Tire & Rubber Co.*, Order Nunc Pro Tunc, in the Eighteenth Judicial District, District Court, Sedgwick County, Kansas, Civil Division, Case No. 78C727, July 11, 1978.

40. From transcript, "The auto repair go-round," aired October 29, 1973.

41. *Ibid.*, aired October 31, 1973.

42. Telephone interview.

43. *Kansas* v. *Firestone Tire & Rubber Co.*, Petition for Civil Penalties, Injunction, and Other Relief, in the Eighteenth Judicial District, District Court, Sedgwick County, Kansas, Civil Department.

44. Lon Teter, "Firestone fined $1,000 for consumer violation," *Wichita Eagle*, May 23, 1979.

45. Telephone interview with Harry Johnson, deputy district attorney, Alameda County, July 31, 1979. See also California Bureau of Automotive Repair, *Newsletter*, June 1979, p. 3.

46. *Alaska* v. *J.C. Penney Company, Inc.*, Assurance of Voluntary Compliance, in the Superior Court for the State of Alaska, Third Judicial District at Anchorage, Civil Action No. 75–6643, September 9, 1975.

47. *California* v. *J.C. Penney Company, Inc.*, Complaint for Injunction, Civil Penalties and Other Relief, in the Superior Court of the State of California, in and for the County of Sacramento, No. 264230, November 24, 1976.

48. *California* v. *J.C. Penney Company, Inc.*, Final Judgement, in the Superior Court of the State of California, in and for the County of Sacramento, No. 264230, January 28, 1977.

49. Telephone interview with Shirley Katt, consumer protection analyst, Washoe County District Attorney's Office, February 1981, and *Nevada* v. *J.C. Penney Company, Inc.*, Stipulation for Entry of Judgement, in the Second Judicial District Court of the State of Nevada, in and for the county of Washoe, No. 2612, Dept. No. 6, March 23, 1981.

50. *Los Angeles Times*, January 21, 1976, Part II, p. 2.

51. *California* v. *Earl Scheib, Inc.*, Second Amended Complaint for Injunction, Civil Penalties and Other Relief, Superior Court of the State of California, for the County of San Diego, No. 340826, February 4, 1974.

52. *California* v. *Earl Scheib, Inc.*, Consent Judgement, Superior Court of the State of California, for the County of San Diego, No. 340826, July 22, 1974.

53. Advertisement, *Wall Street Journal*, July 19, 1979, p. 20.

54. Federal Trade Commission, in the matter of Midas, Inc., Docket 7771, Complaint February 4, 1960, Decision July 7, 1960. See Federal Trade Commission, *Federal Trade Commission Decisions*, 57 F.T.C., pp. 92–96.

55. Letter of February 6, 1978.

56. Interview in 1978.

57. Letter of January 10, 1976

58. Letter of August 20, 1976, obtained from the Federal Trade Commission.

59. *Op. cit.*, note 7 above, p. 51, Figure 15.

60. *Ibid.*, p. 57.

61. *Ibid.*, p. 51.

62. *Ibid.*, pp. 50, 51.

63. *Ibid.*, p. 23.

64. F.G. Ephraim, C.J. Kahane and W.G. LaHeist, *Auto Repair and Maintenance Program to Reduce Consumer Loss*, U.S. Department of Transportation, National Highway Traffic Safety Administration, Office of Program Evaluation, NHTSA Technical Report DOT HS–803 355, May 1978, p. 18.

65. Kenneth E. Johnson Environmental and Energy Center, University of Alabama in Huntsville, *A Critique of Brake Drum Turning Procedures and Practices*, Cooperative Agreement No. DOT–HS–5–01056, September 1977, p. 3.

66. *Ibid.*, p. 2.

67. *Ibid.*, p. 3.

68. *Ibid.*, p. 6.

69. Bernard J. Schroer, William F. Peyton and J.F. Peters, *The Quality of Automotive Repairs for Auto Check Participants*, Kenneth E. Johnson Environmental and Energy Center, University of Alabama in Huntsville, Contract No. DOT–HS–5–01056, January 6, 1978, Appendix C.

70. *Ibid.*

71. *Ibid.*

72. *Op. cit.*, note 7 above, p. 31.

73. *Ibid.*, p. 44.

74. Johnson Center for Environmental and Energy Studies, University of Alabama in Huntsville, *Survey of Automotive Repair Practices*, Draft Report Prepared for the Office of the Secretary of Transportation, Division of Consumer Affairs, Contract No. DOT–OS–90004, May 7, 1979, pp. 81–21, plus additional data detailing on-site results.

75. Joseph J. Innes, P.E. Eder and Leslie E. Eder, *Motor Vehicle Diagnostic Inspection Demonstration Program*, U.S. Department of Transportation, National Highway Traffic Safety Administration, Report No. DOT–HS–802 760, October 1977, pp. 39–41.

76. *Op. cit.*, note 7 above, p. 32.

77. Hearings before the Subcommittee for Consumers of the Committee on Commerce, Science and Transportation, United States Senate, Ninety-fifth Congress,

Second Session, *National Traffic and Motor Vehicle Information and Cost Savings Authorizations of 1979 and 1980*, March 21, 22, and 23, 1978, p. 257.

78. Stephen Fox, "Back with corporate vengeance," *Daily Review* (Hayward, California), July 26, 1979, p. 51.

79. *Op. cit.*, note 1 above, p. 8.

80. *Op. cit.*, note 69 above, p. 25.

81. Prepared statement to U.S. Senate Subcommittee for Consumers, March 23, 1978. For actual testimony, see *op. cit.*, note 77 above, p. 379.

82. *Ibid.*

83. Walt Woron, "Tune-ups," *Motor Trend*, March 1978, p. 102.

84. *Ibid.*

85. *Op. cit.*, note 45 above.

86. Letter of November 29, 1972.

87. California Bureau of Automotive Repair, *Your Car's Ball Joints: How Do They Measure Up?* (pamphlet).

88. California Administrative Code 16 § 3360.1 to 3360.3.

89. Hearings before the Subcommittee on Consumer Protection and Finance of the Committee on Interstate and Foreign Commerce, House of Representatives, Ninety-fifth Congress, Second Session, *Auto Repair*, September 14, 20, 21, 25, October 19, and December 4, 1978, p. 85.

90. *Op. cit.*, note 45 above.

91. *Op. cit.*, note 3 above, p. 27.

92. Stephen La Ferre, "No profit leak with radiator repair," *Modern Tire Dealer*, September 1977, p. 137.

93. *Modern Tire Dealer*, January 1978, p. 57.

94. Moira Johnston, "Hell on wheels," *New West*, May 8, 1978, p. 21.

95. Frances Serra, "Auto repair problems: causes and some safeguards," *New York Times*, December 9, 1975, p. 46.

96. *Op. cit.*, note 7 above, p. 54.

97. *Ibid.*

98. Terry Aaron, Ian Bodell, Jeff Krawitz, Maureen McGinley, Pat O'Brien and Steve Schmerin, *An Investigation of the Practices of Chain Automobile Repair Shops*, University of Pittsburgh, Summer 1974.

99. Frost & Sullivan, Inc., *Strategy for the Automotive Aftermarket 1976–80*, 1975.

100. *Advertising Age*, September 11, 1980, p. 1.

101. *Op. cit.*, note 16 above.

Chapter 4

1. Material contained in letter to American Association of Retired Persons, December 15, 1977.

2. Interview with Lawrence J. Kresky, consumer consultant, American Association of Retired Persons, spring 1978.

3. *60 Minutes*, CBS Television Network, aired 7:00 to 8:00 p.m., September 24, 1978 (from transcript of program prepared by Radio TV Reports, Inc., for the American Petroleum Institute).

4. *Ibid.*

5. Mort Schultz, "Don't get ripped off along the road," *Popular Mechanics*, June 1979, p. 92.

6. *Atlantic Journal*, January 30, 1978, p. 10A.

7. Telephone interview, October 27, 1978.

8. Neil Swan, "Rip-off road," *Atlanta Journal*, January 30, 1978, pp. 1 and 10A.

9. Robert J. Dunphy, "Notes: Who's whoose on the ghost circuit," *New York Times*, July 17, 1977, Section 10, p. 5.

10. *Op. cit.,* note 8 above.
11. *Op. cit.,* note 3 above.
12. Telephone conversation, April 1978.
13. Telephone interview, April 11, 1978.
14. Interview with Robert N. Wiens, chief, California Bureau of Automotive Repair, January 25, 1978.
15. *Mechanix Illustrated,* August 1972.
16. *Op. cit.,* note 3 above.
17. *Op. cit.,* note 15 above.
18. *Op. cit.,* note 8 above.
19. *Op. cit.,* note 14 above.
20. Letter to Ralph Nader, September 2, 1977.
21. Letter, August 25, 1977.
22. Letter, October 5, 1977.
23. Letter to author, July 9, 1978.
24. *Op. cit.,* note 20 above.
25. *Op. cit.,* note 7 above.
26. Telephone interview, April 14, 1978.
27. *Op. cit.,* note 13 above.
28. *Op. cit.,* note 7 above.
29. *Op. cit.,* note 13 above.
30. *Op. cit.,* note 8 above.
31. *Op. cit.,* note 3 above.
32. Letter of April 26, 1974.
33. *Op. cit.,* note 7 above.
34. *Op. cit.,* note 3 above.
35. *Op. cit.,* note 8 above.
36. Hearings before the Subcommittee on Consumer Protection and Finance of the Committee on Interstate and Foreign Commerce, House of Representatives, Ninety-fifth Congress, Second Session, *Auto Repair,* September 14, 20, 21, 25, October 19, and December 4, 1978, p. 370.
37. U.S. Code 15 § 1666i. The act doesn't specifically mention oil companies but applies to franchised dealers of the products or services of the credit card issuer.
38. *U.S. News & World Report,* December 1, 1980, p. 65.
39. Francis J. Gawronski, "Service needs outlined," *Automotive News,* November 21, 1977, p. 71.
40. *Op. cit.,* note 26 above.
41. California State Automobile Association, *Motorland,* March–April 1979, p. 35.
42. Glenn T. Lashley, "Coping with changes," *American Motorist,* January/February 1978, p. 5.
43. *Op. cit.,* note 41 above.
44. Telephone interview, February 20, 1981.
45. Telephone interview, February 8, 1978.
46. C. Lawrence Wiser, "Supreme Court to review oil company law in Maryland," *American Motorist* (American Automobile Association), January/February 1978, p. 5.
47. *Ibid.*
48. *Newsweek,* June 26, 1978, p. 56.
49. *Ibid.*
50. Shell Oil Co., *Announcing a Program to Help Make You the Most Professional Dealer in the Service Station Industry* (pamphlet).
51. *Ibid.*
52. *National Petroleum News,* September 1976.
53. Telephone interview with Judy Anderson, WTVF-TV, November 9, 1978.

Chapter 5

1. *Chicago Tribune,* June 20, 1976, pp. 1 and 12.
2. Better Business Bureau of the Greater New Orleans, Inc., *Bulletin,* July 31, 1974.
3. *New York Times,* December 8, 1975, p. 50.
4. Helen Huntley, "Owners of six auto-repair shops charged with criminal fraud," *St. Petersburg Times,* September 11, 1980.
5. *Op. cit.,* note 3 above.
6. Robert Cherrnay, "Both sides now on TV," *Automotive Rebuilder,* April 1975.
7. Telephone interview, May 9, 1978.
8. Advertisement, *Wall Street Journal,* December 6, 1979, p. 27.
9. Memorandum from Walter F. Moosa, attorney, Washington area field office, Federal Trade Commission, to director, bureau of field operations, Federal Trade Commission, File No. 652 3339, AAMCO Transmissions, et al., February 13, 1967.
10. *Ibid.*
11. *Ibid.*
12. *Ibid.*
13. *Ibid.*
14. Federal Trade Commission, in the matter of AAMCO Automatic Transmissions, Inc., a corporation, and Robert Morgan and Anthony A. Martino individually and as officers of said corporation, Agreement Containing Consent Order to Cease and Desist, Federal Trade Commission Docket No. 8816, July 29, 1970.
15. Letter from James Wynn Chapman, AAMCO director of operations, to Janet D. Saxon, division of compliance, bureau of consumer protection, Federal Trade Commission, September 15, 1971.
16. *Op. cit.,* note 7 above, and letter from Joseph P. O'Sullivan, assistant attorney general, Kansas, to the Federal Trade Commission, September 18, 1974.
17. *Op. cit.,* note 7 above.
18. *Op. cit.,* note 16 above.
19. *Kansas* v. *Stanley Clayton,* d/b/a AAMCO Transmissions, Petition, District Court, Sedgwick County, Kansas, Civil Department Case No. 78C1502.
20. *Kansas* v. *Stanley Clayton* d/b/a AAMCO Transmissions, Journal Entry, District Court, Sedgwick County, Kansas, Civil Department, Case No. 78C1502, Division No. 7, February 7, 1980.
21. *California* v. *Solomon Camhi,* Final Judgement, in the Superior Court of the State of California, in and for the County of Sacramento, No. 223894, September 7, 1973; and *California* v. *Solomon Camhi,* Complaint for Injunction, Civil Penalties, and Other Relief, in the Superior Court of the State of California, in and for the County of Sacramento, No. 223894, June 27, 1972.
22. In Re: John Shelton, Assurance of Voluntary Compliance, 152nd District Court of Harris County, Texas, Case No. 961 437, October 29, 1973.
23. Telephone interview with John R. Roach, Dallas County District Attorney's Office, April 14, 1978.
24. Press release, California Bureau of Automotive Repairs, "Action taken against a Southern California AAMCO shop," December 6, 1977.
25. Telephone interview with Daniel J. Furniss, assistant district attorney; and *California* v. *James Stewart and Sidney Margoles,* Consent Final Judgement (with individual Memorandum of Understanding), Superior Court of the State of California, County of San Mateo, No. 218320, December 29, 1977.
26. Telephone interview with Michael H. Krausnick, deputy district attorney, Stanislaus County; and *California* v. *Valley Industries, Inc., Michael J. Moradian,* Complaint for Injunction, Civil Penalties, and Other Relief and Memorandum of Understanding, Superior Court of the State of California, in and for the County of Stanislaus, No. 158583, March 23, 1978.
27. Telephone interview with Theodore R. Forrest, Jr., deputy district attorney, Fresno County, May 9, 1978; and letter from Mr. Forrest, June 14, 1979.

28. News release, Vermont Office of the Attorney General, "AAMCO sued following undercover operation," February 3, 1976.

29. *Vermont* v. *Burlington Automatic Transmission Co., Inc.*, Final Judgment, Chittenden County Superior Court, Docket No. S59-76 CnC, May 9, 1977.

30. In the matter of: Consolidated Transmissions of Flint d/b/a AAMCO Transmissions, Notice of Intended Action, State of Michigan, Department of Attorney General, File No. 78-1028-CPA, April 4, 1978.

31. Telephone interviews of April 14, 1978, and June 29, 1978.

32. Letter to the Federal Trade Commission, August 12, 1974.

33. *Op. cit*, note 8 above.

34. Frost & Sullivan, Inc., *Strategy for the Automotive Aftermarket 1976–80*, 1975, p. 131.

35. Illinois Legislative Investigating Commission, *Auto Repair Abuses*, June 1975, pp. 57–60.

36. AAMCO Transmissions, Inc., *Report Submitted to George T. O'Brien, Attorney, Division of Compliance Bureau of Consumer Protection Federal Trade Commission*, Federal Trade Commission Docket No. 8816, October 21, 1977, pp. 38–41.

37. Interview, April 1, 1978, and telephone interview, September 28, 1978.

38. *Op. cit.*, note 36 above, pp. 88–95.

39. Telephone interview, September 29, 1978.

40. *Op. cit.*, note 36 above, p. 93.

41. *Ibid.*, pp. 89, 94.

42. Letter to AAMCO, March 23, 1978.

43. *Op. cit.*, note 7 above.

44. *Francis B. Burch, Attorney General of Maryland* v. *Thrifty Diversified, Inc.*, Final Judgment and Consent Decree, Circuit Court of Baltimore County, December 11, 1978.

45. National District Attorneys Association, *Auto Sales and Repair Frauds* (pamphlet).

46. Advertisement by Interstate Automatic Transmission Co., Inc., *Wall Street Journal*, July 19, 1979, p. 20.

47. Telephone interview, August 29, 1979.

Chapter 6

1. Joseph John Bohn, "Mr. Goodwrench goes nationwide," *Automotive News*, April 11, 1977, p. 26.

2. Letter to author from Linda A. Rockford, director of public relations, General Motors Parts Division, October 16, 1978.

3. Washington Center for the Study of Services, *Checkbook Update on Car Repair*, summer 1978, pp. 9–12.

4. Nancy I. Phillips, "Chevy deal uses survey to boost service volume," *Automotive News*, July 17, 1978, p. 20.

5. Washington Center for the Study of Services, *Checkbook Cars*, summer 1976, pp. 30–41.

6. Telephone interview with Frank Faraone, public relations manager of General Motors' Washington, D.C., office, May 11, 1978.

7. Frost & Sullivan, Inc., *Strategy for the Automotive Aftermarket 1976–80*, p. 154.

8. *Ibid.*

9. The survey is contained in a letter from John J. Pohanka to L.G. Kalush, general manager, General Motors Parts Division, May 23, 1975. See: National Automobile Dealers Association, Trial Brief of Intervenor, in the matter of General Motors Corp., Federal Trade Commission Docket No. 9077, March 31, 1978.

10. *Automotive News*, May 7, 1979, p. 1.

11. *Diogenes,* Report by Attorney General Frank J. Kelley in Cooperation with Michigan Citizens Lobby, November 29, 1973, p. 2; and Detroit Testing Laboratory, *Dealer Survey of Costs and Repairs on State Cars with Internal Defects,* November 26, 1973, pp. 18–21.

12. Bernard J. Schroer, William F. Peyton, and J.F. Peters, Johnson Environmental and Energy Center, University of Alabama in Huntsville, *An Evaluation of Component Repair Costs for Auto Check Participants,* Contract No. DOT–HS–5–01056, May 31, 1977, p. 29. The dealers were identified in this report only by the letter designation A through L, but I was able to obtain their actual identities from other sources.

13. Prepared remarks to the annual meeting of the American Automobile Association, September 27, 1978.

14. General Motors Corp., Owner Relations Department, *A Guide to Assist Owners of General Motors Vehicles,* February 1976, p. 2.

15. General Motors Corp., Trial Brief of Respondent, in the matter of General Motors Corp., Federal Trade Commission Docket No. 9077, March 1978, p. 17.

16. Wendell A. Cook, *Repair Industry Response to Diagnostic Inspection Projects,* Society of Automotive Engineers, Inc., Technical Paper Series No. 780030, presented at SAE Congress and Exposition, Detroit, February 27–March 3, 1978, p. 17.

17. *Ibid.,* pp. 17–18.

18. *Ibid.,* p. 17.

19. Hearings before the Subcommittee on Consumer Protection and Finance of the Committee on Interstate and Foreign Commerce, House of Representatives, Ninety-fifth Congress, Second Session, *Auto Repair,* September 14, 20, 21, 25, October 19, and December 4, 1978, p. 265.

20. Interview with Robert N. Wiens, chief of the Bureau, January 25, 1978.

21. *Op. cit.,* note 12 above.

22. *Ibid.,* p. 30.

23. *Ibid.,* p. 28.

24. *Op. cit.,* note 19 above, p. 315.

25. Interview, February 20, 1978.

26. Telephone interview, May 12, 1978.

27. Interview, April 26, 1978.

28. Hearings before the Subcommittee for Consumers of the Committee on Commerce, Science and Transportation, United States Senate, Ninety-fifth Congress, Second Session, *National Traffic and Motor Vehicle Information and Cost Savings Authorization of 1979 and 1980,* March 21, 22, and 23, 1978, p. 303.

29. *Op. cit.,* note 19 above, p. 313.

30. Telephone interview, April 20, 1978.

31. *Op. cit.,* note 26 above.

32. *Op. cit.,* note 5 above, pp. 30–69.

33. Letter to author from Mr. Weissman, May 8, 1978.

34. District of Columbia Code, Regulation 74–3 § 511(c)(6).

35. *Automotive News,* February 13, 1978, p. 28.

36. Letter to author from Earl S. Roberts, May 16, 1978.

Chapter 7

1. Albert Porcelli, "The score: Caruso 1, Allstate 0," *Bulletin* (Auto Body Craftsmen's Guild), November 1974, pp. 4–5; and Frances Cerra, "2 panels probing insurance collusion," *Newsday,* September 20, 1974, p. 15.

2. From letter and material sent to U.S. Office of Consumer Affairs, March 8, 1978.

3. *Consumer Reports,* July 1977, p. 379.

4. Louis Harris and Associates, Inc., and Department of Insurance, Wharton

Notes

School, University of Pennsylvania, *The Sentry Insurance National Opinion Study: A Survey of Consumer Attitudes in the U.S. Towards Auto and Homeowner Insurance,* January 1974, pp. 63–64.

5. *National Underwriter* (Property & Casualty Insurance Edition), May 20, 1977, p. 18.

6. Letter to Ralph Nader, February 6, 1974.

7. Arnold Markowitz, "Repair practices filled with inconsistencies," *Miami Herald,* Auto Insurance Reprint, p. 17 (article originally appeared April 10, 1977).

8. Letter to author from Peter W. Rushton, Public Relations Department, Automobile Association, May 16, 1978.

9. *Op. cit.,* note 7 above.

10. *Ibid.*

11. *Ibid.*

12. *Ibid.*

13. Elizabeth Wolf, "The highs and lows of getting a GEICO estimate," *Hammer and Dolly,* March 1978, pp. 6–8.

14. *Op. cit.,* note 7 above.

15. Remarks to the annual meeting of the Southwestern Insurance Information Service, Inc., Fort Worth, Texas, October 10, 1974.

16. *Ibid.*

17. Letter to the U.S. Office of Consumer Affairs.

18. *Op. cit.,* note 6 above.

19. Illinois Legislative Investigating Commission, *Auto Repair Abuses,* June 1975, p. 144.

20. *Op. cit.,* note 15 above.

21. Testimony before Federal Trade Commission administrative law judge in General Motors antitrust crash parts case, FTC Docket No. 9077, May 15, 1978.

22. Hearings before the Subcommittee on Consumer Protection and Finance of the Committee on Interstate and Foreign Commerce, House of Representatives, Ninety-fifth Congress, Second Session, *Auto Repair,* September 14, 20, 21, 25, October 19, and December 4, 1978, p. 481.

23. *Mitchell Imported Collision Estimating Guide,* January 1977, p. 623.

24. *Washington Post,* July 22, 1976, p. A14.

25. *Op. cit.,* note 22 above, p. 486.

26. Bray & Scarff Sales Inc., when contacted on July 13, 1978, said they charged $17 minimum, which included travel time and the first 15 minutes of work, and after that they charged $6 for every quarter hour or part thereof. GM sold its Frigidaire division in 1979.

27. *Op. cit.,* note 22 above, p. 479.

28. *Op. cit.,* note 21 above, May 24, 1978.

29. *Ibid.,* May 15, 1978.

30. Auto Body Craftsmen's Guild, *Bulletin,* July 1977, p. 19.

31. *Op. cit.,* note 7 above.

32. *Automotive News,* October 16, 1978, p. 12.

33. *Op. cit.,* note 3 above.

34. *Ibid.,* pp. 383–384.

35. Standard & Poor's Corp., *Standard Corporation Descriptions P-S,* June 1979, p. 3847.

36. *Ibid.,* pp. 3847, 3849. The percentage was arrived at by dividing Sears' net income for the year ended January 31, 1978, of $837,982,000 into Allstate's $352 million profit for the year ended December 31, 1977.

37. *Business Week,* May 1, 1978, p. 69.

38. Anthony Feola, "President's Message," in Auto Body Craftsmen's Guild, *Bulletin,* February 1975, p. 5.

39. Letter to the U.S. Office of Consumer Affairs, December 22, 1977.

40. Letter to the U.S. Office of Consumer Affairs, February 16, 1978, and subsequent telephone interview.

41. *Op. cit.,* note 7 above.

42. *Op. cit.*, note 21 above.

43. David W. Vulbrock, *Automotive Repair Shop Survey,* National Association of Independent Insurers, March 1977, pp. 26–28.

44. *Op. cit.*, note 22 above.

45. *Ibid.*

46. *San Francisco Chronicle,* August 6, 1979, p. 5.

47. Suzanne Seixas, "Meeting car crash costs head on," *Money,* May 1976, pp. 120–121.

48. *Op. cit.*, note 32 above, pp. 12, 24.

49. John K. Teahen, Jr., "Cuts by Chrysler trim '78 model count to 252," *Automotive News,* October 10, 1977, p. 1.

50. John K. Teahen, Jr., "Domestic count down in '81," *Automotive News,* November 3, 1980, p. E–27.

51. Hearings before the Subcommittee for Consumers of the Committee on Commerce, United States Senate, Ninety-fourth Congress, Second Session, *Automobile Crash Parts,* March 1, 8 and 12, 1976, p. 182.

52. *Ibid.*

53. *Ibid.*, p. 190.

54. *Ibid.*, p. 91.

55. Donald K. Tenney, FTC attorney, opening statement in GM crash parts hearing, May 15, 1978. See note 21 above.

56. Executive Office of the President, Council on Wage and Price Stability, *Auto Parts Price Behavior: 1971–1976,* Staff Report, May 1977, p. 21.

57. *Ibid.*, p. 18.

58. *Ibid.*, p. 11.

59. *Ibid.*, p. 29.

60. Frances Cerra, "Small car parts costly to replace," *New York Times,* September 24, 1975, p. 38.

61. Arthur C. Mertz, President, National Association of Independent Insurers, at conference, *Making Auto Repair Credible,* Madison, Wisconsin, August 5, 1980.

62. *Op. cit.*, note 60 above.

63. *Op. cit.*, note 46 above.

64. *Op. cit.*, note 51 above, p. 132.

65. United States of America Before Federal Trade Commission, in the matter of General Motors Corporation, Complaint, Docket No. 9077, March 22, 1976, p. 4.

66. *Op. cit.*, note 51 above, p. 155.

67. *Ibid.*, p. 4.

68. *Ibid.*, p. 53.

69. From testimony of various witnesses at GM crash parts hearing. See note 21 above.

70. Letter to author from David W. Vulbrock, assistant to the president, National Association of Independent Insurers, February 22, 1978.

71. *Op. cit.*, note 55 above.

72. *Op. cit.*, note 22 above, p. 501.

73. Helen Kahn, "FTC judge rules against GM in crash-parts case," *Automotive News,* October 8, 1979, pp. 1 & 50.

74. *Op. cit.*, note 51 above, p. 79.

75. *Op. cit.*, note 21 above.

76. *Op. cit.*, note 51 above, p. 79.

77. *Ibid.*, p. 19.

78. Interview in 1978.

79. *Op. cit.*, note 22 above, p. 110.

80. *Op. cit.*, note 51 above, p. 77.

81. *Money,* October 1978, p. 66.

82. Information supplied to author by Albert Benjamin Kelley, senior vice president of the Institute.

83. Hearings before the Subcommittee for Consumers of the Committee on Commerce, Science and Transportation, United States Senate, Ninety-fifth Congress,

Notes

Second Session, *National Traffic and Motor Vehicle Information and Cost Savings Authorizations of 1979 and 1980*, March 21, 22 and 23, 1978, p. 158.

84. William Haddon, Jr., president, Insurance Institute for Highway Safety, prepared statement to the National Highway Traffic Safety Administration public meeting, Docket 74–II, Notice 6; Docket 73–19, Notice 4, Bumper Standard, February 18, 1975.

85. *Op. cit.*, note 51 above, pp. 102, 116.

86. *Op. cit.*, note 83 above, p. 156.

87. Insurance Institute for Highway Safety, *Status Report*, May 17, 1979, p. 1.

88. *National Underwriter* (Property and Casualty Insurance Edition), February 20, 1976, p. 4.

89. *Op. cit.*, note 83 above, p. 166.

90. *Ibid.*

91. Hearings before the Subcommittee on Consumer Protection and Finance of the Committee on Interstate and Foreign Commerce, House of Representatives, Ninety-fifth Congress, First Session, *Motor Vehicle Information and Cost Savings Act of 1972—Oversight*, May 2 and 9, 1977, p. 109.

92. *Op. cit.*, note 43 above, p. 22.

93. James Casassa II, Richard E. Gardner and Wayne Sorenson, *Automobile Crash Damage: Use of Repair Information for Evaluating Automobile Design Characteristics*, State Farm Insurance Companies Research Department (presented at fifth International Congress on Automobile Safety, Cambridge, Massachusetts, July 1977), pp. 8, 28.

94. Hearings before the Subcommittee on Antitrust and Monopoly of the Committee on the Judiciary, United States Senate, Ninety-first Congress, First Session, *Automotive Repair Industry*, Part 3, October 6, 8, 9, 14 and 16, 1969, pp. 1139–1147.

95. Hearings before the Committee on Commerce, United States Senate, Ninety-second Congress, First Session, *Automobile Insurance Reform and Cost Savings*, Part 3, May 6, 7, 10 and 11, 1971, pp. 1421–22.

96. *Op. cit.*, note 91 above, pp. 16, 37, 62.

97. *Ibid.*, p. 168.

98. News Release, U.S. Department of Transportation (NHTSA—41–79), "DOT accepts new safety cars and honors safety pioneers," May 14, 1979.

99. *Ibid.*

100. *Op. cit.*, note 22 above, pp. 393, 396.

101. *Op. cit.*, note 51 above, p. 116.

102. Letter to Ralph Nader, May 3, 1977.

103. General Motors Corp., Trial Brief of Respondent, March 1978, p. 5. See: In the matter of General Motors Corp., Federal Trade Commission, Docket No. 9077.

104. *Ibid.*, p. 1.

105. Based on 1975 automotive product sales of $26,137,300,000. Source: General Motors Corp. *General Motors Annual Report 1979*, p. 26.

106. Public Law 92–513, Title II.

107. *Op. cit.*, note 87 above.

108. Auto Body Craftsmen's Guild, *Bulletin*, September 1975, pp. 18–19.

109. Iowa Code Annotated (1979) § 321.238(13).

110. *Op. cit.*, note 22 above, p. 486.

111. Letter to author, April 4, 1978.

112. Marc Stern, "Dents, dings and dollars," *Automotive Age*, November 1979, p. 40.

113. Regulations of the Commissioner of Motor Vehicles, Sections 82.2(n), 82.3(a) & 82.4(a)(11).

Chapter 8

1. From accounts given to the author by Andra and Ralf Hotchkiss.
2. Public hearing, California State Legislature, Senate Committee on Business and Professions, *Certification of Automobile Mechanics*, Los Angeles, November 26, 1974.
3. Michigan Compiled Laws Annotated § 257.1305.
4. Hawaii Revised Statutes § 437B–24.
5. District of Columbia Regulation No. 74.3, Section 301(b).
6. National Institute for Automotive Service Excellence, *Automobile Mechanic Data*, April 1980.
7. William D. McLean, *Testing and Certifying Mechanics for Automotive Emission Inspection and Maintenance*, paper presented at annual meeting of the Air Pollution Control Association, Toronto, June 4, 1977.
8. *Ibid.*
9. *Ibid.*
10. Hearings before the Subcommittee on Antitrust and Monopoly of the Committee on the Judiciary, United States Senate, Ninetieth Congress, Second Session, *Automotive Repair Industry*, Part 1, December 3, 4 and 5, 1968, p. 145.
11. *Automotive News*, March 20, 1978, p. 33.
12. Elizabeth M. Fowler, "More auto mechanics needed," *New York Times*, May 24, 1978, p. D19.
13. Motor Vehicle Manufacturers Association, *Motor Vehicle Facts & Figures, '78*, p. 32.
14. *Automotive News*, 1980 Market Data Book Issue, p. 22.
15. *Automotive Age*, October 1978, p. 68.
16. Hearings before the Subcommittee for Consumers of the Committee on Commerce, Science and Transportation, United States Senate, Ninety-fifth Congress, Second Session, *National Traffic and Motor Vehicle Information and Cost Savings Authorization of 1979 and 1980*, March 21, 22, and 23, 1978, p. 379.
17. Hearings before the Subcommittee on Consumer Protection and Finance of the Committee on Interstate and Foreign Commerce, House of Representatives, Ninety-fifth Congress, Second Session, *Auto Repair*, September 14, 20, 21, 25, October 19, and December 4, 1978, p. 135.
18. Interview, January 25, 1978.
19. *Op. cit.*, note 14 above.
20. Letter to author from Linda H. Lee, public relations, Ford Parts and Service Division, June 5, 1978.
21. *Ibid.*
22. Jenny L. King, "400 a year graduate from 1,500-hour course," *Automotive News*, July 21, 1980, p. E–23.
23. *Op. cit.*, note 17 above, p. 108.
24. Telephone interview, March 9, 1978.
25. Julie Ann Fitzgerald and Stan Stephenson, "Who will fix the cars of the future," *Motor/Age*, September 1978, p. 112.
26. Letters to author from Robert J. McConnon, administrator, Bureau of Apprenticeship and Training, Employment and Training Administration, U.S. Department of Labor, July 2, 1979, and James P. Mitchell, administrator, Bureau of Apprenticeship and Training, July 23, 1980.
27. Bob Lund, "Funding one solution to the mechanic shortage," *Motor*, July 1978, p. 53.
28. *Op. cit.*, note 26 above.
29. *Ibid.*
30. *Op. cit.*, note 17 above, p. 295.
31. Frances Cerra, "Auto repair problems: causes and some safeguards," *New York Times*, December 9, 1975, p. 43.
32. Interview, April 26, 1978.

Notes

33. U.S. Department of Labor, Employment and Training Administration, U.S. Employment Service, *Occupations in Demand,* July 1979, pp. 3, 14.

34. Earl Quist, coordinator of associate degree apprenticeship program, National Automobile Dealers Association, at NADA convention seminar, February 20, 1978.

35. *Op. cit.,* note 27 above, p. 86.

36. Carol Morgan, "Trouble in the auto repair shop," *Job Safety and Health,* December 1976, p. 22.

37. U.S. Department of Labor, Bureau of Labor Statistics, *Occupational Outlook Handbook,* 1980–81 edition, March 1980, p. 340.

38. *Ibid.,* p. 341.

39. Illinois Legislative Investigating Commission, *Auto Repair Abuses,* June 1975, p. 143.

40. WMAL-TV, Washington, DC, "You and auto repairs," Part One, aired November 12, 1973.

41. *Op. cit.,* note 17 above, p. 262.

42. Statement made at hearing before the Subcommittee for Consumers of the U.S. Senate Committee on Commerce, Science and Transportation, March 23, 1978.

43. *Automotive News,* August 21, 1978, p. 22.

44. *Op. cit.,* note 17 above, p. 443.

45. *Automotive News,* March 19, 1979, p. 18.

46. *Op. cit.,* note 43 above.

47. Report by the Comptroller General of the United States, *Public and Private Coordination Needed If Auto Repair Problems Are to Be Reduced,* January 1, 1980, p. 29.

48. *Washington Post,* August 13, 1978, p. A16.

49. Information supplied by the Virginia Department of Commerce, October 5, 1978.

50. Virginia Commission for Professional and Occupational Regulation, *1974 Report of the Virginia Commission for Professional and Occupational Regulation,* p. 10.

51. Prepared statement to the Senate Business and Professions Committee, November 26, 1974. See note 2 above.

52. California Bureau of Automotive Repair, *Highlights of Consumer Protection, Registration and Licensing Activities,* November 1977, Schedule E.

53. *Op. cit.,* note 17 above, p. 88.

54. *Op. cit.,* note 32 above.

55. Glenn C. Garrett, "The mechanics of an industry rip-off," *Los Angeles Times,* July 18, 1977, Part II, p. 7.

56. Message to author from M. Beth Eakins, director, systems and research, NIASE, February 1981.

57. National Institute for Automotive Service Excellence, *NIASE Tests,* Spring 1978, inside cover.

58. *Op. cit.,* note 16 above, p. 347.

59. National Institute for Automotive Service Excellence, *NIASE Bulletin of Information,* Fall 1980, p. 29.

60. Washington Center for the Study of Services, *Checkbook Update on Car Repair,* Summer 1978, pp. 9, 12.

61. National Institute for Automotive Service Excellence, *Voluntary Certification for Automotive Mechanics.*

62. National Institute for Automotive Service Excellence, *Excelsior,* February 1978, p. 5.

63. *Op. cit.,* note 51 above.

64. National Institute for Automotive Service Excellence, *Fact Sheet* and *Automobile Mechanic Data,* April 1980.

65. *Op. cit.,* note 3 above.

66. Gene Weingarten, "Newly licensed mechanic can barely find the engine," *Detroit Free Press,* June 19, 1978.

67. Interview, September 14, 1978.

68. James Hunsucker at conference, *Making Auto Repair Credible,* Madison, Wisconsin, August 6, 1980.

69. *Op. cit.,* note 4 above.

70. Letter to author from Edward L. Simmons, director, Dealers and Repairers Division, Connecticut Department of Motor Vehicles, February 3, 1978.

71. *Op. cit.,* note 17 above, p. 73.

72. *Op. cit.,* note 68 above.

73. As a trial balloon, a proposal similar in nature was introduced in the state legislature regarding "electronic technicians" (TV repairmen, etc.). See: California Assembly Bill No. 1413 as amended, January 12, 1978.

74. *Op. cit.,* note 16 above, p. 38.

75. State of Wisconsin, Governor's Council for Consumer Affairs, *Report of the Governor's Council for Consumer Affairs Automotive Repair Services Survey, Milwaukee Wisconsin,* March 25, 1974, p. 7.

76. *Op. cit.,* note 3 above, § 257.1305.

77. *Op. cit.,* note 17 above, pp. 108, 110.

78. From interviews with Mr. Van Valkenburg plus written complaint to the Montgomery County, Maryland, Office of Consumer Affairs, January 2, 1978.

79. Motor Vehicle Manufacturers Association, *MVMA Motor Vehicle Facts and Figures '80,* p. 49.

80. U.S. Department of Commerce, Bureau of the Census, *Statistical Abstract of the United States: 1979,* p. 635.

81. Matthew E. Marsh, *California Mechanics' Lien Law Handbook,* edited by Dimitri K. Ilyin, 2nd edition (Los Angeles: Parker and Son Publications, Inc., 1972), p. 1.

82. *Ibid.*

83. *Automotive Age,* February 1979, p. 64.

84. *Op. cit.,* note 80 above, p. 650.

85. T. Pollard Rogers, "Proposed legislation for the licensing of automotive repair facilities and mechanics in Texas," *St. Mary's Law Journal,* Vol. 7, No. 1, 1975.

86. Annotated Code of Maryland § 16–207.

87. Code of Virginia § 43–33.

88. Florida Statutes § 559.917 et seq.

89. General Statutes of North Carolina § 44A–4(a).

90. Alaska Statutes Supplement § 45.45.200 (d).

91. Louisiana Revised Statutes 9 § 4501.

92. Revised Code of Washington Annotated (1981) § 46.71.050.

93. California Business and Professions Code 20.3 § 9884.16.

94. *Op. cit.,* note 3 above,-§ 257.1331.

95. *Op. cit.,* note 4 above, § 437B–20.

96. *Adams* v. *Department of Motor Vehicles,* 11 Cal. 3d 146 & 520 P. 2d 961.

Chapter 9

1. Gerald Gold, "Complaints rise on auto repairs," *New York Times,* June 26, 1974, p. 46.

2. Joseph J. Innes, P.E. Eder and Leslie E. Eder, *Motor Vehicle Diagnostic Inspection Demonstration Program,* National Highway Traffic Safety Administration, No. DOT HS–802 760, October 1977, p. 70.

3. David W. Vulbrock, *Automobile Repair Shop Survey,* National Association of Independent Insurers, March 1977, p. 22.

4. Hearings before the Subcommittee on Consumer Protection and Finance of the Committee on Interstate and Foreign Commerce, House of Representatives, Ninety-

fifth Congress, Second Session, *Auto Repair,* September 14, 20, 21, 25, October 19 and December 4, 1978, pp. 472–473.

5. Letter to Ralph Nader, October 16, 1975.

6. Arthur C. Mertz, president, National Association of Independent Insurers, at conference, "Making Auto Repair Credible," Madison, Wisconsin, August 5, 1980.

7. Press release, Suffolk County Department of Consumer Affairs, September 23, 1976.

8. Marvin Battcher, president, Tech-Cor, at conference, "Making Auto Repair Credible," Madison, Wisconsin, August 5, 1980.

9. Letter of April 5, 1972.

10. Letter of May 19, 1977.

11. *Op. cit.,* note 4 above, p. 114.

12. Letter to author from Linda H. Lee, public relations, Ford Parts and Service Division, May 15, 1978.

13. *Ibid.*

14. Hearings before the Subcommittee for Consumers of the Committee on Commerce, United States Senate, Ninety-fourth Congress, Second Session, *Automobile Crash Parts,* March 1, 8 and 12, 1976, p. 129.

15. *Ibid.,* p. 168.

16. *Op. cit.,* note 4 above, p. 461.

17. *Motor/Age,* September 1978, p. W-14.

18. *Ibid.*

19. *Ibid.,* pp. W-14 to W-16.

20. *Ibid.,* p. W-16.

21. *Op. cit.,* note 4 above, p. 503.

22. Charles P. Schwartz, Jr., president, Champion Parts Rebuilders, Inc. See: Center for Public Representation et al., *Making Auto Repair Credible: A Conference on Approaches,* Madison, Wisconsin, August 5–6, 1980.

23. *Automotive News,* January 29, 1979, p. 40.

24. *Automotive News,* January 31, 1977, p. 115.

25. Helen Kahn, "AAA blasts towability problems," *Automotive News,* November 14, 1977, p. 17.

26. *Op. cit.,* note 2 above, p. 71.

27. Letter from Mr. Baum to A.P. Caputo, Cadillac Motor Car Division, January 3, 1978.

28. Federal Trade Commission, *Automobile Policy Session* (edited version), April 17, 1978, p. 28.

Chapter 10

1. Information gathered from telephone interviews with Messrs. Campos and Sweitzer in 1978; correspondence between Mr. Sweitzer and Ford Motor Co.; Ted Thackery, Jr., "Anaheim man pounds his '72 Pinto to pieces," *Los Angeles Times,* January 2, 1974, Part II, p. 1.

2. Letter to U.S. Senator Wendell Ford, December 19, 1977.

3. Letter to U.S. Senator Wendell Ford, December 13, 1977.

4. Hearings before the Subcommittee for Consumers of the Committee on Commerce, Science and Transportation, United States Senate, Ninety-fifth Congress, Second Session, *National Traffic and Motor Vehicle Information and Cost Savings Authorizations of 1979 and 1980,* March 21, 22, and 23, 1978, pp. 113–114.

5. *Advertising Age,* September 11, 1980, p. 1. This was the amount spent for advertising in 1979 just by General Motors, Ford, Chrysler, Toyota, Nissan (Datsun), Volkswagen, American Motors, Honda and Mazda.

6. Motor Vehicle Manufacturers Association, *MVMA Motor Vehicle Facts and Figures '80*, p. 45.

7. *New York Times,* November 11, 1978, p. 30.

8. The balance sheet appeared in the *Sunday Times* (London), February 12, 1978, p. 1, and details of the case in Philip Jacobson and John Barnes, "£66m damages: the car that carried death in the boot," *Sunday Times* (London), February 12, 1978, p. 4. The balance sheet originally appeared in Ford Motor Co., Environmental and Safety Engineering Division, *Fatalities Associated with Crash-Induced Fuel Leakages and Fires.*

9. News release, U.S. Department of Transportation, "DOT announces recall of Pintos and Bobcats," June 9, 1978.

10. *San Francisco Chronicle,* February 8, 1978, p. 5, and *Consumer Reports,* July 1978, p. 412.

11. Gregory Skwira, "Ford knew fan risk, delayed recall," *Detroit Free Press,* September 1, 1977, pp. 1 & 4.

12. Helen Kahn, "Ford knew of transmission trouble," *Automotive News,* September 11, 1978, p. 48.

13. *Automotive News,* January 5, 1981, p. 1.

14. Ford Motor Co., *North American Automotive Operations Quality Meeting,* November 16, 1973, p. 24.

15. Office of Business Research and Analysis, Bureau of Domestic Commerce, U.S. Department of Commerce, *Impact of Environmental, Energy, and Safety Regulations and of Emerging Market Factors upon the United States Sector of the North American Automotive Industry,* August 1977, p. 421.

16. This figure is the total of expenses for amortization of special tools claimed in each company's income statement. For General Motors, the amortization was $1,855,700,000 (*General Motors Annual Report 1978*, p. 20); Ford, $578,200,000 (*Ford Annual Report 1978*, p. 18), and Chrysler, $198,200,000 (*Moody's Industrial News Reports,* April 24, 1979, p. 2417).

17. James J. Flink, *The Car Culture* (Cambridge, Mass.: MIT Press, 1975), p. 206.

18. Marjorie Sorge, "UAW absenteeism issue blossoming," *Automotive News,* November 27, 1978, p. 60.

19. Interview, August 5, 1980.

20. *Op. cit.,* note 14 above, p. 27.

21. Larry Tuck, "Transit damage: trouble along the way," *Automotive Age,* June 1979, p. 59.

22. *Automotive News,* December 4, 1978, p. 3.

23. *Consumer Reports,* April 1977, p. 239.

24. Letter from Norman D. Shultler, deputy assistant administrator for mobile source and noise enforcement, U.S. Environmental Protection Agency, to D.A. Jensen, director of Automotive Emissions Office, Ford Motor Co., January 31, 1978.

25. *Op cit.,* note 4 above, p. 301.

26. John A. Russell, "N.J. tackles prep charges," *Automotive News,* November 5, 1979, p. 34.

27. Telephone interview with Curtis R. Hoffman, deputy district attorney, Contra Costa County, April 20, 1978.

28. *Ward's Auto World,* March 1978, p. 130.

29. *Automotive News,* May 15, 1978, p. 3.

30. *Ibid.*

31. National Automobile Dealers Association, *1976 Warranty Survey Findings,* p. 12.

32. *Ibid.,* p. 2.

33. Hearings before the Subcommittee on Consumer Protection and Finance of the Committee on Interstate and Foreign Commerce, House of Representatives, Ninety-fifth Congress, Second Session, *Auto Repair,* September 14, 20, 21, 25, October 19, and December 4, 1978, p. 227.

34. *Op. cit.,* note 29 above.

35. *Car Dealer Insider Newsletter,* June 5, 1978.

36. *Op cit.*, note 4 above, p. 129.

37. *Op. cit.*, note 29 above.

38. *Ibid.*

39. Telephone interview.

40. *Op cit.*, note 31 above, p. 8.

41. Greg Conderacci, "Three are convicted in 'motorgate' case over false warranty claims made to GM," *Wall Street Journal*, December 24, 1976, p. 3.

42. *Op. cit.*, note 33 above, p. 225.

43. *Ibid.*, p. 91.

44. Bob Hall, "Saab 99 Turbo," *Motor Trend*, March 1978, p. 79.

45. *Op. cit.*, note 31 above, p. 10.

46. Nancy I. Phillips, "Chicago dealers charged with warranty fraud," *Automotive News*, June 6, 1977, p. 3.

47. Telephone interview with Mr. Campos.

48. Letter to U.S. Senator Harrison A. Williams, January 30, 1978.

49. John William Riley, "GM warranty will cover paint problem in Northeast," *Automotive News*, September 18, 1978, p. 57.

50. *Automotive News*, August 22, 1977, p. 30; Dan Miliott, "The consumer's shining knight," *Florida Trend*, October 1977, p. 79; and *Automotive News*, April 6, 1981, p. 54.

51. Ford Motor Co., *North American Automotive Operations Reliability/Quality Meeting*, October 19, 1973, pp. 39–40.

52. *Fortune*, May 4, 1981, p. 324.

53. *Moody's Industrial Manual*, 1976, p. 583; General Motors Corp., *General Motors Annual Report 1978*, p. 1; and *Wall Street Journal*, February 3, 1981, p. 34.

54. Joseph J. Bohn, "GM said to be toughest on warranty claims," *Automotive News*, January 3, 1977, p. 2.

55. *Op. cit.*, note 31 above, p. 3.

56. *New York Times*, August 29, 1974, p. 27.

57. *Op. cit.*, note 23 above.

58. Ford Customer Service Division, General Field Bulletin No. 550, August 25, 1972.

59. *New York Times*, July 10, 1975, p. 60.

60. *Op. cit.*, note 4 above, p. 213.

61. Federal Trade Commission, *Complaint*, In the matter of Ford Motor Co., Docket No. 9105, January 10, 1978.

62. Helen Kahn, "No secret warranties, Ford agrees," *Automotive News*, October 20, 1980, p. 2.

63. *Automotive Age*, February 1978, p. 107.

64. Letter from Esther Peterson, Special Assistant to the President for Consumer Affairs, to U.S. Senator Wendell Ford, February 2, 1978.

65. *Op. cit.*, note 4 above, p. 204.

66. *Ibid.*, p. 130.

67. Letter to U.S. Rep. Tom Steed, March 2, 1978.

68. *Op. cit.*, note 4 above, p. 124.

69. Public Law 93–637 (15 USC 2301 et seq.).

70. Letter to U.S. Senator Wendell Ford, January 5, 1978.

71. *Wall Street Journal*, January 8, 1981, p. 12.

72. *Op. cit.*, note 69 above, Section 104(a)(4).

73. 16 Code of Federal Regulations 433. See also: *Federal Register*, November 18, 1975, Part III, pp. 53506 to 53530.

74. Maine Revised Statutes Annotated 11 § 2–316(5).

75. Annotated Code of Maryland § 2–316.

76. Massachusetts General Laws Annotated 106 § 2–316.

77. Vermont Statutes Annotated 9A § 2–316(5).

78. West Virginia Code Annotated § 46A–6–107.

78a. Mississippi Code Annotated § 75–2–719(4).

79. Kansas Statutes Annotated § 50–639.

80. *Op. cit.*, note 4 above, p. 207.

81. Ford Motor Co., *North American Automotive Operations Quality Meeting,* September 21, 1973, p. 7.

82. *Op. cit.*, note 53 above, *Moody's*, p. 521.

83. *Op cit.*, note 69 above, Section 110(a)(1).

84. *Ibid.*, Section 102(b)(3).

85. California Civil Code § 1793.1 & 1795.6.

86. *Op. cit.*, note 21 above.

87. Mo Mehlsak, "Warranty administration," *Automotive Age*, June 1979, p. 63.

88. Puerto Rico Department of Consumer Affairs, *Regulation to Regulate the Guarantee Which Should Be Given in the Sale of New and Used Motor Vehicles,* May 1972.

89. Massachusetts Office of the Attorney General, Consumer Protection Division, Motor Vehicle Regulations, 940 CMR § 5:03(5).

Chapter 11

1. Joseph A. Slobodzian, "Auto inspections: accident curb or ripoff," Philadelphia *Evening Bulletin*, August 24, 1980.

2. Steve Lawrence, "Car repairs: going to rack and ruin," *New York Daily News,* May 13, 1979.

3. Letter to author from James P. Melton, New York State commissioner of motor vehicles, March 9, 1978.

4. Letter to author from James E. Forrester, director, Office of State Vehicle Programs, NHTSA, June 29, 1979.

5. Gunter David, "Repair ripoffs weaken car inspection system," *Philadelphia Evening Bulletin*, March 24, 1974.

6. David Long, "Clearing the air in Arizona," *Bee-Hive* magazine (United Technologies Corp.), Winter/Spring 1977, pp. 18, 21.

7. Gale Cook, "Auto smog checks: why state stalled," *San Francisco Sunday Examiner and Chronicle*, September 9, 1979, p. A9.

8. Hearings before the Subcommittee for Consumers of the Committee on Commerce, Science, and Transportation, United State Senate, Ninety-fifth Congress, Second Session, *National Traffic and Motor Vehicle Information and Cost Savings Authorizations of 1979 and 1980*, March 21, 22, and 23, 1978, p. 17.

9. Report to the Congress by the Comptroller General of the United States, *Effectiveness of Vehicle Safety Inspections Neither Proven Nor Unproven*, December 20, 1977, p. 20.

10. California Highway Patrol, *Mechanical Factors Study*, February 1970, pp. 3, 52.

11. Hearings before the Subcommittee on Consumer Protection and Finance of the Committee on Interstate and Foreign Commerce, House of Representatives, Ninety-fifth Congress, Second Session, *Auto Repair*, September 14, 20, 21, 25, October 19, and December 4, 1978, pp. 153–154.

12. Robert Hickox, "Motor vehicle inspection: its time is now," *Motor Service*, September 1977, p. 22.

13. *Op cit.*, note 11 above, p. 152.

14. AB Svensk Bilprovning, *Weak Points of Cars*, 1975.

15. AB Svensk Bilprovning, information sheet supplied with *Life Expectancy of Passenger Cars in Sweden*, calculated in 1975.

16. *Op. cit.*, note 14 above.

17. *Op. cit.*, note 15 above.

Chapter 12

1. Hearings before the Subcommittee on Oversight and Investigations of the Committee on Interstate and Foreign Commerce, House of Representatives, Ninety-fifth Congress, Second Session, *Safety of Firestone Steel-Belted Radial 500 Tires,* May 19, 22, 23, and July 10, 1978, p. 170.

2. Report together with Additional and Dissenting Views by the Subcommittee on Oversight and Investigations of the Committee on Interstate and Foreign Commerce, House of Representatives, Ninety-fifth Congress, Second Session, *The Safety of Firestone 500 Steel Belted Radial Tires,* August 16, 1978, p. 1.

3. *Op. cit.,* note 1 above, p. 288.

4. News release, Office of Public and Consumer Affairs, U.S. Department of Transportation, "Final settlement in Firestone 500 recall," NHTSA—110–78, November 29, 1978.

5. *Op. cit.,* note 1 above, p. 304.

6. *Ibid.,* p. 216.

7. *Ibid.,* pp. 215–216.

8. *Ibid.,* p. 305.

9. *Op. cit.,* note 2 above, p. 52.

10. *Op. cit.,* note 1 above, p. 218.

11. *Ibid.,* p. 200.

12. *Automotive Age,* July 1977, p. 9.

13. *Consumer Reports,* April 1977, p. 239.

14. *Op. cit.,* note 1 above, p. 215.

15. Harry M. Philo and Arnold D. Porter, "170 million defective tires per year," *Trial* magazine, November 1976, p. 51.

16. U.S. Department of Transportation, National Highway Traffic Safety Administration, *Appendices to the Five Year Plan for Motor Vehicle Safety and Fuel Economy Rulemaking Calendar Years 1980–1984,* April 20, 1979, p. 62.

17. U.S. Department of Transportation, National Highway Traffic Safety Administration, *Five Year Plan for Motor Vehicle Safety and Fuel Economy Rulemaking Calendar Years 1980–1984,* April 20, 1979, p. 48.

18. *Automotive News,* July 30, 1979, between pp. 28 and 29.

19. *Op. cit.,* note 15 above, pp. 52–53.

20. Letter to newspaper columnist Jack Anderson, May 8, 1978.

21. Walter Rugaber, "Auto tire safety: the Detroit role," *New York Times,* July 7, 1966, pp. 1, 23.

22. Letter to U.S. Representative John E. Moss, May 5, 1978.

23. Interview, November 2, 1978.

24. Letter to Ralph Nader, October 25, 1977.

25. *Consumer Reports,* March 1978, p. 156.

26. *Op. cit.,* note 24 above.

27. *Ibid.*

28. *Op. cit.,* note 25 above.

29. *Status Report* (Insurance Institute for Highway Safety), July 14, 1978, p. 8.

30. Hearings before the Committee on Commerce, United States Senate, *Tire Safety,* June 7, 1965, p. 100.

31. ICF Inc., *The Uniform Tire Quality Grading System: A Case Study of the Government Regulatory Process,* the National Center for Productivity and Quality of Working Life, April 1977.

32. *Ibid.*

33. *Modern Tire Dealer,* January 1981, p. 35. Goodrich is listed as a supplier to General Motors and Ford, but the company stopped making original equipment tires in 1981.

34. Contained in press release, Center for Auto Safety, "CFAS releases results of DOT tire survey suppressed by Firestone in court," March 31, 1978.

35. *Automotive News,* April 2, 1979, p. 34.
36. Tire Industry Safety Council, *Consumer Tire Guide,* p. 4.
37. *Op. cit.,* note 1 above, p. 301.
38. *Tire Review,* February 1978, p. 18.
39. *Automotive News,* October 17, 1977, p. 39.
40. *Ibid.*

Chapter 13

1. Complaint to Broward County Department of Business and Consumer Affairs, September 22, 1976.
2. Federal Trade Commission, *Staff Report On the Used Motor Vehicle Industry,* December 1975, pp. 25, 27 & 30.
3. *Ibid.,* p. 45.
4. *Ibid.*
5. *Ibid.,* p. 46.
6. *Automotive News,* March 14, 1977.
7. National Analysts, *A Survey of Buyers of Used Cars,* March 1977, p. 19.
8. Aptco Auto Auction (Taylor, Michigan), *Welcome to Aptco Auto Auction* (leaflet distributed in 1978).
9. *Op. cit.,* note 2 above, p. 40.
10. Harvey A. Farberman, "A criminogenic market structure: the automobile industry," *Sociological Quarterly,* Autumn 1975, p. 445.
11. *Op. cit.,* note 2 above, p. 50.
12. John William Riley, "Boston consumers list used-car beefs for FTC," *Automotive News,* January 3, 1977, p. 2.
13. *Op. cit.,* note 2 above, p. 52.
14. Letter to the Federal Trade Commission, March 9, 1976.
15. Bill Davidson, "King of the iron merchants," *New York Times Magazine,* March 2, 1975.
16. *Ibid.*
17. Center for Auto Safety, *Sale of Used Motor Vehicles, Dealer Disclosure Practices Survey,* presented to the Federal Trade Commission, April 26, 1977, p. 22.
18. Standford Research Institute, *Relationship Between Vehicle Defects and Vehicle Crashes,* Final Report, July 1970, Vol. II, p. 64. See also note 2 above, p. 58.
19. *Op. cit.,* note 17 above, p. 27.
20. Center for Public Representation, *An Investigation of the Retail Used Motor Vehicle Market: An Evaluation of Disclosure and Regulation,* p. 85.
21. *Ibid.*
22. *Automotive News,* February 20, 1978, p. 142.
23. *Op. cit.,* note 20 above, p. 87.
24. *Automotive News,* April 16, 1979, p. 46.
25. Maine Revised Statutes Annotated 10 § 1471 et seq.
26. *Op. cit.,* note 2 above, p. 57.
27. *Consumer Reports,* December 1977, p. 375.
28. *Hot Rod,* June 1976, p. 99.
29. *Op. cit.,* note 2 above, p. 42.
30. Milton Moskowitz, "The biggest auto seller," *San Francisco Chronicle,* August 7, 1980, p. 30.
31. Jenny L. King, "Hertz used-car sales grow," *Automotive News,* March 12, 1979, p. 14.
32. *Ibid.*
33. Advertisement, *San Francisco Chronicle,* August 17, 1979, p. 31.
34. Helen Kahn, "Simpler but tougher used-car regulation proposed by FTC," *Automotive News,* November 13, 1978, p. 45.

35. Maryland Annotated Code (1976) § 11.02.03, paragraph .83C.

36. Puerto Rico Department of Consumer Affairs, *Regulation to Regulate the Guarantee Which Should Be Given in the Sale of New and Used Motor Vehicles,* May 1972.

37. *Op. cit.,* note 25 above.

Chapter 14

1. Hearings before the Subcommittee for Consumers of the Committee on Commerce, Science and Transportation, United States Senate, Ninety-fifth Congress, Second Session, *National Traffic and Motor Vehicle Information and Cost Savings Authorizations of 1979 and 1980,* March 21, 22, and 23, 1978, pp. 113–114. Former FTC chairman Michael Pertschuk said a warranty survey showed that nearly 30% of motor vehicles purchased had some problems covered by warranties, and of those about 30% took over a month to resolve and then not to the satisfaction of most of the car owners.

2. *Consumer Reports,* April 1979, p. 240.

3. *Changing Times,* September 1980, pp. 21–22.

4. Hearings before the Subcommittee on Consumer Protection and Finance of the Committee on Interstate and Foreign Commerce, House of Representatives, Ninety-fifth Congress, Second Session, *Auto Repair,* September 14, 20, 21, 25, October 19, and December 4, 1978, p. 298.

5. *Autobody and the Reconditioned Car,* July 1980, p. 39.

6. *Motor Trend,* March 1978, p. 19.

7. Letter to author, June 14, 1979.

8. Evelyn Bash, "Florida study profiles buyers of new autos," *Automotive News,* August 21, 1978, p. 20.

9. Joseph J. Innes, P.E. Eder and Leslie E. Eder, *Motor Vehicle Diagnostic Inspection Demonstration Program,* National Highway Traffic Safety Administration, NHTSA Technical Report DOT–HS—802–760, October 1977, p. 32.

10. *Automotive News,* March 3, 1980, p. 1; *Automotive News,* April 27, 1977, p. 97 (49,173 dealerships on January 1, 1949), and R.L. Polk & Co. (4,838,342 new cars registered in 1949).

11. Interview, February 20, 1978.

12. *Automotive Age,* February 1978, p. 25.

13. *Op. cit.,* note 11 above.

14. *Money,* February 1978, p. 27.

15. Maryland Center for Public Broadcasting, "Consumer Survival Kit," aired KQED-TV, San Francisco, February 20, 1978, 11:30 p.m.–midnight.

16. *Consumer Reports,* April 1978, p. 200.

17. Phil Edmonston, *Lemon-Aid* (Don Mills, Ontario: Musson Book Co., 1977).

18. Paul Travis, "Rust-wary car owners should note warranty," *Dayton Daily News,* March 1, 1980.

19. *Op. cit.,* note 16 above.

20. Federal Trade Commission, *Automobile Policy Session* (Edited Version), April 17, 1978, p. 29.

21. Speech at conference, "Making Auto Repair Credible," Madison, Wisconsin, August 5–6, 1980.

22. Joseph J. Bohn, "Warranty-claim costs vary widely," *Automotive News,* December 16, 1976, pp. 1 & 38.

23. Letter to White House Office of Consumer Affairs, February 1, 1978.

24. Letter to E.A. Cafiero, President, Chrysler Corp., May 25, 1977.

25. Letter of September 15, 1977.

26. Telephone interview with Curtis R. Hoffman, deputy district attorney, Contra Costa County, April 20, 1978.

Chapter 15

1. B.J. Schroer and J.F. Peters, *An Evaluation of Vehicle Repair Costs for Auto Check Participants,* Center for Environmental and Energy Studies, The University of Alabama in Huntsville, Contract No. DOT–HS–5–01056, February 1, 1977, p. 63.

2. Interview, January 25, 1978.

3. Hearings before the Subcommittee on Consumer Protection and Finance of the Committee on Interstate and Foreign Commerce, House of Representatives, Ninety-fifth Congress, Second Session, *Auto Repair,* September 14, 20, 21, 25, October 19, and December 4, 1978, p. 333.

4. Washington Center for the Study of Services, *Checkbook Cars,* Summer 1976, p. 8.

5. Gerry Haddon, "Don't let a bugged car bite you," *Automotive Service Reports* (Automotive Service Councils, Inc.), October–November 1977, p. 2.

6. *Midwest Motorist,* December 1974, p. 11.

7. Better Business Division, Greater Tampa Chamber of Commerce, *Auto Repair Guide* (pamphlet).

8. Johnson Center for Environmental and Energy Studies, University of Alabama in Huntsville, *Survey of Automotive Repair Practices,* draft report, Contract No. DOT–OS–90004, May 7, 1979, p. 22, and data on individual shops visited.

9. Erik H. Arctander, "Pros tell how to avoid an auto-repair ripoff," *Popular Science,* January 1975, pp. 61–63.

10. U.S. Code 15 § 1666i. See also: Board of Governors of the Federal Reserve System, Regulation Z, 12 Code of Federal Regulations 226.13(i).

11. *Op. cit.,* note 3 above, p. 495.

12. WMAL-TV, Washington, DC, "You—and auto repair," Part Two, aired November 13, 1973.

13. Francis J. Gawronski, "Most cars waste fuel, pollute air," *Automotive News,* January 31, 1977.

14. News release, Car Care Council, May 1, 1977.

15. *Ibid.*

16. John Goodman, *Anatomy of a Complaint,* September 1973, p. 11.

17. Sandra Bundy, *The Breakdown Book,* Shell Answer Book No. 2.

18. *Ibid.*

19. Business Communications Co., Inc., *Home & Auto Do-It Yourself Market,* p. 3.

20. *Consumer Reports,* April 1976, p. 202.

21. Communiqué from David Friedrichs, president, Co-Op Auto, February 24, 1981.

22. Telephone interview, October 5, 1978.

23. Telephone interview, March 14, 1978.

24. Telephone interview with mechanic Jeff Kessler, October 5, 1978.

25. F.G. Ephraim, C.J. Kahane and W.G. La Heist, *Auto Repair and Maintenance Programs to Reduce Consumer Loss,* National Highway Traffic Safety Administration, NHTSA Technical Report DOT–HS–803–355, May 1978, p. B–20. See also: N.J. Taubenslag, *Concept Design Study of a Vehicle Inspection/Maintenance Organization (VIMO),* First Phase, Prepared for Office of State Vehicle Programs, National Highway Traffic Safety Administration, January 25, 1978.

26. *Ibid.,* p. B–21.

27. Telephone interview with Ralph Ferrara, April 19, 1978.

28. *Op. cit.,* note 4 above, p. 63.

29. *Op. cit.,* note 3 above, p. 310.

30. Prepared statement to the House Subcommittee on Consumer Protection and Finance, Sptember 21, 1978.

31. *Op. cit.,* note 3 above, p. 312.

32. *Op. cit.,* note 30 above.

33. *Ibid.*

34. Telephone interview with Mark Vogeler of Cincinnati Experience, 1978.
35. *Op. cit.*, note 25 above, p. B–6.

Chapter 16

1. B.J. Schroer and J.F. Peters, *An Evaluation of Vehicle Repair Costs for Auto Check Participants,* Center for Environmental and Energy Studies, University of Alabama in Huntsville, DOT–HS–5–01056, February 1, 1977, p. 39.
2. *Ibid.,* p. 42.
3. Joseph J. Innes, P.E. Eder and Leslie E. Eder, *Motor Vehicle Diagnostic Inspection Demonstration Program,* National Highway Traffic Safety Administration, NHTSA Technical Report DOT–HS–802–760, October 1977, p. 5.
4. Hearings before the Subcommittee for Consumers of the Committee on Commerce, Science, and Transportation, United States Senate, Ninety-fifth Congress, Second Session, *National Traffic and Motor Vehicle Information and Cost Savings Authorizations of 1979 and 1980,* March 21, 22, and 23, 1978, p. 17.
5. *Op. cit.,* note 3 above, p. 60.
6. Interview with receptionist Sharie Soriano, February 1978.
7. The Auto Club of Missouri, Diagnostic Car Clinics, *Historical and Operating Information for Our Diagnostic Car Clinics.*
8. Larry A. Pipes, *Auto Club of Missouri Diagnostic Clinic,* Society of Automotive Engineers, Inc., Technical Paper Series 780034, February 27–March 3, 1978, p. 2. See also note 4 above, p. 262.
9. Washington Center for the Study of Services, *Checkbook Cars,* Summer 1976, pp. 87–92.
10. Automobile Club of Southern California, Automotive Engineering Department, *Criteria for the Approval of Diagnostic/Repair Facilities.*
11. F.G. Ephraim, C.J. Kahane and W.G. La Heist, *Auto Repair and Maintenance Program to Reduce Consumer Loss,* National Highway Traffic Safety Administration, NHTSA Technical Report DOT–HS–803–355, May 1978, p. 9.
12. *Ibid.,* pp. B–14, B–15.
13. *Op. cit.,* note 3 above, p. 80.
14. *Op. cit.,* note 11 above, p. B–14.
15. *Ibid.,* p. B–15.
16. *Ibid.,* pp. B–15 to B–17.
17. Interview, August 7, 1980.
18. *Op. cit.,* note 11 above, pp. B–18 to B–20.
19. *Op. cit.,* note 3 above, p. 31.
20. *Op. cit.,* note 7 above.
21. *Op. cit.,* note 3 above, p. 32.
22. *Ibid.,* p. 36.
23. B.J. Schroer and W.F. Peyton, *The Effects of Automobile Inspections on Accident Rates,* Johnson Environmental and Energy Center, University of Alabama in Huntsville, August 31, 1977, Technical Report Documentation Page.
24. *Op. cit.,* note 3 above, p. 22.
25. *Op. cit.,* note 1 above, p. 3.
26. *Oakland* (California) *Tribune,* February 26, 1981, p. B–5.
27. Hearings before the Subcommittee on Consumer Protection and Finance of the Committee on Interstate and Foreign Commerce, House of Representatives, Ninety-fifth Congress, Second Session, *Auto Repair,* September 14, 20, 21, 25, October 19, and December 4, 1978, p. 181.
28. Wendell A. Cook, *Repair Industry Responses to Diagnostic Inspection Projects,* Society of Automotive Engineers, Inc., Technical Paper Series No. 780030, February 27–March 3, 1978, p. 18.

29. Information supplied by Larry Pipes.
30. *Op. cit.*, note 4 above, p. 43.
31. *Op. cit.*, note 29 above.
32. *Op. cit.*, note 17 above.
33. *Op. cit.*, note 27 above, p. 180.
34. *Ibid.*, p. 45.
35. *Ibid.*, p. 109.
36. *Motor Trend,* March 1978, p. 9.
37. *Op. cit.*, note 27 above, p. 180.
38. Interview, September 20, 1978.
39. *Op. cit.*, note 27 above, p. 194.

Chapter 17

1. Information supplied by the American Automobile Association.
2. Hearings before the Subcommittee for Consumers of the Committee on Commerce, Science and Transportation, United States Senate, Ninety-fifth Congress, Second Session, *National Traffic and Motor Vehicle Information and Cost Savings Authorizations of 1979 and 1980,* March 21, 22, and 23, 1978, p. 218.
3. Automobile Association, *About Technical Services,* 1976, p. 9.
4. *Ibid.*
5. American Automobile Association, *Approved Auto Repair Services Program,* Background Report, undated.
6. Letter to author from Peter W. Rushton, Public Relations Department, Automobile Association, May 16, 1978.
7. *Ibid.*
8. *Op. cit.*, note 3 above, p. 5.
9. *Ibid.*
10. *Ibid.*, p. 8.
11. *Op. cit.*, note 6 above.
12. *Op. cit.*, note 3 above, p. 14.
13. Automobile Association, *The AA Seal of Approval,* March 1978.
14. Letter to author from M.A. Reddaway, technical manager, Royal Automobile Club, February 1, 1978.
15. *Ibid.*
16. American Automobile Association, *AAA at a Glance,* 1977.

Chapter 18

1. Case history supplied by the Michigan Bureau of Automotive Regulation.
2. U.S. Department of Health, Education and Welfare, Office of Consumer Affairs, *Consumer Auto Repair Problems,* Draft Study Report, August 1974.
3. Interview, January 25, 1978.
4. Interview with Robert N. Wiens, chief of the bureau, January 25, 1978.
5. Letter to author from Robert N. Wiens, February 4, 1981.
6. *Ibid.*
7. California Business and Professions Code 20.3 § 9884.9(a).
8. California Administrative Code 16 § 3353 & 3354.
9. *Ibid.*
10. *Ibid.* and *op. cit.*, note 7 above.

11. *Schreiber* v. *Kelsey*, 62 Cal. App. 3d Supp. 45; and *Bennett* v. *Hayes* (1975), 53 Cal. App. 3d 700.

12. *Op. cit.*, note 7 above.

13. California Bureau of Automotive Repair, *Estimates and Invoices.*

14. *Op. cit.*, note 4 above.

15. *Op. cit.*, note 7 above, § 9884.7(c).

16. *Ibid.*, § 9884.8.

17. *Ibid.*, § 9884.10.

18. *Ibid.*, § 9884.7.

19. Hearings before the Subcommittee on Consumer Protection and Finance of the Committee on Interstate and Foreign Commerce, House of Representatives, Ninety-fifth Congress, Second Session, *Auto Repair,* September 14, 20, 21, 25, October 19, and December 4, 1978, p. 84.

20. Interview with Douglas Laue, September 14, 1978.

21. *Op. cit.*, note 4 above.

22. *Op. cit.*, note 5 above.

23. *Op. cit.*, note 20 above.

24. Based on 15,157,000 licensed drivers (source: Motor Vehicle Manufacturers Association, *MVMA Motor Vehicle Facts and Figures '80,* p. 46).

25. *Op. cit.*, note 5 above.

26. Telephone interview, April 11, 1978; and interview, September 14, 1978.

27. Telephone interview, September 19, 1978.

28. Prince George's County Code § 2–148(3).

29. Connecticut General Statutes Revised 14 § 246 Sec. 14-51a.

30. Hawaii Revised Statutes § 437B–12.

31. Consolidated Laws of New York Annotated, Vehicle and Traffic Law (1980), 12A § 398–e(2).

32. *Op. cit.*, note 28 above, § 26A–104.

33. *Op. cit.*, note 29 above, Sec. 14–64.

34. From files of Michigan Bureau of Automotive Regulation.

35. Michigan Compiled Laws Annotated § 257.1333.

36. *Op. cit.*, note 19 above, p. 75.

37. Minnesota Statutes Annotated (1980) § 325.973 Subd. 1.

38. Montgomery County Code § 31A–6(a)(2).

39. District of Columbia Regulation 74–3 § 505(b)(5).

40. Broward County Code § 20–162.

41. Dallas Ordinance § 50–122.

42. *Op. cit.*, note 39 above, § 511(c)(6).

43. Florida Statutes Annotated § 559.905(1)(1).

44. Alaska Statutes Supplement § 45.45.200(d).

45. *Op. cit.*, note 43 above, § 559.917 et seq.

Chapter 19

1. Information from news release, California New Motor Vehicle Board, January 6, 1977; State of California New Motor Vehicle Board, *Jennings* v. *Quality Motors and American Motors Sales Corp.*, Petition No. P–25–76; complaint of Mr. Lambert to the board, August 9, 1976; and declaration of Bradshaw F. Perkins, Bureau of Automotive Repair, September 23, 1976.

2. Letter to author, March 8, 1978.

3. Telephone interview with Don Krohn, May 5, 1978.

4. Telephone interview, October 5, 1978.

5. Telephone interview with Russell Harding, executive director, Texas Motor Vehicle Commission, October 5, 1978.

6. Hearings before the Subcommittee on Consumer Protection and Finance of the Committee on Interstate and Foreign Commerce, House of Representatives, Ninety-fifth Congress, Second Session, *Auto Repair,* September 14, 20, 21, 25, October 19, and December 4, 1978, pp. 347–348.

7. *Op. cit.,* note 5 above.

8. Letter to author from G.W. Odom, public relations, Ford Parts and Service Division, February 17, 1981.

9. General Motors Corp., *Fact Sheet on General Motors Third-Party Arbitration,* February 1981.

10. Marc Stern, "GM's arbitration system working," *Automotive News,* May 19, 1980, p. 18.

11. *Automotive Age,* January 1977, p. 29.

12. William M. Bulkeley, "Chrysler wins a bid to issue new stock, is blasted by holders for its performance," *Wall Street Journal,* May 3, 1978.

13. *Op. cit.,* note 6 above, p. 119.

14. Charles Dunsire, "Local Chrysler recall repairs hit bottleneck," *Seattle Post-Intelligencer,* May 24, 1978.

15. From material supplied by the Center for Auto Safety.

16. Letter to E.A. Cafiero, President of Chrysler Corp., July 27, 1978.

17. Ralph Blumenthal, "Parade of defective vehicles seeks 'lemon' aide," *New York Times,* March 5, 1978.

18. Hearings before the Subcommittee for Consumers of the Committee on Commerce, Science and Transportation, United States Senate, Ninety-fifth Congress, Second Session, *National Traffic and Motor Vehicle Information and Cost Savings Authorizations of 1979 and 1980,* March 21, 22, and 23, 1978, p. 212.

19. *Ibid.*

20. *Ibid.,* pp. 211–212.

21. *Coronet,* March 1977, pp. 67–68.

22. Speech to Conference on Transportation, Washington, D.C., May 1979.

Chapter 20

1. Barry Siegel, "The nuts and bolts of an auto-repair suit," *Los Angeles Times,* January 8, 1978, Part LX, pp. 1, 14 & 15. Additional information from attorney Glickman's secretary.

2. *Ibid.,* p. 15.

3. Texas Code Annotated Business and Commerce Code (1980), 2 § 17.46, 17.50.

4. Michigan Compiled Laws Annotated (1980 Supplement), § 445.903, 445.911 Sec. 11(2).

5. *Ibid.,* § 257.1336.

6. New Jersey Statutes Annotated (1980 Supplement) § 56:8–2, 56:8–19.

7. Florida Statutes Annotated (1980 Supplement) § 501.204, 501.2101; General Laws of Idaho Annotated § 48–603, 48–608(3); Louisiana Statutes Annotated (1980 Supplement) 51 § 1405, 1409A; Maine Revised Statutes Annotated 5 § 207, 213.2; Mississippi Code 1972 Annotated (1979 Supplement) § 75–24–5, 75–24–15(2); and Code of Laws of South Carolina 1976 § 39–5–20, 39–5–140(a).

8. *Zabriskie Chevrolet, Inc.* v. *Smith,* 240 A.2d 195 (N.J.).

9. *Ibid.*

10. *Asciolla* v. *Manter Oldsmobile-Pontiac, Inc. and General Motors Corp.,* 370 A.2d 270 (N.H.).

11. *Automotive News,* May 22, 1978, p. 32.

12. *Ronald Pavesi* v. *Ford Motor Co. and Larsen Ford, Inc.,* Superior Court of New Jersey, Chancery Division, Middlesex County, Docket No. C–2369–79, January 11, 1978.

13. Beverly Edwards, "Trailerist sues GM and wins—round one," *Automotive Age,* June 1979, pp. 73–74.

14. Maine Bureau of Consumer Protection, *Down Easter's Lemon Guide,* 1977, pp. 6–7.

15. Mo Mehlsak, "Dealers' dilemma: refund or fix," *Automotive Age,* April 1978, p. 32.

16. *Oakland* (California) *Tribune,* April 8, 1980, p. C–5.

17. Illinois Legislative Investigating Commission, *Auto Repair Abuses,* June 1975, pp. 101–102.

18. Sylvia Porter, "Small claims breakthrough," *San Francisco Chronicle,* July 6, 1979, p. 61.

19. Sylvia Porter, "Small claims victory may not pay off," *Washington Star,* December 11, 1977, p. C8.

20. *Op. cit.,* note 18 above.

21. Harold C. Wright, "Dealers *can* win in small claims court," *Automotive Age,* February 1978, p. 126.

22. *New York Times,* November 9, 1975, p. 40.

23. U.S. Code 15 § 16661. See also Board of Governors of the Federal Reserve System, Regulation Z, 12 Code of Federal Regulations 226.13(i).

Chapter 21

1. Interview, April 10, 1978.

2. *Ibid.*

3. Letter to author from Richard E. Lerner, associate general counsel, American Arbitration Association, June 14, 1979.

4. *Op. cit.,* note 1 above.

5. *Ibid.*

Chapter 22

1. Donald W. King and Kathleen A. McEvoy, *A National Survey of the Complaint-Handling Procedures Used by Consumers,* King Research, Inc. (under subcontract from TARP, Inc.), p. 77.

2. Telephone interview with Michael Mustokoff, district attorney's office, April 19, 1978.

3. *Ibid.*

4. Interview, April 12, 1978.

5. Hearings before the Subcommittee on Consumer Protection and Finance of the Committee on Interstate and Foreign Commerce, House of Representatives, Ninety-fifth Congress, Second Session, *Auto Repair,* September 14, 20, 21, 25, October 19, and December 4, 1978, p. 77.

6. Telephone interview, April 18, 1978.

7. *Op. cit.,* note 5 above, p. 202.

8. Telephone interview, October 5, 1978.

9. Telephone interview, February 6, 1978.

10. Letter to author from Emmanuel E.M. Feuerwerker, Consumer and Corporate Affairs Canada, May 22, 1978.

Chapter 23

1. *Maclean's,* September 20, 1976, p. 58.
2. Automobile Protection Association, *Consumer Communiqué,* Spring 1976, p. 11.
3. *Ibid.*
4. *Ibid.*
5. *Wall Street Journal,* September 27, 1976, p. 38.
6. News release, Consumer and Corporate Affairs Canada, December 8, 1977.
7. Interview in 1978.
8. *Ibid.*
9. *Ibid.*
10. Goody L. Solomon, "Car complaints get attention," *Washington Star,* August 15, 1977, Section D.
11. John Sherwood, "Vega haters bust up a lemon," *Washington Star,* August 22, 1976, Section D.
12. Letter to author from Mr. Richardson, February 1, 1978.

Chapter 24

1. Telephone interview, September 29, 1978.
2. Telephone interview, May 31, 1979.
3. *Oakland* (California) *Tribune/Eastbay Today,* February 18, 1981, p. E-2.
4. Telephone interview, April 27, 1978.

Chapter 25

1. Federal Trade Commission, *Automobile Policy Session* (edited version), April 17, 1978, pp. 3, 4.
2. National Highway Traffic Safety Administration, *The Contributions of Automobile Regulation,* Preliminary Report, June 1978, p. ii.
3. *Hayward* (California) *Daily Review,* January 29, 1981, p. 30.
4. General Motors Corp., *General Motors Annual Report,* 1978, p. 20 (listed as expense for amortization of special tools).
5. *Op. cit.,* note 2 above, p. 12.
6. *Ibid.*

Appendix A

1. Alaska Statutes (1979 Cumulative Supplement) § 45.45.130 et seq.
2. Colorado Revised Statutes (1980) § 42–11–101.
3. Connecticut Motor Vehicle Laws of the 1977 Revision of the General Statutes 14 § 14–51 et seq.
4. District of Columbia Regulation 74–3 § 505(b)(5) et seq.
5. Florida Statutes Annotated § 559.901 et seq.
6. Broward County Code § 20–162.

7. Dade County Ordinance No. 71–20, Sec. 8A-154 et seq.

8. Hawaii Revised Statutes § 437B–1 et seq. and Regulations of the Motor Vehicle Repair Industry Board.

9. Idaho Consumer Protection Regulations § 12.1 et seq.

10. Municipal Code of Chicago § 156.2–1 et seq.

11. Maine Revised Statutes Annotated 29 § 2601 et seq.

12. Annotated Code of Maryland § 14–1001 et seq.

13. Montgomery County Code § 31A et seq.

14. Prince George's County Code § 26A–101 et seq. § 2–142 et seq.

15. Motor Vehicle Regulations of the Massachusetts Department of Attorney General.

16. Michigan Compiled Laws Annotated § 257.1301 et seq.

17. Minnesota Statutes Annotated § 325.968 et seq.

18. Minneapolis Code § 158.10 et seq.

19. St. Paul Legislative Code § 331.01, § 363.01, 345.01 to 345.03.

20. Montana Department of Business Regulation, Regulation § 8–2.4(2)–S410 et seq.

21. Nevada Trade Regulations and Practices § 598.690 et seq.

22. New Hampshire Revised Statutes Annotated § 358–D:1 et seq.

23. New Jersey Department of Law and Public Safety Regulation 13:45A–7.1 et seq.

24. Consolidated Laws of New York Annotated Vehicle and Traffic Law 62A § 398; Regulations of the Commissioner of Motor Vehicles § 82.2 et seq.

25. Ohio Substantive Rules of the Director of Commerce § COcp–3–01.05 et seq.

26. Oregon Revised Statutes § 746.292 et seq.

27. 37 Pennsylvania Code § 301.1 et seq.

28. General Laws of Rhode Island Business & Professions Code § 5–38–1 et seq.

29. Dallas Ordinance § 50–113 et seq.

30. Regulations of the Utah Trade Commission.

31. Code of Virginia § 59.1–207.1 et seq.

32. Revised Code of Washington Annotated § 46.71.010 et seq.

33. Wisconsin Administrative Code § AG 132.01 et seq.

Index